DIGITAL BUSINESS NETWORKS

DIGITAL BUSINESS NETWORKS

Allen Dooley
Santa Ana College,
Santa Ana,
California

PEARSON

Boston   Columbus   Indianapolis   New York   San Francisco   Upper Saddle River
Amsterdam   Cape Town   Dubai   London   Madrid   Milan   Munich   Paris   Montréal   Toronto
Delhi   Mexico City   São Paulo   Sydney   Hong Kong   Seoul   Singapore   Taipei   Tokyo

Editor-in-Chief: Stephanie Wall
Executive Editor: Bob Horan
Senior Editorial Project Manager: Kelly Loftus
Editorial Assistant: Ashlee Bradbury
Director of Marketing: Maggie Moylan
Executive Marketing Manager: Anne Fahlgren
Marketing Assistant: Gianna Sandri
Production Project Manager: Clara Bartunek
Senior Art Director: Jayne Conte
Cover Designer: Suzanne Behnke

Text Permission Specialist: Brooks Hill-Whilton
Cover Art: Fotolia
Media Director: Allyson Graesser
Senior Media Project Manager: Alana Coles
Full-Service Project Management: Integra Software Services, Pvt Ltd.
Printer/Binder: Edwards Brothers Malloy
Cover Printer: Lehigh/Phoenix-Hagerstown
Text Font: ITC Garamond Std

Credits and acknowledgments borrowed from other sources and reproduced, with permission, in this textbook appear on the appropriate page within text.

Library of Congress Cataloging-in-Publication Data
Dooley, Allen.
    Digital business networks/Allen B. Dooley.
        p. cm.
    ISBN-13: 978-0-13-284691-2
    ISBN-10: 0-13-284691-8
    1. Business networks—Computer network resources.   2. Business enterprises—Computer networks.
    3. Digital communications—Economic aspects.   4. Communication in organizations—
Computer network resources.   I. Title.
    HD69.S8.D66 2014
    004.6—dc23
                                                                                2012031844

10 9 8 7 6 5 4 3 2 1

ISBN-10:   0-13-284691-8
ISBN-13: 978-0-13-284691-2

In memory of my parents, Irene and Ben Dooley

BRIEF CONTENTS

CONTENTS

PREFACE

Wireless technologies and social networking applications are dramatically transforming tele-communication as well as data communication. The universal availability of these tools and their multifaceted uses are unusual compared to former technologies, and yet their underlying infrastructure remains mysterious to most. Cloud architectures are rapidly making the storage, access, and retrieval of any type of data available at the push of a button to the casual end-user. Today's legions of mobile-device consumers expect instant information, entertainment, analysis, discussion, and a host of other functionalities from the growing array of technologies they carry in their pockets or purses.

And yet, for network administrators and networking professionals, the very invisibility of these technologies, how they are deployed, configured, and supported, to a good extent indicates how successful these technologies are. The world of even 10 years ago would seem almost archaic to today's youth, who, for example, mostly have no experience with a land phone line's rotary dial. By the scale of human history, however, that time was barely yesterday.

This text explores emerging technologies, such as 4G mobile wireless, the advent of social networking applications from a business perspective, the underlying layer of architecture functionalities of the TCP/IP model, and IPv6. Discussion of cloud architectures also threads throughout the text.

Directed primarily toward undergraduate CIS/MIS college/university majors, this text also provides practical content to industry professionals or those who want to be. Using clear, concise language, with engaging examples and exercises, as well as informative graphics and illustrations, the material is geared to both students and faculty.

My intent is to provide the essential components needed for undergraduate students, and yet present contextually driven examples and language required by today's career professional.

UNIQUE FEATURES OF THIS TEXT

1. This text covers the *social networking* explosion. It presents real business context questions that need to be addressed. As with many technologies, including the Internet itself, how a technology is presented at its inception can often differ from how it eventually is used, leading to sometimes surprising and unexpected alternative uses.

   Initially, and up through the present, social networking applications such as Facebook, YouTube, Yelp, and many others, have been viewed primarily as a means of creating connectivity between individual users and their extended social network. That is changing. These very technologies are now being viewed and utilized by businesses to gain competitive advantage. Important to this topic and presented in the "Social Networking" chapter of this text is a discussion, as an example, of social networking analytics, what it is, and why it is important in business.

2. A theme running throughout the text is *cloud architectures.* The introduction of cloud-based infrastructures has significantly changed how end-users view and interact with a business's networking capability. This end-user expectation of cloud services has in turn challenged networking professionals to deliver critical

business resources seamlessly, accurately, rapidly, and, perhaps most importantly, securely.

3. Every chapter starts with a brief vignette titled "The Business Benefit." This feature will inform students, before the chapter begins, how and why the succeeding content of the chapter is important from a business perspective. Students want to know "how" something is relevant and "why" they should be mastering the content of the chapter. For example, the text regularly presents the student with the sometimes opposing concepts of effectiveness versus efficiency. For a business, in what ways may the business derive a greater benefit if it must choose between the effective use of a technology or an efficient use of the same technology? As presented in ongoing chapter discussions, sometimes a business, depending on the benefit gained or objective desired, will have to give greater weight to one of the two.

4. The technology presented in the text has a larger *social implication*. Every chapter includes a feature titled "The Ethical Perspective." This feature asks the student to reflect on not just the technical and business aspects of the content but the societal context as well. For example, what ethical responsibility does a business have for securing and recovering critical customer and/or employee data and information? Is it sufficient for a business to meet strictly minimum specifications in this regard? What about the data captured regarding customers? Does a business have the right to use these data in any manner the business sees fit—for example, selling the data to vendor partners with whom the customer has no connection? Even if such use of customer data were legal, is it ethical? Such a feature can spark lively class discussions, whether in a brick-and-mortar classroom or by use of "threaded" discussion boards in an online class.

5. While describing in detail the *open systems interface (OSI)* model, this text will focus on the *transmission control protocol/Internet protocol (TCP/IP)* networking model. The TCP/IP model is the most popular networking model used in the world today; it is to some extent familiar to virtually all students who are web-centric and connected to many types of social networking applications. For well-rounded discussions, analog concepts are also presented. Students will find an immediate comfort level with "Digital" in the title. Furthermore, digital technologies are at the forefront of today's business data and information communication infrastructures.

6. At the end of every chapter are a minimum of four *"Research in Brief"* assignments. The intent is to enable students to research and report, in a technology updated manner, on a current topic of relevance to the chapter and of interest to the student. This is an engaging way to have students begin thinking of research and its implications.

7. The text incorporates an ongoing *case study* that provides context from one chapter to another. Case study questions relate to the chapter content provided. For example, what type of backbone would be most effective for Sheehan Marketing, the business on which the case study is based? The key purpose of the case study is to give students a sense of continuity from one chapter to the next as to how the entire topic, class, and technology are related. It can be completed individually or in teams. The case study unites and ties the text together.

8. At the conclusion of every chapter is a discretionarily assignable *"Topic in Focus."* The intent is to extend the chapter content and, if time allows, further explore that content. The "Topic in Focus" can be optional, extra credit, or required, based on faculty requirement. For example, the chapter that presents material related to "subnetting" offers a "Topic in Focus" that describes the ANDing processs.

END-OF-CHAPTER MATERIALS

The following appear at the end of every chapter:

- Chapter Summary
- Keywords
- Short-Answer Questions
- Hands-On Projects
- Research in Brief
- Topic in Focus

Each chapter ends with a Chapter Summary. The summary is then followed by a list of Keywords taken from the chapter's content.

Short-Answer Questions require a brief response of about a paragraph's length. Answers to these brief questions can be found in the content of the associated chapter. The intent is for the student to revisit selected chapter topics and test for comprehension.

The Hands-On Projects provide an immediate context to the material. This feature asks the student to produce, evaluate, describe, illustrate, or in some fashion demonstrate a practical understanding of the material presented.

The Research in Brief encourages students to investigate a chapter topic in greater detail. As with any text regarding the topic of data communications, there are many areas that cannot be explored in depth within the text. This feature allows the student to choose from a range of topics in a brief report of about three or four pages, and to provide more content and exploration on that topic.

The text emphasizes the importance of teamwork in an enterprise environment. In both traditional and online classes, team projects can be highly effective in establishing student engagement. A Case Study within the text binds the chapters of the text together in an ongoing analysis and works well as a group or team project.

Each chapter concludes with a Topic in Focus. This feature may be optional, part of the regular class material, a form of extra credit, or a forum for additional class discussion. The idea behind the Topic in Focus is to explore and offer more content on a given chapter topic.

HOW THE TEXT IS ORGANIZED

The text is divided into five parts, each containing a set of content-related chapters. This approach allows students to see how a digital/analog data communication infrastructure builds from standards to protocols and successively to networks of various sizes and purposes, all to meet a business need.

The text also includes graphics, illustrations, and appropriate artwork. Visual elements are critical to student comprehension of sometimes difficult and complex technologies.

Part One: Data Communication Essentials

Chapters 1 and 2 is where the two major networking models, OSI and TCP/IP, are addressed. Also in Part One is the discussion of the "analog" portion of the essential content. While the OSI model is explored, these chapters focus and set up the later discussions on the TCP/IP architecture.

Part Two: Layer Services

Chapters 3 through 7 explore the TCP/IP model in a five-layer approach. Due to its complexity, the data link layer is presented in two chapters: Chapter 3 on data link layer concepts and components, and Chapter 4 on data link layer media and devices. Then Chapters 5, 6, and 7, respectively, explore the network layer, the transport layer, and the application layer of the TCP/IP model.

Part Three: Networking Implementations

Chapters 8 and 9 address varying networking implementations: local area networks, backbone, metropolitan, and wide area networks. Topics presented include how these networking models vary, are implemented, and yet are related. Content covered includes gigabit Ethernet, backbone architectures and fault tolerance, wiring closets, circuit versus packet switching, the versions of DSL, trunk services, frame relay, ATM, and other related topics.

Part Four: Enterprise Solutions

Chapters 10, 11, and 12 give students an opportunity to address complete enterprise business needs. Chapter 10 focuses on servers in the enterprise; Chapter 11 presents integrating technologies within the enterprise; and Chapter 12 targets security issues.

Part Five: Current and Emerging Digital Business Technologies

Chapters 13 and 14 address our immediate present and the emerging future. Topics include convergence technologies such as unified messaging, various wireless implementations, social networking, and careers for data communication technologists.

SUPPLEMENTAL MATERIALS

The following supplements are available at the Online Instructor Resource Center, accessible through *www.pearsonhighered.com/dooley*.

Instructor's Manual

The instructor's manual includes a sample syllabus, chapter outlines, a list of key terms, and answers to the Short Answer Questions.

Test Item File

The Test Item File, prepared by Mansour Sharha of Capella University, contains over 1,400 questions, including multiple-choice, true/false, and essay. Each question is followed by the correct answer, page reference, and difficulty rating.

TestGen

Pearson Education's test-generating software is available from *www.pearsonhighered.com/irc*. The software is PC/MAC compatible and preloaded with all of the Test Item File questions. You can manually or randomly view test questions and drag and drop to create a test. You may also add or modify test-bank questions as needed. Our TestGens are converted for use in several popular course management systems, including BlackBoard, WebCT, Moodle, D2L, and Angel. These conversions can be found on the Instructor's Resource Center.

PowerPoint Presentations

The PowerPoints, prepared by Mansour Sharha of Capella University, highlight text learning objectives and key topics and serve as an excellent aid for classroom presentations and lectures.

Image Library

This collection of the figures and tables from the text offers another aid for classroom presentations and PowerPoint slides.

CourseSmart

CourseSmart eTextbooks were developed for students looking to save on required or recommended textbooks. Students simply select their eText by title or author and purchase immediate access to the content for the duration of the course using any major credit card. With a CourseSmart eText, students can search for specific keywords or page numbers, take notes online, print out reading assignments that incorporate lecture notes, and bookmark important passages for later review. For more information or to purchase a CourseSmart eTextbook, visit *www.coursesmart.com.*

ACKNOWLEDGMENTS

I thank and acknowledge the reviewers of this text for their valued comments, criticisms, and recommendations:

- Irena Bojanova, University of Maryland
- Jerry Chang, University of Nevada–Las Vegas
- James W. Gabberty, Pace University
- Timothy Klaus, Texas A&M University–Corpus Christi
- Robert Lipton, Pennsylvania State University
- Masoud Naghedolfeizi, Fort Valley State University
- Myron Sheu, California State University–Dominguez Hills
- Dwayne Whitten, Texas A&M University

I especially thank my executive editor, Bob Horan, and his senior editorial project manager, Kelly Loftus, both of whom were very patient and supportive. Thanks as well to the Pearson staff for smoothing a rough draft manuscript into a polished product.

ABOUT THE AUTHOR

Allen Dooley completed his doctorate in Education and his master's degree in Professional Writing at the University of Southern California in Los Angeles. In addition, he received his master's and bachelor's degrees in Business Administration from California State University Los Angeles.

Dr. Dooley has been in the field of postsecondary higher education for more than 18 years. Thirteen of those years were at Pasadena City College as a tenured professor in Computer Information Systems, lecturing particularly in the areas of networking, data communications, database theory, and other areas of information literacy. He has also served as a guest lecturer on networking topics at California Polytechnic University in Pomona, California, and at Woodbury University in Burbank, California. (California Polytechnic University is part of the California State University system in California. Woodbury University is a private four-year university.)

Also, Dr. Dooley has an additional six years' experience as an academic administrator in a variety of roles, including Dean of Business, Dean of Enrollment Management, and Dean of Academic Support. Currently he is Dean of Business at Santa Ana College, Santa Ana, California. Prior to his career in education, Dr. Dooley worked as a banking information technologist at such institutions as Security Pacific Bank, Tokai Bank, Great Western Bank, and other financial institutions.

DIGITAL BUSINESS NETWORKS

Chapter

1

Elements of Data Communications: Analog and Digital

The Business Benefit

ACME Corporation produces three styles of living room furniture: Santa Fe, English Traditional, and French Modern. Wireless Radio Frequency Identification (RFID) tags are placed on each piece of furniture manufactured by ACME. The furniture is stored in warehouses on stacked inventory pallets. The telemetry tags, tracked by satellite, enable the production manager to quickly analyze which products are moving out of the warehouse and which are not. She adjusts her production schedule accordingly, knowing the company needs to produce more of those items that are selling and fewer of those that are not. The production manager's schedule will also affect her orders for parts from outside vendors as well as other ACME departments.

The ACME marketing department manager has access to the same production schedule. With this information, the marketing staff makes decisions on how to better market slow-moving inventory and how to increase the market share of those items selling successfully. Senior management, on the other hand, uses both production and marketing data to set strategic goals for ACME. At the heart of all this is wireless telemetry technology used on ACME's inventory. Marketing management, based on the data derived from this networked telemetry technology, calculates that the Santa Fe line is on its way out due to poor sales. ACME stops production of Santa Fe and pursues another, more promising, furniture line, Mediterranean. Figure 1.1 demonstrates ACME's use of telemetry. This example typifies how businesses can benefit from networked technologies that allow them to better leverage their inventory and marketing resources.

Learning Objectives

After studying this chapter, you should be able to:

- Identify five phases in the evolution of data communications.
- Explain the difference between data communications and telecommunications.
- Understand what a protocol is and why protocols are used.
- Recognize the importance of standards and standards-setting bodies.

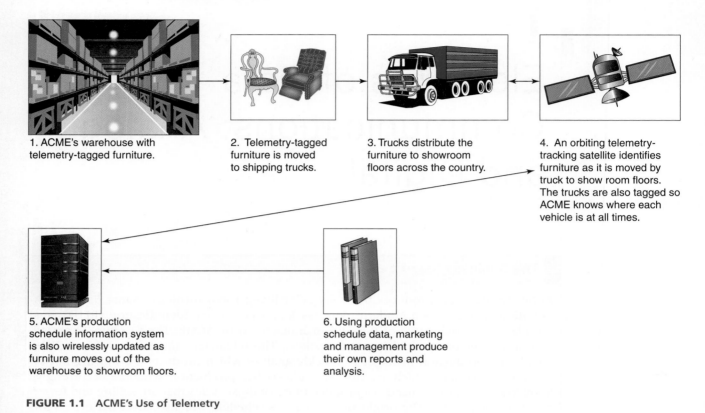

1. ACME's warehouse with telemetry-tagged furniture.

2. Telemetry-tagged furniture is moved to shipping trucks.

3. Trucks distribute the furniture to showroom floors across the country.

4. An orbiting telemetry-tracking satellite identifies furniture as it is moved by truck to show room floors. The trucks are also tagged so ACME knows where each vehicle is at all times.

5. ACME's production schedule information system is also wirelessly updated as furniture moves out of the warehouse to showroom floors.

6. Using production schedule data, marketing and management produce their own reports and analysis.

FIGURE 1.1   ACME's Use of Telemetry

THE CHANGING WORLD OF COMMUNICATIONS

It is 5 A.M. and you are soundasleep. On your front lawn, however, something curious is occurring. Silently, an electronically controlled sprinkler head with a sensor containing a small microchip rises inches above ground level. The sprinkler sensor's microchip controller has been programmed to activate the twice-a-day watering of your lawn. Using wireless communications, the sprinkler's sensor controller sends an inquiry to an orbiting weather satellite. In response, the weather satellite informs the sprinkler's sensor controller that your area has an 85 percent probability of rain. Previously, you had programmed your sprinkler's sensor controller to activate watering only if the likelihood of rain is less than 75 percent. Based on your programmed commands, the sensor controller directs your sprinklers to postpone watering. The sensor controller then, like you, goes back to sleep until its next programmed activation. A light rain begins to fall.

This is but one example of how networked data communications are changing our world. In fact, this technology is available now from such vendors as HydroPoint Data Systems (*www.hydropoint.com*). How much have things changed? In 700 BC, the Greeks used homing pigeons to carry messages. Today, programmed devices, such as smart sprinkler systems, work invisibly based on wireless communications. One very popular option for automobiles that you have likely used is a global positioning system (GPS) that can provide instant directions and assistance, regardless of where the driver is, at the push of a dashboard button. Our automobiles have become mobile communication devices. Of course, these technologies took time to evolve, even though they evolved very rapidly. The evolution of data communications can be divided into five phases:

1. Digitization in the 1960s
2. Growth of data communications in the 1970s
3. An era of deregulation in the 1980s
4. The Internet as a common tool in the 1990s
5. Pervasive computing in the 2010s

Phase 1: Digitization

In the 1960s, computer technology began to transform our social, economic, and governmental infrastructures. Data, formerly transcribed or maintained primarily in paper form, were instead being captured electronically as binary digits understandable to computers. The process of transcribing data into binary form is called **digitization**. This period witnessed the beginnings of extensive digitization, with processing and communications being highly centralized.

The computers in use at that time, called *mainframes,* were very large and expensive and used proprietary architectures that did not support cross-platform communications. The term **proprietary** generally refers to a technology or product that is copyrighted and not available for use without some type of fee or payment to its owner. As a result, an organization's mainframe from one vendor could not directly interact with the software and hardware of a different vendor's mainframe, creating a closed architecture technology. Such "closed" architectures made it challenging and difficult for businesses to select the most cost-effective technology solutions. A closed architecture technology does not permit competing technologies to directly interface or interact with it.

Because they were large, expensive, and complex, mainframes were used mostly by governments, major research institutes, and large corporations. Users connected to the mainframe by way of so-called dumb terminals. All work and communications were controlled through the mainframe. The dumb terminals were simply the way that users accessed the mainframe's computing power.

In this environment, when a business bought into a computer vendor's technology, it bought into one vendor's implementation of that technology. Today, for both software and hardware, as well as data communications models and protocols, the trend has been toward open architecture systems. These systems enable the use of technologies that are conversant across platforms. For consumers, open architecture systems offer many advantages, including greater competition for their dollars as more vendors enter the market.

Phase 2: Growth of Data Communications

Electronic data must be transported from one location to another over some type of transmission infrastructure in order to be widely available. An infrastructure is like a transportation route in that it conveys data from one location to another. The first data communications infrastructures used the existing circuit-based telephone system. This system was owned and run as a monopoly by Bell Telephone/AT&T, meaning that Bell was the only provider of this critical infrastructure.

As technology improved in the 1970s, and as the importance of computer technology became apparent, especially to the business world, solutions were pursued that would enable computers to more efficiently communicate and share information with each other. Smaller-scale computers, called minicomputers, were introduced. Processing and communications became more decentralized. The microprocessor became commercially available. Also, packet-switching networks, first created in the 1960s, began to be extensively deployed and implemented.

Briefly stated, packet-switched circuits are more efficient for transporting data, whereas circuit-switched circuits are more efficient for voice transmission. (We find out why in a later chapter.) With increased digitization of data through computer technology, communication networks were needed that could support more than voice. The development of packet-switching technologies was the solution to this problem. Packet-switching networks, in turn, because of their ability to more efficiently transport digitized data, ignited the growth of extensive data communications networks. Users of technology now expected their communications systems to provide real-time, online capabilities over great distances.

Phase 3: Deregulation

As the economic impact and power of capable and reliable data communications infrastructures became apparent, more players sought to enter the field of providing data communication technologies for profit. Until 1968, Bell Telephone/AT&T, operating as a monopoly, controlled the entire U.S. telephone system. A series of legal battles, beginning in the late 1960s and continuing into the 1970s, introduced an era of **deregulation** that in 1984 resulted in the federally mandated breakup of Bell Telephone/AT&T into two components. One component resulted in seven regional Bell operating companies (RBOCs) that were to provide only local telephone services to businesses and homes. The second component created a new AT&T that was permitted to provide only long-distance telephone services, but in competition with other providers. A key goal of deregulation is to allow competitors to enter a market so that consumers in that market can have a wider selection of service providers from which to choose.

The 1980s saw the beginnings of much greater competition among service providers in the areas of telecommunications and data communications. In 1996, the U.S. Congress passed the Telecommunications Competition and Deregulation Act. This law resulted in changing the highly regulated and monopolistic industry of providing local telephone service into one of open competition. The issue of deregulation is politically charged and has become a global topic of concern. International competition to provide telecommunication services has intensified as for-profit organizations seek to increase their market share. The trend, in the United States and elsewhere, has been toward greater deregulation.

Phase 4: The Internet as a Common Tool

In 1958, in response to the Soviet Union's launch of *Sputnik,* the U.S. Department of Defense established the Advanced Research Projects Agency (ARPA). One of ARPA's primary missions was to find a way for computers to communicate with each other, regardless of the computers' manufacturers. Recall that in the 1960s, mainframe computers were not cross-platform conversant and were a closed architecture technology. Researchers knew that by designing a communication model that enabled different types of computers to communicate with each other over great distances, researchers could more easily exchange ideas and knowledge, thus reducing duplication of effort.

By 1969, ARPA would evolve into **ARPANET**. That same year, the first two nodes of ARPANET, which would eventually become the Internet, were connected to each other. One node was located at the Stanford Research Institute and the second was at University of California Los Angeles (UCLA). Things have changed.

According to IMS Research (*www.imsresearch.com*), the number of devices connected to the Internet was expected to exceed 5 billion by August 2010. With the explosive growth of mobile device technology, and in particular telephones, that number was far exceeded. Another way of stating this is that the **Internet** is a great network of networks based on a common architecture. From its origin as a research tool, the Internet has been transformed into an infrastructure that is increasingly viewed as the single-most important universal information transport and service tool ever created. However, the Internet's very success has led many to believe that the Internet as we now know it is nearing a meltdown.

The Internet mostly in use today, especially in the United States, is known as version **IPv4 (Internet protocol version 4)**. When this version of the Internet was created, researchers had no way of knowing how wildly successful the Internet would become. Also, the types of data that IPv4 was designed to carry did not include relatively resource-intensive kinds of files such as those carrying video and sound. Users have come to expect a rich multimedia experience, and they expect computer and communication infrastructures to support such use. In addition, today's users increasingly want to connect many other types of devices to the Internet, including computers, cell phones, pagers, cameras, cars, and other devices, so that users are always "plugged-in."

Business has also been an aggressive adopter of Internet technologies. Through the Internet, businesses seek solutions that allow hardware, software, and services to be integrated into one secure, reliable, and scalable infrastructure. The Internet is evolving into an intelligent network capable of providing Web services, policy management, network management, security, and mobility. In the long run, for all of this to happen, IPv4 will ultimately be replaced with the new improved **IPv6** (Internet protocol version 6). This transition is taking place now. IPv6 is viewed by many technologists as a solution to the significant problems that IPv4 cannot address.

Phase 5: Pervasive Computing

The nature of what we mean by communications and how we communicate is rapidly changing. A major discussion under way in today's business world revolves around the convergence of communications. The Internet, and wireless technologies, are playing a major role in how this convergence is being implemented. We are fast approaching a society in which pervasive—and some say invasive—computing is the norm. From your wristwatch to your phone to perhaps the buttons on your shirt—all of which could serve as digital receivers—we are an increasingly connected society and carry our connections with us wherever we go. A technology so commonly used that it is taken for granted within a society is referred to as a **pervasive technology**. A famous example of a commonly used pervasive technology in industrial countries is the traditional telephone system. Residents of the United States expect to hear a dial tone when they pick up a traditional "land line" telephone, whether they are in a metropolis such as Los Angeles or a tiny rural community in the mountains of Montana. The following discussion of telemetry provides a few examples of this relatively new pervasive technology.

Telemetry is the wireless transmission and reception of data for the purpose of remotely monitoring environmental conditions or equipment parameters. Telemetry is used with mobile robots, satellites, and space probes. As with the former spaceshuttle, the International Space Station uses telemetry to monitor the physical condition of astronauts and ensure the maintenance of their working environment.

Telemetry can be used to monitor security and fire alarm systems, read utility meters, track and locate vehicles or inventory, or poll remote candy vending machines to determine if they require stocking. Industrial manufacturers use telemetry to streamline maintenance tasks, prolonging machine life and reducing product support, and to improve asset utilization. The health-care industry uses telemetry to minimize human error in recording patient data at their point of capture, to improve doctor–hospital workflow processes, and to better manage individual patient health-care services and data. For businesses, telemetry is an efficient way to control and access critical data, saving time and money. Each of these examples is a form of pervasive computing, and demonstrates, again, how businesses benefit from this technology.

The Internet has become be an essential medium for such communications convergence. Originally used for remote access, file sharing, and e-mail, the Internet, by way of the World Wide Web (WWW), has become an information repository. The Internet has made e-commerce a multi-billion-dollar reality. Common communications today include instant messaging as well as online gaming, music, movies, and voice/video conferencing.

Increasingly, users expect to use these communications anywhere and everywhere they go, sometimes to the displeasure of those around them. Of course, supporting these types of communications presents a number of challenges, especially those relating to privacy, security, cost, and access.

DEFINING DATA COMMUNICATIONS

Data communications is formally considered as a subset of telecommunications, meaning that data communications is included within telecommunications, not the other way around. Even so, data communications covers a very large territory. Let's look first at what is meant by telecommunications, so that we can then see why data communications has had a more narrow focus.

The prefix *tele* comes from the Greek word for "distant," and in telecommunications, we are usually talking about great distances. **Telecommunications** includes many different types of communication besides data, such as voice and video, and includes telephony, telegraphy, and television. Therefore, telecommunications historically has supported other purposes beyond communications between computers and networks. A number of standards-setting bodies, both national and international, specify how, where, when, what, and who can provide telecommunications services. A few of these standards organizations will be identified in a moment.

Data communications, as the name implies, is focused on the communication of data and information between computers and computer networks. Today, the term *data* encompasses a much broader range of elements, no longer consisting of just numbers and text. Data might include graphic images, sound files, or video elements. Because of the broader context that data now includes, and with technologies such as voice-over IP (VoIP), the distinction between the worlds of telecommunications and data communications is blurring. The difference between telecommunications and data communications may soon be one that is no difference at all.

Regardless of the kind of data, that data will ultimately be expressed in **binary** code (a coding notation covered later in the text) so that computers can process it. Binary coding schemes, using elements called *bits,* represent the data in the form of zeroes and ones, as shown in Figure 1.2. One binary coding scheme in particular that will affect data communications technologies is Unicode, a relatively new technology that has received a lot of attention.

After being expressed in binary format, the data may need to be transmitted from one computer to another or from one network to another, in order to be processed. Data communications networks have been built to handle this transition. Indeed, data communications networks may use many different types of computers and other devices that enable data to be processed and routed. A data communications network may also have many different types of transmission media that permit the data to be carried from one location to another. The medium may be wired or wireless. Besides the devices

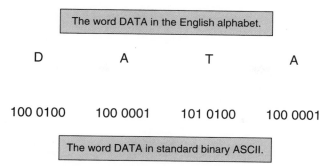

FIGURE 1.2   DATA in Standard Binary ASCII

that process the data, and the transmission media that carry the data, the data communications network will also have rules or protocols that determine how the devices and transmission media work with each other. These rules and protocols are defined by standards that are set by formal and informal controlling organizations; many of these organizations are the same ones that define telecommunication standards.

All of these elements affect and determine the quality of the data communications infrastructure. The three questions that must be considered with regard to data communications are (1) how the data are delivered, (2) how accurate the data are when delivered, and (3) how accessible the data are to those who need to use it. This text will discuss the many types of devices, transmission media, rules or protocols, and standards that allow the data communications infrastructure to exist. As you can see, data communications is itself a vast topic.

PROTOCOLS

Simply stated, a **protocol** is a set of rules that determine how something is performed or accomplished. Many kinds of protocols rule our daily lives, some formal, some casual. For example, when a customer goes into a bank to make a transaction, protocol states that the customer politely wait in line until it is his or her turn to speak with a teller. We have language protocols, called rules of grammar, which make it possible for people who speak and read the same language to understand each other. Without human protocols, our lives would be even more complicated than they already are, and social institutions as we know them would not be possible. Like people, computers, and the networks they use, need protocols in order to understand and work with each other. Also, as with human protocols, different types of protocols exist for different needs.

In data communications, protocols must possess four key characteristics in order for communications to successfully and effectively occur. First, an agreement, or protocol, must specify how the data are to be packaged, or formatted, so that they can be sent between sending and receiving devices. If a person were to write an English-language letter and send it to a business associate in Spain, that person would follow the formatting, or syntax, protocol rules for English grammar. Having a formatting protocol, however, does not necessarily imply that the sender and receiver will understand each other. For example, the Spanish business associate may not read English. The same is true with communicating devices. Such devices, of course, will not be using a language such as English or Spanish to communicate, but rather some type of binary encoding scheme, as discussed earlier. An **encoding scheme** is a way of transforming one type of data or information into another. Translating English into Spanish, for example, requires an encoding scheme (Figure 1.3) that follows a formatting protocol. A binary encoding scheme will also follow a formatting protocol.

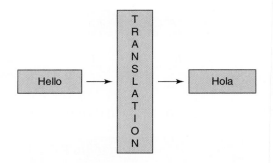

In this social encoding example the English word "Hello" is translated into its Spanish equivalent of "Hola." Communicating devices in a network perform similar types of translation from one binary encoding scheme to another.

FIGURE 1.3   Social Encoding Scheme

However, if a receiving device does not understand the binary data format of the sending device, communication will not occur. Just as someone who reads only Spanish would not be able to understand a letter written in English, so, too, a protocol should address a second characteristic—that is, the ability of the communicating devices to understand the formatting protocols being used. Within the binary encoding schemes, or protocols, that are in use, sending and receiving devices will have to agree, for the sake of understanding, as to what particular patterns of bits mean within the bit stream being sent. Formatting of the data according to a protocol is one thing; the two communicating devices must also understand the meaning of the format. For the Spanish associate discussed earlier, when the sender sends the letter, the sender better also send an English-to-Spanish dictionary and grammar book so that the Spanish business associate can understand and interpret what has been written.

A third characteristic that data communication protocols should address is the speed of the communication. When a sending device sends its data to a receiving device, the two devices must agree on the rate of speed that will be used in the transmission. For example, one device may be faster than the other, and without controlling for this, transmission overload could occur. Imagine what would likely happen if all the cars driving on a busy highway were suddenly detoured to a two-lane country road! The two-lane country road would suffer serious transmission overload. Protocols determine the speed at which sending and receiving devices can communicate based on the capabilities of each device.

Finally, when two devices need to communicate, one of the devices may not be available for a variety of reasons: hardware failure, a downed communication link, system repair, or software upgrading. Communication protocols determine when, and if, communications can occur. Devices are not like people; they require specific control over not only the *speed* at which they can communicate but also *when* they can communicate. A sending device needs to know if a receiving device is available for communications. Both sender and receiver have to agree on the speed of the communication, if available.

Technology continues to provide us with increasing convenience. Yet, this very convenience in many ways may require that we surrender, knowingly or not, data and information that many of us might consider to be private. How much management over a technology should a user, or consumer, of that technology be able to regulate and control? The issue of control and access over data and information involves a code of conduct, or code of ethics, for those who manage this data and information.

The Ethical Perspective

Evolving data communications technologies, which are pervasive or invasive depending on how one views them, are having dramatic effects on the ethical standards of conduct within our society. These technologies are changing our society's standards of what is ethically considered right and wrong in terms of the use of data and information. Consider the following: Should a clothing manufacturer be able to stitch tags into the labels of its garments that potentially track, through wireless technology, where the garments go when they are taken off store shelves? This technology is already available through the use of Radio Frequency Identification (RFID) tags, a type of telemetry referred to at the beginning of this chapter. From a business perspective, such tracking makes a lot of sense. A business wants to be able to keep accurate records of its inventory. If a business knows what is in its warehouse or selling from retailers' shelves, it will have a better understanding of whether the production of certain items should be increased or decreased. And RFID can help a business do that. Yet, as a consumer of that clothing product, when you buy a shirt, jacket, or pair of socks, are you concerned about the possibility of your movements being tracked and identified?

What do you think about this? What implications, beyond clothing, do you foresee? Might this affect our legal system? What about our medical system? Is this type of market tracking what you had in mind when you bought your last pair of shoes? From a business perspective, though, how is this type of tracking beneficial? Can data of this type be ethically used? How might it be ethically abused?

The Electronic Privacy Information Center, a nonprofit organization located in Washington, DC, has posted a warning regarding RFID technology on its website, *www.epic.org/privacy/rfid*. The warning makes for interesting reading.

STANDARDS AND STANDARDS-SETTING BODIES

Protocols, as stated earlier, are the rules that determine how devices communicate. The question becomes, Who determines the rules? The answer is that **standards** are defined that establish the essential rules, functionalities, and operations a protocol must fulfill. Standards-setting organizational bodies *usually* create and define the standards. The word *usually* is used because there are two kinds of standards: formal and informal. First, let's describe why standards are desirable.

Standards provide well-known and published guidelines upon which a technology can be based. By following standards, providers of data and telecommunications technologies ensure the interoperability of their software and hardware. Owing to this interoperability, consumers of the technology have a more competitive and open market from which to select their services and products. Developers of a technology know that by following standards they will create a product of much greater appeal to their market of interest. Managers of a technology appreciate standards because it makes for easier maintenance, upgrade, and troubleshooting of their technology infrastructures. Standards are well documented, and, in general, rigorously tested and evaluated before they can become standards.

Formal standards are those standards that have been authorized by either an officially recognized body or by law and regulation. It is not unusual for formal standards to evolve from informal *de facto* standards. **De facto standards** are either proprietary or nonproprietary. The trend in most industries over the past couple of decades has been toward **nonproprietary**, meaning "open," standards. A technology may, because of its pervasiveness, or because it is the only model of that technology, become a de facto standard simply by its existence and use. These types of de facto standards will occasionally evolve into formal standards. A famous example of a de facto standard that later became a formal standard is the Ethernet protocol. Ethernet was created by Xerox Corporation and later formalized by the Institute of Electrical and Electronics Engineers (IEEE; *www.ieee.org*) as the 802.3 standard.

The IEEE is one example of a standards-setting body; there are many more. In addition, many standards-setting bodies are managed by professional organizations, not by formal governmental agencies. This text will identify only those that are of primary importance in North America, but be aware that there are standards-setting bodies for Europe, Asia, and other parts of the world. The following lists the key North American standards-setting groups:

- The International Standards Organization (ISO; *www.iso.org*)
- The International Telecommunications Union-Telecommunication Standards Sector (ITU-T; *www.itu.int*)
- The American National Standards Institute (ANSI; *www.ansi.org*)
- The Institute of Electrical and Electronics Engineers (IEEE; *www.ieee.org*)
- The Telecommunications Industry Association (TIA; *www.tiaonline.org*)
- The Internet Society (ISOC; *www.isoc.org*)
- The Internet Engineering Task Force (IETF; *www.ietf.org*)
- The Internet Engineering Steering Group (IESG; *www.iesg.org*)
- The Internet Architecture Board (IAB; *www.iab.org*)
- The Internet Assigned Numbers Authority (IANA; *www.iana.org*)

The ISO is an international body of voluntary organizations with great influence in the field of information technology. The organization attempts to create international technological compatibility by supporting and establishing worldwide standards.

The ITU-T concerns itself with international telecommunications issues. Its particular areas of interest are phone and data systems. The ITU-T has established standards that define data transmission over phone lines, e-mail and directory services, and transmission over public digital networks.

The American National Standards Institute represents the United States on the ISO. However, ANSI does not have a formal affiliation with the federal government; it is a nonprofit, private corporation. The membership list of ANSI includes industry associations, consumer groups, governmental bodies, professional associations, and other interested parties. It is the principal standards-setting body in the United States.

The IEEE defines many standards for both local area networks (LANs) and backbone networks (BNs). Emphasizing electronics and electrical engineering, the IEEE is the world's largest professional engineering society. This organization plays a critical part in establishing new wireless communication standards. (See this chapter's "Topic in Focus" to find out more about the IEEE.)

The TIA is a nonprofit organization accredited by the American National Standards Institute (ANSI) to develop voluntary industry standards for a wide variety of telecommunications products. The TIA plays a fundamental role in the defining of standards for electrical and functional characteristics of interface equipment.

There are numerous Internet-related organizations, each with its particular responsibility and area of interest; here we identify just a few. The ISOC, an open-member professional society, meaning you could join it if you wanted to, is the closest the Internet has to an owning organization. It represents more than 100 countries. The IETF is also an international community, consisting of researchers, vendors, and network designers. Its concern is with the evolution of the Internet's architecture and its efficient functioning. The IETF spearheaded the development of the Simple Network

Management Protocol (SNMP) and reviews performance standards for bridges, routers, and router protocols. The Internet Engineering Steering Group (IESG) is the technical, management arm of the IETF. The IESG is responsible for actions associated with, and the final specifications of, Internet standards. It manages the Internet standards process. The Internet Architecture Board (IAB) provides strategic direction and guidance to the IESG and IETF. Finally, the IANA governs the assignment of IP (Internet Protocol) numbers.

Although not a standards-setting body, the powerful United States Federal Communications Commission (FCC; *www.fcc.gov*) is a very important regulatory agency. The FCC oversees and authorizes interstate and international electrical communication systems originating in the United States. Before a piece of communication technology equipment can be marketed in the United States, FCC approval is required. The FCC plays a major role in ensuring that the national telephone system operates effectively.

Besides standards-setting bodies, data communication networks also, of course, depend on design, configuration, implementation, and maintenance. Hardware and software components will both be required. Networks also usually follow guidelines based on models. Several data communications network models have been developed, but two in particular have won wide acceptance. One is the Open Systems Interconnection, or OSI, model. The second is the Transmission Control Protocol/Internet Protocol, or TCP/IP, model. We cover these models in detail in Chapter 2.

Chapter Summary

Five phases characterize the evolution of data communications over the past five decades: (1) digitization, (2) expansion, (3) deregulation, (4) Internet as a common tool, and (5) pervasive computing. Technology continues to change, altering our definition of what is meant by "communications." Data communications is a subset of telecommunications. Whereas telecommunications involves such technologies as telephony and television, traditional data communications is more concerned with the transmission of data between computers and computer networks. In the transmission of data from one location to another, data are first transformed using binary coding schemes. Binary coding schemes use the binary digits 0 and 1, which are called bits, to represent data.

Data communications uses protocols, or rules, that establish how the communications occur. There are many different types of protocols that fulfill different purposes and functionalities. Protocols state how the data are to be formatted, how the format is to be interpreted, the rate at which the data are to be transmitted, and whether communications between two devices can be established.

Protocols become established or defined through a standards process. Both formal and informal standards exist. The trend is for standards to be open and publicly available for all to use. There are numerous standards-setting bodies; many of them are nongovernmental, private nonprofit organizations.

Networks have both physical and logical components—respectively, the hardware devices that make them up and the software that drives them. Networks are also based on models. Two major models used in data communications are the Open Systems Interconnection, or OSI, model and the Transmission Control Protocol/Internet Protocol, or TCP/IP, model.

Keywords

ARPANET *4*
Binary *6*
Data communications *6*
De facto standard *9*
Deregulation *4*
Digitization *3*

Encoding scheme *7*
Internet *5*
IPv4 *5*
IPv6 *5*
Nonproprietary *9*
Pervasive technology *5*

Proprietary *3*
Protocol *7*
Standards *9*
Telecommunications *6*
Telemetry *5*

Chapter Questions

Short-Answer Questions

1. What are open standards, and what, if any, are the advantages of such standards?
2. What is a protocol and why would one be used? Provide an example of a technological protocol or a society-based protocol.
3. How do formal standards differ from de facto standards?
4. What are the five phases associated with the evolution of data communication networks?
5. With what scale of network is the IEEE associated?
6. What organization is the principal standards-setting body in the United States?
7. What is an encoding scheme?
8. What is telemetry?

Hands-On Projects

1. At your college, university, or workplace, interview a manager in networking administration. From this manager, find out what job duties and responsibilities are involved. What parts of the job are most challenging? What parts are most satisfying? After the interview, report to your instructor and/or class as to what you discovered.
2. Look at an online or printed job site. Find job descriptions for a network administrator. What types of skill sets and preparation are required to obtain the position?
3. Review the catalog of a college or university that offers coursework in networking and data communications. Identify and describe three courses related to these topics.
4. Many technical organizations provide student resources. Other than the IEEE, which is the Topic in Focus for Chapter 1, contact one of the standard-setting bodies identified in this chapter. Find out, if possible, if this organization provides any student resources, incentives, tutorial assistance, specialized programs, or other services. If such services are provided, what are they? Is there a student membership? If so, is there a cost or fee? Are tutorials or other educational materials available? Report to your instructor and/or class on what you have discovered.

Research in Brief

As a data communications professional, your researching skills will be very important, whether in troubleshooting a jabbering network host, finding the latest software driver, or providing a cost-benefit analysis for a technical solution to your management. At the end of every chapter, questions will be presented that require additional research and analysis on your part. For one or more of the following questions, provide a three-to four-page report based on your findings.

1. Describe what a protocol is and detail the process of how a protocol might become a standard. Discuss the advantages of open protocols.
2. Unicode provides for extensive new character-set definitions. Visit and explore the Unicode website at *www.unicode.org*. Answer the following based on your findings:

   • Who belongs to the Unicode consortium?
   • What is the current version of Unicode and what does it include or not include?
   • What future changes to Unicode are planned?
   • What are the benefits of a coding scheme such as Unicode?

3. Pervasive computing is transforming how we think of communications technology. The following three websites address pervasive computing: *www.computer. org*, *www.ibm.com/pvc*, and *www.nist.gov*. Visit these sites, or others that you find, and answer the following questions:

   • What organizations are involved in pervasive computing?
   • How do you think pervasive computing might change a society?
   • What types of issues are being discussed with regard to pervasive computing?

4. Select any standards-setting body or organization, other than the IEEE (discussed in the following Topic in Focus), and describe the primary functions of that body or organization.

Topic in Focus

A CLOSER LOOK AT THE IEEE

Earlier in this chapter you were introduced to a number of standard-setting bodies. One of the most influential of these bodies is the IEEE (Institute of Electrical and Electronics Engineers). The IEEE refers to itself as "the world's largest technical professional society—promoting the development and application of electrotechnology and allied sciences for the benefit of humanity, the advancement of the profession, and the well-being of our members." The IEEE helps to develop, modify, and maintain standards that have a national and international impact.

As a professional organization, the IEEE relies on an international group of elected and appointed volunteer members. According to the IEEE's website (*www. ieee.org*), the organization's "governance structure includes boards for operational areas as well as bodies representing members in the 45 societies and technical councils and ten worldwide geographic regions." Central to what this organization does is to encourage technological innovation, particularly in the areas of networking and data communications. The IEEE sponsors many local chapters as well as publications and journals. This is an open-membership society for professional technologists.

More than 90,000 students belong to the IEEE, which maintains 1,855 student branches in 80 countries, and 483 student branches at various colleges and universities. The organization offers student membership discounts and special services, and is particularly targeted at students from particular areas of study: Engineering, Computer Sciences, Information Technology, Physical Sciences, Biological and Medical Sciences, Mathematics, Technical Communications, Education, Management, and Law and Policy.

From the IEEE's primary home website, students can find links that provide information on scholarships, competition, conferences, and student branch locations.

The IEEE dates back to 1884, when it was referred to as the American Institute of Electrical Engineers (AIEE). This was at a time when electricity was just beginning to have a major impact on social life in the United States. Among the IEEE's early members were Thomas Edison and Alexander Graham Bell. Today, the membership numbers into the hundreds of thousands from across the globe, and is no longer strictly an "American" group. As of this writing, the IEEE numbers more than 395,000 members from more than 160 countries. It sponsors a "Global History Network," *http://www.ieeeghn.org*, to which members and invited guests are able to add postings and other types of content. An interesting feature of this global history website is an interactive timeline that permits users to identify IEEE articles chronologically.

Of particular relevance to our text is the IEEE's outline of its standards development process; it may be found at *http://standards.ieee.org/resources/development/index.html*. In fact, within the IEEE is a "Standards Association," *http://standards.ieee.org*, with its own membership. The standards development process allows members to initiate, produce, and/or manage standards. Members may actively participate in all steps in the process, or only in the step of specific interest to themselves. Currently the IEEE has more than 1,300 standards that are in one or more stages of the development process. These standards address a wide range of technology, both wired and wireless.

From its primary website, a user can find links to a variety of features of interest, including:

- Membership
- Publications
- Conferences
- Standards
- Education and Careers
- Grants
- Awards

2

Networking Models: OSI and TCP/IP

The Business Benefit

ACME is a business with 1,000 employees and 50,000 customers. As a business, ACME includes such departments as Human Resources, Marketing, Fiscal Services, Facilities, Research and Planning, and Legal. All of these are important functions that are needed by ACME to be an effective business. Each organizational layer has its own specific responsibilities. For example, the accounts receivable manager doesn't have to know what the marketing manager's job duties are or how they are done. Each functional area is responsible for its own duties, although each functional area still needs to communicate with other functional areas in the organization in order for the organization to be effective. Let's look at this in a possible business scenario.

A secretary gathers financial sales data from individual department employees. He uses the data to type, in a company-required format, a financial analysis statement he then passes up to his manager. The secretary is not required or expected to explain or understand the analysis he has typed. The secretary is responsible only for accurately typing the financial analysis into the exact format required by his manager and then passing the analysis up to his manager.

The manager accepts the printed analysis. He is not concerned with how the analysis was typed, who typed it, and on what computer. He is only concerned that the data on the report is accurate and produced in a timely manner. The manager takes the analysis and other data and summarizes the information for the vice president of finance.

The vice president of finance, who wants her data in a specific summarized format, also does not care or ask who typed the data or how. What she wants is that the data be in an accurate format appropriate to her level in the organization. She will then process the data and pass it up to the next level of organizational hierarchy. Here, we see that one layer of the organization does not need to know the detail of how a different layer produced its results. And yet, organizational layers that touch, or interact, do require that data that are passed back and forth be in a specific format and delivery for the information to be usable.

Business efficiency requires that organizational layers interact effectively and in a manner that allows the business to prosper. This is the same concept used by the networking models presented in this chapter.

Learning Objectives

After studying this chapter, you should be able to:

- Explain networking models.
- Describe open architectures.
- List the benefits of layered architectures.
- Understand the OSI networking model.
- Understand the TCP/IP networking model.
- Identify four general categories of networks.

NETWORKING MODELS

Computers and other devices process data and then may route that data from one location to another. In order to get the data from point A to point B, an infrastructure must be used. Recall that an infrastructure is like a highway that provides a means of transporting goods from one city to another. In data communications, various types of networks are used as a transporting infrastructure.

Networks have both physical and logical components: the hardware devices that make them up and the software that drives them. The physical aspects of a network will also include the media used to transport data from one location to another. The media are either wired or wireless. Many of the physical components that make up a network can be seen and touched, but not all. For example, microwave transmissions are not visible to the human eye, and yet microwaves are a physical reality. Consider that dogs can hear sound frequencies that humans cannot. The fact that we cannot hear these sound frequencies does not mean that they do not physically exist. Physical and logical components within the network work with each other based on standards and protocols. Above and beyond their standards and protocols, networks have another dimension that describes how they function. This extra dimension is the **networking model** on which the network is based.

When a builder wants to build a house, he or she usually starts with an architectural blueprint. The blueprint is not the house itself, of course, but rather a conceptual, logical model of what the house will be. As a model, the blueprint can be modified, perhaps as the builder adds or removes rooms during the design process. Eventually, the house is built based on the final model described by the blueprint. The end result may vary from the model as originally drawn, because the concept, in this case the blueprint, which is logical, and the physical construction, the house, are not the same thing.

The model is a guideline. Depending on what is being built, the builder may follow the model precisely, to its last detail, or more generally, deviating from the model's specifications. If the model is good, it provides good guidelines, and the builder will end up with, in this example, a sound building. If the model is bad, then the house will also be bad or flawed. In this case, the house may not survive the next big storm.

OPEN ARCHITECTURES

Open architecture models share similar advantages to open standards in that they are available for public comment, review, and varying implementations. Open models provide a common basis of understanding because their functionalities are documented and available. Open models lend themselves to duplication; this means that the designers of technologies who use these models do not have to take on the cost and labor of creating new ones. Models, because they are conceptual, can be modified to fit varying conditions. **Open architecture technology** based on established models provides known advantages and disadvantages. Software and hardware vendors who create products based on accepted models can produce products that have a wider consumer appeal.

Data communications networks, like houses, are also built from models. Several data communications network models have been developed, but two in particular have won wide acceptance. One is the **open systems interconnection (OSI) model**. The second is the **transmission control protocol/Internet protocol (TCP/IP) model**. Perhaps these models are new to you. However, if you have ever used a bank's automated teller machine (ATM) machine, paid for gasoline at an automated gas pump using a charge card, made an airline reservation over the phone, paid a restaurant check using a credit card, or browsed the World Wide Web, then you have used a data communications network that is based on one of these two models.

Both models have several characteristics in common. First, they are both open architecture models. This means that anyone, anywhere, at any time, can freely design or create technologies based on these models, which is a real advantage. Second, both models are based on a layered architecture. This means that each model can be broken into several distinct components, called layers. Each layer within the model has its own particular and specific responsibilities and functionalities. A major topic discussed throughout this text is what these layers do, how they do it, and why. And finally, each model is well established and accepted by the data and telecommunications industries as models that provide clear guidelines as to how to build a data communications network that works. But remember, models are conceptual guidelines; how they are physically implemented can vary.

This chapter introduces you to both the OSI and the TCP/IP models, but the emphasis in this text will be on the TCP/IP model. The TCP/IP model has become the model of choice throughout the world not only for wide area networks (WANs) but also for metropolitan area networks (MANs), local area networks (LANs), and backbone networks (BNs). Throughout the text we attempt to point out the similarities between the two models. And, in fact, they have much in common. Perhaps the most important feature they share is that both the OSI and the TCP/IP models have layered architectures. Let's discuss briefly why this layered architecture is so advantageous.

LAYERED ARCHITECTURES

In a **layered architecture**, each layer is assigned a specific set of functionalities and responsibilities. This means that one layer does not have to do the work of all the other layers or understand what the other layers are doing. Instead, each layer is responsible only for its assigned duties, no more, no less.

As noted at the beginning of this chapter, different business functional areas are responsible for their specific duties. This works for networking models as well as for human organizations. In the layered network model approach, each layer has a set of functions that that layer is responsible for. Each layer only needs to be able to communicate with the layer immediately above or below itself. The layer does not have to understand what happens above or below it, but it must know the proper format to pass information up or down.

The network layer models we discuss in this chapter work in much the same way. Let's take a closer look at the layers that make up the OSI and TCP/IP models.

THE OSI MODEL

Developed by the ISO, one of the major standards groups we presented earlier, the open systems interconnection (OSI) model has seven distinct layers. Each layer has a specific set of functionalities and responsibilities. Starting from the bottom of the model, the physical and data link layers are low-level layers that are responsible for placing the data on a physical medium and then framing, or formatting, the data bits into a form that can be passed from one computer to another. The mid-level layers, which are the network and transport layers, are responsible for the complete delivery of a message, and the data packets that make up the message, between the sender and receiver. The top, high-level layers—the application, presentation, and session layers—represent functions that involve the user or user applications. The order of these layers, from top to bottom, is shown in Figure 2.1.

Notice in Figure 2.1 that the sender and receiver have the same set of layers in the exact same order. We call this type of architecture a **layer stack**, which is like a stack of pancakes. (In a later chapter, you will learn that there are also stacks called *protocol stacks*.) The layers on the sender's side do the same work as the layers on the receiver's side. A good phrase for remembering these layers in their correct order is: All People Seem To Need Digital Power. Each layer represents a type of function that a protocol should support if that protocol is designed to work at that particular layer.

(Upon examining each layer more closely, you will probably find that there are terms or concepts that are unfamiliar or that you do not yet understand. Don't be too concerned at this point; remember, this is only Chapter 2. As you move through the remainder of the text, these terms, concepts, and functionalities will be described in much greater detail.)

Application Layer

Here, the term *application* does not refer to an end-user application, such as a spreadsheet or word processor, but instead refers to how a user or a user application would gain network access. Users and end-user applications gain network access by cooperating with a process running at the application layer of the OSI. Three key services provided at the **application layer** include (1) synchronizing the services between a user application and the protocol(s) it may use, (2) ensuring that necessary resources required by an application service is available, and (3) making sure that the correct communication protocol or service is available to the application.

Some of the services supported at this layer include e-mail, remote file access and transfer, printing services, various messaging services, and shared database management.

Sender	Receiver
7. Application	7. Application
6. Presentation	6. Presentation
5. Session	5. Session
4. Transport	4. Transport
3. Network	3. Network
2. Data link	2. Data link
1. Physical	1. Physical

FIGURE 2.1   Seven Layers of the OSI Model

Presentation Layer

The **presentation layer** ensures that data passed up to the application layer is in a format understandable to that layer. This layer is responsible for the interoperability between a sender and receiver who might be using different encoding schemes. Recall that data have to be encoded into some binary form so that the data can be used by computer systems. The presentation layer might perform translation, but it can also, if required, perform encryption and compression.

Encryption scrambles data so that only those with a decryption key can use the data. Encrypted data must be unscrambled in order for the data to be available for use. **Compression**, which occurs at the sender's end, reduces the number of bits to be transmitted based on some type of compression scheme. The receiver would have to have the proper decompression software to then use the transmitted data in its original, uncompressed form.

Session Layer

The sender and receiver may need to establish a connection, or session, before they can begin to communicate. The **session layer** is responsible for establishing, maintaining, and terminating communications running between processes or applications across the network. In essence, the session layer manages the dialog that occurs between two communicating devices.

Transport Layer

The **transport layer** ensures that the entire message sent from a sender to a receiver has been delivered. By providing connection control, the transport layer can be either connectionless or connection-oriented. (Explaining *connectionless* or *connection-oriented* at this point would be too involved, but you will see in later chapters exactly what is meant by these terms.) In addition, the transport layer disassembles or reassembles data based on whether it is passing the data down (disassembly) or passing the data up (reassembly) the layer stack.

Network Layer

Whereas the transport layer is responsible for determining if the entire message has been delivered, the **network layer** is concerned about the delivery of individual packets across network links. This layer is responsible for ensuring that each packet that makes up a message gets from its point of origin, the sender, to its final destination, the receiver. The network layer also handles the **logical addressing** of a packet, attaching to the packet the logical addresses of both the sender and receiver. Something that is "logical," as in a logical address, can be changed or modified. Something that is "physical," as in a physical address, is fixed, or set, and cannot be changed. Based on where the sender and receiver are in relation to each other, on the same or different logical networks, the network layer may also perform routing services. Routing services will be explained in a later chapter.

Data Link Layer

The **data link layer** has several key responsibilities. This layer takes unpackaged bit stream data arriving from the physical layer and packages the bits into units called *frames*. The data link layer attaches a physical address to each frame. This layer is responsible for getting each frame from one node to another on its way from sender to receiver. This layer also provides for flow control, error control, and access control. In this way, the network layer provides for logical addressing, and the data link layer provides for physical addressing. In data communications, as you will discover, there are many types of addressing schemes, each serving a particular purpose.

Physical Layer

The **physical layer** concerns itself with transmitting an unpackaged bit stream over some type of physical medium. The medium might be wired or wireless. This layer deals with the mechanical and electrical/optical specifications that define the connection between devices and the transmission medium they use. The physical layer is also responsible for the synchronization of bits, line configuration, physical topology, and the transmission mode. (Again, it is not expected at this point that any of these terms are meaningful to you, but by the end of this text they will be.)

The Ethical Perspective

Enterprise Wiring and Safety

Wiring a network, especially a large one, isn't just a matter of having things work and look nice. Real-world fire, health, and safety issues are also involved. Several government bodies set building regulations and safety standards. One such body is the U.S. Department of Labor's Occupational Safety and Health Administration, or OSHA (*www. osha.gov*). Many OSHA regulations and standards cover wiring methods, components, and how and where equipment is deployed. Businesses are expected to follow OSHA regulations, as well as those set by local governing bodies, such as those at the state, county, and city levels.

Meeting all of these regulations costs money. Staff must be hired to determine where a business may or may not be in compliance. For areas not in compliance, necessary modifications must be made, again at a cost, to ensure that a business meets the legal requirements. Some businesses may reduce the incurred costs by meeting only the minimum legal requirements. Other businesses may go above and beyond regulatory agency requirements, perhaps as a quality of service feature for employees or clients. Of course, the staff employed should have the proper training to ensure that all wiring, electrical, and other infrastructure work is of good quality. It may surprise you to know that many of the courses on network wiring completed by networking technologists have an ethics component.

The ethics component often discusses quality of work, honesty, the technician's ability to follow instructions, integrity, and other interpersonal skills. Assume that ACME Corporation has requested that you present a bid to do the installation wiring for their entire enterprise network. You have visited several of their facilities and have noted that many of the networks do not comply with current fire and safety regulations. ACME has made it clear that they want the work done for the lowest possible cost. After completing your analysis, you provide your estimate.

Later, one of ACME's managers informally, not in writing, tells you that you can have the job if your bid were lower, perhaps through the use of lower-quality materials. This is a job that you and your employees would really like to have, because it could lead to other jobs. What would you do in this scenario? If you do not accept the job at ACME, should you alert a government agency about ACME's lack of compliance? What if other firms will not hire you should they discover that you reported ACME for lack of compliance? Does this situation involve business ethics?

THE TCP/IP MODEL

The transmission control protocol/Internet protocol (TCP/IP) model was developed prior to the OSI model. The layers of the two models are similar, but they are not exactly the same. One feature shared by TCP/IP and OSI is that they are both layered models. One difference, however, is that although everyone agrees that the OSI model has seven layers, TCP/IP, depending on who you speak to or what reference you are reading, may be presented as either a four- or a five-layer model. Either approach will include all of the functionalities of the TCP/IP model; the difference is in how some of those functionalities are divided between the layers. For purposes of clarity, this text will present TCP/IP as a five-layer model.

Another significant difference between TCP/IP and OSI is that with TCP/IP, several of the protocols associated with TCP/IP are relatively independent of the layer with which they are generally associated. This means that some protocols, depending on the needs of the network, can appear in one or another of the TCP/IP layers. With the OSI model, protocol functions are dependent, or tied, to the layer with which they are associated.

Each TCP/IP layer, as with the OSI model, has a set of functionalities and responsibilities. Also as with the OSI model, the lower-level layers (the physical and data link layers) are responsible for placing the data on a physical medium and then framing, or formatting, the data bits into a form that can be passed from one computer to another. The mid-level layers (the network and transport layers) are responsible for complete delivery of a message, and the data packets that make up the message, between sender and receiver. The top-most layer (the application layer) represents functions that involve the user or user applications. The application layer of TCP/IP includes the functionalities of the OSI application, presentation, and session layers. Figure 2.2 shows the layers, from top to bottom, of the TCP/IP model.

Let's look at each of these TCP/IP layers. You probably will not be surprised to discover that they have many of the same functionalities as those already identified in the OSI model.

Application Layer

The TCP/IP application layer is equivalent to the application, presentation, and session layers of the OSI model. In TCP/IP, this layer is also sometimes referred to as the *process layer,* because this is where a protocol stack interfaces with processes on a host machine, enabling that host to communicate across the network. Simply stated, this layer is the user's access to the network.

Transport Layer

The transport layer of the TCP/IP model has two key protocols that are identified with it: TCP (transmission control protocol) and UDP (user datagram protocol). Both TCP

Sender	Receiver
5. Application	5. Application
4. Transport	4. Transport
3. Network	3. Network
2. Data link	2. Data link
1. Physical	1. Physical

FIGURE 2.2 Five Layers of the TCP/IP Model

and UDP are responsible for the delivery of a message from one process to another—in other words, from the sender to the receiver. (A later chapter explores how TCP and UDP differ in this delivery.) This layer's primary responsibility is establishing and maintaining end-to-end communication between the sender and receiver.

Network Layer

The network layer of TCP/IP supports IP, or *Internet protocol*. Four protocols are associated IP: the address resolution protocol (ARP), the reverse address resolution protocol (RARP), the Internet control message protocol (ICMP), and the Internet group message protocol (IGMP). The key here is that IP, working within the network layer, is the transmission mechanism used by the other TCP/IP protocols. Formally, IP is called an "unreliable" and "connectionless" protocol, but that does not mean that it is bad or weak. The Internet protocol is used at the network layer to send units of data called *datagrams* from one network to the next. You will learn more about datagrams in a later chapter.

Data Link Layer

As in the OSI model, the data link layer is responsible for moving data from one host to the next in the network path from the sender to the receiver. Bear in mind that between the sending host and the receiving host there may be, and probably are, many intermediary hosts. The data link layer will frame the data bits and perform flow and error control.

Physical Layer

This TCP/IP layer serves the same purpose as in the OSI model. At the physical layer, the physical connections between the sender and receiver are specified. The physical layer will detail all of the hardware devices and physical mediums used to transport data from one host to another.

Networking Categories

Up to this point, you have discovered that there are data communication protocols, standards, and models, each of which is logical, defined, and documented. That is all very well and good, but as of yet nothing physically exists. You have the theory but not the product. What we must do next is implement the theory into a real, live, physical data communications network. But it is not, of course, quite that easy. The reality is that a one-size-fits-all network solution is not practical. In the physical implementation of the logical theory, many factors must be considered in order to determine the type of network that will be built.

Very likely, as a curious professional networking technologist, you are already asking several questions: What is the purpose of the network? What services will this network be expected to provide? What types of connectivity, 10 people or 100,000, are required? What are the physical dimensions the network? Is the network limited to the size of a room or the expanse of a country? What type of business and user applications will this network have to support? Are the applications online real-time, 24/7, or are they batched? Based on business requirements, what bandwidth and transmission issues need to be addressed? Will there be a need for remote accessibility? What size budget is available? Will there be a qualified staff to support the network? Does management understand the types of resources the network might require, and is management willing to support those needs? Do any regulatory issues—city, state, county, national, and/or international—need to be addressed? Have we run out of questions yet? The answer is, No.

There will always be more questions with more problems, or, as an optimist would say, more challenges. But these are just a sampling of the questions networking professionals ask themselves when designing a network. Likely, the answers will require more than one type, or category, of network. Answering the questions just presented will go a long way toward defining what category of network is needed. In many cases, several different types of networks may be required.

A network will fall into one of four categories:

- Local area network
- Backbone network
- Metropolitan area network
- Wide area network

Each type of network will be discussed in much greater detail in later chapters. This introductory chapter provides a very simple set of characteristics associated with each type of network. Keep in mind that each category of network is in itself a very large topic. Entire courses are designed around subtopics relating to each of these four categories. In today's world, a networking technologist will usually end up concentrating his or her technical skills in one of these four networking categories, and probably within a subtopic area of the category. It is to the advantage of the technologist, however, that he or she understands, at least in general, something about each of the four categories of networks that make up a complete data communications system.

This text provides a detailed overview of the critical factors that touch on each of these networking categories. Keep in mind that sometimes the distinction between where one category of network begins and another ends can be blurry. This is especially true when technologies designed to support one category of network are applied to a different category.

Local Area Networks

A **local area network (LAN)** is a network that is usually bounded by a relatively small geographical space—for example, a room, a building, or a complex of buildings. Generally, LANs are inexpensive to set up, especially compared to the other types of networks. Of great importance is that, because LANs typically do not cross public thoroughfares or property, they are not regulated by the FCC or state public utility commissions. Depending on the type of LAN, a LAN might include devices such as printers, microcomputers, workstations, servers, hubs, bridges, and routers. We describe these different devices in greater detail in later chapters. For now, be aware that a LAN can have differing configurations based on the specific needs of a business. An organization may have one LAN, or hundreds, based on business needs. Figure 2.3 illustrates a simple LAN.

Backbone Networks

Organizations that have more than one network, and especially more than one LAN, will probably want to connect these networks so that they can share resources. All of the networks that belong to one organization are collectively called the **enterprise**. An organization's enterprise network may consist of dozens, hundreds, or thousands of individual networks. The networks of the enterprise are typically connected through a **backbone network (BN)**. A BN is usually a high-speed circuit that connects all of the networks within the enterprise, allowing them to communicate with each other. Figure 2.4 demonstrates how a BN might be used.

FIGURE 2.3 Simple
Local Area Network
(LAN)

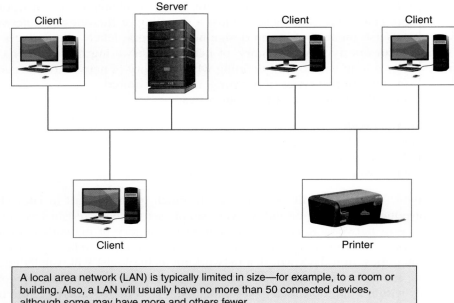

Client   Server   Client   Client

Client   Printer

A local area network (LAN) is typically limited in size—for example, to a room or building. Also, a LAN will usually have no more than 50 connected devices, although some may have more and others fewer.

FIGURE 2.4 Simple
Backbone Network
(BN) in a Single
Building

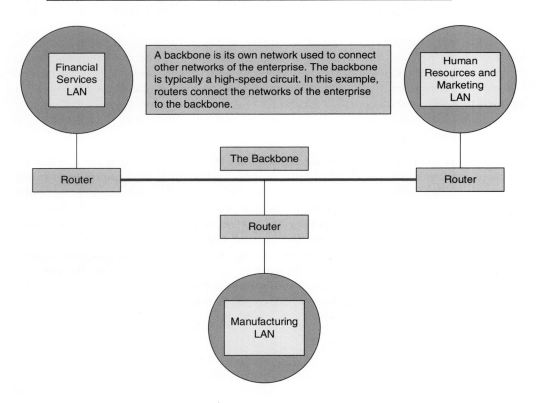

Financial
Services
LAN

A backbone is its own network used to connect other networks of the enterprise. The backbone is typically a high-speed circuit. In this example, routers connect the networks of the enterprise to the backbone.

Human
Resources and
Marketing
LAN

The Backbone

Router   Router

Router

Manufacturing
LAN

Metropolitan Area Networks

A **metropolitan area network (MAN)** is a network that generally spans a city or a county. An organization can use a MAN to cover greater distances at higher data rates than those offered by a LAN. A MAN can be used to connect BNs and LANs. An organization may find, if justified by transmission-volume needs, that having a private MAN may be less expensive than leasing these services from a local telecommunications company. A MAN is between a LAN and a WAN (wide area network) in terms of its geographic scope. However, MANs, unlike LANs, are usually subject to federal and state regulations.

At this point, the term **cloud** must be introduced. To many people, a cloud is a fluffy, beautiful object floating in a blue sky. To a data communications technologist, however, a cloud is a term used to logically represent connecting to a network infrastructure without being concerned as to how that infrastructure is configured, maintained, or controlled. For many users of MAN and WAN infrastructures, how the infrastructure works is not their concern. These users are simply leasing or renting the right to use the infrastructure, and they generally leave the details of how it works to others. The inner workings of the infrastructure, the details that are hidden from the user, are called the *cloud*. We return to the topic of cloud architectures in a later chapter. Figure 2.5 shows a three-LAN organization connecting through a MAN cloud.

Wide Area Networks

Business data communication needs may require that data be transported over great geographic distances, such as across a state, several states, a country, or even around the world. A network on this scale is called a **wide area network (WAN)**. A WAN will very commonly use circuits provided by common carriers. In our discussion, a **common carrier** is a business or company that provides communication services of varying types to the general public. Common carriers include such organizations as Sprint, MCI, and AT&T, among others. A WAN can connect BNs and MANs. The infrastructures that create and support a WAN are heavily regulated. Figure 2.6 illustrates a WAN that spans a continent.

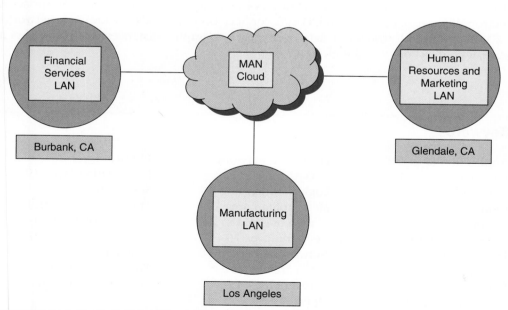

FIGURE 2.5 A Simple Metropolitan Area Network (MAN). Los Angeles County is a very large metropolitan area that includes the cities of Burbank, Glendale, and Los Angeles.

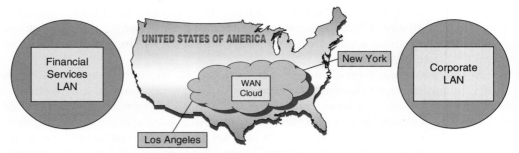

FIGURE 2.6   Simple Wide Area Network (WAN). A WAN spans great geographic distances, including states, provinces, countries, continents, and the globe.

Chapter Summary

Networks have both physical and logical components: the hardware devices that make them up and the software that drives them. Networks are also based on models. Open architecture models have some of the same advantages as open standards. Two major models used in data communications are the open systems interconnection, or OSI, model and the transmission control protocol/Internet protocol, or TCP/IP, model. The two models share several characteristics, and each model is well established and accepted by the data and telecommunications industries. One of the most important features they share is that both models are based on the concept of layered architectures.

   A model is based on theory. The theoretical model must then be implemented into a physical data communications network. In general, a network falls into one of four categories, based on the network's characteristics. A local area network (LAN) is usually contained within a limited geographic area. A backbone network (BN) is usually a high-speed circuit that connects the various LANs within an enterprise. A metropolitan area network (MAN) can connect BNs and LANs. Wide area networks (WANs) are used to transport data over great geographic distances, such as across a state, a country, or even the globe.

Keywords

Application layer *18*
Backbone network
   (BN) *23*
Cloud *25*
Common carrier *25*
Compression *19*
Data link layer *19*
Encryption *19*
Enterprise *23*
Layer stack *18*
Layered
   architecture *17*

Local area network
   (LAN) *23*
Logical addressing *19*
Metropolitan area
   network (MAN) *24*
Network layer *19*
Networking model *16*
Open architecture
   technology *17*
Open system
   interconnection (OSI)
   model *17*

Physical layer *20*
Presentation layer *19*
Session layer *19*
Transmission control
   protocol/Internet
   protocol (TCP/IP)
   model *17*
Transport layer *19*
Wide area network
   (WAN) *25*

Chapter Questions

Short-Answer Questions

1. What are open standards, and what, if any, are the advantages of such standards?
2. In general, why would a layered architecture be viewed as beneficial?
3. What is a protocol and why would one be used?
4. What are the four different types of networks?
5. How many layers make up the OSI model?

6. Which layer in the TCP/IP model is closest in alignment with the OSI model?
7. What is the purpose of the application layer in the TCP/IP model?
8. What is the largest scale networking category?

Hands-On Projects

1. Identify for two layers of the OSI or TCP/IP model two hardware devices associated with those layers and what functions they perform.
2. Identify for two layers of the OSI or TCP/IP model two protocols or services associated with those layers and what function they perform.
3. Interview a network administrator at your place of employment, school, or elsewhere regarding one of the networking categories presented in this chapter: LANs, BNs, MANs, or WANs.
4. For one of the networking categories presented in this chapter identify a job or career position for that category and three of its associated functions or responsibilities.

Research in Brief

For one or more of the following questions, provide a one- to two-page report based on your findings.

1. What is the general history of the TCP/IP model?
2. How are the OSI and TCP/IP models similar? How do they differ?
3. Identify and describe an example of a technological protocol or a society-based protocol.
4. For any layer of the OSI or TCP/IP models, research any single standard-setting body associated with that layer.

Case Study

Starting with this chapter and continuing through Chapter 11, a case study is presented. The case study presents a scenario that will be a continuing work in progress, building from one chapter to the next using the same business problem. As you work through the case study at the end of each chapter, you will create a total business solution that will enable you to understand how the information you are learning fits into the "big picture." You can work on this case study alone or in small groups.

Sheehan Marketing and Public Relations

Sheehan Marketing and Public Relations (SMPR) is a mid-sized public relations firm that focuses on the entertainment industry, primarily film and music. Based in Los

Angeles, SMPR also has branch offices in New York and Chicago, with plans for expansion in Miami and Nashville. Each office has an internal network; the offices' internal networks are not currently connected to one another. SMPR's office networks were implemented six years ago. Each office network is based on UTP Ethernet 10 Mbps traffic.

Tom Sheehan, SMPR president, recognizes that to remain competitive, the corporate and branch offices need much greater integration of their technology and improved communications between branch offices. Each office has data and information resources that the others do not. The offices must be able to collaborate and share music, video, and text files. Each office currently maintains its own database of clients and projects. However, SMPR account executives working from different offices increasingly need to work, as a team, on a given client's marketing and public relations program.

Each SMPR branch has a manager who reports directly to the company's president. Each branch manages its own payroll, accounting, and other services. Only the Los Angeles office has a dedicated LAN administrator. However, the LAN administrator, Karla, was never trained in her job, but "grew" into it because "she understands computers." The New York and Chicago offices are frequently frustrated by the lack of on-site technical support, which is needed to keep their LANs up and running. At the last quarterly branch managers' retreat meeting, held off-site in Phoenix, a major discussion topic was how data communications technology could help SMPR not only improve but also survive. President Sheehan informed his managers that he would aggressively pursue solutions to their problems. He stated that one of his first goals would be hiring a network technologist who would oversee and manage SMPR's data communication technology operations.

Although pleased with this decision, the branch managers also expressed concern that their individual offices would be neglected or not have their needs immediately addressed. In fact, Sheehan was surprised at how strongly each branch manager insisted that his or her branch office must be the first linked to the Los Angeles office. There was also much discussion about what skills a corporate networking technology manager should have. Before ending the retreat, it was agreed that a major strategic goal of SMPR would be the integration and coordination of data communication technology needs across all offices. As he concluded the session, President Sheehan reflected that he would need to know much more about the data communications industry in order to guide his business wisely.

CASE STUDY QUESTIONS

Using the information just provided, answer the following questions.

1. What are SMPR's data communication needs?
2. Based on the information provided, do you foresee any significant problems in integrating and coordinating the needed networks? If so, what are they?
3. What skills do you think should be included in a job description for SMPR's new corporate networking technology manager?
4. How much do you think the owner of a business like SMPR needs to know about data communications? Detailed information? General information? Justify your answer.
5. Mr. Sheehan is also contemplating the creation of a mission statement for his organization that would describe how SMPR uses client data. List three things you believe should be addressed by such a statement.

Topic in Focus

HOW THE LAYERS WORK

The following discussion is simplified in order to make the topic more approachable. Most significantly, the term *envelope* is used to describe how data might be processed in a layered model. Many students relate to the intent of a private letter being enclosed in an envelope, stamped, and only, ideally, being read by those meant to read it! The layered models are in some ways similar to the concept of addressing private hand-written mailed communications. Greater detail as to how the data communications layers work is provided in later chapters.

This chapter introduced two of the world's most popular data communication models: OSI and TCP/IP. Both models use a layered architecture. In a layered architecture, each layer is responsible for a particular set of functions and operations. A given layer is required to communicate only with the layers immediately above or below it. This means, in the seven-layer OSI model, layer 3 needs to communicate only with layers 2 and 4. Layer 3 has nothing directly to do with layers 1, 5, 6, or 7. In fact, layer 3 doesn't know, or care, that the other layers, other than 2 and 4, exist.

With this highly conceptual topic, understanding how these layers work can be challenging. By placing the layers into the context of a common business need—for example, sending a payments-due-and-paid report electronically from one network in an organization to another—we expect to make clearer just what these mysterious layers are doing and why. The following discussion focuses on the OSI model and its seven layers, detailing how and what each layer is doing and why. Also, because the focus of this text is on TCP/IP, this OSI example will provide needed exposure to this model. TCP/IP layers, though, operate in a manner similar to how the OSI layers operate.

In the OSI model, the seven layers, from top to bottom, are application, presentation, session, transport, network, data link, and physical. The sender and receiver each have identical layer stacks on their networked workstations. With the OSI model, the seven layers can be divided into two categories: end-to-end layers and chained layers. The top four layers are the end-to-end layers: application, presentation, session, and transport. These four layers are "end-to-end" because the layers on the sender's "end" and receiver's "end" directly communicate with each other. The four top layers on each "end" establish a communication. This communication provides an "end-to-end" connectivity.

The remaining three lower layers—network, data link, and physical—are the chained layers. These three layers are "chained" in that they are used to link, or chain, one physical device to another in a communication path. The number of devices that need to be linked, or chained, depends on the number of intermediary devices or networks between the sender and receiver of a communication. In a network or enterprise, there may be many intermediary devices or networks between a sender and receiver. The lower three layers provide the chain of links that permits the sender and receiver to have a communication. Figure 2.7 shows the OSI layers in an end-to-end and chained illustration. Notice in this figure how the end-to-end layers appear only in the layer stacks of the sender and receiver, whereas the chained layers are on all devices, especially those that "link" the sender and receiver to each other. Let's consider how this might work with a common business application.

Carlos and Rita are both employed by ACME Corporation. Carlos works in Accounts Payable (AP) at the Chicago branch office. Rita works in Financial Services (FS) at the company's Denver office. From his workstation in Chicago on the AP LAN, Carlos sends a large report file to Rita regarding outstanding payments owed and amounts paid to

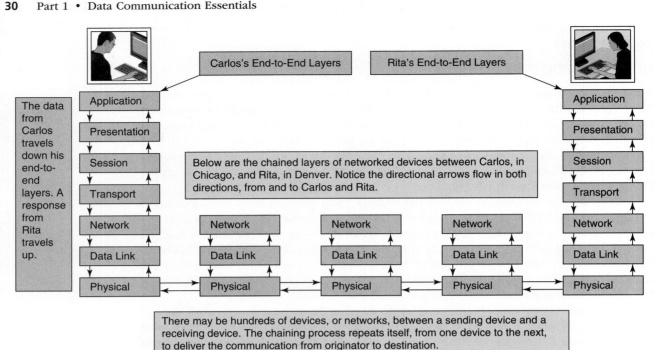

FIGURE 2.7   OSI End-to-End and Chaining Layers

various vendors for the last fiscal quarter. Rita, in Denver, receives the report file at her workstation, which is part of the FS LAN. As you can imagine, there are likely numerous intermediary devices and networks between Carlos's workstation in Chicago and Rita's in Denver. How does Carlos's report file get to Rita? And how do the OSI layers assist in this process?

In Chicago, at his "end," Carlos's workstation has a report-generating program associated with a database, such as Microsoft's SQL Server or Oracle's Oracle9i. At her "end," Rita has the same, or similar, reporting program and database. To send his large report file, Carlos uses a file transfer protocol program. The user interface in this file transfer program serves as the "application layer" mechanism that permits Carlos and Rita to exchange the data file over the network. (Other common types of application layer protocols include e-mail and Web browsers, which are covered in detail elsewhere in the text.) From his workstation, Carlos uses the file transfer program to submit his data for transmittal. When Carlos clicks the Send button or presses the Enter key on his keyboard, the file transfer application layer protocol takes over.

As Carlos's data travels down the layers, each layer envelopes and adds its own stamp or header. As the data travel up the layers on Rita's device, each layer recognizes the "header" created by its equivalent layer from Carlos's end, as demonstrated in Figure 2.8. For example, the presentation layer header from Carlo's devices will be recognized and interpreted by the equivalent presentation layer on Rita's device.

The file transfer program at the application layer of Carlos's workstation puts his data into what we can think of as an "envelope." The program also writes a stamp, or header, on this electronic envelope. The matching file transfer application layer protocol on Rita's receiving "end" workstation reads the header and data created by Carlos's application to interpret the application protocol being used. (Because the sender might be using one of many application layer protocols, an e-mail client or Web browser, for example, a header provides specific information on the protocol being used.)

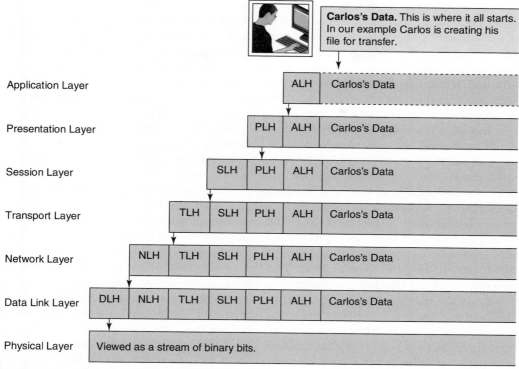

Carlos's Data. This is where it all starts. In our example Carlos is creating his file for transfer.

Application Layer					ALH	Carlos's Data
Presentation Layer				PLH	ALH	Carlos's Data
Session Layer			SLH	PLH	ALH	Carlos's Data
Transport Layer		TLH	SLH	PLH	ALH	Carlos's Data
Network Layer	NLH	TLH	SLH	PLH	ALH	Carlos's Data
Data Link Layer	DLH NLH	TLH	SLH	PLH	ALH	Carlos's Data
Physical Layer	Viewed as a stream of binary bits.					

FIGURE 2.8 OSI Layers with Enveloping and Headers

Other layers ignore this application layer header, recognizing that it is not addressed to their level. An envelope created by one layer is read and processed only by its matching layer on the other side of the communication. This is the magic of how the layers work with each other. From the sender's perspective, each layer accepts an "envelope" of data from the layer above it. Upon acceptance, without reading the contents of the envelope, each accepting layer puts the unread envelope into a new envelope that it creates. The accepting layer then attaches its own header and other relevant information to the envelope it creates. An envelope created at one layer is not processed or read by the other layers. The different layers recognize which layer created an envelope by reviewing the attached header information. Let's continue with Carlos's file transfer.

Carlos's application layer file transfer protocol puts his data into an envelope, stamps the envelope with a header, and then hands that stamped envelope down to the presentation layer. You may recall that the presentation layer takes application layer data and transforms it into a form agreeable to both the sender and receiver. The presentation layer can also encrypt the data if it is flagged as being sensitive. In our example, Carlos creates his report file using an English-character-based alphabet, meaning simply the report is in text, not binary. After all, the report is not for a machine to read, but for Rita! Even so, as discussed earlier in this chapter, data must be encoded into a binary form before it can be transmitted over a communication infrastructure. This is where the presentation layer comes in. Carlos's presentation layer transforms the received application layer's English text data into binary data, encrypts it, packages the transformed data into a presentation layer envelope, stamps the envelope with its own presentation layer header, and passes this newly created envelope down to the session layer.

The job of the session layer on Carlos's end is to ensure that the session layer at Rita's end is available for a communication. If, for some reason, Rita's workstation is not available for communication (a bad data link, her workstation is turned off, some type of hardware or software failure, etc.), a session will not be established and the process will stop. But let's assume that Rita's workstation is up and running properly and ready for communications. Carlos's session layer makes the initial contact with Rita's session layer, establishes a connection, monitors its progress throughout the communication, and eventually terminates the communication. If the connection is not terminated when the data transfer is finished, valuable bandwidth or circuit capacity could be wasted. However, for the session layer to be successful in establishing a communication, the session layer hands down a "connection request" to the transport layer. Once the connection request has been fulfilled, meaning a successful connection has been established, the session layer on Carlos's end creates an envelope. Carlos's session layer places his presentation data into a session layer envelope, stamps the envelope with a session layer header, and hands the envelope down to the transport layer.

The transport layer, as we just saw, assists the session layer by first making the initial connection request. In our example, we need to connect Carlos's workstation in Chicago to Rita's in Denver. Once the link is established, the session layer hands down its stamped envelope to the transport layer. If the session layer data envelope is too large, the transport layer may need to segment the data into smaller units. In fact, this is one of the transport layer's essential duties. On Carlos's end, the transport layer takes Carlos's session layer data and disassembles this data into segments and then sequences these segments with a number. The disassembled segments must be given a sequence number so that they can be put back into correct order by the transport layer on Rita's receiving end. In this way, the transport layer on the sender's end creates segmented envelopes; each envelope is stamped with a sequence number and other transport layer header information. These transport layer enveloped segments are then passed down to the network layer.

In our example, the end-to-end layers have done their work, and now the chained layers take over. The chained layers are concerned with getting the data from one device to another in the chain of devices between a sender and receiver. In Carlos and Rita's case, there are likely many intermediary devices and networks between them. The network layer on Carlos's workstation receives its transport layer data, places the data into an envelope, and stamps the envelope with the network layer header routing information. (Later chapters discuss how this routing information is determined. For now, let's simply say that the network layer maintains routing information that allows it to know where to send a data envelope on its way from the original sender to the ultimate receiver.) With this routing information, the network layer is ready to pass down its stamped header envelopes to the data link layer.

The network layer may need to route data from one network to another. The data link layer, however, is concerned only with passing data from one single device to another. The data link layer places the data into an envelope, stamps it with a header, and then passes the data down to the physical layer. The physical layer is the one layer that does not create an envelope and stamp it with a header. Instead, the physical layer, which we look at in greater detail in Chapter 3, is simply a means of getting the physical data bits from one point to another, whether the two computers are five feet or 500 hundred miles apart. The physical layer does not evaluate or analyze the data bits; it is concerned only with transmitting these bits along a physical media.

Let's assume that there are 100 networks between Carlos and Rita, and that each network has 20 devices. A communication between Carols and Rita must go through multiple devices and networks to get to where it needs to go. The number of devices and networks between Carlos and Rita depends on how the enterprise is set up. The important idea here is that there is a chain of devices and networks between Carlos and Rita that have to be navigated in order for a communication to be delivered. Imagine that you are telling friends in Miami how to drive to your house in Los Angeles. Such a trip would require several days, with different "linking" or "chaining" highways or roadways to get from point A to point B. That is a chaining process. You are describing to your friends, by road and highway links, how to get to your house. Our data communication example is not so different, except that instead of friends in a "car" envelope we have data bits in an "electronic" envelope. This chaining process continues over and over again (network, data link, physical) until eventually the data arrives at its ultimate destination—in our example, to Rita's computer in Denver from Carlos's computer in Chicago.

This discussion has described the flow of data from the application layer to the physical layer. From the sender's end, each layer envelopes and attaches headers (except at the physical layer). Once the receiver receives the data, the opposite occurs. Instead of headers being attached as they pass down through the layer stack, as they do at the sender's end, the reverse occurs as data flows up the layer stack at the receiver's end. For the receiver, headers are evaluated and stripped off as the data passes up the layer stack on the receiver's end. Each layer in the stack processes the envelope appropriate to its layer, identified by the envelope header, and then strips off, or removes, its own layer header and envelope before passing the data up the stack to the next higher layer.

The physical layer at the receiver's end, in this case Rita's workstation, takes the binary bits coming in from her physical layer and passes them up to her workstation's data link layer. Rita's data link layer evaluates the data received in their appropriate data link layer format. Assuming no problems are encountered, the data link layer removes its layer-specific information and passes the data up to the network layer. The network layer does the same, evaluating and removing its layer-specific information and passing the data up to its next-higher layer, the transport layer. The other layers continue the process. Eventually, Rita is looking at a report on her workstation's display screen in an application-friendly format, very likely without realizing the amount of layer-stack teamwork required to get it there. But that is, after all, how it should be in a well-run enterprise.

Chapter

3

Physical Layer Fundamentals: Concepts and Components

The Business Benefit

Growth-oriented businesses seek to increase revenue and profits. Such businesses also strive to decrease cost and inefficiency. Increased costs are often associated with inefficient business practices, whereas efficient practices can lead to cost savings. How a business utilizes its resources—whether human, financial, or technical—can have a great impact as to how well a business succeeds in its goal of cost reduction and revenue and profit increase.

In today's world, most modern businesses rely on networking and data communications technology to improve their effectiveness of operation while at the same time achieving technical efficiencies that can result in decreased cost and higher profits. How businesses design, configure, maintain, and improve their networking infrastructures can have a direct impact on their cost of doing business.

Data communication networks allow businesses to trim costs and reduce expenses by making key resources—including hardware, software, and data—available across a common infrastructure or enterprise. Such sharing of common resources can lead to higher efficiency of use as potentially expensive equipment, software, and data will not need to be replicated across the enterprise. Well-configured networks can permit businesses to leverage their resources such that unneeded redundancies and their associated maintenance can be significantly reduced.

Users of the enterprise's data communication infrastructure will be able to share common equipment, software, and data. Such networked sharing also simplifies the administration, maintenance, and securing of these resources. Businesses benefit from streamlining of operations, resulting in lower costs, while still being able to provide, more efficiently, the resources essential to staff and customers.

Connecting these networked resources, however, in a manner that is both effective and efficient will require physical layer implementations, which are addressed in this chapter.

Learning Objectives

After studying this chapter, you should be able to:

■ Understand the general purpose of the physical layer.

■ Identify four components of the physical layer.

■ Describe the differences between analog and digital signaling.

■ Understand amplitude, frequency, and phase modulation in analog signaling.

■ Describe the differences between simple and complex analog signaling.

■ Understand general digital signal encoding schemes.

■ Describe two digital transmission modes.

■ Explain two circuit configurations.

■ Explain three methods of data flow.

Chapter 2 described how physical data communications networks are based on logical models. These models propose that physical networks be built using a layered approach. Both the OSI and TCP/IP models identify lower-level layers. These lower-level layers are responsible for the physical media and the devices that make up a network and the initial framing of data bits so that these bits can be passed from one computer or network to another. The two lower-level layers are the physical and the data link layers.

PHYSICAL LAYER CONCEPTS

The physical layers of the OSI and TCP/IP models serve the same function in a very similar manner. Both identify the physical characteristics of the network. The physical layer interfaces directly with the data link layer. The data link layer passes frames of data bits down to the physical layer. The physical layer then transmits these frames as an unformatted stream of electrical, optical, or electromagnetic signals represented by the binary bits 0 and 1. (A **frame** is a specially formatted sequence of bits. Framing occurs at the data link layer and is discussed in the next chapter.) In effect, the physical layer does not "see" a frame; rather, it sees only a stream of data bits. The physical layer is responsible for transmitting this unformatted bit stream across a transmission medium, from one device to another, until ultimately the data bits travel from sender to receiver.

Data bits are frequently passed through pins in the connectors. It is the physical layer's function to make pin-signal assignments for the cable and connectors. ISO (*www.iso.org*) standard 2110 defines connector-pin assignments for 25-pin serial connectors. This means that each of these 25 pins has a particular purpose and function. The DB-25 connector, for example, is frequently used in modems, and each of its pins is associated with a particular signal.

Transmission properties that indicate how a binary 0 or 1 signal is to be represented in either an analog or digital encoding scheme are also defined at the physical layer. A 0 or 1 can be represented either electronically or optically. Most networks make use of some type of digital encoding scheme. We take a closer look at a couple of digital encoding schemes later in this chapter.

Note that the physical layer assigns no meaning to the data bits it is transferring. This means that the physical layer does not interpret the bit stream; that is not its job.

The physical layer serves as a means of getting the data bits from point A to point B. It is the function of the higher-level layers of the OSI and the TCP/IP models to provide meaning to the bits being transmitted.

PHYSICAL LAYER COMPONENTS

The four physical layer components are: (1) the signaling methods used for conveying or representing data and translating between them; (2) the circuit configuration that carries the data; (3) the transmission medium used, which is wired or wireless, on which the circuits are based; and (4) the devices typically associated with this layer.

Each component is equally important in fulfilling the functions of the physical layer. Understanding what these components do, and why, will be essential in designing a networking infrastructure that is both effective and efficient.

In terms of management, when an action is **effective**, it is performed correctly. When something is **efficient**, it is cost-effective. The two terms are not the same, and a networking technologist must pay close attention to both. Furthermore, from a business perspective, we want our data communication systems to be a balance of efficiency and effectiveness. Achieving an ideal balance can be challenging, especially when there are so many varying technologies from which to choose.

SIGNALING

A **signaling method** defines a set of rules for illustrating how a 0 or 1 is to be represented electromagnetically. The question is: Why would one need to do that? Recall that networks transmit data from one location to another. A physical transmission medium connects the devices with the networks. However, the data are not always in a form that can be transmitted across the medium. For example, the data may initially take the form of a paper document, such as a sales invoice. Because a paper document cannot be directly transmitted across a network in its original form, the original data must be encoded into a form that the medium can support.

The binary bits 0 and 1 are used to encode the data. However, our transmission medium is a physical path that conducts energy in the form of electromagnetic signals, not literally 0s and 1s. Therefore, these binary bits will have to be further transformed into an electromagnetic form. This transformation turns the physical layer's data bit stream into energy in the form of electromagnetic signals. These signals may be either analog or digital. Let's look more closely at each type of signal representation, beginning with analog.

Analog Signaling

The term **analog** refers to a measure, form, or expression that is continuous and has a range of magnitude between one value and another. Temperature, for example, is analog. If we had a finely calibrated Fahrenheit thermometer, we could measure a continuous range of temperatures from 98.000 to 98.999. In fact, humans live in an analog world. Things such as smell, sound, and touch, as we experience them, are all analog. When using analog transmission, the signal sent over the transmission medium will continuously vary from one state to another in a smooth, wavelike pattern. An analog wave is capable of having an infinite number of values as it travels along its path.

Analog communications are used extensively. Phones (both landline and cellular), modems, fax machines, cable television, and many other devices and network services are based on analog communications. Our first telephone networks were designed for analog communications—human speech, not data. When we speak, our voices generate sound waves. The plain old telephone system, or POTS, was originally built to transmit voice sound waves in an electrical form. A telephone on the sender's end translates the sound wave produced by a human voice into electrical signals. These signals are then passed to and travel along a voice communication circuit. A telephone on the receiving end then reverses the process, taking incoming electrical signals and converting them back into sound for the listener to hear.

In analog communications, signals flow across a copper wire in the form of electromagnetic waves. Analog signals can also use fiber-optic or wireless (e.g., radio, microwave, infrared) transmission media. Taking the form of a sine wave, analog signals may be simple or complex. A sine wave is usually represented as a smooth oscillating curve with a continuous rolling flow, as shown in Figure 3.1. Whether simple or complex, sine wave analog signals have three basic characteristics that can be manipulated, or modulated, to represent the binary bits 0 and 1. These modulated characteristics are amplitude, frequency, and phase. Let's look at each of these characteristics, first in their simple form, and then as a complex signal.

AMPLITUDE MODULATION   The amplitude of a sound wave defines the height, or strength, of the wave. In terms of your own voice, if you speak loudly, amplitude increases; when you speak softly, amplitude decreases. **Amplitude modulation (AM)** takes place when the height of a sound wave is manipulated to encode a binary 0 or 1. Amplitude modulation is also called *amplitude shift keying (ASK)*. Simple amplitude modulation defines one amplitude or height of a wave as representing a binary 0 and the second amplitude as defining a 1. Amplitude modulation is measured in watts, volts, or amperes, depending on the type of signal. See Figure 3.2 to see how amplitude is used to encode 0s and 1s.

In the figure, note that different ranges of amplitude, measured in voltage, can be used to identify equivalent binary 0s and 1s. Voltage values between 0 and up to and including 5 are identified as a binary 0, any voltage value greater than 5 is a binary 1.

FREQUENCY MODULATION   When you speak in a higher or lower pitched voice, you are demonstrating a form of frequency modulation. **Frequency modulation (FM)** uses frequency, the number of waves per second, to differentiate between 0

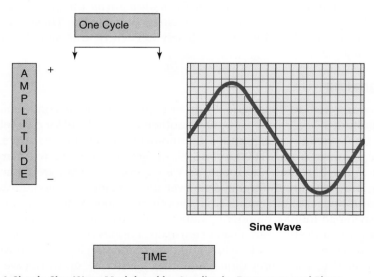

FIGURE 3.1   A Simple Sine Wave Modulated by Amplitude, Frequency, and Phase

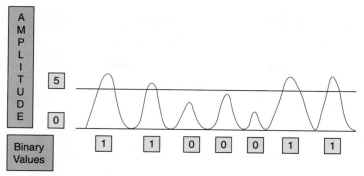

FIGURE 3.2 Amplitude Measured in Voltage. Note in this figure that different ranges of amplitude, measured in voltage, can be used to identify equivalent binary 0s and 1s. Voltage values between zero and up to and including five are identified as a binary 0; any voltage value greater than five is a binary 1.

and 1. Frequency modulation is also called *frequency shift keying (FSK)*. With simple frequency modulation, the amplitude of the wave remains constant and only two different frequencies are defined. One frequency encodes a 0, the second encodes a 1. Frequency modulation also has an element called the **period**, which is the amount of time, in seconds, that a signal needs to complete one cycle. A **cycle** is the completion of one full pattern of a wave. Thus, frequency modulation is based on two concepts: frequency and period. Figure 3.3 shows how FM is used to encode 0s and 1s to depict both period and frequency.

The communications industry has defined five units of measurement for both frequency and period. Frequency is measured in hertz, kilohertz, megahertz, gigahertz, or terahertz. A **hertz** is a unit of frequency. The following prefixes are also used: *kilo* for thousand, *mega* for million, *giga* for billion, and *tera* for trillion. A **kilohertz**, then, has a unit frequency of 1,000. A period is measured in seconds, milliseconds, microseconds, nanoseconds, or picoseconds. See Table 3.1 to see how these values are expressed exponentially.

It just so happens that frequency and period are the multiplicative inverse of each other, so if you know one, you can determine the other. Following are a few examples. Let's assume we have a wave with a frequency of 8 hertz. Its period, expressed as a

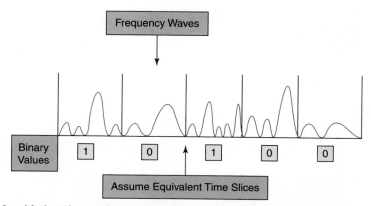

FIGURE 3.3 Considering Time with Frequency Modulation. In this example, assume that within the same time period, if four or more frequency waves are generated, a binary 1 is represented. If three or fewer frequency waves are generated, a binary 0 results.

Table 3.1   Frequency and Period Unit Measurements

Frequency Unit	FU Exponential	Period Unit	PU Exponential
Hertz (Hz)	1 Hz	Seconds (s)	1 s
Kilohertz (KHz)	10^3 Hz	Milliseconds (ms)	10^{-3} s
Megahertz (MHz)	10^6 Hz	Microseconds (μs)	10^{-6} s
Gigahertz (GHz)	10^9 Hz	Nanoseconds (ns)	10^{-9} s
Terahertz (THz)	10^{12} Hz	Picoseconds (ps)	10^{-12} s

multiplicative inverse, is 1/8, or .125, second. A wave with a frequency of 8 kilohertz has a period of 1/8000, or .000125, second. A wave with a period of 8 seconds has a frequency of 1/8, or .125, hertz.

PHASE MODULATION   **Phase modulation**, also called *phase shift keying (PSK)*, is a bit more complicated than AM or FM. With phase modulation (PM), a wave begins in a given direction, called its *phase*, and then creates a *baseline,* or *reference wave.* Look at Figure 3.4 as you read so that you can see what is being described. As shown in Figure 3.4, the baseline begins at zero. As the wave starts at the baseline and moves up and to the right, it reaches phase degree zero (0°). As the wave starts at the baseline and moves down and to the right, it reaches phase degree 180 (180°). We can define phase *0°* as being a binary 0 and phase *180°* as being a binary 1. As the phase shifts, or modulates, it changes from 0 to 1, and then back again. In Figure 3.4, the first time period wave is the baseline wave and is defined as binary 0. When the phase shifts, in time period two, a binary 1 is expressed. Unlike amplitude or frequency modulation, phase modulation is not readily intelligible to the human ear. Fortunately, electronic devices can easily recognize phase changes.

Of the three modulation techniques, amplitude modulation is the most susceptible to noise and distortion during transmission. Amplitude, frequency, and phase modulation can all be used in radio and television broadcasting. For satellite communications, though, only frequency and phase modulation are used. With simple signal

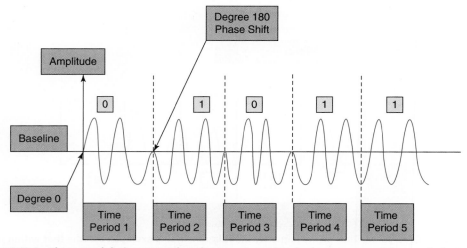

FIGURE 3.4   **Phase Modulation. Note that the wave's amplitude, frequency, and time periods are the same. The phase shift causes the change in value from 0 to 1.**

modulation, which is what has been discussed thus far, each signal sent represents only one binary bit. In this case, the bit rate and the symbol rate are the same. The term **bit rate** refers to the number of bits transmitted per second, per signal. The **symbol rate** refers to the number of bits that can be encoded in a single signal.

With simple signal modulation, the ratio is one-to-one, meaning that one signal symbol represents one bit. Some techniques, however, allow a single signal symbol to represent more than one bit. Such techniques are referred to as *complex signal modulation*.

Digital Signaling

Digital signaling is, in several ways, more straightforward than analog signaling. Digital signaling uses only two values: 0 and 1. These values are represented electronically. Because digital signals are one value or the other, with no variance in between, they are a discrete representation. This **discrete** representation means that digital signals have only a given, specific value. Digital signaling is usually less expensive than analog signaling because it requires less-complex circuitry. Noise interference is less of a problem in digital signaling, making error detection and correction easier. A disadvantage is that digital signals are more susceptible to attenuation. **Attenuation** can be defined as the weakening of a signal's strength as it travels through a circuit. This weakening of the signal is caused by friction. The longer the distance that a signal needs to travel though a circuit, the more probable attenuation becomes. Different media, however, suffer from attenuation at varying distances. Digital signals can be carried over copper or fiber-optic cables.

Two other characteristics of digital signaling are bit interval and bit rate. **Bit interval** is the time required to send a single bit. *Bit rate* is the number of bit intervals per second. It is usually measured in bps (bits per second).

One of the most common ways of electronically encoding digital signals is to use two different voltage levels, one for each of the two binary digits. A positive voltage is usually used for 0 and a negative voltage for 1. A number of digital encoding schemes are available; each has advantages and disadvantages. To better understand these advantages and disadvantages, we first discuss signal timing and the ability of an encoding scheme to be self-clocking.

SIGNAL TIMING AND CLOCKING

Each bit signal sent in a digital transmission has a specific duration. This duration, called the bit interval, is the time required to send one single bit. The sender and receiver in a communication can use the bit interval to clock their transmission with each other. **Clocking** allows the sender and receiver to synchronize their transmission. In a communication, a sender and receiver need to clock, or synchronize, each bit's duration because the bit stream transmitted may, and likely will, contain a string of bits in a series with the same value. This presents a problem.

Bits of the same binary value are identified using the same voltage. So if 20 binary 1s are in a series in the bit stream, one after the other, and each binary 1 is represented by –5 volts, how does the receiver know when one binary 1 ends and another binary 1 begins, since they all look the same? If the bits are clocked, meaning each bit's duration is known, the receiver will be able to determine when one bit begins and ends. This is where the bit interval comes into play.

The sender and receiver may rely on their own external clocks to keep data bits synchronized, based on the bit interval, but would require resynchronizing millions of times per second, which eats up valuable transmission time. Alternatively, extra clocking bits could be inserted into the data stream. But this means that the amount of data will have to be increased, eating up valuable transmission capacity. Both are inefficient solutions. It would be better if the encoding scheme itself had a self-clocking mechanism built into it. An encoding scheme that has clocking "built into" it is referred to as being **self-clocking**. And in fact, many encoding schemes are self-clocking, making external clocks or additional clocking bits unnecessary.

Some encoding schemes use a more sophisticated method called **transition coding**. With transition coding, a value is encoded by means of a voltage transition during the bit interval, not before or after it. The advantage of transition-coding schemes is that they are less susceptible to noise. Noise can distort or corrupt the data bits on a transmission line. Vendors that provide physical layer hardware that use encoding schemes should be able to provide sample timing diagrams for their products; however, you may have to ask for one. Following are brief descriptions of several digital encoding schemes.

Unipolar encoding has a direct current (DC) component. It uses either a positive or negative voltage, but never both, to represent one value, usually a binary 1, and zero voltage to represent a second value, usually binary 0. Unipolar does not provide transition coding but does require communicators to use their own external clocks for synchronization. As an encoding scheme, unipolar is mostly obsolete because it is fairly primitive, has problems with synchronization, and cannot be used on media that do not support DC components.

Bipolar encoding uses positive, negative, and zero voltages. Generally, zero voltage is used to represent one value and a nonzero voltage the other. The bipolar encoding schemes non-return-to-zero level (NRZ-L) and non-return-to-zero invert (NRZ-I) do not use transition coding; they require external clocks. Both of these forms of NRZ have a disadvantage in that it is difficult to determine within a bit stream where one bit ends and another begins. However, NRZ is inexpensive to implement and does not suffer the DC-component problem presented by unipolar encoding. Figure 3.5 provides examples of NRZ-L and NRZ-I.

Biphase encoding includes at least one transition per bit interval and provides for a self-clocking mechanism, giving these encoding schemes an advantage over NRZ ones. Also, transition coding makes it easier for these schemes to detect errors. Two common biphase schemes in use are Manchester and Differential Manchester.

Manchester is used in Ethernet and other LANs, whereas Differential Manchester is used in token ring LANs. With Manchester, the direction of the transition in mid-interval, negative to positive or positive to negative, indicates the binary bit value.

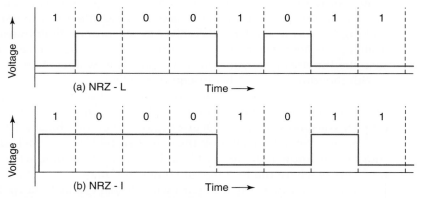

FIGURE 3.5 Non-Return-to-Zero Level and Non-Return-to-Zero Invert

Manchester Encoding: With Manchester, the direction of the transition in mid-interval, negative to positive or positive to negative indicates the binary bit value.

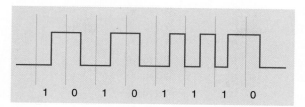

Differential Manchester Encoding: With Differential Manchester, the presence or absence of a transition at the beginning of a bit interval indicates the bit value.

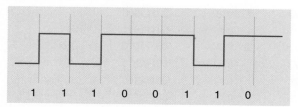

FIGURE 3.6   Manchester and Differential Manchester Encoding

For a 1 bit, the transition is always from negative to positive; for a 0 bit, it is from positive to negative. This mid-bit transition not only represents data but it also provides clocking. With Differential Manchester, the presence or absence of a transition at the beginning of a bit interval indicates the bit value. The transition in mid-interval is used only for self-clocking, not to provide data, which is an advantage. Figure 3.6 illustrates Manchester and Differential Manchester.

DIGITAL TRANSMISSION MODES

Digital signaling has another characteristic: the transmission mode, which is either serial or parallel. The transmission mode determines how many bits will transmit at one time as a block. The block is usually one or eight bits. Recall that binary bits are used to represent digital data. These binary bits are organized into units called *bytes*. Each byte is able to represent one, and only one, character, such as the characters *a, A, 1, 9, #,* and *$,* among others. Binary bits are put together into bytes based on an encoding scheme.

Two widely used encoding schemes are ASCII (American Standard Code for Information Interchange) and EBCDIC (Extended Binary Coded Decimal Interchange Code). EBCDIC was created by IBM for use with its large-scale mainframe computers and is based on an eight-bit byte. ASCII is the more common encoding scheme and has been used much more extensively, especially by terminals and microcomputers. ASCII has two versions: Standard ASCII, based on a seven-bit byte, and Extended ASCII, based on an eight-bit byte. Of the two, Extended ASCII is used more often.

In EBCDIC or Extended ASCII, a byte has eight bits. Both EBCDIC and Extended ASCII are capable of encoding, or defining, up to 256 different characters using these eight bits. The limit is 256 because there is a maximum of 256 different ways that eight 0s and 1s can be put together. Two possible ways are 00000000 and 11111111. See Figure 3.7 for other possible ASCII combinations.

Decimal	Octal	Hex	Binary	Value
000	000	000	00000000	NULL
048	060	030	00110000	0
049	061	031	00110001	1
050	062	032	00110010	2
051	063	033	00110011	3
052	064	034	00110100	4
053	065	035	00110101	5
054	066	036	00110110	6
055	067	037	00110111	7
056	070	038	00111000	8
057	071	039	00111001	9
058	072	03A	00111010	: (colon)
059	073	03B	00111011	; (semi-colon)
060	074	03C	00111100	< (less than)
061	075	03D	00111101	= (equal sign)
062	076	03E	00111110	> (greater than)
063	077	03F	00111111	? (question mark)
064	100	040	01000000	@ (AT symbol)
065	101	041	01000001	A
066	102	042	01000010	B
067	103	043	01000011	C
068	104	044	01000100	D
069	105	045	01000101	E
070	106	046	01000110	F
071	107	047	01000111	G

FIGURE 3.7 A Sampling of Some of the Extended ASCII Binary Characters

In digital transmissions, a byte with its eight bits is transmitted in one of two modes, serial or parallel. In **serial transmission mode**, which is more common because it only requires one wire, each bit of the byte is sent single file, one after the other. In **parallel transmission mode**, all eight bits of the byte are sent at one time in parallel, thus this mode is eight times as fast as serial mode. The catch is that parallel mode requires eight separate wires for each of the eight bits of the byte to travel on.

Because of the need and expense for additional wiring, parallel mode is used almost exclusively within the confines of the computer's internal architecture or to connect a computer to a high-speed device, such as a laser printer. Parallel mode is also sometimes used to connect two high-speed devices that are in close proximity to each other. Serial mode, because it requires only one wire, is the more common form used by communication circuits. See Figure 3.8 to see how these two modes differ in how they transmit a byte.

A third encoding scheme, Unicode (*www.unicode.org*), uses a 16-bit character code that can support up to 64,000 different characters. This is a big enough character set to represent most, if not all, human languages, something not possible with EBCDIC or ASCII. In addition, Unicode contains the EBCDIC and ASCII coding schemes. Technologies that use Unicode can be **backward compatible** with the proper software

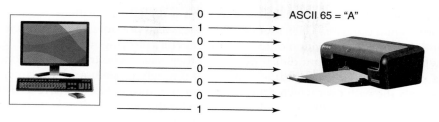

With the serial transmission of the same letter, note the bits are sent one at a time in single file.

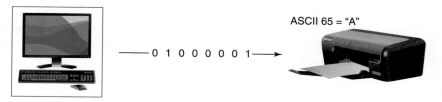

FIGURE 3.8 Parallel Transmission of the Letter "A" from a Computer to a Printer. In ASCII, which is binary, the capital letter "A" is represented by the value 01000001. (This value, 010000010, also equates to 65 in decimal.) Note that all the bits travel together at one time.

Source: http://aa.uncwil.edu/ward/chm255/chapters/chpt4/chpt04b.htm

engineering. A backward-compatible technology is one that can function with earlier versions of that technology. This type of technology will cost a business less because older hardware and/or software may not need to be immediately replaced.

From your reading, you now understand that data signals can be either analog or digital and that both are important in data communications. Digital signals have several advantages over analog signals. Because digital signals are binary, with only two values, they produce fewer errors. Higher maximum transmission rates are possible with

The Ethical Perspective

Businesses need to economize in order to be profitable. Without effective cost controls a business may find that it cannot operate. Sometimes a business may choose to do with less of a resource (staffing, equipment, software, supplies, etc.) or other element of cost in order to trim expenses. There is a balance, however, as to when trimming a particular element of cost may have unwanted consequences.

Customers generally expect a business to have adequate staffing, resources, and support to provide them a certain level of quality in service, security, and responsiveness. Many businesses rely on their networking technologies to fulfill such essential customer expectations. Considerable analysis has to be given by that business to ensuring that these technologies are robust enough to continue operation when an error or other problem arises.

Particularly with networking technologies, systems such as bandwidth capacity, server redundancy, wiring quality, and physical plant security and safety must be considered. What if a business, due to cost, chooses to use less expensive, lower quality technology in any of these areas? Redundant systems, for example, cost money, but they also ensure a degree of recoverability.

Does a business have an ethical requirement to ensure its technology, or lack of it, will not harm its customers, even if there is a significant cost involved? If you were trying to balance cost and savings, what approach would you take?

digital signaling. More data can be sent through a digital circuit than an analog one; therefore, digital transmission is more efficient. It is also possible with digital circuits to combine data, voice, and video onto the same circuit, allowing for greater integration.

Whether the signals are digital or analog, they have to be transmitted along some type of physical medium. A signal is transmitted through a medium over a circuit. A circuit is simply the path over which data and information travels. Circuits have to be configured in a manner that is effective and appropriate for the network. The next section looks at circuit configuration, the second physical layer component covered in this chapter.

CIRCUIT CONFIGURATION

A circuit is the link that provides the physical means by which data are transferred. **Circuit configuration** affects the way in which two or more communicating devices share their connection or link with each other. The two basic circuit configurations are point-to-point and multipoint.

Point-to-Point Configuration

In a **point-to-point** configuration, a dedicated circuit is established between two devices. *Circuit dedication* means that the circuit's entire capacity is reserved for the two communicating devices; no other devices can use that dedicated circuit. This type of link is most efficient when the two communicating devices are using most, if not all, of the circuit's capacity. If this were not the case, then the circuit's capacity would be seriously underutilized. A point-to-point circuit might also be appropriate between two devices that must be able to communicate with each other whenever they need to. Most point-to-point circuits use a length of wire or cable to connect two devices, but other media are possible, such as microwave, satellite, or infrared. For example, if you use an automatic garage door opener, the device you click, the door opener, is using a wireless point-to-point circuit to communicate with its controller. Figure 3.9 offers an example of point-to-point wired connections.

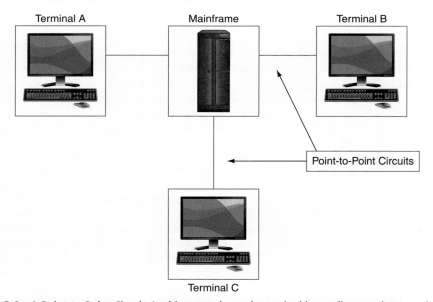

FIGURE 3.9   A Point-to-Point Circuit. In this example, each terminal has a direct, point-to-point link, or "circuit," to the mainframe computer. For A to communicate with B, A must go through the mainframe—likewise for B and C. Also, A, B, and C do not share their circuit with each other. This type of circuit is common with mainframe and terminal configurations.

In a typical network, most devices are not in constant communication with other devices. Someone sitting at a typical networked computer is not constantly pressing the Send button or Receive button every 10 seconds to do his or her work. Instead, most users of these devices only need to send or receive a communication once in a while, not constantly. Therefore, having point-to-point circuit configurations for all devices is not only expensive, because of wiring and other hardware costs, but inefficient as well. Point-to-point circuits should be reserved for devices that require a dedicated link because their communication needs demand it. A pair of multiplexers will, for example, need to be connected by a single link. Multiplexers are devices that let other slower devices share a higher-speed circuit. Sharing a high-speed circuit is more efficient in terms of utilizing that circuit's capacity.

Multipoint Configuration

Most devices in a network do not require the dedicated capacity of a point-to-point circuit. For the organization, then, it is more efficient and cost-effective for devices to share a circuit. Multiple devices sharing a single circuit are using a **multipoint** configuration. Multipoint is also sometimes referred to as a *multidrop*. With a multipoint circuit, many devices can be connected to the same physical circuit.

Multipoint circuits require that a method be established that determines how devices will share a single circuit resource. One common way for sharing this single resource is for devices to wait turns to use the circuit. The next chapter will describe how media access controls specify how devices share a single physical circuit. Figure 3.10 shows an example of a multipoint configuration.

BANDWIDTH

Whether point-to-point or multipoint, every circuit has a key characteristic associated with it called **bandwidth**. For many, the mysterious concept of bandwidth is irritatingly vague and confusing. It can be difficult to grasp something that cannot be seen

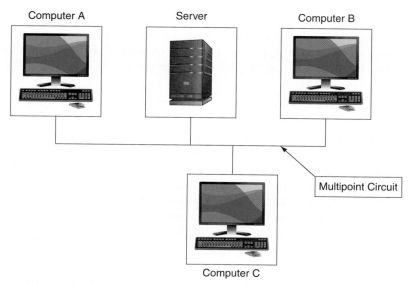

FIGURE 3.10 All devices share the same circuit, making it a multipoint, or multidrop, circuit. Multipoint circuits are common in LANs.

or touched. Simply stated, bandwidth is the capacity of a circuit to carry data. The more data that a circuit can carry, the greater that circuit's bandwidth capacity. Also, different types of data require different types of bandwidth capacity.

Consider a river that carries water, with the water being the river's data. A small river will have less capacity, or bandwidth, to carry water than a large river. A small river will also be limited in the types of boat traffic that it can handle. For example, a small river might accommodate a canoe very easily but not be able to support an ocean-going cruise ship. A geographer comparing the water capacity of the Potomac River in the United Sates with the Amazon River in Brazil would say that the capacity, or bandwidth, of the gigantic Amazon to carry water is far greater than that of comparatively tiny Potomac. Data communication circuits are conceptually similar, but of course they carry data, not water or canoes. And the data of a small, simple text file will require far less capacity, or bandwidth, than the data of even a small video file.

With an analog circuit, bandwidth is the difference between the circuit's highest and lowest frequencies. The wider this value, the greater the bandwidth. With a digital circuit, bandwidth is usually measured in bps (bits per second). A formula to determine bps using bit interval and bit rate is: bps = 1/(bit interval * period unit exponential value). The higher the result, the greater the bandwidth.

DATA FLOW

Whether using a point-to-point or multipoint circuit, data flows over the circuit. The **data flow** may occur in one or two directions, based on how the circuit is configured. Data can flow over a circuit in three ways: simplex, half-duplex, or full-duplex. The method chosen depends on how the circuit is to be used. Each method is appropriate under particular circumstances, and a medium- to large-scale network will likely utilize all three.

Simplex

With **simplex** communication, data travel in one direction only; data can be sent or received, but not both. The direction depends on the purpose of the communication. It may be that a central computer receives data from remote sources on a simplex circuit but never sends data back out. When you drive a car and listen to the car stereo, you are experiencing a simplex transmission—you receive but do not send sound. Keyboards and monitors are two common examples of simplex devices; one is used for input, the other for output. The entire bandwidth is used either for input or output.

Half-Duplex

A **half-duplex** circuit can transmit data in either direction, but in only one direction at a time. The circuit is either used to send or receive, but never simultaneously. An example of a half-duplex communication is the use of walkie-talkies that permit two users to speak or listen, but not both at the same time. A network may have a central computer that remotely receives data but that cannot send data while it is receiving. After analyzing the received data, the central computer sends the data back to its source for correction or modification; but while transmitting, it cannot receive new data.

Full-Duplex

In a **full-duplex** communication, data can be sent and received simultaneously. An everyday example of full-duplex is a telephone conversation. It may not be polite, but you and your friend can both be talking, or listening, at the same time. To permit this simultaneous two-way communication, one of two things must occur. Either two physically separate transmission paths can be established, in effect creating two circuits, one for sending and one for receiving, or the capacity of the circuit is divided so that the sending and receiving signals can travel together but in opposite directions.

Depending on the needs of the network, simplex, half-duplex, or full-duplex might each be appropriate. Circuits, though, regardless of the type of data flow selected, have to be based on some type of wired or wireless physical medium. Wired media are often referred to as *conducted;* wireless media are often called *radiated.* The next chapter will examine the third and fourth components of the physical layer: media and devices.

Chapter Summary

The physical layers of the OSI and TCP/IP models are virtually the same. The physical layer identifies the physical characteristics of the network. These characteristics include the types of cables and connectors used to link devices. Transmission properties are also defined at the physical layer that indicates the ways in which a binary 0 or 1 signal is to be represented in either an analog or digital encoding scheme. A 0 or 1 can be represented either electronically or optically.

Four important physical layer components are: (1) the signaling methods used for conveying or representing data and translating between them; (2) the circuit configuration used to carry the data; (3) the transmission medium used, wired or wireless, on which the circuits are based; and (4) the devices typically associated with this layer.

Data can be represented as analog or digital signals. In analog communications, signals flow across a copper wire in the form of electromagnetic waves. Analog signals can also use transmission media such as fiber-optics or wireless (radio, microwave, infrared). Digital signaling is more straightforward than analog signaling. With digital signaling, only two values are used: 0 and 1. With analog signaling, modulation techniques include amplitude, frequency, and phase. These modulation techniques can be simple or complex. For digital signaling, encoding schemes such as bipolar, biphase, Manchester, and Differential Manchester are used.

Whether analog or digital, signals are carried over a transmission medium. The transmission medium has a circuit configuration—point-to-point or multipoint—and a data flow—simplex, half-duplex, or full-duplex. Based on the needs and size of the network, one or all of these might be used.

Keywords

Amplitude modulation *38*
Analog *37*
Attenuation *41*
Backward compatible *44*
Bandwidth *47*
Biphase *42*
Bipolar *42*

Bit interval *41*
Bit rate *41*
Circuit configuration *46*
Clocking *41*
Cycle *39*
Data flow *48*
Discrete *41*
Effective *37*
Efficient *37*

Frame *36*
Frequency modulation *38*
Full-duplex *48*
Gigahertz *40*
Half-duplex *48*
Hertz *39*
Kilohertz *39*
Megahertz *40*

Multipoint *47*

Parallel transmission
   mode *44*

Period *39*

Phase modulation *40*

Point-to-point *46*

Self-clocking *42*

Serial transmission
   mode *44*

Signaling method *37*

Simplex *48*

Symbol rate *41*

Terahertz *40*

Transition coding *42*

Unipolar *42*

Chapter Questions

Short Answer Questions

1. In general, what purpose does the physical layer serve?
2. Describe at least three ways in which digital signaling differs from analog.
3. How does a point-to-point circuit differ from a multipoint one?
4. What is meant by attenuation?
5. What other layer does the physical layer interface directly with?
6. What relationship do frequency and period have with regard to frequency modulation?
7. Which modulation method is most susceptible to noise and distortion during transmission?
8. In what critical way does bipolar encoding differ from unipolar encoding?

Hands-On Projects

1. Using either amplitude or frequency modulation draw an example that can differentiate 4 bits per amplitude or frequency. Indicate the bits being represented.
2. If you have a frequency wave at 5 hertz, what is its period?
3. If you have a period of 6 seconds, what is its frequency?
4. Using the word "DATA" in uppercase, what is its standard ASCII equivalent and then demonstrate with a simple drawing how the binary bits would be transmitted in serial and in parallel transmission modes.

Research in Brief

For one or more of the questions below, provide a one- to two-page report based on your findings.

1. Explore bandwidth in greater detail. Describe throughput. Explain how throughout and bandwidth together affect utilization.
2. Research the use of Unicode and how it is currently being deployed.
3. Write a brief report detailing when a point-to-point configuration would be appropriate and why.
4. Review the history of the Manchester encoding scheme. When was it developed? Describe any advantages and disadvantages that are associated with Manchester encoding.

Case Study

Sheehan Marketing and Public Relations

Congratulations. You have just been hired by Sheehan Marketing and Public Relations (SMPR) as their new networking technologist. Your first order of business will be to evaluate the current status of SMPR's networks. SMPR has three offices, one in Los Angeles, which is the corporate headquarters, one in Chicago, and another in New York City. You are aware that there are plans to open two additional offices in Miami and Nashville.

You have asked Karla, the L.A. office LAN administrator, for help in your analysis. However, Karla has told you that she is very busy and not able to provide you with much support. She also indicates that there is little written documentation as to how the various offices are set up. Following is her brief description of the L.A. office. Later you will visit the Chicago and New York offices to determine how they are configured. For now, Karla tells you they have a similar, though smaller, set-up: Chicago has 10 computers and New York has 15.

The corporate office in Los Angeles is the oldest. It has 24 computers; 19 of them have licensed versions of Windows Vista and the 5 newest machines have licensed versions of Windows 7 Workstation. Karla has configured the computers to run as a peer-to-peer network, so depending on the particular computer it may function as either a server or a client. Karla admits that it has become complicated for her to keep all the machines current with the various user privileges that are shared across the network. For example, there are three laser printers, each connected to a separate computer. Fifteen other machines have been set up to share these printers, so there are 18 machines with rights to use the printers. The other 6 computers also need to be configured for printer sharing.

All the computers have various data, files, and resources that are shared across the network. All computers have licensed copies of Microsoft Office—but different versions. Again, Karla isn't clear as to which versions are on which machines. Also, individual users have installed many of their own programs on their local computers. The resources (data, files, software) have not been documented in writing as to what is installed where or whether everything is correctly licensed. Karla simply "knows" where things are.

CASE STUDY QUESTIONS

Using the information just provided, answer the following questions.

1. Interpersonal relations can be an important factor in whether you can successfully do your job or not. How would you describe the situation regarding Karla? How do you plan to proceed in working with her? It can be difficult to work with users who are accustomed to "running their own computers"—installing what they want when they want on their local machines. How do you plan to address this? Is this a problem? If so, why?

Topic in Focus

COMPLEX SIGNAL MODULATION

In complex signal modulation, the symbol rate and the bit rate are not the same. Instead, the bit rate becomes a multiple of the symbol rate. Before continuing, let's look again at what we mean by the symbol rate.

The *symbol rate* is also called the *baud rate*, but *symbol rate* is the term recommended for use by the ITU-T (*www.itu.int*). In simple signal modulation, one bit is encoded per symbol, so the bit rate and the symbol rate are the same, one-to-one. Complex signal modulation, however, allows a single signal symbol to encode more than one bit. In that case, one symbol may have two, four, or more bits encoded within it. This can be accomplished in several ways.

With amplitude modulation, it is possible, for example, to define not two, but four different amplitudes. Each of the four amplitudes would represent one pair of two

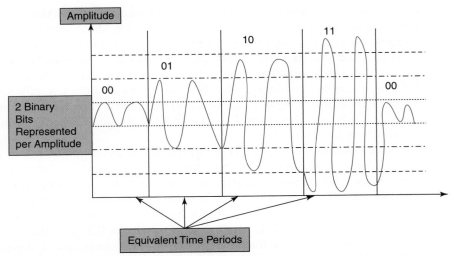

FIGURE 3.11   Complex Signal Amplitude Modulation Expressing Two Bits per Symbol Instead of One

bits: 00, 01, 10, or 11. Figure 3.11 shows the definition of four distinct amplitudes. Each single amplitude, or symbol, represents two bits. If eight amplitudes were defined, four bits per symbol could be encoded. At some point, though, if too many amplitudes are defined, it may become difficult for services to differentiate between them. If a communication system cannot differentiate one amplitude from another, the significance of the different amplitudes becomes lost and the communication fails.

This concept also works with frequency and phase modulation. Defining four frequencies or four phases allows each single frequency or phase to represent two bits. Modulation techniques can also be combined. *Quadrature amplitude modulation (QAM)* is one popular combination method. It uses two different amplitudes and eight different phases. Each amplitude is capable of representing one bit and each phase three bits, for a total of four bits. The bit rate would be four times the symbol or baud rate. A major advantage of combination techniques such as QAM is that more bits can be sent at the same time, resulting in faster transmissions.

A tremendous volume of data is carried on analog communication circuits. From this discussion, you can see that it is possible for analog signals to be translated into digital signals. This translation is necessary so that analog signals can be processed by computers, which are digital. However, computers frequently need to send their digital signals across analog lines, again requiring a translation, but in this case the translation is digital to analog. Both analog and digital signaling are important. Now that we know something about analog signaling, let's take a closer look at digital signaling in the next chapter.

Physical Layer Fundamentals: Media and Devices

The Business Benefit

One of the key reasons that businesses deploy and use networks is to share resources. The resources shared may be of benefit to employees, customers, vendor partners, governmental agencies, or other entities. Also, the type of resources to be shared can vary; they may be primarily textual, audio, video, graphical, and so on. The various servers and client devices that store these resources must also be considered.

For example, textual data can be maintained on a relatively low-end less costly networked device. Database or graphic data, however, will require a more high-end and expensive device. In addition, these devices will need to be connected to the network utilizing some type of transmission media, which might be wired or wireless. So, depending on the primary type of resources to be shared, thought must be given as to the best-fit hardware and media for those resources.

The resources to be shared, the devices they are stored on, the media that connect the devices, and the staff who support them, all have a cost. Businesses will want to evaluate and analyze their network resource distribution requirements in order to put in place a networked solution that is both effective and efficient. This chapter looks at media and devices, both of which are essential to the successful delivery of shared resources to the parties just mentioned. Spending too much on hardware and media that are not necessary to support business needs is wasteful and drains profits. Spending too little on hardware and media such that key constituent groups, such as customers, are not having their needs met puts that business at a competitive disadvantage. To get the solution right will benefit the business.

Learning Objectives

After studying this chapter, you should be able to:

■ Identify common types of conducted media.

■ Describe cable components.

■ Identify common types of radiated media.

■ List the factors that affect medium selection.

■ Be familiar with the relative advantages and disadvantages of different media.

■ Identify common physical layer devices.

■ Understand the purpose for multiplexing.

■ Describe three types of multiplexing.

In Chapter 3 we introduced four components of the physical layer: (1) the signaling methods used for conveying or representing data and translating between them; (2) the circuit configuration that carries the data; (3) the transmission medium used, which is wired or wireless, on which the circuits are based; and (4) the devices typically associated with this layer. In this chapter we continue our discussion of the physical layer but now concentrate on the last two components: media and devices.

TRANSMISSION MEDIA

Transmission media make up the physical path that data travel over to get from point A to point B. This medium might be wired, or conducted, and be one of several different types of cable. The medium might be wireless, or radiated, in which case the physical path is said to be "in the air." Data can be radiated in several different ways. Each of these two categories of media, conducted and radiated, have advantages and disadvantages. Based on the needs of the network, both types of media might be required. Some of the characteristics that must be considered when selecting a medium are security, cost, bandwidth, distance, and susceptibility to error.

Certain types of transmission media are used for *baseband communications* and others are used for broadband. In networking, a *baseband connection* is one that uses digital signals. With baseband connections, one digital stream is transmitted over the single baseband channel. Baseband, by definition, has only a single channel, although within that channel there may be multiple, interleaved signals. (This is examined more closely later in the chapter during the discussion on multiplexing.) In a traditional sense, *broadband communication* sends analog signals over multiple frequency channels at the same time. Today, however, broadband is widely marketed and viewed as a digital technology. Broadband offers multiple channels, and each channel is allocated a specific frequency range or bandwidth. Therefore, one physical cable might have separate channels for sound, video, and data. Figure 4.1 illustrates the concepts of baseband and broadband. The next section considers different types of conducted and radiated media.

CONDUCTED MEDIA

Conducted media are composed of some type of cable. We will look at three types of cable: twisted-wire pair, coaxial, and fiber-optic. Of these three, twisted-wire pair and fiber-optic are used extensively in data communication networks. Coaxial is more likely to be found, if at all, in much older, legacy networks. Networking technologists need to be familiar with all three types of conducted media. Regardless of the cable type, every cable has a conductor, insulation, and sheathing.

Common Cable Components

First, a cable must have a conductor over which a signal can be conducted. The conductor will either be copper wire for twisted-wire pair and coaxial cables or glass or plastic strands for fiber-optic cables. For copper, the conductor, called the *carrier*

Baseband

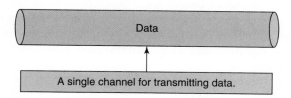

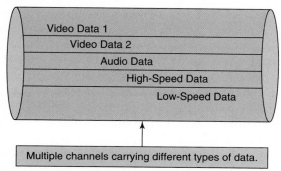

FIGURE 4.1 Contrasting Baseband and Broadband Channels

wire, might be solid or stranded, and the conductor's diameter might be measured in inches, centimeters, or millimeters. The American Wire Gauge (AWG) is another common means for specifying the diameter of a wire conductor. For fiber-optic cables, the conductor is called the *core.* The core can be either a glass or plastic tube that runs through the cable. The core's diameter is measured in microns, which are millionths of a meter.

Second, a cable's conductor has some type of insulation that is used to keep the signal in and external interferences out. For electrical wire, the insulation is usually made from some type of nonconductor, such as polyethylene. Fiber-optic insulation is called *cladding.* The cladding is made of a material with a lower refraction index than the core's material. The refraction index measures the ability of a material to reflect light rays. For fiber-optic cables, a cladding with a refraction index lower than the core ensures that light bounces back off the cladding and remains in the core.

Finally, an outer sheath, or jacket, encases the cable's elements and keeps them together. The sheath also provides protection from environmental forces such as water, pressure, or heat.

Twisted-Wire Pair

The signal wires for **twisted-wire pair** come in pairs that are wrapped around each other. By twisting wires around each other at regular intervals, usually between 2 and 12 twists per foot, noise on an individual wire is significantly reduced. A twisted-wire pair cable might contain 2, 4, 6, 8, 25, 50, or 100 twisted pair bundles. The more pairs there are per bundle, the more care that must be given to prevent *crosstalk,* defined later in this chapter, by providing adequate shielding and proper wire termination to the connector.

Unshielded twisted-wire pair cables are connected to network devices using a snaplike plug-in called an RJ-45 connector. These connectors are slightly larger than standard telephone jacks because they contain more wires. RJ-45s have eight conductors, one for each wire of four twisted pairs. Connectors of any type have *plugs* and *jacks*. A plug fits, or is inserted, into a jack. (In the past, plugs were referred to as male and the jacks as female.)

For networking, two- and four-pair cables are the most common. Twisted-pair wire comes in two flavors: shielded twisted pair (STP) and unshielded twisted pair (UTP). Of the two, UTP is by far the most commonly used. The cost of UTPs is significantly less than the cost of STPs. Also, because STP uses more shielding to protect its internal copper wiring, it is bulky and can be difficult to work with in tight spaces. Unshielded twisted pair wire, however, is very inexpensive, easy to install, and highly flexible. One potential problem with both types is a moderate risk of security violation. An unauthorized individual could, with the right equipment and opportunity, tap into the copper cabling on which UTP and STP are based. The signals that flow over the copper wire make no distinction between authorized and unauthorized taps. Security is thus a factor to be considered.

Unshielded twisted pair wire is far more susceptible to noise and electromagnetic interference than either coaxial or fiber-optic cabling. Also, UTP signals cannot travel as far as signals on the other cable types before they need to be boosted. Even so, due to its low cost and ease of installation, UTP is the most common medium used in data communications networks. A UTP cable has two conductors, each with its own colored plastic insulation. The colors provide information about the specific conductors in the cable and show which wires belong in pairs. For a standard UTP segment, the length of the cable should not be greater than 100 meters (about 330 feet).

Untwisted twisted pair wire is standardized by category using guidelines from such standard setting bodies as the Telecommunications Industry Association (*www.tiaonline.org*). The categories range from one to seven, from lowest to highest quality. Because UTP is inexpensive, many networks use Category 5, or Cat 5, which supports data transmission speeds of up to 100 Mbps (million bits per second). Standard Cat 5 has four pairs of 24 American Wire Gage copper wire. Category 1 is basic twisted-wire pair cable used in telephone systems. More than adequate for voice, Category 1 UTP is not suitable for data communications.

Coaxial Cable

For home use, a type of **coaxial cable**, RG-11, is a popular choice for connecting to cable television broadcasting and for linking to the Internet. But for data communications networks, coaxial cable is more likely to be encountered, if at all, in older, legacy systems. Two of the most common forms of coaxial cable are *thinnet* (RG-58) and *thicknet* (RG-8). In enterprise networks, thinnet has mostly been replaced by UTP, whereas fiber-optic cables have replaced thicknet. Recall that the term *enterprise* refers to the collection of all networks of a single organization.

Fiber-Optics

Fiber-optic cable, unlike twisted-wire pair or coaxial, transmits signals using light rather than electricity. Because light signals are used, fiber-optic cables do not suffer from electromagnetic interferences—a major advantage. Also, fiber-optic cables experience much less resistance to the signals they carry; therefore, signals travel much farther before they need to be boosted or regenerated. Consequently, fiber-optic signals encounter much less attenuation than those transmitted over a copper medium—a second major advantage. In addition, fiber-optic cable provides excellent bandwidth. Speeds of up to 100 Gbps (billion bits per second) are possible—a third advantage. (Recent research has tested fiber cable at 100 terabits per second!) And finally, fiber-optic cables are extremely hard to tap into—a fourth advantage. With a fiber-optic strand, if the strand is broken, which will likely occur if someone tries to tap into it, the link itself is broken, and communication stops. Fiber-optic circuits provide excellent security. Given all these advantages, why then isn't everything fiber-optic? One word answers that question: cost.

Fiber-optic technology, with all its benefits, is also quite expensive. Network interface cards (NICs), discussed in later chapters, for fiber connections can cost hundreds of dollars per card. An NIC is essential for connecting to the network. An NIC for a UTP connection might cost as little as $20. If 1,000 devices must be connected to the network, and each device must have an NIC, you can see how cost might be an important decision factor. In evaluating their needs, businesses often select to go with the technology that is the most cost-effective rather than the most technology-efficient. Recall that effectiveness and efficiency are two different considerations. They must be balanced.

Fiber-optic cables have one or more glass or plastic fibers through which light moves. Plastic is less expensive to manufacture, but works over shorter distances. Glass is more expensive, but works over greater distances. Distance, then, may be a deciding factor over what type of fiber-optic cable is selected. Do you need to connect a campus of a few buildings or branches across a state? In either case, the fiber core will range from 2 to several hundred microns. One micron is about 1/25,000 of an inch. Most core sizes for networking are 60, 62.5, and 100 microns. Also, most fiber-optic cable has at least two strands in its core, one for receiving and one for sending. You may recall that fiber-optic cable has a cladding for its insulation. The core and the cladding are frequently manufactured as a single unit. The fiber-optic cable can be either single mode or multimode. A mode is a possible path through which light can travel through a cable.

When **single-mode** fiber-optic cable is used, the core is very narrow, usually less than 10 microns. Single-mode cable has the least signal attenuation, but it is the most costly to install. Using single-mode cable, speeds of greater than 50 Gbps are possible. To put this in context, one 10 Gbps line can carry up to 130,000 voice channels. Because there is only one transmission path, distortion of the signal (which can occur with multimode) will not happen. Single-mode fiber-optic cable with a glass core and cladding will be of the highest quality and the highest expense.

Multimode cabling has a wider core. Because the core is wider, multiple beams of light have more paths to follow, resulting in the transmission of greater amounts of data. However, in a multi-light path, signal distortion at the receiving end of the transmission is also more likely. Multimode is particularly useful in wavelength division multiplexing (WDM).

The light source for fiber-optic is either a laser or a light-emitting diode (LED). Although laser light sources provide better quality, LEDs are cheaper. Also, LEDs are less likely to fail, and thus are more reliable. Because of cost and reliability, LEDs are more commonly used. Whether single- or multimode, fiber-optics has become the medium of choice for backbone networks.

So far we have discussed conducted, or wired, media. The other category type of media is radiated, or wireless. Whereas conducted media can be physically seen and touched, radiated media is, under normal circumstances, invisible to the human eye and said to be "in the air." For certain data communication needs, radiated media may provide the best, and only, alternative for transmission.

RADIATED MEDIA

Radiated or wireless media have four general forms: earth-based terrestrial micro-wave, space-based satellite microwave, radio, and infrared. All these forms are based on frequency waves, electromagnetic or light. Radio and microwave transmission and reception are achieved by use of antenna. During transmission, the antenna radiates electromagnetic energy into the air. For reception, the antenna picks up the electromagnetic energy. With infrared media, transmitters and receivers are used that modulate infrared light. As with the different conducted media, each type of radiated medium has advantages and disadvantages.

One disadvantage that all radiated media share is low security. Because transmissions are carried in the air, anyone with the proper equipment can intercept these transmissions. Therefore, for data that are sensitive or critical, some type of encryption is typically used. Data that are encrypted are scrambled or altered in order to prevent unauthorized users from understanding the message. Encrypted data, how-ever, require that both the sender and the receiver have the necessary software keys to unlock the meaning of the scrambled messages. Encryption has a time element. It takes time to encrypt and then unencrypt data so that the data can be used; time is money. Encryption is used with selected data, not all data. The same is true with compression, when data are squeezed into a smaller form so that the data can be transmitted more quickly. Again, compressed data must be uncompressed before it can be used. Again, this takes time.

TRANSMISSION IMPAIRMENT

Many factors can negatively affect a medium's transmission performance. Cable performance can be impaired by attenuation, crosstalk, and distortion. Radiated media are affected by fog, rain, snow, and solar disturbances. **Transmission impair-ment** can result in the transmission signal sent not being the transmission signal received.

The Ethical Perspective

Satellites and You

Satellite technology has proven to be an invaluable tool for modern man, assisting in weather tracking, global communications, environmental research on global climate change, and exploration of the universe, as well as other uses. Satellite technology, however, also allows the users of that technology—primarily governments, major research institutions, and large businesses—to use the technology in ways that people don't always agree. For example, one country may use its satellite technology to observe and track events taking place in another country, in a highly detailed manner. Buildings, vehicles, and people can be tracked with almost pinpoint accuracy from anywhere in the world.

Some are concerned that a government might use this technology to track its own population in ways that its citizens are unaware. Many consider the use of satellite technol-ogy for such purposes to be a violation of a government's international sovereign rights and an invasion of privacy of the populace at large.

What do you think? Should international law stipulate how satellite technology is used? Are there ethical issues of conduct related to privacy and security that should be considered by those who either control or have access to satellite technology? What is your ethical perspective?

ATTENUATION

Attenuation is the decrease of a signal's strength as it travels over a wire. This happens because the signal loses some of its energy as it tries to overcome the resistance of the cable. The greater the distance the signal must travel over a segment of cable, the more likely it is that a loss of signal strength, or attenuation, will result. Attenuation occurs more often in transmissions of higher frequencies or when the cable's resistance is higher. Devices such as repeaters can prevent attenuation. Repeaters intercept and boost a signal before passing it on to the next cable segment. However, repeaters may also boost any noise traveling on the cable.

CROSSTALK

Crosstalk occurs when one cable or circuit's transmission interferes with the transmission of a different cable or circuit. For example, different pairs of twisted wire in an UPT cable may interfere with each other. If this occurs, the signals from each pair of wires, in effect, step on each other, making one or both of their transmissions unintelligible. One means of correcting for crosstalk is to use cables that have additional shielding so that the wires and circuits are better protected from each other. For radiated media, guardbands, or buffer frequencies, can be used to separate signals from each other.

DISTORTION

Sometimes a signal changes its form or shape as it travels from its source to its destination. The signal arrives, but not as it was originally sent. This is called **distortion**. Distortion is a particular problem with complex signals. Recall that a complex signal may include multiple types of modulation, such as QAM, which uses amplitude and phase modulation. Individual signal components that make up a complex signal each have their own propagation speed. Propagation speed is the distance a signal can travel through a medium in 1 second. Distortion could occur if all of the signals that make up a complex signal do not arrive at their destination at the same time.

Now that we know something about the common components and problems that might affect transmission, let's look more closely at how to select a medium.

CHOOSING A MEDIUM

After examining both conducted and radiated media, the question becomes: How do you choose a medium for a particular data communication need? To answer that, five factors need to be considered:

1. *Cost*. Cost includes not only the materials but also the labor for installation, which is often one of the most expensive elements in implementation.
2. *Bandwidth*. What are the data speed requirements? Bandwidth should be based on business needs. Which medium provides sufficient bandwidth to support organizational requirements?
3. *Security*. Is security critical, or is it just desirable?
4. *Transmission impairment*. What level of transmission impairment can be tolerated? What physical environment will the medium be placed into?
5. *Distance*. Does the medium need to provide transmission between rooms in a building or between states or provinces in a country? Is the medium for a LAN, BN, MAN, or WAN?

Table 4.1   Advantages and Disadvantages of Different Major Medium

Type of Medium	Security	Transmission Distance	Cost	Error Potential	Difficulty of Installation
Twisted Wire Pair	Moderate	Short	Low	Moderate	Low
Coaxial Cable	Moderate	Short	Moderate	Low	Low
Fiber Optic	High	Moderate to Long	High	Very Low	High
Radio	Low	Short	Low	Moderate	Moderate
Terrestrial Microwave	Low	Long	Moderate	Low to Moderate	Low to Moderate
Satellite	Low	Long	Moderate	Low to Moderate	Low to Moderate

In a large enterprise, you will likely need several types of media, and they should be placed where they are used best. Again, efficiency and effectiveness are important, and your recommendation may need to balance the two. Table 4.1 summarizes the advantages and disadvantages of the various media that have been considered. Keep in mind that the medium selected must address economic business requirements. Most likely, a business will use a variety of media throughout its enterprise. One of your jobs might be advising the enterprise as to where and why a particular medium would or would not be appropriate.

PHYSICAL LAYER DEVICES

The selected transmission medium is one element in the overall design of a data communications network. You also need to be aware of the many types of devices that allow a data communications network to function. Each layer of the OSI and TCP/IP models has devices that are either specifically or generally associated with that layer. Some devices are more flexible in their functionality and thus can be positioned or used in more than one layer of the model. Several devices are associated with the physical layer.

Hubs, also referred to as *repeaters,* are devices that pass signals that transmit through them to an adjoining section of the same logical network. Hubs connect devices that share a common architecture, such as Ethernet or token ring. These architectures are explored later in the text.

A hub is either active or passive. If active, the hub not only transmits signals but also boosts and cleans the signals before it passes them on. In order to do this, an active hub must have its own power supply. A passive hub does not clean or boost the signals, so it does not have its own power supply. A passive hub simply passes the signals on to the next segment of transmission medium it is connected to. Another term for *boosting* a signal is *amplifying.* Because they have no power supply, passive hubs are limited to connecting shorter segments of the network.

Modems are devices that modulate a digital signal into an analog signal on the sending end, and then, at the receiving end, demodulate the signal from analog back to digital. A digital device is at each end of the communication. The term *modem* stands for modulator/demodulator. As you read earlier, analog signals can be modulated using amplitude, frequency, or phase modulation. Modems also use simplex, half-duplex, or full-duplex connections, depending on the type of modem.

Codecs do the reverse of what a modem does. They take analog signals on the sending end, convert them to digital signals for transmission, and then translate the signals back from digital to analog on the receiving end.

A **multiplexer** is a device that can take communications from several slow-speed devices on the sending end and combine them so that these several communications can pass over a single high-speed circuit. Another multiplexer is at the receiving end. Its job is to take the single high-speed circuit's combined communications and break it back down into the original individual communications. Multiplexers are frequently used with multiples of four slower circuits that have devices connected to them. Sending and receiving multiplexers might be assembling and disassembling communications from 4, 8, 16, or more slower-speed circuit devices.

Frequency-division multiplexing (FDM), Figure 4.2, divides a single high-speed circuit horizontally, creating a series of separate channels, each on a different frequency. Frequency-division multiplexers can use either amplitude or frequency modulation. Each sending device connected to the frequency-division multiplexer has its own channel, sharing the single high-speed circuit. The combined bandwidth of the individual channels cannot be greater than the total bandwidth of the single high-speed circuit. And, in fact, the combined bandwidths need to be less due to the need for guardbands.

The tradeoff here is that between each of the frequency channels, a guardband of frequency has to be inserted. The *guardband* is an unused portion of the circuit. It ensures that individual channels remain distinct within the single circuit. This means that the total capacity of the circuit cannot be used because guardbands are required to ensure that individual channels maintain their integrity. Guardbands are also a form of overhead. *Overhead* is an additional element that must be added to a technology in order for that technology to work. As a rule, lower overhead is more

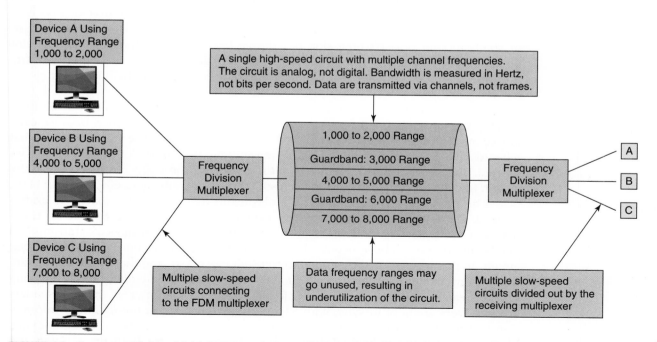

FIGURE 4.2 Frequency Division Multiplexing. Each device has an allocated frequency range that it uses. A range may go unutilized if a device has nothing to send or receive. Guardbands carry no data, and are used only for separating data ranges from each other.

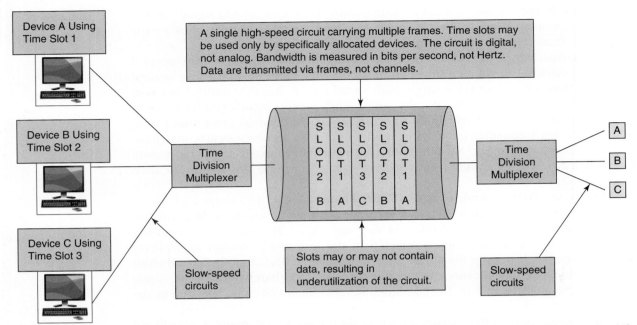

FIGURE 4.3   Time Division Multiplexing. Each device has an allocated time slot that only it can use. Slots may go unutilized if a device has nothing to send or receive.

desirable because it is more efficient. No data are carried in the guardbands. Their purpose is to prevent the separate channels from interfering with each other, which would result in crosstalk.

Time-division multiplexing (TDM), Figure 4.3, divides the circuit vertically into time slots. Each of the slower devices connected by time-division multiplexing is given an allocated, specific time slot over which it can communicate. Devices cannot use or share another device's time slot. If a device has nothing to transmit, its time slot goes unused. Time-division multiplexing is useful when the data rate capacity of the high-speed circuit is greater than the data rate required by the individual sending and receiving devices.

Keep in mind that the time slots are preallocated: Each time slot can be used only by the device defined for it. For TDM, guardbands are not needed because each device owns a predetermined portion of the high-speed circuit. The tradeoff here is that when devices are not communicating or transmitting, their time slot of the circuit goes unused. So, even if a device has nothing to send, it will be granted a time slot on the circuit. Idle devices cause overhead. Even so, TDM is generally more efficient than FDM.

The problem with time-division multiplexing is that circuit capacity is underutilized if a device has nothing to send over its allotted time slot. **Statistical time-division multiplexing (STDM)**, Figure 4.4, can evaluate each device's transmission needs and, based on those needs, allocate or not allocate a portion of the high-speed circuit. In this way, devices that need to transmit can do so, and those that are idle are not wasting circuit capacity. In order to do this, statistical time-division multiplexing encodes each individual transmission it sends with an identifier so that the senders and receivers are kept in sync. With STDM, the overhead is in the identifier information that must be encoded on each signal. Recall that with any type of multiplexing, identification of the individual devices must be provided for both the sending and receiving ends. Even so, statistical time-division multiplexing is more efficient than time-division multiplexing.

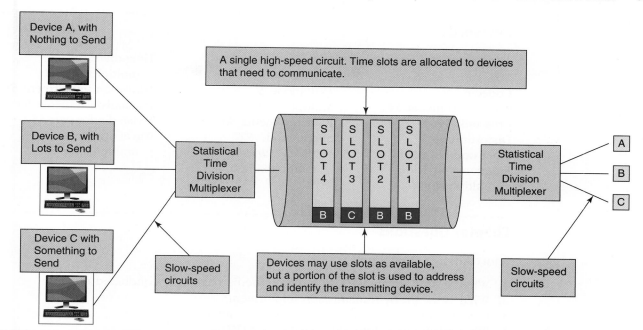

FIGURE 4.4 Statistical Time Division Multiplexing. Time slots are used by those devices that need to communicate. Time slots are not preallocated, but are distributed based on the need of a device to communicate.

Wavelength-division multiplexing (WDM) is used with fiber-optics in a manner similar to how frequency-division multiplexing is used with copper. Wavelength division multiplexing uses lasers to transmit different frequencies of light through the same fiber-optic cable. At the sending end, narrow bands of light are combined into a wider band. The wider band is the high-speed circuit. At the receiving end, the signals are separated. A more complex form of wavelength division multiplexing is dense wavelength division multiplexing. Dense wavelength-division multiplexing (DWDM) combines wavelength division multiplexing with time-division multiplexing. Using DWDM, one fiber-optic cable can send up to 400 Gbps (billions of bits per second).

Chapter Summary

Whether analog or digital, signals are carried over a transmission medium. The transmission medium has a circuit configuration, point-to-point or multipoint, and a data flow, simplex, half-duplex, or full-duplex. Based on the needs and size of the network, one or all of these might be used. Transmission media fall into one of two categories: conducted or radiated. Conducted media use cables: twisted-wire pair, coaxial, or fiber-optic. Radiated, or wireless, media include microwave, radio, or infrared. Each type of transmission medium has advantages and disadvantages. Factors to consider when selecting a medium include cost, bandwidth, security, transmission impairment, and distance.

A number of different devices are associated with the physical layer. These include hubs, modems, codecs, and multiplexers. Multiplexers at the sending end of a communication combine several slower-speed circuits onto one high-speed link. At the receiving end, multiplexers disassemble the high-speed transmission back into its slower-circuit component parts. Multiplexers are frequently configured with multiples of four slower-speed circuit devices. Types of multiplexing include frequency-division, time-division, statistical time-division, and wavelength-division multiplexing.

Keywords

Attenuation *59*
Coaxial cable *56*
Codec *61*
Conducted media *54*
Crosstalk *59*
Distortion *59*
Fiber optic cable *56*
Frequency-division
   multiplexing *61*

Hub *60*
Modem *60*
Multimode *57*
Multiplexer *61*
Radiated media *58*
Single-mode *57*
Statistical time-division
   multiplexing *62*

Time-division
   multiplexing *62*
Transition impairment *58*
Transmission media *54*
Twisted-wire pair *55*
Wavelength-division
   multiplexing *63*

Chapter Questions

Short Answer Questions

1. What, if any, advantages do radiated media have over conducted media?
2. What is meant by transmission impairment?
3. Describe one type of transmission impairment.
4. What advantages does UPT have over STP?
5. Describe a baseband channel.
6. Why would a copper-based transmission cable have insulation?
7. What is the purpose for an RJ-45 connector?
8. Describe one disadvantage of a radiated media.

Hands-On Projects

1. Describe the steps you could take when using Cat-5 UTP to prevent crosstalk, attenuation, distortion, or other physical problems that might occur when using this type of cabling medium.
2. Visit either a physical or online hardware networking supply store. Identify three types of cabling tools, their cost, purpose, and the physical layer functions they are associated with.
3. Assume you need enough Cat-5 UTP cabling and connectors for a 15 station LAN. What is the approximate cost?
4. Interview a network administrator at your college, university, or place of work. How does he or she decide on media used for the networks they support?

Research in Brief

For one or more of the following questions, provide a one- or two-page report based on your findings.

1. What factors would you consider when recommending a data communications medium for a network? Explain why these factors affect your recommendation and what advantages and disadvantages different media have.
2. Search the Internet to find at least three vendors of fiber-optic hardware components. Compare and report on price, service, warranty, or other related topics for at least three different types of hardware: cable, NICs, tool kits, etc.
3. Wireless has rapidly become a preferred physical media. Three standards for wireless include 802.11a, 802.11b, and 802.11g. What standards-setting body (or bodies) is involved with these specifications? How do the standards differ? How are they similar? What implementation issues might there be with wireless media?

Case Study

Sheehan Marketing and Public Relations

The networked computers that are used by Sheehan Marketing and Public Relations are cabled together with Cat-5 UTP Ethernet. The Los Angeles facility is composed of a separate room for the president, a reception area for the secretary, and a large open floor space for the rest of the staff. The total office is approximately 2,000 square feet. Three passive hubs connect all the computers together. The hubs are in the general office space. Wires connecting the computers to the hubs run along the perimeters of the wall and, in a few cases, cross floor space where staff frequently walk.

Over the past two years, SMPR has acquired more clients who are involved in video and audio work. Currently, because these files do not transport well across the network, when someone needs access to a client's video or audio file, the person must physically access the file from the computer on which it is stored. The staff is finding it difficult to work cohesively as a team because only one person at a time can access a particular file. Also, the different branch offices need to be able to access resources remotely.

CASE STUDY QUESTIONS

Using the information just provided, answer the following questions.

1. Focusing on the physical part of the Los Angeles network, research and prepare a report on the costs of upgrading a 24-computer network with Cat-5e UTP, NICs capable of 10/100 Mbps, and 3 active hubs. Include in your report the cost of a standard tool kit for yourself. Are there any problems with how the wiring is currently set up? If so, what do you plan to recommend? Don't forget to include in the report any labor costs for installing the new Cat-5 wiring. Assume you can hire a wiring technician for $40 an hour.
2. Do you have any concerns with the level of documentation at SMPR? If so, what steps would you take to improve the situation and why?

Topic in Focus

RADIATED MEDIA

Terrestrial Microwave

In a terrestrial microwave application, a microwave signal is beamed over a line-of-sight path to a parabolic antenna, as conceptualized in Figure 4.5. Microwave frequencies follow a straight line and do not bend with the curvature of the Earth. Because microwave frequencies do not bend, line-of-sight antennas are required. The sending antennas must be precisely placed in order for the transmitting frequency to be passed and caught by the receiving antenna. If the antennas are not in line of sight of each other, a transmitting frequency will continue on a straight line into space, and ultimately into the next galaxy and beyond—not a good sign when we are trying to communicate here on Earth.

Transmission frequencies used in terrestrial microwave generally range from 2 to 40 GHz (Gigahertz, billions of hertz). Higher frequencies provide higher potential bandwidth and data rates. But, higher data rates are also more likely to experience errors. As is true with any transmission medium, attenuation can be a problem. Microwave boosters are usually placed 10 to 100 kilometers apart. These boosters, or repeaters,

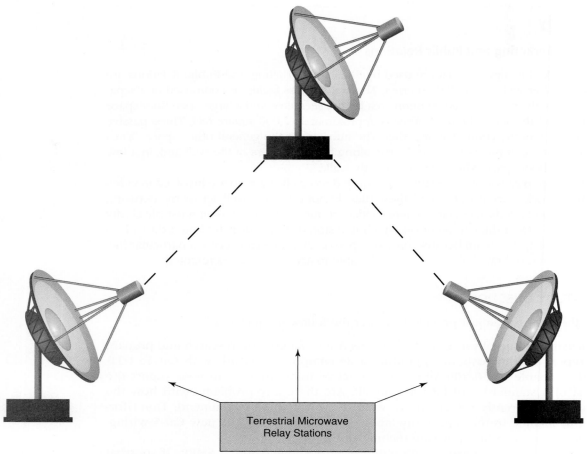

FIGURE 4.5   Terrestrial Microwave Relay Stations. Terrestrial microwave relay stations must be "in line of sight" of each other. The microwave frequencies they transmit do not bend with the curvature of the earth, but instead travel in a straight line. One relay station captures and passes on a transmission to the next relay station. The dotted lines represent data being transmitted.

can be installed with each antenna. Environmental influences such as heavy rain, snow, or fog can negatively impair a microwave's performance, whether terrestrial or satellite. Terrestrial microwave is an essential and critical component in global telephone systems.

Microwave relay stations are typically placed at high positions, such as on sky-scrapers or hills or mountains, in order to extend the range between the sending and receiving antennas. For long distances, a series of microwave relay towers are required. This type of transmission, as with satellite transmission, crosses public thoroughfares and is highly regulated. Cost in establishing a microwave network is high.

Satellite Microwave

Satellite microwave is also a line-of-sight technology, but in this case one of the stations is on Earth and the other is in orbit. Figure 4.6 illustrates the concept of satellite transmission. The satellite, in effect, is the antenna and the receiver. The satellite also serves as an amplifier, so intermediate amplifiers are not needed as they are with terrestrial microwave. When transmission signals need to span a continent or an ocean, satellite is a good choice. However, satellite microwave can also be negatively affected by the same environmental conditions as terrestrial microwave: heavy rain, fog, snow, or solar flares.

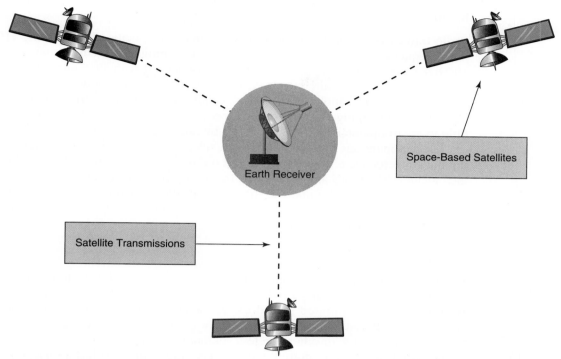

FIGURE 4.6   Three Geosynchronous Satellites Required for Full Communication Coverage of Earth. An Earth-based station communicates with its space-based satellite companion and can then relay that communication to another space-based satellite. The satellites are in line of sight with their Earth-based receiver.

Transmitting over two bands, satellites have an uplink and a downlink. The uplink is from an Earth station to the satellite. The downlink is from the satellite to an Earth station. The optimum frequency range for satellite communications is from 1 to 10 GHz. A satellite in geosynchronous orbit is fixed about 23,000 miles above the Earth's surface. Note that there are only a limited number of spaces available to place satellites in geosynchronous orbit. It takes at least three geosynchronous satellites, equally spaced from one another, to provide complete global coverage.

The long distances traveled by signals transmitted by satellite results in propagation delay. Propagation delay is the time it takes a transmission to get from Earth to the satellite, or vice versa. This delay is significant enough that it can be noticed in a satellite-based telephone conversation. Propagation delay can also result in problems related to data flow and error control. As with terrestrial microwave, satellite communications are heavily regulated and very expensive to implement. Most users of microwave technologies, whether terrestrial or satellite, lease the use of the infrastructure from a common carrier rather than build their own. Leasing the infrastructure is only moderately expensive.

Because of cost and the limited number of locations to position geosynchronous satellites, low-Earth-orbiting satellites, or LEOs, are another option. These satellites are much closer to the Earth, typically between 435 and 1,500 miles. This closer distance means that propagation delay is not a problem. However, LEOs also cover a much smaller area of the Earth in terms of communications capability. This, in turn, means that many more LEOs are required to cover the same amount of territory that a geosynchronous satellite could cover. In addition, LEOs travel faster than the rotation of the Earth. This means that a ground station that uses a LEO must track the satellite before beginning a communication.

Radio

Radio transmissions, in terms of data communications, generally fall in the VHF (very high frequency) and UHF (ultrahigh frequency) ranges. Together, they range from 30 MHz to 1GHz. Very high frequencies are associated with VHF television, FM radio, aircraft AM radio, and aircraft navigational aids. Ultrahigh frequencies are associated with UHF television, mobile telephones, cellular radio (which can be used in wireless networks), and paging. Because of their low frequencies, VHF and UHF are less susceptible to environmental attenuation caused by rain, fog, and snow.

The tremendous popularity of mobile telephones and other mobile devices is driving the convergence of the telephone and the Internet. Emerging radio-based technologies include Bluetooth and IEEE 802.11g—two topics we return to in a later chapter. Radio solutions can accommodate the relatively short distances associated with a LAN. In addition, such technologies are low in cost. However, the speed of data transmission is also slow—from 1 to 10 Mbps.

Infrared

Infrared communications use transmitters and receivers, which have to be in line of sight of each other. The frequency used is just below the visible light spectrum. Unlike microwave transmissions, infrared light does not penetrate or pass through solid substances such as walls. Because transmission does not go beyond a room, security problems are lessened compared with other wireless solutions. However, this also limits the mobility of the user linked to an infrared network. Like radio, infrared has a relatively low cost and is used for short distances appropriate to a LAN. Although infrared might provide significant bandwidth, as a technology it can be difficult to implement, especially with its line-of-sight requirements.

5

Data Link Layer Fundamentals

The Business Benefit

Organizations utilize their enterprise networking technologies to get critical data from one location of the enterprise to another, whether that other location is across the street in another building or across the globe in another country. Businesses depend on the accuracy of these data not only for commercial advantage but also for supporting all components of the organization: research, sales, marketing, customer services, inventory control, governmental reporting, and more. However, even with the best and most expensive underlying networking technology, the value of the data is lost if the data are not accurate to begin with, or if the data become corrupted as they are routed through the enterprise. Not only do the data, if inaccurate, lose their own intrinsic value, but the business will find that other costs are created as well.

In a 2010 report produced by Ovum (*http://ovum.com*), an independent data research and consulting firm, Madan Sheina, a lead analyst, stated, "Bad data is a growing problem for businesses due to the sheer volume and pace at which it is now moved between organizations....We now estimate that bad data costs US companies 30 percent of their revenue—a massive $700 billion per year and a figure that is set to increase....With such a high cost, it is imperative that businesses get to grips with this issue. If more did, the economy would be in a better position to recover from the downturn, and emerge more competitive when the upturn arrives."

Inaccurate data can lead to customer disputes, user and business partner frustration, business risk, late reporting, cost of redoing an order or transaction, and, perhaps most significantly, bad business decisions that can result in the failure of the business itself.

One of the key topics presented in this chapter on the data link layer relates to error detection and correction as a means of helping to ensure that data are accurate.

Learning Objectives

After studying this chapter, you should be able to:

- Identify the components that make up the IEEE 802 implementation.
- Understand the concept of flow control at the data link layer.
- Describe stop-and-wait flow control.

- ■ Describe sliding windows flow control.
- ■ Identify three types of error detection.
- ■ Identify two types of error correction.
- ■ Explain asynchronous and synchronous data link protocols.
- ■ Describe how a bridge or switch might be used.

As you learned in the last chapter, the lowest-level layer, the physical layer, assigns no meaning to the data bits of the message that it transmits. The physical layer is only concerned with getting the sender's message bits from the originating source device to the final destination device. It is at the data link layer, the second lowest-level layer, that meaning and organization are associated with the bits being transmitted. The data link layer frames message data bits so that they can be passed to the next-higher layer, the network layer. A message can be composed of one or many frames. The data link layer not only frames the data bits but it also controls how the frames are moved from one networked device to another.

THE DATA LINK LAYER

One of the major functions of the data link layer is to frame binary bits received from the physical layer. A **frame**, then, is the structure given to binary bits at the data link layer. A frame may have to pass through many intermediary devices and networks on its path from the originating source to the final destination device. Think of it as a relay in which one runner passes the baton (in this case a frame) to the next runner (in this case the next device). While moving the frames between each sending and receiving device in the relay, the data link layer ensures that one device does not overwhelm the other with too much data at one time. Flow control is used so that the sending device does not overwhelm the receiving device in a communication. Imagine a single clerk in a store with 20 customers to serve. Without flow control (in this case a single-file line that the customers must wait in), the clerk could be overwhelmed with customer demands. Flow control is important for many human as well as data communications applications.

An associated type of control is line discipline. **Line discipline** controls which device can communicate and when. It is like a professor in a class specifying which student may speak in what order to give his or her opinion or observation. If everyone spoke at once, not much would be accomplished. Instead, the professor enforces line discipline to ensure orderly discussion. The data link layer also performs *error control,* the goal of which is to enable a receiving device to recognize, and potentially correct for, a transmission error.

This chapter also introduces the topic of addressing. Physical addressing is an important function of the data link layer. It may seem odd that physical addressing takes place at the data link layer rather than the physical layer, but that is how it is done. In later chapters, you will learn that other forms of addressing are equally critical. This chapter will identify the devices and components associated with the data link layer. In addition, the chapter will present an entire alphabet soup of new acronyms and terms you will need to know. You will find that the data link layer is a fascinating, challenging layer with many important activities.

Components of the Data Link Layer

In 1985, the IEEE developed Project **802**, an implementation specification for the data link layer used by both the OSI and the TCP/IP networking models. (The IEEE

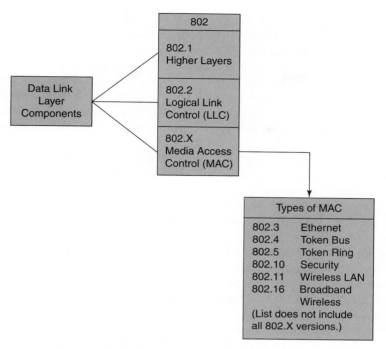

FIGURE 5.1   Components of the 802 Standard for the Data Link Layer

was introduced in Chapter 1. Visit this body's website at *www.ieee.org*.) The IEEE divided the data link layer into two parts: logical link control and media access control. In the IEEE 802 implementation, the **logical link control (LLC)** sits above the media access control (MAC). The data link layer in effect contains its own miniature layer stack. The 802 specification is modular, which is one of its strengths. Figure 5.1 shows how the components of the 802 specification fit together. Each module under the 802 umbrella has a number that identifies that module's specific functionality for specific types of MAC: **802.1** for inter-networking; **802.2** for LLC; **802.3** for CSMA/CD (Carrier Sense Multiple Access/Collision Detection) **802.4** (token bus), and **802.5** (token ring). We review the last three MAC protocols listed later in the chapter.

Keep in mind as you read through the chapter that the data link layer sits between the physical and network layers. The data link layer not only passes data down to the physical layer for transmission but it also must pass data up to the network layer in a form the network layer will recognize and accept. Together, LLC and MAC make this possible. Let's see how.

Logical link control, also designated as 802.2, provides three types of frame delivery service: Type 1, Type 2, and Type 3. A **delivery service** is a method of getting a frame from point A to point B. Type 1 is a connectionless service that does not provide acknowledgment. In this case, an **acknowledgment** means that the receiver responds to the sender regarding a communication. If acknowledgment is not provided, the receiver does not tell the sender whether a frame arrived or not. **Connectionless** means that, first, no predefined path or permanent circuit is established between sender and receiver. Second, because there is no acknowledgment, the sender has no direct or immediate way of knowing whether a frame has reached its destination.

These two characteristics mean that Type 1 delivery is the fastest but least reliable service offered by LLC. Type 1 service is like putting a postcard in the mail without a return address. You do not know what route the postcard takes. You hope it gets there, but there is no guarantee. (With a return address, if the postcard comes back you know it did not get delivered.) And, you cannot know for sure that it has arrived unless you call the person you sent the postcard to, which defeats the purpose of sending the postcard in the first place. Even so, Type 1 delivery is the most popular delivery service because higher-level layer protocols often provide their own delivery and error checking.

The opposite of Type 1, Type 2 is a **connection-oriented** delivery service that provides acknowledgment. In a connection-oriented service, a transmission circuit must be established between the sender and receiver before they can begin to communicate. Also, the receiver eventually acknowledges to the sender whether the frame was received. The circuit established between the sender and receiver does not have to be permanent, and often it is not. However, the circuit is maintained long enough for the communication to take place. With a connection-oriented service, flow control is especially important, but not the kind of flow control that takes place at the physical layer. Two of the most common forms of data link layer flow control managed by LLC are stop-and-wait and sliding windows, which are discussed later in this chapter.

A connection-oriented service is similar to a registered letter that has a guarantee of delivery and that also requires the receiver to sign for receipt, thereby acknowledging that he or she has received your letter. Sending a registered letter is more expensive than sending a postcard. The same is true with regard to Type 1 and Type 2 delivery service requirements.

A Type 3 delivery service is connectionless but offers acknowledgment, thereby providing some of the advantages of both Type 1 and Type 2 services. Even so, Type 3 is the least often used of the three types of delivery service.

To accomplish its work, LLC uses a unit of data called a **protocol data unit (PDU)**. A good website that describes PDUs and other protocols can be found at *www. protocols.com*. A PDU can contain up to four elements: (1) a destination service access point (DSAP), (2) a source service access point (SSAP), (3) a control field, and (4) a data or information field.

The DSAP is an 8-bit field that identifies the higher-level protocol using the LLC's services. Remember, the frame has been passed down to the data link layer from a higher-level layer in the TCP/IP layer stack. That higher-level layer uses a specific type of protocol. The first bit of the eight-bit DSAP field indicates whether the frame is meant for an individual host or a group of hosts. A host is any device that can communicate with and is connected to a TCP/IP network.

The SSAP is also an eight-bit field that indicates the local user of the LLC service. The SSAP's first bit indicates whether the protocol data unit communication is a command or a response type of frame.

The control field, the third element of a PDU, is a one- or two-byte field that indicates the type of PDU. Protocol data unit frames are one of the following: information (I), supervisory (S), or unnumbered (U). Only Type 2 connection-oriented delivery services use I and S frames. All three delivery types use U frames. Information frames are used to transmit connection-oriented data. Supervisory frames are used to supervise and manage the information frames. Unnumbered frames are used for connectionless data and to terminate the logical link between hosts using Type 2 services.

The fourth protocol data unit element, the data field, is of variable length and contains the data or information received from the network layer protocol. The length

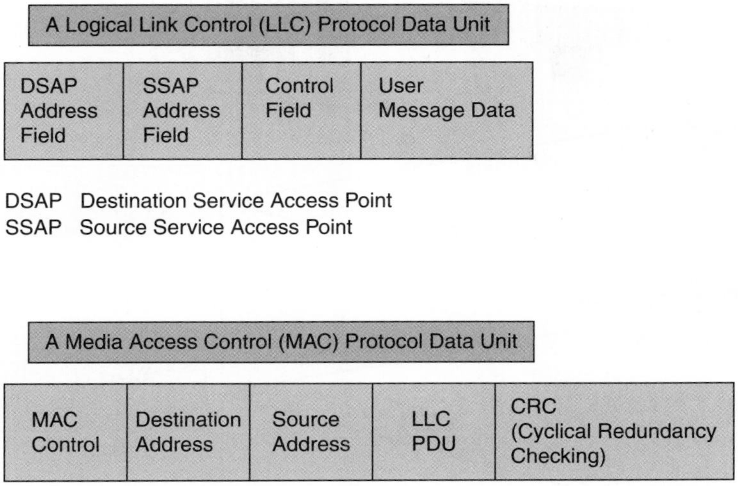

A Logical Link Control (LLC) Protocol Data Unit

DSAP Address Field	SSAP Address Field	Control Field	User Message Data

DSAP   Destination Service Access Point
SSAP   Source Service Access Point

A Media Access Control (MAC) Protocol Data Unit

MAC Control	Destination Address	Source Address	LLC PDU	CRC (Cyclical Redundancy Checking)

FIGURE 5.2   Elements of a Protocol Data Unit (PDU)

of the data field will be determined by the media access method used—for example, token or contention. We explore both later when we discuss MAC in more detail. Of the three types of PDU frames, supervisory frames do not have a data field. Figure 5.2 illustrates the components of a PDU.

FLOW CONTROL

With a Type 2 connection-oriented delivery service, a sender and receiver must agree on establishing their communication before transmission can begin. Part of their agreement is that the sender will not overwhelm the receiver with the data being transmitted. A faster sending device, without flow control, could overwhelm a slower receiving device. How might this happen? A receiving device typically has a temporary and limited amount of storage memory, called a buffer, available to it for acceptance of incoming data. If, from a faster-sending device, a slower-receiving device has more data coming in than it can hold in its buffer, transmission overload results on the receiver's end. Data loss can be expected.

In order to ensure that the sender does not overwhelm the receiver (causing transmission overload), flow control is required. Flow control, which is managed by LLC, restricts the amount of data a sender can send until the sender receives an acknowledgment from the receiver that the receiver is ready for data. In the previous example, if the receiver's buffer is filled, the receiver so alerts the sender. The sender then halts transmission until given the go-ahead by the receiver to continue. Two common flow control methods at the data link layer are stop-and-wait and sliding windows. Let's take a closer look at each.

Stop-and-Wait Flow Control

With **stop-and-wait** flow control, each individual frame that the sender transmits requires an individual acknowledgment back from the receiver that that specific frame has been received. Only after each individual frame has been acknowledged can the sender transmit the next sequential frame. A message could be composed

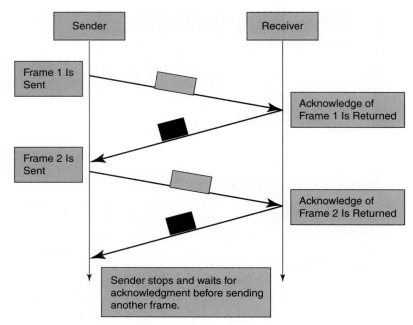

FIGURE 5.3 Stop-and-Wait Flow Control

of 1,000 frames. With stop-and-wait flow control, the sender would ultimately get back, assuming no transmission problems occurred, 1,000 acknowledgments from the receiver, or one for each of the 1,000 frames sent. Therefore, the sender sends frame 1 and then stops and waits for acknowledgment from the receiver that frame 1 has been received and accepted. Then the sender sends frame 2 and again stops and waits for an acknowledgment from the receiver that frame 2 has been received and accepted. Then the sender sends frame 3, and so on. Figure 5.3 illustrates this process.

Stop-and-wait flow control has one major advantage: It is very straightforward and simple. For messages composed of a few large frames, stop-and-wait flow control can be very efficient over a short link. But this is not a typical situation. Also, the more, and the smaller, frames there are, the more inefficient stop-and-wait becomes as a flow control mechanism. Furthermore, the longer the link between the sending and receiving devices, the more serious the inefficiency becomes in gaining full utilization of the circuit. It does, after all, take time for acknowledgments to travel back and forth across a link. The longer the link, the more time required to transmit acknowledgments. So, except under certain limited circumstances, stop-and-wait flow control is not a first choice. Sliding windows is the more popular flow control method.

Sliding Windows Flow Control

If one acknowledgment could be used for multiple frames, instead of one acknowledgment per frame, the result would be more efficient utilization of the communication circuit. This is the objective behind sliding windows. With **sliding windows**, several frames can be sent before an acknowledgment is required, making for a more complicated method.

Earlier you read that the receiver has a memory buffer into which frames are received in order to be processed. The sender also has a memory buffer holding the frames to be sent. These memory buffers on the sender's and receiver's ends are, in effect, the sliding windows. Window refers to the memory buffer storage area that is used to hold frame data. The window on either the sender's or receiver's end can slide to become wider or more narrow based on the communication. The acknowledgment going back and forth between sender and receiver controls the communication and causes the windows to adjust their size, sliding open or sliding closed. Before a sender's **sliding windows buffer** can expand, the sender must receive an acknowledgment back from the receiver. Before a receiver's sliding windows buffer can expand, the receiver must send an acknowledgment. Figure 5.4 illustrates the sliding windows concept.

The sliding windows method uses a sequencing number scheme to control the number of frames being transmitted and received based on the acknowledgments going back and forth. This sequencing number scheme controls the size of the sender and receiver's sliding windows buffer. The sender and receiver must use the same sequencing number scheme to stay in sync with each other. The sequencing number is a field that is part of the frame being sent and received. The sequencing number field must have a specific bit size. The bit size of the field must be the same for sender and receiver. The number of bits used to define the field depends on network needs as well as the size of the sender's and receiver's buffers. To know more about how sliding windows works, see the "Topic in Focus: The Secrets of Sliding Windows" at the end of this chapter.

Another type of circuit control the data link layer performs is line discipline, a straightforward concept. Line discipline controls the give and take (i.e., who talks when) between two devices that are communicating.

Assume that a point-to-point, half-duplex circuit connects two devices. From Chapter 3, you know that a device using a half-duplex circuit can send or receive, but not both at the same time. With this example, because there is a point-to-point circuit, only one device at a time can use the half-duplex line to either send or receive. What determines which device can send or receive and when? If both devices attempt to send or receive at the same time, their communications would fail because the transmissions would collide. This is similar to having two cars on a one-way road driving in the opposite direction toward each other; an accident is going to happen. A half-duplex line can only be used by one device at a time. Line discipline is required to enforce rules of communication, controlling who can communicate when.

Line discipline is associated with two types of network environments. One is a point-to-point connection between two devices using either a half-duplex or full-duplex

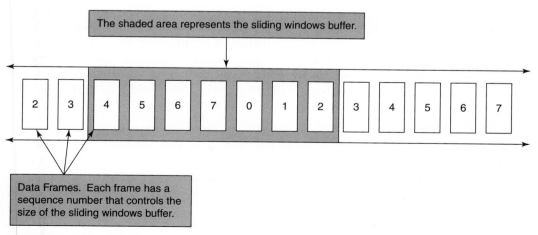

FIGURE 5.4 Sliding Window

line. Whether half- or full-duplex, before communication can occur, a session must be established between the two devices. If half-duplex, the devices have an additional requirement in that they must take turns using the line. The form of line discipline used in this scenario is called *enquiry/acknowledgment (ENQ/ACK)*. Let's consider how this might work.

The sending device, device A, initiates a communication by transmitting an enquiry frame to the receiving device, device B. Device A then waits to hear from device B if it is available and accepting communications. Device B, if available and ready for communication, transmits an acknowledgment frame to the sender, device A. At that point, a session is established and device A begins its communication with B. When finished, device A transmits an end of transmission (EOT) frame, terminating the session. If device B were not available for communication, it would transmit an NAK (negative acknowledgment) frame to device A. Device A will have to try again later. If device B, because it is disconnected or down, does not send an acknowledgment frame to A, after a specified time, device A will issue another enquiry to device B. After three failed enquiry attempts, A assumes that B is completely unavailable and terminates communication entirely until a later time.

The second type of network environment requiring line discipline occurs when multiple devices on a multipoint line communicate through a central controlling communication device. This is fairly common with terminals connected to a mainframe computer. The terminals do not communicate directly with each other. Instead, they must pass their communications through the mainframe. The mainframe, or other similar central controlling device, controls the multipoint circuit and determines when and if devices can communicate. The central controlling device does this through a process called polling.

With **polling**, the controlling device is the key initiator of all communication processes, even when the controlling device has nothing to communicate. This may sound odd. What this means is that all the other devices wait for the central controlling device to "poll" them to see if they having something to communicate. The controlling device is often called the *primary device;* the multipoint-attached devices are referred to as *secondary devices*. The secondary devices wait for the primary device to contact them. If a secondary device has a communication need, it makes this known to the primary device, which then carries out the communication.

ERROR CONTROL

Besides flow control duties, the data link layer also performs various types of **error control**. We do not live in a perfect world—neither do data communication systems. For that reason, errors will find their way into any data communications environment. Error control is essential. Error control at the data link layer has two elements: detection and correction. If an error can be detected, it might be corrected. Let's first consider error detection and then how such errors might be corrected.

Error Detection

In data communications, **error detection** and correction requires that additional overhead be attached to the core message data being transmitted. The overhead takes the form of added data elements, above and beyond the core message data itself. The added overhead, referred to as *redundant data,* is a necessary burden used to ensure data accuracy.

Users of communications technologies rely on the accuracy of their data to make informed decisions. Businesses rely on data accuracy to give them a competitive advantage. Whereas human error can be challenging, and in some cases impossible to control for, error-detection techniques are available that can be used to ensure that within a communications system the data sent are the data received. Common error-detection techniques include parity checking, longitudinal redundancy checking, checksum checking, and cyclical redundancy checking.

PARITY CHECKING   Parity checking is a very simple but not very accurate method of error detection. It is sometimes referred to as *vertical redundancy checking*. Other newer and more complicated techniques offer much higher rates of error detection. With parity checking, an extra parity bit is added to a byte. For example, an additional eighth parity bit is added to a seven-bit standard ASCII byte, thereby creating an eight-bit unit. The parity bit added is either a 0 or a 1, depending on the type of parity used, even or odd. **Even parity** is usually used with synchronous transmissions and **odd parity** is generally used with asynchronous transmissions, both of which will be addressed later in the chapter.

Whether even or odd, both the sender and receiver must agree to use the same parity type. In even parity, the number of 1 bits transmitted in the eight-bit unit must always add to an even number. For odd parity, the number of 1 bits transmitted in the eight-bit unit must always add to an odd number.

Assume that two devices are set for even parity. On the sending end is a seven-bit ASCII uppercase character, "A," whose binary value is 1000001. The parity bit is set to 0 or 1 depending on the number of 1 bits in the core ASCII character. Currently, ASCII character A has two binary 1s. Therefore, the parity, or eighth, bit should be set to 0 in order to keep the number of binary 1s an even number. The following eight bits are transmitted: 10000010. The last bit is the parity bit; it is set to 0 to maintain even parity. On the receiving end, the receiver adds the number of binary 1s in the eight-bit unit and determines if the total is even or odd. If it is even, the receiver assumes the data are good; if it is odd, the receiver assumes that a transmission error has occurred. The problem with parity checking is that it is only good for single-bit transmission errors.

Using this same example with even parity, if 10000010 is what is sent, but 10000110 is what is received, the receiver will recognize that an error has occurred

The Ethical Perspective

Error Detection and Correction: Who Is Responsible?

Businesses rely on the accuracy of their data as a competitive advantage. Consumers also require business data communications systems to be truthful and accurate regarding the data captured and stored about them. However, if the data should, for whatever reason, be inaccurate due to technical error or human error, and a business has discovered this within its own system, should that business be ethically or legally bound to inform its customers of this issue? Some businesses claim that such disclosures could be so damaging, even if the errors were slight, that the future of their business would be at stake. And yet, the data captured and utilized by a business involve real people who may be affected by such errors.

In your view, to what degree must a business disclose any errors that its data communications systems may create? What would be your opinion from a business owner's perspective versus your opinion as a customer? Is there a conflict of interest? Should there be legal ramifications for data that are in error? If so, how moderate or severe should these ramifications be? Should customers be informed of data errors in a system even if over the long term no real harm will result to them?

because the number of 1 bits is odd. But if 10000010 is sent and 10011010 is what is received, the receiver does not recognize an error because the number of binary 1s adds up to an even number. To the receiver, the data are good, although you can see that it is not. With parity checking, the probability of detecting an error is about 50 percent, not very good when you consider you could get the same odds with the toss of a coin.

LONGITUDINAL REDUNDANCY CHECKING   Simple parity relies on a single bit to detect errors in a single byte. In contrast, **longitudinal redundancy checking (LRC)** generates an entire additional byte, called a **block check character (BCC)**, based on all the bytes in a message. All the bytes that make up the message are the "block." (Be aware that longitudinal redundancy checking works with either Standard or Extended ASCII. You might also find the following website of data communications terms, including longitudinal redundancy checking, to be useful: *www.nickara.com/glossary_v0.htm*.) On the sending end, the block check character is calculated and attached to the end of the block of data being sent. Parity is still used, again either even or odd, but in a more complex manner.

Using longitudinal redundancy checking, the bytes in the message that make up the block are evaluated in a row/column manner. Using parity, based on the row/column evaluation, a block check character is calculated. The receiver performs the same block check character calculation on the block of data received and compares its generated block check character with the one sent. If they are not the same, a transmission error is recognized. Evaluating the block of data in a row and column manner generates the block check character. This is difficult to visualize, so let's take a look at a concrete example.

In this example, the word "BYTE" is the data block that needs a block check character. This example will use even parity. The word "BYTE" is a block of four characters. Each character occupies one byte, so the block has four bytes. First, each character is converted into its Extended ASCII binary equivalent. The data block is now expressed as a stream of bits: 01000010 01011001 01010100 01000101. For purposes of longitudinal redundancy checking, let's place these binary values in a table of rows and columns (see Table 5.1). Each character, or byte, has its own row. There are eight columns, one for each bit in the byte. Note that the last row is reserved for the block check character, which has yet to be calculated. To perform the calculation, each column of binary bits is evaluated lengthwise, top to bottom, for even parity. (The term *longitudinal,* by the way, literally means "lengthwise.")

Even parity requires that the number of 1 bits, if present, add up to an even value. Column 1 does not have any 1 bits. Therefore, the first bit value of the block check character byte is set to 0. Column 2 has four binary 1s. Consequently, the second bit

Table 5.1   The Word BYTE in ASCII

Character	Col 1	Col 2	Col 3	Col 4	Col 5	Col 6	Col 7	Col 8
B	0	1	0	0	0	0	1	0
Y	0	1	0	1	1	0	0	1
T	0	1	0	1	0	1	0	0
E	0	1	0	0	0	1	0	1
BCC								

Table 5.2   Bit Values of the Word BYTE According to the Rule for Even Parity

Character	Col 1	Col 2	Col 3	Col 4	Col 5	Col 6	Col 7	Col 8
B	0	1	0	0	0	0	1	0
Y	0	1	0	1	1	0	0	1
T	0	1	0	1	0	1	0	0
E	0	1	0	0	0	1	0	1
BCC	0	0	0	0	1	0	1	0

value of the block check character is also set to 0. Table 5.2 shows all the bit values of the block check character BYTE filled in according to the rule for even parity.

Once calculated, the block check character is now attached to the end of the core message data block. The data block stream is now: 01000010 01011001 01010100 01000101 00001010. When the receiver gets the transmitted data block, the receiver's data link layer will perform its own block check character calculation on the core message data. The receiver will then compare its own calculated block check character with the block check character that was transmitted. If they are the same, the data are assumed to be good. If they are not the same, the data transmitted are assumed to be bad. When longitudinal redundancy checking is used in addition to simple parity, the probability of detecting transmission errors increases to 98 percent. It's not perfect, but it's much better than the 50 percent detection capability of simple parity checking.

CHECKSUM CHECKING   **Checksum checking (CC)** works by computing a running total based on the byte values transmitted in a message block and then applying a calculation to compute the checksum value. A common technique is for checksum to add the decimal value of each byte in the message block to obtain a total. The total is then divided by 255. The remainder becomes the checksum value, which is attached to end of the message block being transmitted. The receiver also performs a checksum computation on the core message block received and compares its computed checksum with the checksum sent. If the two values are the same, the receiver assumes the transmission was error free. Checksum has a 99.6 percent probability of detecting errors in a transmission.

CYCLICAL REDUNDANCY CHECKING   If longitudinal redundancy checking is good, and checksum checking is better, then **cyclical redundancy checking (CRC)** is the best. Cyclical redundancy checking has a 99.9 percent or higher probability of detecting errors in a transmission. The most powerful of the error-detection techniques we have considered, cyclical redundancy checking is based on binary division. Cyclical redundancy checking adds an 8-, 16-, 24-, or 32-bit calculated value to the end of the core message block.

The core message data are treated like one long binary number. This binary number is then divided by another unique, fixed prime binary number. The remainder generated is the cyclical redundancy checking value attached to the end of the message block. The receiver, as you probably can guess by now, makes a similar calculation and comparison. The same fixed prime binary number is used by the receiver when it divides the transmitted message's binary number value. If the receiver's computed cyclical redundancy checking value is the same as the sender's cyclical redundancy checking value, the transmission is assumed to be successful and error free.

ERROR CORRECTION METHODS

When detected, transmission errors need to be corrected. The most common *error correction* technique is also the least complicated. The data are simply retransmitted. If errors are to be corrected by **retransmission**, a technique called *acknowledgment repeat request (ARQ)* is used. An acknowledgment repeat request takes one of two forms: stop-and-wait acknowledgment repeat request or continuous acknowledgment repeat request. Of the two, stop-and-wait is simpler but less efficient than continuous acknowledgment repeat request.

If using stop-and-wait acknowledgment repeat request, the sending device does not send its next sequential frame until it has been advised by the receiving device that the current frame has been received and accepted. This method of error correction uses stop-and-wait flow control. Continuous acknowledgment repeat request uses sliding windows flow control. With continuous acknowledgment repeat requests, the sender does not wait for individual frame acknowledgment. Instead, a continuous stream of frames is sent. The sender will, however, expect acknowledgment from the receiver that all frames were successfully received.

If frames were damaged or not received, the sender will get a negative acknowledgment from the receiver. In that case, the sender retransmits the damaged or missing frames. As with sliding windows flow control the sender must keep a copy of all frames sent until those frames have been acknowledged. Continuous acknowledgment repeat request also requires a full-duplex circuit.

ERROR CORRECTING CODES

Another means of correcting for error is for the receiver to correct the error on its end through the use of *error-correcting codes (ECC)*. This method, sometimes called **forward error correction (FEC)**, requires redundant data to be carried in the message block in the form of error-correcting codes. Similar in concept to error-detection codes, error-correcting codes require more redundant data bits because they are more complicated. The advantage of error-correcting codes is that they can eliminate the need to retransmit erroneous data. The receiver, by evaluating the error-correction data, can determine and, if needed, fix a transmission error. The disadvantage is the overhead of carrying extra data bits for achieving error correction.

The amount of redundant data needed by the error-correcting codes varies by the technique used. The most common techniques correct for one-, two-, or three-bit errors in a byte. This means, for example, that every 7-bit character byte might need an additional 3 to 4 bits for error correction, translating into a 10- or 11-bit character. The overhead required for higher bit-error correction is generally considered too great to be efficient even if it is effective. This is a good example of how efficiency and effectiveness differ. In an ideal environment, a business would like to have both—but that is not always possible.

DATA LINK PROTOCOLS

Communicating devices express their communication as a stream of bits transmitted over a medium. As discussed earlier, this stream may include not only the core data message bits but also bits used for such purposes as error detection or correction. Recall that ultimately the bits represent characters of data. How do communicating devices determine where one character of data begins and ends within this bit stream? The answer is that the data link protocols delineate the data in the bit stream.

Delineate means to mark out. Data link protocols are used to mark out in the bit stream where characters begin and end, whether one character at a time or within groups of characters. This delineation is essential in order to give meaning to the bits transmitted. The two types of data link protocols that delineate data in a bit stream are asynchronous and synchronous.

Asynchronous Protocols

Asynchronous protocols are used almost exclusively today by modems or terminals connecting to a mainframe. Popular asynchronous protocols include XModem, YModem, ZModem, and Kermit. (See *www.faqs.org/faqs* to find out more about these asynchronous protocols.) In general, asynchronous protocols are simple and relatively inexpensive to implement. However, they are not very efficient. Here is why. An asynchronous protocol requires that every data byte include a start and a stop bit before and after it. This means that each character's byte begins with a start bit and ends with a stop bit. Start bits are always 0, and stop bits are always 1. This is illustrated in Figure 5.5.

Asynchronous communications are generally less efficient than synchronous ones, but they are more resistant to disruption. Each character in an asynchronous transmission is transmitted independently of all the other characters. And, because the communication is asynchronous, the sender can transmit whenever it is convenient, with no need to coordinate with the receiver. However, because each character in a transmission must be evaluated independently, asynchronous protocols are much slower than synchronous ones.

Synchronous Protocols

Synchronous protocols evaluate groups of characters instead of one byte or character at a time. Because these protocols are synchronous, the sender and receiver must use timing to control their transmissions with each other. To establish the timing, a transmission will start with a series of initial synchronization bits. These synchronization bits put the sender and receiver in sync with each other with regards to the transmission they are sharing. Both the sender and receiver must also be aware of the coding scheme being used, such as EBCDIC or Standard or Extended ASCII. Therefore, after they have processed the initial synchronization data, the sender and receiver can each count off the number of bits that define a byte based on the coding scheme used—EBCDIC or ASCII. In this way, an entire string of data characters can be sent as a group without requiring the individual start and stop flags needed in asynchronous

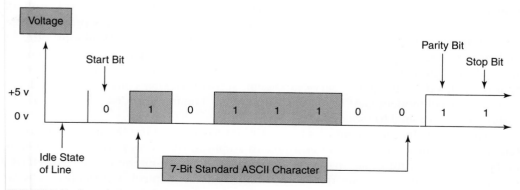

FIGURE 5.5 Asynchronous Transmission

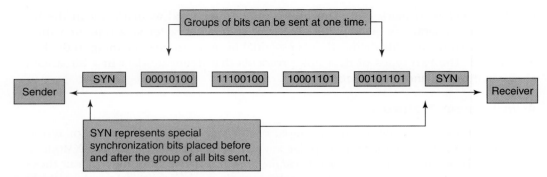

FIGURE 5.6   A Very Simplified Synchronous Transmission

communications. For LANs, BNs, MANs, and WANs, the superior speeds of synchronous transmission make it the preferred protocol choice. Figure 5.6 illustrates a very simple synchronous transmission.

Synchronous protocols are either byte- or bit-oriented. Byte-oriented protocols are sometimes referred to as being character oriented. Of the two, bit-oriented protocols are more flexible because they do not require that frames use eight-bit byte units. Byte-oriented protocols evaluate a frame as a series of characters. Bit-oriented protocols evaluate a frame as a series of bits. Two common examples of byte-oriented protocols are Ethernet 802.3 and Point-to-Point (PPP). In years past, telephone dial-up users connecting to an Internet service provider (ISP) most frequently used PPP. The most popular bit-oriented protocol is **high-level data link control (HDLC)**, which has several variants. Additional information on HDLC can be found at *www.webopedia .com/TERM/H/HDLC.html.*

One byte-oriented protocol is **Ethernet**. Ethernet 802.3 is popular primarily because it is used extensively in LANs. Ethernet uses a contention-based form of MAC that is discussed later in greater detail. An Ethernet 802.3 frame has four components. The first component is an 8-byte preamble that marks the beginning of the frame and also enables the sender and receiver to synchronize their transmission. Following the preamble is the second component, a 14-byte header. This header contains a length field that specifies the length of the message portion of the frame. The length field, therefore, delineates where the message is inside of the frame and is a key reason why Ethernet 802.3 is a byte-oriented protocol. The header is followed by the third component, the message data. After the message data is the fourth component, a four-byte trailer. The trailer contains a cyclical redundancy checking value for error detection.

The bit-oriented HLDC protocol is a formal standard that is defined by the International Standards Organization (ISO). High-level data link control, unlike Ethernet, uses a controlled-access form of MAC. A variety of link access protocols has been developed based on HLDC, including LAPB, LAPD, and LAPM, among others. Link access protocol-balanced (LAPB) is used to connect a device to a packet-switching network, a technology addressed later in the text. LAPD, Link access protocol-D (LAPD) channel is used in Integrated Services Digital Network (ISDN) communications. Link access protocol-modem (LAPM), is used in modem communications, allowing HDLC features to be applied to modems.

High-level data link control supports point-to-point or multipoint circuits over either half- or full-duplex communications. In addition, HLDC supports all three kinds of Type 2 frames: information (I), supervisory (S), and unnumbered (U). An HLDC frame may contain up to six fields: start flag, address, control, information, check sequence, and ending. An HLDC communication has three stages. First, a sender must request session set-up by issuing one of six set-mode commands. Next, after initialization has been accepted, a logical connection is established between sender and receiver. Both sides can now exchange I frames. The S frames are used for flow and error control. Finally, the session is terminated. Frames exchanged might include RR (receive ready) and RNR (receive not ready), among others.

High-level data link control makes use of an eight-bit control field flag that is composed of six binary 1s enclosed within two binary 0s, as follows: 01111110. It is possible that a message data element might also have six or more binary 1s. To accommodate for this, a technique called *bit stuffing* is performed. Bit stuffing ensures that message bit data are not mistaken for control bit data. Bit stuffing inserts an extra binary 0 after the fifth binary 1 in a series of a message data values. This means that if a binary message has the bit configuration string 01111111100, an extra 0 bit would be inserted, or stuffed, so that the message data would not be mistaken for a control field. The result looks like this: 01111101100. The receiver recognizes the stuffed bit and discards it. This is just one of the many types of technical tricks used to ensure proper data communications.

MEDIA ACCESS CONTROL

As discussed earlier in the chapter, line discipline determines for particular types of data communications circuits how devices get access to the transmission media in order to communicate. Within a LAN, devices share a circuit using a multipoint configuration. **Media access control (MAC)** protocols, the second half of the data link layer, use this common circuit. Media access control protocols fall into one of two categories: contention or controlled access. For **contention**, Ethernet 802.3 is the most common implementation. For *controlled access,* a form of token passing is used, such as token ring or fiber distributed data interface (FDDI). The MAC sublayer is LAN dependent, meaning that the MAC frame has a specific structure if used with an Ethernet, token ring, or FDDI LAN.

ETHERNET 802.3

Ethernet's contention-based MAC protocol is referred to as **CSMA/CD**, which stands for *carrier sense multiple access with collision detection.* The term *contention* is used because devices contend for use of the circuit. Devices sharing a common line have to take turns to communicate over it. *Carrier sense* occurs when devices "listen" to the line to see if it is currently being used or if it is free. If the line is free, meaning that no voltage is detected, that device can then use the line to transmit. *Multiple access* refers to the multiple devices connected to the common circuit, and, if the line is available, any one of these device can use the line. It can happen, however, that two or more devices listening to the line simultaneously discover that the line is free. These devices will then begin to transmit. When this happens, *collision detection* informs the devices by putting a jamming signal on the line. The jamming signal takes the form of a very high-voltage signal. Devices know when they "hear" the jamming signal that their communications did not succeed. Figure 5.7 shows a simple Ethernet 802.3 LAN.

Only one device at a time can transmit over the circuit. If collision detection occurs, each device that wants to communicate waits a randomly determined interval and then tries for the line once again. It is likely that one device out of all the others will select a shorter amount of time to attempt retransmission. That device, in effect, wins the line and uses it to transmit. As the other devices eventually begin to listen in on the line, they discover that it is occupied and understand that they will have to try retransmitting later.

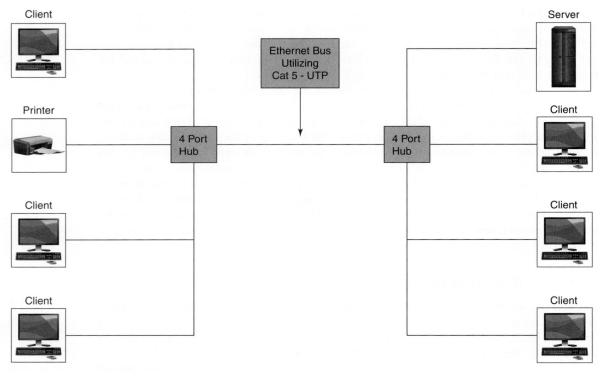

FIGURE 5.7 A Simple 803.3 Ethernet LAN

It is possible on a shared circuit with many devices or on a circuit with a high volume of traffic that collisions will happen repeatedly. In this case, network performance begins to degrade, because no device is able to communicate. Chapter 7 will discuss how different LAN topologies can help to alleviate or even eliminate excessive collisions. It is also possible on a traditional busy 802.3 LAN that one or more devices, because of bad timing, may never, or very infrequently, get access to the circuit, which can be very frustrating to the user of that device. Contention is not a fair-access protocol. However, on a network where there a few devices or where traffic is light, CSMA/CD is very efficient because each device on the circuit would likely get immediate access to the circuit whenever it is needed.

The IEEE 802.3 MAC frame contains seven fields: preamble, start frame delimiter (SFD), destination address (DA), source address (SA), length/type of protocol data unit, 802.2 frame (logical link control), and cyclical redundancy checking. Figure 5.8 shows a standard 802.3 frame. Notice the source and destination address fields. These are the physical addresses associated with the data link layer. These physical addresses are bit patterns physically encoded on each device's network interface card.

A **network interface card (NIC)** (pronounced "nick") is usually an expansion card plugged into a device's motherboard circuitry. These NICs can also take the form of PC cards used in laptop computers or other types of mobile devices. Every NIC has a unique physical address that distinguishes it from every other NIC. If the ultimate receiver of a transmission is on a different logical network, the DA within the frame will be the address of the router connecting the current LAN to the next. The SA within the frame can also be the physical address of the sender or the address of the most recent router to receive and forward the frame.

SFD or Preamble	DA	SA	Length	User Data	FCS

SFD or Starting Frame Delimiter indicates that the frame is about to begin.

DA or Destination Address of where the frame is to be sent.

SA or Source Address of the frame's sender.

Length, indicating the number of bytes in the user data.

User Data is the information content data from the originating user.

FCS or Frame Check Sequence is a value used to check for errors in the transmission.

FIGURE 5.8   A Standard 802.3 Frame

Do not confuse the frame and its address contents with the encoded addresses on a device's NIC. As a frame is passed from one network to another and is handed off from one device to another, the addresses in the frame are changed to reflect this. Remember the comparison made earlier in the chapter of how the passing of frames from source to destination is like a relay? The addresses on a NIC are physical and part of the NIC. Furthermore, all LAN-connected devices, regardless of the type of MAC, have a NIC. The addresses in a frame are logical and can be modified to reflect a frame's journey from the original sender to the ultimate receiver.

Other types of addressing schemes, such as network layer addressing, are also important in data communications. In addition, Ethernet continues to evolve. Some of the active work groups developing standards related to Ethernet 802.3 can be found at *grouper.ieee.org/groups/802/3/*. Data link layer addressing is just one piece of the puzzle, but all of the pieces fit together to create a communications system.

TOKEN RING

Of the MAC controlled-access forms, **token ring**, or 802.5, is the most common within the 802 structure. However, 802.5 is not very popular nor widely implemented. Even so, a brief description of this protocol is described in case you encounter it.

Token ring makes use of a "token" for media access control. A **token** is a specially designated frame that is passed from one LAN device to another. In order to transmit, a device on the LAN must have, or control, the token. A token can be free or busy. If the token is busy, the device that wants to use it must wait until the token is freed. An advantage of 802.5 is that every host eventually does get access to the network within a given length of time, usually within a few hundred microseconds or milliseconds. This characteristic makes controlled-access MAC more efficient in networks that experience heavy traffic. This type of MAC is called *fair-access MAC*. With token ring, a time limit is placed on any host that needs to use the ring to transmit; therefore, no one host can tie up the ring. Figure 5.9 illustrates a simple token ring LAN.

In a standard token ring, a free token frame circles the ring in one direction only. A host that needs to transmit can intercept the free token frame. The sending

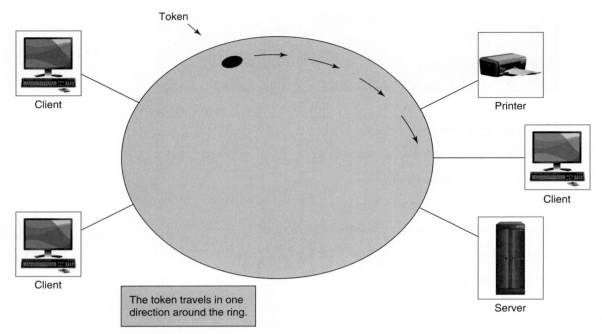

Token

Client

Printer

Client

Client

The token travels in one direction around the ring.

Server

FIGURE 5.9   A Simple 802.5 Token Ring LAN

host attaches its message and then puts the busy token with the message back onto the ring for transmittal. The message and busy token circle the ring, continuing in the same direction. As the busy token and its attached message pass each host on the ring, the message is evaluated to see if it is addressed to that host. If yes, the message is processed. If no, the message is simply ignored. As you might imagine, the token is a very important element in this type of MAC. No token means no communication. Occasionally a token can be damaged or lost. When that occurs, a new token must be generated.

Generating a lost or damaged token is the job of a device on the ring designated as the *active monitor*. One or more standby or passive monitors may also be assigned if, for some reason, the active monitor fails. Should this happen, the passive monitor becomes the new active monitor. The active monitor keeps track of the token. If necessary, the active monitor can regenerate another free token and place it back on the ring.

Token ring uses three types of frames: data/command, token, and abort. Of the three, only the data/command frame can carry a PDU and be addressed to a specific destination. The data/command frame has nine fields: start delimiter flag (SD), access control (AC), frame control (FC), destination address (DA), source address (SA), logical link control protocol data unit (PDU), cyclical redundancy checking (CRC), end delimiter flag (ED), and frame status (FS). As was described with 802.3 Ethernet, the destination and source address are associated with the physical addresses of NICs. The token frame uses only three fields: SD, AC, and ED. The abort frame has only two fields: SD and ED. Figure 5.10 is an example of a data/command frame.

A token bus (802.4) MAC specification also exists, but is seldom used. By far, the majority of LANs use some version of Ethernet.

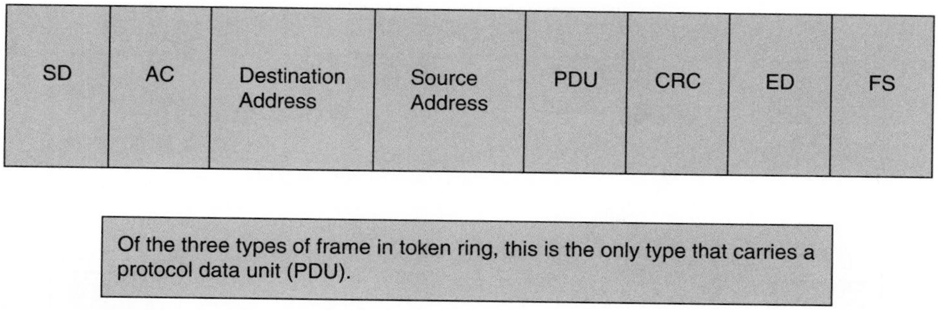

SD	AC	Destination Address	Source Address	PDU	CRC	ED	FS

Of the three types of frame in token ring, this is the only type that carries a protocol data unit (PDU).

FIGURE 5.10   A Data/Command Frame

DATA LINK LAYER DEVICES

Physical devices are frequently associated with a particular OSI or TCP/IP layer. However, as technology has advanced, devices that once were strictly associated with one layer have become configurable for multiple layers. This is especially true with the two most typical data link layer devices: bridges and switches. Both can be configured or programmed to operate with more than one layer of a networking model, usually the data link and network layers. Of course, the right kind of bridge or switch is needed to be multilayer conversant. Generally, devices that can be configured for more than one layer are not only more intelligent devices but are also more complex and expensive. Once again, cost may be a deciding factor in what type to use.

For these reasons—and keep in mind that devices are no longer as functionally specific to a layer as they used to be—it is still appropriate that a chapter on data link layer services introduce bridges and switches. In Chapter 7, the types and job duties of bridges and switches are revisited along with other LAN devices. First, however, we discuss another data link layer component, the network interface card (NIC).

Network Interface Cards

Although a component rather than a device, a NIC is an extremely important part of the network. A NIC is a critical data link layer component that provides the physical address required by networked devices in order to identify and communicate with each other. Also referred to as a *LAN adapter, LAN card, network adapter,* or *network board*, these cards allow a device to connect to and access a network. No two NICs should have the same manufactured physical address. If they do, problems result. A NIC's address identifies its manufacturer. Each NIC has a unique serial number that is assigned according to guidelines specified by the IEEE.

Bridges

Bridges provide a means of dividing larger LANs into smaller segments. A bridge connects segments of a network. Larger LANs are broken into smaller segments in order to reduce the amount of traffic experienced on each side of the LAN connected by the bridge. Bridges have multiple ports into which devices are plugged. Devices are recognized as being on one or the other side of the bridge. A bridge reduces traffic by serving as a traffic cop. Let's discuss how it works.

A frame sent out on a multipoint circuit, without special intervention, will go to all devices on that multipoint circuit whether addressed to those devices or not. In a large LAN with moderate to heavy communications, a lot of traffic is generated that ends up being ignored by many, if not most, devices. Even so, this ignored traffic

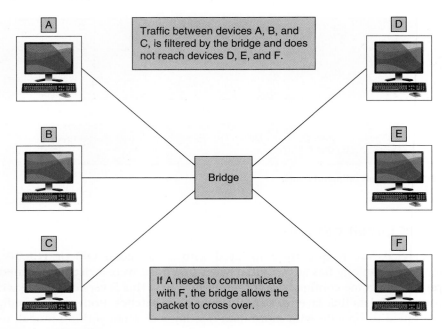

FIGURE 5.11   Bridge Filtering

takes up valuable bandwidth capacity. When a bridge is used to connect segments of the network, the bridge acts as a filter. Frames that enter the bridge are evaluated, or filtered, by their destination address. The bridge can determine whether the destination device is on one side or the other of the bridge. Based on that knowledge, the bridge either passes the frame through the bridge to the other network segment or disallows it from crossing over. This filtering reduces traffic on both sides of the bridge.

Consider Figure 5.11. Assume that host node A wants to communicate with host node B. The bridge will intercept A's communication and, recognizing where B is located, not pass A's transmission over to the other segment of the network. In this way, host nodes D, E, and F are not bothered with A's traffic. If A had wanted to communicate with F, the bridge, knowing F's location, would pass A's transmission over to the other network segment.

On a multipoint circuit, all host devices on the circuit intercept the frame or packet transmitted. If the frame or packet is not addressed to the host, the host simply ignores it, but traffic still results. Sometimes people use the terms *frame* and *packet* interchangeably. Others consider a *packet* to be the unit of storage used at the network layer and reserve the term *frame* for a data link layer unit. In this text, *frame* is used as a data link layer unit and *packet* is used as a network layer unit to clearly differentiate the processes discussed. In conversations with networking colleagues, you may have to ask them exactly what they mean when they use the term *packet*. See *www. practicallynetworked.com* to learn about wireless bridges.

Switches

Switches are similar to bridges but have additional functionality that gives them greater efficiency. Like bridges, they have multiple ports into which devices are plugged. Generally, switches connect two or more LAN segments that use the same data link and network protocols; for example, if LAN segment A is Ethernet and TCP/IP and is connected to LAN B using a switch, LAN B must also be Ethernet and TCP/IP. In this example, Ethernet is the data link protocol and TCP/IP the network protocol.

Switches are most often used to direct traffic over multiple Ethernet networks. Usually having multiple processors, switches also have memory storage buffers that can store frame and/or addressing table information. One important aspect of switches is that each device connected to a switch port uses that connection as a point-to-point circuit. This means that even with an Ethernet contention-based protocol, devices connected to a switch do not compete for their connection to the switch. Each device has an independent or point-to-point connection to the switch.

One common type of switch is called *store-and-forward*. A store-and-forward switch will store all the frames that make up a packet before sending them out as a group. In addition, this type of switch will check each packet for errors before releasing it. Checking for errors in a high-traffic volume network can be time consuming, resulting in network degradation. Another choice might be to use a *cross-point*, sometimes called a *cut-through, switch*. A cross-point switch directs packets without checking for errors. Consequently, this switch will be much faster than a store-and-forward one. It will be necessary, however, for higher-layer protocols to perform error checking. Cisco is famous for its switching technology. Find out more about switching by visiting the Cisco website at *www.cisco.com*.

Chapter Summary

The data link layer frames message data bits so that they can be passed to the next higher layer, which is the network layer. A message can be composed of one or many frames. The data link layer not only frames the data bits but it also controls how the frames are moved from one computer or network device to another. A frame may pass through many intermediary devices and networks on its path from the originating source and the final destination device. The data link layer performs error control and physical addressing as well. A top-priority goal of error control is to enable a receiving device to recognize, and potentially correct for, a transmission error.

The IEEE has divided the data link layer into two parts: logical link control (LLC) and media access control (MAC). In the IEEE 802 implementation, the LLC sits above the MAC. The logical link control, also designated as 802.2, provides three types of frame delivery service: Type 1, Type 2, and Type 3. Type 1 is a connectionless service that does not provide acknowledgment. Type 2 is a connection-oriented delivery service that provides acknowledgment. Type 3 is a connectionless service that provides acknowledgment. Type 1 is the most often used type of delivery service. The three types of frames supported are information (I), supervisory (S), and unnumbered (U). Only Type 2 uses the I and S frames. All service types use U frames.

The two types of data link flow control are stop-and-wait and sliding windows. Stop-and-wait is simple but inefficient. Sliding windows is more complex and more efficient. With stop-and-wait flow control, each individual frame the sender transmits requires an acknowledgment from the receiver that the frame has been received. With sliding windows, several frames can be sent and be in transit before an acknowledgment is required.

Another type of circuit control performed at the data link layer is line discipline. Line discipline is associated with two types of network environments. One is a point-to-point connection between communicating devices using either a half-duplex or full-duplex line. The second occurs when multiple devices on a multipoint line communicate through a central controlling communication device. The central controlling device is often a mainframe with terminals connected to it.

Error control at the data link layer has two elements: detection and correction. Common error-detection techniques include parity checking, longitudinal redundancy checking, checksum checking, and cyclical redundancy checking. Parity checking is a very simple but not very accurate method of error detection. Parity checking is also sometimes referred to as vertical redundancy checking. Longitudinal redundancy checking (LRC) generates an entire additional byte called a block check character (BCC) based on all the bytes in a message. When longitudinal redundancy checking is used with simple parity, the probability of detecting transmission errors increases to 98 percent. Checksum checking (CC) works by computing a running total based on the byte values transmitted in a message block and then applying a calculation to compute the checksum value. Cyclical redundancy checking (CRC), the most powerful of the error-detection techniques, has a 99.9 percent or higher probability of detecting errors in a transmission. It is based on binary division.

The most common correction technique is also the least complicated: The data are simply retransmitted. Another means of correcting for errors is for the receiver to correct the error on its end. This method, sometimes called forward error correction, requires redundant data to be carried in the message block in the form of error-correcting codes.

Two types of data link protocols delineate data in a bit stream: asynchronous and synchronous protocols. Asynchronous data link protocols are used almost exclusively by modems or terminals connecting to a mainframe. Synchronous protocols evaluate groups of characters rather than one byte or character at a time. Because these protocols are synchronous, the sender and receiver must use timing to control their transmissions with each other.

Synchronous protocols are either byte- or bit-oriented. Byte-oriented protocols are sometimes referred to as character oriented. Of the two, bit-oriented protocols are more flexible because they do not require that frames use eight-bit bytes. Byte-oriented protocols evaluate a frame as a series of characters. Bit-oriented protocols evaluate a frame as a series of bits. Ethernet is an example of a byte-oriented protocol. High-level data link control (HDLC) is a bit-oriented protocol.

Within a LAN, devices share a common circuit through a multipoint configuration. Media access control (MAC) protocols are used to determine how devices share a common circuit. The MAC protocols fall into one of two categories: contention or controlled access. With contention-based MAC, Ethernet 802.3 is the more common implementation. With controlled access, a form of token passing is used, such as token ring or FDDI (fiber distributed data interface). The MAC sublayer is LAN dependent, meaning that if Ethernet, token ring, or FDDI are used on a LAN, the MAC frame will have a specific structure.

Although a component rather than a device, a NIC is a critical data link layer hardware element that provides the physical address that net-worked devices require in order to identify and communicate with each other. A NIC's address identifies its manufacturer, has a unique serial number, and is assigned according to guidelines specified by the IEEE.

Bridges provide a means of dividing larger LANs into smaller segments. A bridge connects segments of a network. A larger LAN is divided into smaller segments in order to reduce the amount of traffic experienced on each side of the LAN connected by the bridge. Switches are similar to bridges but have additional functionality, giving them greater efficiency. Like bridges, switches have multiple ports into which devices are plugged. Generally, switches connect two or more LAN segments that use the same data link and network protocols. A store-and-forward switch will store all of the frames that make up a packet before sending them out as a group. In addition, this type of switch checks each packet for errors before releasing it. A cross-point switch sends packets without checking for errors.

Keywords

802 *70*
802.1 *71*
802.2 *71*
802.3 *71*
802.4 *71*
802.5 *71*
Acknowledgment *71*
Asynchronous
    protocol *81*
Block check character
    (BCC) *78*
Bridge *87*
Checksum checking *79*
Connectionless *71*
Connection oriented *72*
Contention *83*
CSMA/CD *83*
Cyclical redundancy
    checking *79*

Delineate *81*
Delivery service *71*
Error control *76*
Error detection *76*
Ethernet *82*
Even parity *77*
Flow control *73*
Forward error
    correction *80*
Frame *70*
High-level data link
    control *82*
Line discipline *70*
Logical link control *71*
Longitudinal redundancy
    checking *78*
Media access control
    (MAC) *83*

Network interface card
    (NIC) *84*
Odd parity *77*
Parity checking *77*
Polling *76*
Protocol data unit *72*
Retransmission *80*
Sliding windows *74*
Sliding windows
    buffer *75*
Stop-and-wait *73*
Switch *88*
Synchronous
    protocols *81*
Token *85*
Token ring *85*

Chapter Questions

Short-Answer Questions

1. In general, what are the functions of the data link layer?
2. Why is flow control necessary?
3. How do asynchronous and synchronous data link protocols differ?
4. Briefly describe MAC and why it is used.
5. What two components make up the data link layer?
6. Describe one component of error checking.
7. What elements make up error control?
8. In what key way does stop-and-wait flow control differ from sliding windows?

Hands-On Projects

1. Visit either a land-based or web-based retailer of networking equipment. Identify, then compare and contrast, two different vendor bridging devices. What are their relative advantages and disadvantages?
2. From two different vendors, provide an example of two NIC addresses.
3. Visit at least two websites of vendors who provide NICs. How does someone download or access updated drivers from each site? Compare the usability of each site. Was there an area for frequently asked questions (FAQs)? If so, was it useful and easy to navigate? If not, why not?
4. Describe at least two different and current topics from the IEEE related to the 802 project.

Research in Brief

For one or more of the following questions, provide a one- to two-page report based on your findings.

1. Further explore and report on connection-oriented delivery services.
2. Research the following data link protocols and explain how they are used, how they are different, and how they are similar: XModem, YModem, ZModem, and Kermit.
3. Briefly describe how Ethernet and token ring function. What are their advantages and disadvantages?
4. Contrast stop-and-wait flow control with sliding windows.

Case Study

Sheehan Marketing and Public Relations

After continued evaluation of SMPR's L.A. office, you decide to recommend that bridges be replaced with switches. Prepare a report for the president that explains what this might cost and what the advantages are. Provide examples of switches from at least three vendors that show the price and functionality of each switch. Make a recommendation, explaining your reasoning, as to which switch vendor to select. Your reasoning might include such factors as cost, warranty, support, and vendor reputation. Also, SMPR's president wants to know why it was necessary to upgrade the old 10-Mbps NICs with new NICs. In your report, include a rationale for this change.

Over the last month, you have arranged for Karla to receive formal training in basic networking analysis and troubleshooting. In a memo to SMPR's president, explain why you believe this cost was justified.

In addition, you attended a $500 seminar on fine-tuning Ethernet networks. Include in your memo why you believe a networking technologist should attend professional seminars.

SMPR's president would also like you to prepare a simple description, no more than one page, for the rest of the staff on how Ethernet functions. He has asked you to use nontechnical jargon so that your description will be easy to understand.

Topic in Focus

THE SECRETS OF SLIDING WINDOWS

Sliding windows is a form of flow control. Allowing for a single acknowledgment for multiple frames, sliding windows makes more efficient utilization of a communication circuit. Sliding windows requires the use of a sequencing number field that is part of the frame that is being sent and received. The sequencing number field has to be defined with a specific bit size. The bit size of the field must be the same for both the sender and the receiver. The number of bits used to define the field depends on network needs as well as the sender's and receiver's buffer size.

Because the sequence number field will be a specific bit size, the range of values that it can take within that size is limited. As an example, the range of values that a two-bit binary field can contain is from 0 to 3 in decimal. The range of values that a three-bit binary field can contain is from 0 to 7 in decimal. This concept is critical because the bit size of the sequence number field determines the maximum number of frames that a window can contain. The following description uses a three-bit sequencing number field.

Chapter 5 discusses binary numbering in much greater detail and shows how to convert between binary and decimal. For now, trust that the range of a three-bit binary field is from 0 to 7 in decimal. This allows for eight unique values: 0, 1, 2, 3, 4, 5, 6, and 7. The maximum size of a sliding window buffer is $n - 1$. Here, n is the number of unique numeric values that can be assigned, determined by the sequence number field bit size. Given a three-bit sequence field, n equals 8. The maximum window size then becomes: $8 - 1 = 7$. With this example, the maximum number of frames that a sliding window's buffer can hold is seven. Therefore, frames in our transmission example will be numbered sequentially from 0 to 7. Frames are always numbered in sequence, and the sequence numbers are reused in a circular fashion.

Because this example uses sliding windows as its flow control mechanism, the sender can send none, some, or all of the frames it holds in its sliding windows buffer. The sender does not have to wait for individual frame acknowledgments from the receiver. Each frame the sender transmits has a number attached to it. The numbers are used in sequential order, are continuously reused as transmission proceeds, and are based on the sequence number field. When the receiver sends an acknowledgment, the acknowledgment will contain the sequence number of the next frame that is expected. Let's see how this works.

The following discussion uses several figures to illustrate the sliding windows process. At the beginning of the transmission, both the sender and receiver have a sliding windows buffer space that allows for seven frames, based on a three-bit sequence number field. Look at Figure 5.12. The figure shows a sender and a receiver. From the left, the frames zero through six represent the sender's and receiver's views of their sliding windows buffer space. The sender is holding seven frames, and the receiver is capable of accepting seven frames.

As the sender's frames are transmitted, the sender's sliding windows buffer shrinks from the left edge, going from left to right, starting with frame F0. Only when

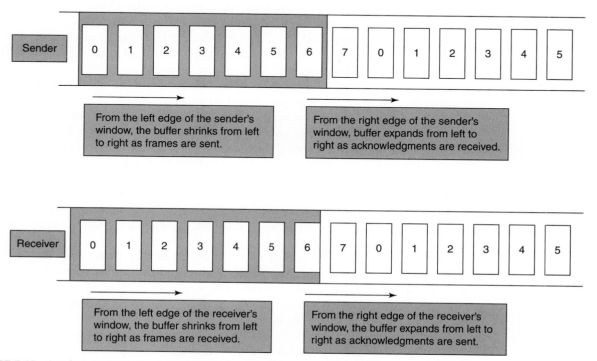

FIGURE 5.12 Sender's and Receiver's Sliding Windows Buffer Space Shaded in Gray

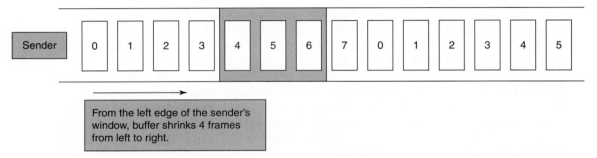

FIGURE 5.13   Sender's Shrinking Sliding Windows Buffer after Sending Four Frames. No acknowledgments yet received from the receiver

the sender gets an acknowledgment from the receiver can the sender's sliding windows buffer expand from the right edge, from left to right.

How many frames the sender's window shrinks or expands depends on the acknowledgment sent back from the receiver. From the receiver's perspective, the sliding windows buffer also shrinks from the left edge, going from left to right, as frames are received. Based on the last frame processed, the receiver sends an acknowledgment to the sender, and the receiver's sliding window expands from the right edge, from left to right. Before the receiver's sliding windows buffer can expand, it must send an acknowledgment.

Assume the sender initially transmits four frames: F0, F1, F2, and F3. The sender's sliding window shrinks by four frames from the left edge. Figure 5.13 shows the sender's now shrunken sliding window. (The sender also keeps a copy of the frames that have been transmitted in a different memory buffer location, just in case one or more of the transmitted frames has to be retransmitted. Not until the frames have been successfully acknowledged does the sender completely drop them.) At this point, the sender has not received an acknowledgment from the receiver for the four frames that have been sent. Even so, the sender could send the remaining three frames held in its sliding windows buffer, beginning with frame F4, without having to wait for an acknowledgment. This is the benefit of sliding windows.

However—and this is important—the sender's sliding windows buffer does not expand, and will not expand, until acknowledgment is received from the receiver. Sending frames that remain in the sliding windows buffer and expanding the sliding windows buffer are two separate events. The sender's sliding windows buffer can shrink without waiting for the receiver's acknowledgment. However, the sender's sliding window buffer cannot expand without acknowledgments from the receiver.

In the meantime, assume that the receiver begins to receive the sender's first four frames. As the frames arrive, they occupy available sequential frame slots in the receiver's sliding windows buffer. Once occupied, these slots are not available for other incoming frames. The receiver's sliding windows buffer shrinks accordingly by four frames from the left edge, from left to right, to reflect that these slots are no longer available. The result is that the receiver's sliding windows buffer now has only three frames' worth of space available for use. The receiver's sliding windows buffer does not expand, and will not expand, until the receiver sends an acknowledgment to the sender. Figure 5.14 shows the receiver's and the sender's sliding windows buffer pre-acknowledgment status.

Now assume that the receiver finally transmits a "ready to receive 4" (RR4) acknowledgment to the sender. This acknowledgement tells the sender, "I have received

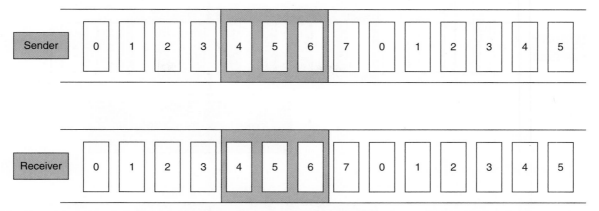

FIGURE 5.14   Pre-Acknowledgment Buffer Status of Sender and Receiver. The sender has sent 4 frames. The receiver has received 4 frames. At this point no acknowledgment from the receiver has yet been sent

frames F0 through F3 and am ready for the next sequential frame." Based on sending this acknowledgment, the receiver's sliding windows buffer now expands by four, from the right edge, from left to right, as shown in Figure 5.15.

In time, the sender gets the RR4 acknowledgment from the receiver. The sender, based on this acknowledgment, knows that frames F0 through F3 have been received. The sender's sliding windows buffer in response now expands, from the right edge, from left to right, by four frames. Figure 5.16 shows the sender and receiver's post-acknowledgment sliding windows buffer status.

A receiving device can also send a "receive not ready" (RNR) frame, which tells the sending device to stop transmitting until further notice. A RNR closes the sliding windows, and a "receive ready" (RR) frame will have to be sent by the receiver to reopen them. The frame sequence numbers in sliding windows are reused in a circular manner. Thus, sliding windows is a continuous cycle, controlled by acknowledgments between the sender and receiver, of memory buffers shrinking and expanding, shrinking and expanding, and so on.

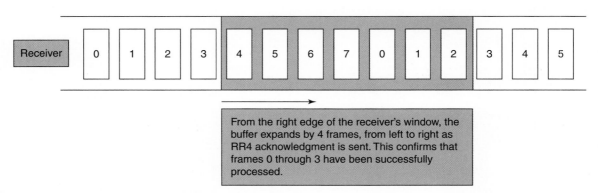

FIGURE 5.15   The Receiver's Expanding Sliding Windows Buffer after Sending Acknowledgment "Ready to Receive 4" (RR4) to the Sender

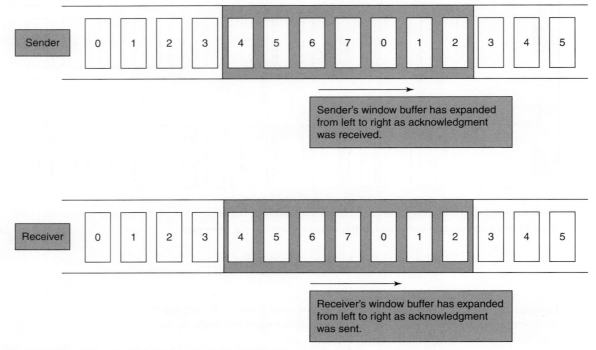

FIGURE 5.16 Post-Acknowledgment Status of Sliding Windows Buffers of Sender and Receiver

6

Network Layer Services

The Business Benefit

Whether a business is a small Mom-and-Pop retail store or an international conglomerate with a thousand branches, today virtually all organizations of all scales rely on rapid and up-to-date access to data and information. Much of this has become possible through "cloud computing," which we return to in a later chapter. The point here is that up-to-date and easily accessible data and information have become a strategic business competitive factor.

Not only must the data and information be accurate but they must also be readily, if not almost instantly, available. Business managers require such rapid data resource access to give them a real-world/real-time view of business processes such that they are able to respond immediately to market conditions and customer interests.

The business that has the better, faster, more reliable ability, by means of its underlying networking infrastructure, to access, distribute, and share essential data and information to multiple sources will have a strong competitive edge. Indeed, the business of the business may be providing this underlying networking infrastructure to other small- and medium-scale businesses.

Efficient businesses strive to reduce costs in order to trim expenses and grow profit. Effective and well-designed data networks can help achieve that goal. A core topic presented in this chapter is the means by which data packets get from point A to point B, and why network design is of essential importance. The efficiency and speed of this delivery for a business can have a direct impact as to how timely the data are as they travel from sender to receiver. In many transactionally based applications, time can truly be of the essence.

Learning Objectives

After studying this chapter, you should be able to:

- Understand the purpose of the network layer.
- Describe components of the network layer.
- Identify network layer services.
- Understand network layer addressing.
- Recognize IP address formats.

■ Identify IP address classes.

■ Understand how an IP address class can be configured and assigned.

■ Know the advantages of the subnetwork architecture.

In a later chapter you will find that a local area network, or LAN, is composed of both logical and physical components. These components work together so that resources can be shared and network devices can communicate. A business may, of course, have more than one LAN and will need for its multiple LANs to be able to communicate and share resources. For such communication and sharing to occur, network devices require two critical pieces of information.

First, a sending device needs to know the network address of the receiving device. Second, the sending device must also know the specific, individual address of the receiving device within the receiving device's network. Addressing is critical to any network, regardless of the type of network model used. This chapter explores, among other things, how logical addressing is accomplished in the TCP/IP model.

MID- AND HIGH-RANGE SERVICES

Originally designed as a collection of protocol suites to support very large networks—and what could be larger than the Internet—TCP/IP has emerged as the network model of choice for LANs as well as WANs. (Visit *www.isoc.org/internet/history* for an interesting history of the Internet.) The network, transport, and application layers of the TCP/IP model perform mid- to high-level services. From previous material you now know that the physical and data link layers perform lower-level services. The network, transport, and application layers each make use of protocols to fulfill their particular functionalities. In an earlier chapter, a *protocol* was defined as a set of rules or procedures that specify how something works or performs. By defining standards, protocols enable communication to occur, whether between people or between machines. In communications between people, the protocols or languages used can be very sophisticated and complex, far more so than the relatively straightforward protocols that enable machines to talk to each other.

This chapter explores the various protocols used by network layer services in the TCP/IP model. Figure 6.1 shows the layers of the TCP/IP model. This chapter

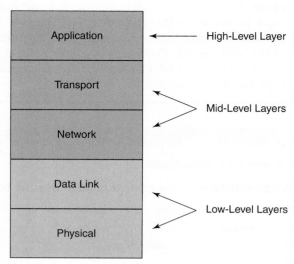

FIGURE 6.1   The TCP/IP Layers

also presents the network layer Internet protocol (IP) and explores how it is used to implement communications not only within a LAN but also between LANs and WANs. You will discover that the process is very logical and that the rules, based on the IP portion of the TCP/IP protocol suite, create a communication infrastructure that make it possible for LANs and networked devices to recognize and talk to each other. In Chapter 7 we will present transport and application layer services.

Throughout this discussion, remember that the collection of all networks owned by a single organization is commonly referred to as the *enterprise*. An organization's enterprise might include dozens, hundreds, or thousands of LANs, BNs, MANs, and WANs. The scale of the enterprise depends on the business. The larger the scale, the more important—and the more complicated—addressing becomes.

NETWORK LAYER SERVICES

Sitting just above the data link layer and below the transport layer is the TCP/IP **network layer**. At the heart of the network layer is IP, the Internet protocol, which in turn is supported by four other protocols: (1) address resolution protocol (ARP), (2) reverse address resolution protocol (RARP), (3) Internet control message protocol (ICMP), and (4) Internet group message protocol (IGMP). Think of IP as being in charge of a team of dedicated assistants whose only concern is getting the job done. Figure 6.2 shows how these protocols fit into the overall architecture of the TCP/IP model. Each of these four protocols helps IP at the network layer by performing the specific duties to which they are assigned.

Address Resolution Protocol

The **address resolution protocol (ARP)** is used to relate a logical IP address with a physical address. Much of this chapter concentrates on what is meant by a logical IP address. For now, understand that each host device in a TCP/IP network is assigned a **logical IP address**. Because an IP address is a logical address, it can be changed or modified. Each IP address in turn will be associated with a particular physical address. The **physical address** is the MAC layer address that comes from the host device's NIC. The MAC address is physical in that it cannot be modified. (You may also recall from a previous chapter that each NIC address is unique.)

In a TCP/IP environment, logical IP addresses must be associated with their physical MAC address counterparts. The process of associating a specific logical address to a specific physical address is called "resolving" the address. The address resolution protocol is the TCP/IP protocol that resolves logical TCP/IP addresses to physical MAC addresses. Like a detective, ARP tracks down and finds the matching physical address for a known logical IP address. When two TCP/IP devices need to communicate, both the logical and physical addresses of each device are required. When the sending device knows the logical IP address of the receiving device but not

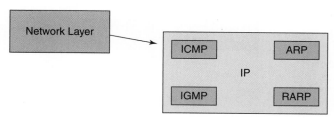

FIGURE 6.2   **The IP Protocol Suite at the Network Layer**

the receiving device's physical address, ARP is used to determine that device's physical address. ARP is the dedicated IP assistant that resolves addresses.

Here is how ARP works. You now know that communicating devices at the data link layer use physical, or MAC, addresses. Also remember that both the sender and receiver have multiple layers in their protocol stacks. The different layers have different requirements. Consequently, a logical IP address, which is required at the network layer, must still be associated with a physical address, which is required at the data link layer. The data link and network layers work together.

Assume that a sending device wants to communicate with a receiving device. Also assume that the sending device has the receiving device's logical IP address. The sending device must also, however, have the receiving device's physical address. The sending device, which has IP in its network layer stack, issues an ARP request. As you have just learned, ARP comes bundled with IP at the network layer.

The sender's ARP first checks the sending device's memory storage to see if the requested information, the receiving device's physical MAC address, is already available. The sender may have recently communicated with the receiver and may therefore still have the receiver's physical MAC address information in its memory. If this is true, no further effort is required. The address resolution protocol immediately resolves the address, matching the physical address with the logical address, and the sender sends its data packet. But what if the sender has never communicated with the receiver? Or, what if any previous communication happened so long ago that the receiver's physical MAC address information has been flushed from the sender's memory buffer?

This would mean that the sender no longer has the receiver's physical address information, which is required. ARP comes to the rescue!

The sender's local network layer IP stack broadcasts an ARP data packet. A broadcast goes to all the devices on the local network. Each device on the local network receives and evaluates the broadcasted ARP request. If one of the devices has the requested information, that device sends the information to the originating device's ARP. If none of the local devices has the requested information, the originator's ARP request is passed on to the network routers to be sent to other networks in the enterprise. Eventually, if all goes well, the requested information is brought back to the sending device, and the sender's ARP completes its job by resolving the address request. The sender can now forward its packet to the receiver. Figure 6.3 illustrates this process. For even more on ARP, visit *whatis.techtarget.com.*

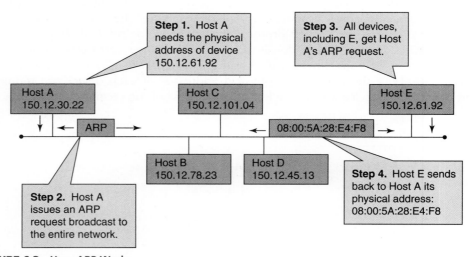

FIGURE 6.3 How ARP Works

Reverse Address Resolution Protocol

Reverse address resolution protocol (RARP), as you might guess from its name, does the opposite of ARP. When a sending device knows the physical address of the receiving device but not the receiving device's logical IP address, RARP is used. It is also used when a host device is connected to a network for the first time or when a diskless computer is powered up. When a host device connects to a TCP/IP network for the first time, it must resolve its own logical IP address. A device that is networked must, by definition, have a NIC. The NIC, in turn, provides the device's MAC physical address. Therefore, a host will know its own physical layer address.

Diskless computers do not have hard drives. A diskless computer's physical address can be stored in a read only memory (ROM) chip. However, a diskless computer on a TCP/IP network still needs a logical IP address for it to function at the network layer. The reverse address resolution protocol is used to resolve the diskless computer's logical IP address. When the diskless machine boots or powers up, an RARP request is initiated and broadcasted to the network. Another device on the network that has a table of IP addresses assigned to all devices on the network responds and sends the diskless device its IP address information. The diskless device stores its logical IP address information in its temporary memory. When the diskless device powers down and reboots, it must again go through the RARP process.

You may be asking, Why would a business use a diskless device? Diskless devices have several advantages. They are particularly useful when security is essential. Without a disk drive, or, more precisely, a drive that a user can write data to, it becomes very difficult to copy data and remove it from the premises. Also, one of the most common ways of spreading a virus throughout an organization is through the use of disk drives. Removing a systemwide virus can be very difficult. Without a local storage device or drive, the network administrator has a much easier job of controlling the spread of malicious programs. Of course, users will likely be less than thrilled at having no secondary storage devices available for storing data. Secondary storage devices include hard drives, and other devices to which data can be saved. Cost can also be a consideration for using diskless client stations, because such stations are typically less expensive than their more fully featured alternatives.

Internet Control Message Protocol

By itself, IP has no error-reporting or error-correcting controls, so if something goes wrong with an IP datagram, as can happen, IP has no direct way of compensating for the error. A **datagram** is a packet of data used by an IP network. Internet protocol also does not directly support management functions, so, for example, if a host is trying to determine whether a router is available, no management mechanism is available to assist it. This is where Internet control message protocol comes into play.

The **Internet control message protocol (ICMP)** supports IP by providing two important functions: error reporting and query management. It only reports errors, it does not correct them. For example, if a datagram, for whatever reason, is unable to reach its final destination, then an error has occurred. The ICMP can report to IP that a "destination unreachable" error has occurred for that packet.

Five types of errors can be reported by ICMPs: (1) destination unreachable; (2) source quench, which notifies a sending host that a datagram has been discarded due to congestion; (3) time exceeded, which is sent when a datagram's time-to-live value has counted down to zero (without this value a lost datagram could circle the network endlessly); (4) parameter error, which is sent when a datagram's header has a problem; and (5) redirection, which is used by routers to inform a sending host that the sending host has directed a datagram to the wrong router.

Internet Group Message Protocol

Internet group message protocol (IGMP) is used primarily by IP when multicasting is required. Two types of communication can occur over a TCP/IP network: unicasting and multicasting. **Unicasting**, Figure 6.4, is the more common and is a communication between one sender and one receiver.

Multicasting, Figure 6.5, occurs when a sender wants to send to many receivers. In a TCP/IP environment, it is possible to set up a multicasting group. A multicast address can only be used as a destination, not as a source address. The IGMP helps multicast routers identify the hosts in a network that are part of a multicast group. The multicast router maintains a list of group multicast addresses.

Internet group message protocol supports two types of messages: reporting and query. *Reporting messages* are sent from a host to a router. *Query messages* are sent from a router to a host. An IGMP packet is very simple and includes a field for group address identification.

From our discussion so far, we have seen that a key responsibility of the network layer of the TCP/IP model is determining how host devices use logical and physical addressing to identify each other so that they can communicate. Without this addressing identification, communication would not be possible.

Imagine that you send a letter to a distant friend but write no forwarding or return address on the envelope. Do you think your letter will arrive? Most likely, your letter will arrive, but if it does not arrive, how could you be notified? If your friend for some reason does not receive your letter, there is no way you will be informed of

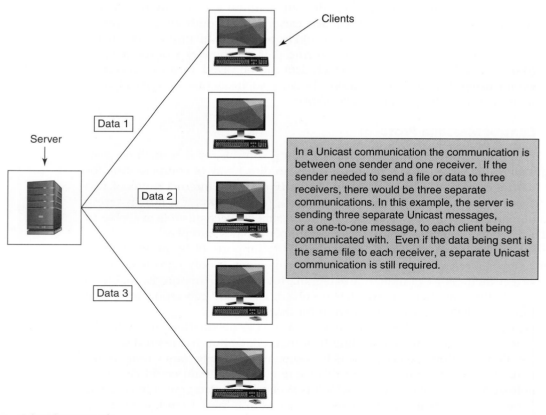

In a Unicast communication the communication is between one sender and one receiver. If the sender needed to send a file or data to three receivers, there would be three separate communications. In this example, the server is sending three separate Unicast messages, or a one-to-one message, to each client being communicated with. Even if the data being sent is the same file to each receiver, a separate Unicast communication is still required.

FIGURE 6.4   Unicasting Example

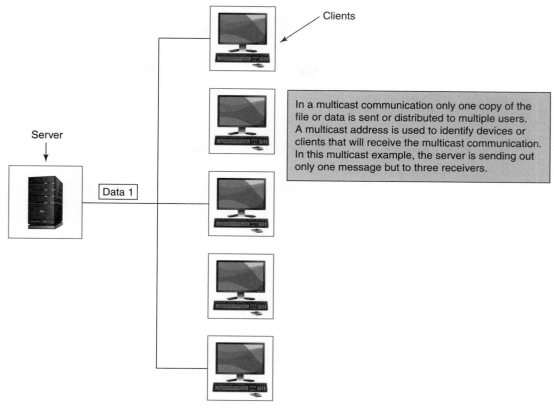

In a multicast communication only one copy of the file or data is sent or distributed to multiple users. A multicast address is used to identify devices or clients that will receive the multicast communication. In this multicast example, the server is sending out only one message but to three receivers.

FIGURE 6.5 Multicasting

The Ethical Perspective

Only a phone? Or is there something more?

The use of mobile hand-held devices, especially cell phones, has exploded in use. These so-called smart phones have become multipurpose tools that perform many functions: texting, photography, video capture, e-mail access, location tracking and assistance, web-based browsing, shopping, and gaming, to name a few. Oh, and yes, making a phone call.

For all this to happen, particularly regarding texting or phoning, addressing of the device, meaning where it is in order for services to be sent to the device, is essential. Without a known location, or address, your cell phone service provider could not send to your specific phone the data that you are either requesting to receive or to send. Marketers have become all too well aware of this.

Today's technology allows cell phone usage to be easily tracked, including not just your location but also the various uses and functions you employ on your cell phone. What are you shopping for? What locations do you frequent and how often? What "apps" are you most likely to use? What types of messages, by key stroke capture, are you sending? How often do you text as oppose to talk? What are you texting? How often, where, and for how long do you use your mobile device? As you may suppose, much controversy surrounds what communication service providers are and are not capturing, and analyzing, regarding their customers.

What do you think? Are the "business needs" of your communication service providers valid? Should such providers be allowed to sell or share this rich marketing data? Should there be formal policies or laws regarding the capturing and recording of any data from a cell phone? Do you see any privacy issues related to this thriving technology?

the failure. A full communication, assuming that you want your friend to write back or acknowledge receipt, requires complete addressing from the source, you, and the destination, your friend. This same addressing principle is true for networked devices. For an application layer service to send and receive data, two communicating hosts must be able to identify each other. They identify each other through addressing. The rest of this chapter examines this critical topic, exploring how addressing is implemented in a TCP/IP network.

THE IMPORTANCE OF ADDRESSING SCHEMES

As you read at the beginning of this chapter, an organization's enterprise may be very large. The larger the enterprise, the more critical addressing within the enterprise becomes. In a TCP/IP network, each device connected to the network can also be referred to as a host. Each **host** device on the network has a unique address that identifies it specifically and uniquely throughout the entire enterprise. Without unique addresses, devices in an enterprise would not be able to be individually identified.

The need for identification requires that each network in the enterprise also have a unique logical address. Again, an enterprise may have many networks. So, not only must each host device within each specific network have a unique logical address within its network, but each network must also have a logical address. If designed correctly, the network and host addresses together enable the unique identification of each device in the enterprise. Such identification is especially crucial in an enterprise that has many networks. In such a scenario, the organization will very likely want the hosts on the different networks to be able to communicate with each other. Figure 6.6 shows a possible enterprise configuration with five network addresses.

In TCP/IP, the combined network and host addresses of each device make up what is called an **IP address**. A country's postal service usually organizes postal addresses through an addressing scheme. For example, in the United States, a zip code is used to route mail, whether between cities or across states. TCP/IP networks must also have an addressing scheme.

The larger and more complex the enterprise, the more critical the design of the organization's IP addressing scheme becomes. To implement communication over any TCP/IP network, small or large, an IP addressing scheme must be developed, configured, and then implemented. In this addressing scheme, the IP address contains a LAN or network identifier as well as a host or device identifier. Each host device's IP address reveals two things: the network address the host is on and the address of the host within the network.

Let's consider our regular letter postal service example again. Typically, for a letter to be delivered to you, the sender needs to know your state, city, zip code, street, and house or apartment number and to write that information on the outside of the letter's envelope. Think of the letter inside the envelope as the original user application layer data. In the IP address scheme, the enterprise network can be compared with your city, which likely has many streets. The network portion of the IP address compares with your specific street, on which there are likely many houses or apartments. The host portion of the same IP address compares with your house or apartment number, which is specific to you and your household. The result is that you have been identified by your individual address within a street, within a city, and now you can send or receive a letter! A networked host device is within a network, within an enterprise.

Routers connect the networks that make up the enterprise and the Internet. They are the "post offices" that make sure that your letter gets from one post office

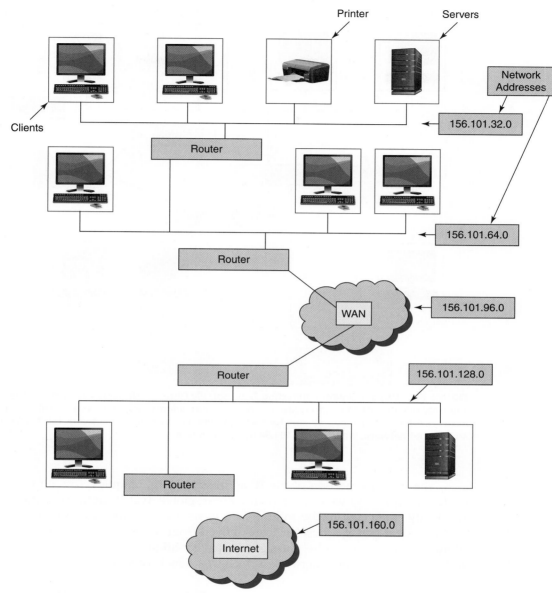

FIGURE 6.6 A Five-Network Enterprise Configuration

to another and eventually to your friend's mailbox. Routers, though, instead of delivering letters, deliver a data packet from one network to another. Routers, discussed in Chapter 7, are primarily used to segment and subdivide network traffic. Network and subnetwork boundaries are created using routers. Routers use internal address tables to discover which networks they can reach. Routers make the Internet and the organization's enterprise appear as one single network. Also, routers are devices that make use of IP addresses to determine where to send a data packet. In our paper mail example, a post office functions in a similar way as a router, determining where next to send a letter. Figure 6.7 shows how a router might be used to connect different networks.

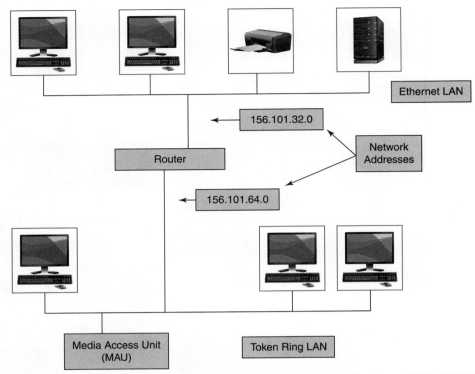

FIGURE 6.7 Use of a Router Connecting Two Logically Different Networks: Network 156.101.32.0 and Network 156.101.64.0. This router has two network address assignments and will have two network interface cards as well, one for each network. In this example, network 156.101.32 could be an Ethernet network, whereas 156.101.64.0 is a token ring.

The network portion of the IP address must be unique across all the networks of the enterprise as well as across the entire global TCP/IP network if the enterprise is directly connected to the Internet. All hosts on the same network share the same network identifier. If a host device is moved from one network to another, the host's IP address will have to be reassigned and reconfigured. The newly reconfigured IP address will have a new network as well as a new host identifier.

SUBNETS

In practice, most businesses that use TCP/IP refer to each separate network in the enterprise as a *subnet*. Rather than have one very large network, with hundreds or thousands of hosts, most organizations segment or subdivide a single network address through a process called **subnetting**. With subnetting, a single network identifier is subdivided into multiple uniquely identified segments, which is why we call this subdivision a subnet. Subnetting is accomplished by borrowing bits from the host portion of an IP address and reassigning those bits for use as network address identifiers.

In order to subnet, something called a **subnet mask** is used. Subnet masks use binary 1s to represent the network portion of an address and 0s to represent the host portion. Before describing how subnetting and submasking work, let's examine a few advantages of the subnetwork architecture.

Advantages of the Subnetwork Architecture

Subnetworks offer several advantages, one of which is allowing networks with different topologies to be supported. For example, a router can connect an Ethernet subnet with a token ring subnet. Subnets also resolve the problem of the physical limitations of a network's capacity. An Ethernet network can accommodate only so many devices. Through subnetting, the physical limitations of an Ethernet LAN are overcome. If a network becomes too large, management and configuration can become quite complicated, if not impossible. Subnets allow a greater number of hosts to be provided for and more easily managed over the entire enterprise. Another advantage of subnets is that they can reduce traffic. Reducing traffic improves the overall performance of the network, allowing for faster response.

The construction of a well-structured subnetting enterprise requires careful analysis and good planning. However, with additional networks comes additional complexity, especially in maintaining an IP addressing scheme that is accurate, reliable, and easy to modify across the entire enterprise. With more hosts, maintenance and configuration efforts will likely be affected. Several factors should be considered when designing a subnet architecture.

First, how many network address identifiers will be required? Each subnet requires its own unique IP address. When determining the number of network addresses, you should plan for the future growth of the organization. A separate network identifier will be required for every network bordered by a router, including any WAN connections bordered by routers. Once the total number of network addresses has been determined, the number of hosts to be supported per subnet must be evaluated.

Second, each device with a NIC will require a unique host IP address. As with network identifiers, future growth in the number of hosts within a subnet must be considered. The decision as to how many hosts should be supported within a subnet will directly affect the subnet mask that must be defined for the enterprise. (The subnet mask is explained in more detail soon.) "Measure twice and cut once," said the wise tailor, saving expense and customer irritation caused by measuring error. The same might be said for a wise network administrator in charge of designing the overall networked enterprise. Performing the necessary planning and analysis right the first time will prevent you from having to reconfigure every host device with a new subnet mask in the future.

Figure 6.8 illustrates an enterprise with five subnets. The numbers shown in the figure are unique subnet addresses.

The subnet mask will determine the number of network address identifiers the organization will have available for use. When selected, the subnet values need to be well documented so as to verify and document that they are already in use. In this way, when a new network identifier is required, all of those already in use will be known. After subnet network identifiers have been selected, host identifiers within each subnet can be appended to the network address. As with network identifiers, host identifiers should be well documented to ensure that no duplicate or invalid addresses are used within a subnet.

A network administrator may want to develop a numbering range scheme that allocates particular ranges of IP addresses to particular types of devices—for example, routers, switches, and servers, as well as static and dynamic clients. With such a preplanned numbering range scheme, the IP address allocated immediately identifies the type of device supported. Subnetting is common among businesses that use the TCP/IP IPv4 networking model. To better understand this concept, let's now turn to IP address configuration and subnet masking.

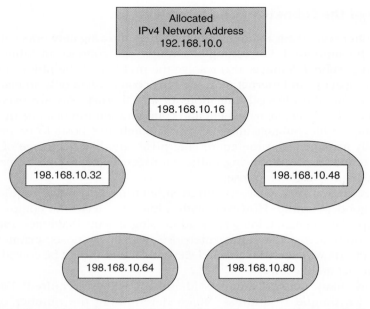

FIGURE 6.8 An Enterprise with Five Small Subnet Networks. Assume the organization has been allocated the following IPv4 class C address: 192.168.10.0. From that single address, five subnets identified in the diagram could be configured. Each of the subnets would have a very limited number of hosts that they could support. These subnet addresses are for internal use only.

IP ADDRESSING

Internet protocol addresses can be represented in both binary and decimal formats. Network administrators, being people and not machines, generally work with the decimal equivalent of an IP address, because the decimal equivalent is much more convenient and easily understandable. However, it is important that network technologists understand both the binary and decimal representations of an IP address and be able to work and convert between the two. To understand how IP addresses are resolved—meaning how a sending host discovers whether a receiving host is on the same logical network or not—you first must understand binary numbering.

Converting Binary Numbers to Decimals and Back Again

Decimal IPv4 addresses are composed of four numbers, each of which is referred to as an octet. The term **octet** is used because each decimal number has an 8-bit, or octet, equivalent. With binary numbering, a **bit** is represented by either a 0 or a 1—that's it, no other values are used. A sequence of eight 0s or 1s, in any combination, is called a **byte**. Further, each of the four decimal numbers making up the IP addresses is tied, or anchored, to its neighboring decimal number with a dot; hence, we have the dotted-decimal notation that is associated with an IPv4 address. (We see in a later chapter that discusses IPv6 that colons are used in IPv6 addresses to denote information.) Therefore, an IPv4 address is composed of four bytes, each having eight bits. Because computers use binary numbers, a computer will view a dotted-decimal IPv4 address as a 32-bit binary number. The decimal values that a given octet can take range from 0 to 255, for a total range of 256 different values, because 0 is also a value. Table 6.1 shows an example of a dotted-decimal IP address with its binary, or computer, equivalent.

Table 6.1 Dotted-Decimal and Binary Equivalent

Dotted Decimal	Binary Equivalent
192.01.36.240	11000000.00000001.00100100.11110000

In an eight-bit octet, each bit can have a value of either 0 or 1. The decimal value for each bit position in the octet can be determined using the equation 2^{n-1}, where n is the position of the binary bit from the right of the octet. A value of 1 in the octet indicates that the decimal value is to be accumulated into the total; a value of 0 indicates that the decimal value equivalent is not accumulated. Consequently, in the octet, only the 1s have to be accumulated. For example, the binary octet 00010110 has the following position accumulations, going from right to left in the octet:

$$2^{2-1} + 2^{3-1} + 2^{5-1} \text{ OR } 2 + 4 + 16 = 22 = 00010110$$

The maximum value that any octet can take is 255, as demonstrated in Table 6.2.

Every IP address within an enterprise or directly on the Internet must be unique. Organizations with no plans to connect their networks directly to the Internet need not be concerned with allocation or duplication of addresses already on the Internet. In effect, such organizations have private IP addresses. A key problem with private IP addresses is that they cannot be routed across the public Internet unless the devices that sit on the boundary of the private and public networks use additional software. Few organizations go to the labor of developing an enterprise network that does not connect directly to or utilize the Internet.

For this reason, it is critical that an organization use validated, authenticated IP addresses. The **Internet Corporation for Assigned Names and Number (ICANN)** (*www.icann.org*) is the major official body responsible for allocating, coordinating, and assigning the IP addresses, domain names, and protocol parameters that enable organizations to connect their networks to the Internet. In turn, ICANN uses commercial vendors to assist it in the management of its responsibilities.

Duplicate IP addresses are not allowed within an intranet or on the Internet. An **intranet** is an internal TCP/IP network owned by a given organization. Intranets are used by staff within the business and are not meant for outside user access.

Table 6.2 Octets and Their Corresponding Bit and Decimal Values

Binary Octet	Octet Bit Value	Octet Decimal Value
00000000	0 + 0 + 0 + 0 + 0 + 0 + 0 + 0	0
10000000	128 + 0 + 0 + 0 + 0 + 0 + 0 + 0	128
11000000	128 + 64 + 0 + 0 + 0 + 0 + 0 + 0	192
11100000	128 + 64 + 32 + 0 + 0 + 0 + 0 + 0	224
11110000	128 + 64 + 32 + 16 + 0 + 0 + 0 + 0	240
11111000	128 + 64 + 32 + 16 + 8 + 0 + 0 + 0	248
11111100	128 + 64 + 32 + 16 + 8 + 4 + 0 + 0	252
11111110	128 + 64 + 32 + 16 + 8 + 4 + 2 + 0	254
11111111	128 + 64 + 32 + 16 + 8 + 4 + 2 + 1	255

This means that the customers and vendors with which the business works usually do not have access to the organization's intranets. The portion of the enterprise that a customer or vendor is given access to is called an **extranet**. An enterprise differs from both an intranet and extranet in that it is the collection of all of the networks owned by an organization, which may include any intranets and extranets. Most hosts within an organization's enterprise that require an IP address do not need public IP addresses, because most hosts function as clients and do not provide services that need to be accessible over the Internet. Today, due to the scarcity of public IPv4 addresses, organizations typically lease their public IP addresses from an Internet service provider.

IP ADDRESS CLASSES

Internet protocol version 4, or IPv4, has been the most widely implemented version of TCP/IP. Currently, however, IPv4 is being rapidly replaced by its newer and improved version, IPv6. We return specifically to the topic of IPv6 in a later chapter this text. Even so, IPv4 is still a present-day reality and widely deployed, particularly in the United States. Under IPv4, IP addresses are divided into five **address classes**, ranging from Class A through Class E. Of these classes, D and E are reserved for special and/or research use, leaving Classes A, B, and C for public use. For Classes A, B, and C, each class reserves a portion of its IP address for network identification and the remaining portion for host identification. Depending on the class, more or less of the IP address is available for more or less of the network or host identifier. Recall that for a communication to occur between a sender and a receiver, both a network and a host address must be provided. An IP address contains elements of both.

Regardless of the class, each IPv4 address will always have four octets. The octets used for network identification and those used for host identification differentiate the classes from each other. The network portion of an IP address always begins from the left-most octet. A standard Class A IP address uses its first octet from the left for network identification and its last three right-most octets for host identification. A standard Class B address uses its first two left-most octets for network identification and its last two right-most octets for host identification. A standard Class C address uses its first three left-most octets for network identification and its last right-most octet for host identification. Table 6.3 illustrates the portion of an IP address used for network identification and the portion used for the host.

From the left, the first three bits of the first octet will clearly tell into which class an IP address falls. For a Class A address, the first high-order bit (the left-most bit of the left-most byte) of the first octet is always zero. For a Class B address, the first two high-order bits of the first octet are always 10. Finally, the first three high-order bits of the first octet for a Class C address are always 110. Because the first three high-order bits are used to identify the class of an IP address, they also affect the range of values that the first octet can take for each of the class addresses. Furthermore, each class can support only a specific number of networks and hosts. Depending on the class, more

Table 6.3   IP Address by Class, Showing Network and Host Portions

Class	Address Octets	Network	Host
A	$1^{st}.2^{nd}.3^{rd}.4^{th}$	$1^{st}.$	$2^{nd}.3^{rd}.4^{th}$
B	$1^{st}.2^{nd}.3^{rd}.4^{th}$	$1^{st}.2^{nd}.$	$3^{rd}.4^{th}$
C	$1^{st}.2^{nd}.3^{rd}.4^{th}$	$1^{st}.2^{nd}.3^{rd}.$	4th

Table 6.4	Address Classes, Showing Network and Host Values Available					
Address Class	First Octet in Binary	Decimal Values of First Octet	Number of Network Octets	Number of Host Octets	Networks Available	Hosts Available
Class A	01111111	1 – 126	1	3	126	16,777,214
Class B	10111111	128 – 191	2	2	16,384	65,534
Class C	11011111	192 – 223	3	1	2,097,152	254

networks or hosts can be supported. Table 6.4 shows the number of networks and hosts available for each class.

IP Address Classes and the Number of Hosts on a Network

In a Class A address, the high-order bit of the first octet is always set to 0. That leaves only seven bits in the first octet for use by network addresses. These seven bits provide a maximum decimal value of 127, or 01111111 in binary. However, network address 127 is reserved for what is referred to as a *network adapter loopback function*. For that reason, only 126 Class A networks are, or were, in fact, available. All 126 public Class A addresses were assigned long ago. (If you want to know what organizations were lucky enough to get those priceless Class A addresses, visit *www.iana.org/assignments/ ipv4-address-space.*)

For Class A IP addresses, 24 bits (the last three octets) are available for host address assignment. This allows for $2^{(24 - 2)}$, or 16,777,214, host addresses. The reason that 2 is subtracted from the 24 is that a host address of all 0s or all 1s is not allowed. The use of all 0s in a host address indicates that the communication is for a particular network without specifying a host. All 1s in the host address indicate that the communication is for all hosts on a particular network.

As it happens, a network address of all 0s and all 1s is also not allowed. All 0s in a network address indicate that the host is on the local network, so the communication will not be routed. All 1s in the network address indicate a broadcast whereby all hosts on the network receive the communication. In addition, all 0s and all 1s are used in particular combinations in an IP address to define a subnet mask.

The first two octets of Class B addresses are for the network identifier. Of the remaining 16 bits, only 14 may be used for host addressing, again because a host of all 0s or all 1s is not allowed. Using 14 bits provides for a possible 65,534 hosts per Class B network. Using its first three octets for network identification, Class C addresses use the last eight bits, minus 2, or 282, for host addressing, giving a decimal value of up to 254 hosts per Class C network.

IP Addressing Guidelines

Connecting a network to the Internet requires an authenticated and validated public IP address. Due to the scarcity of IPv4 addresses, organizations have little choice with regard to the network IDs they are assigned. When planning a TCP/IP enterprise, IP addressing guidelines become critical for effective communication by the networks that make up the enterprise. Several factors need to be considered when selecting IPv4 addresses. For example, organizations should choose a class address that reflects the current size of the enterprise, as well as one that will accommodate future expansion of the network. Each intranet in the organization must be given a unique, accurately documented network address. The larger the enterprise, the more important full and accurate documentation becomes.

Table 6.5 Use of Address Ranges to Identify Types of Host Devices	
IP Address	**Type of Host**
120.x.x.10 to 120.x.x.30	DCHP and DNS Servers Fall into the Range of .10 to .30
120.14.68.10	DHCP Server in the Accounting LAN
120.50.72.11	DHCP Server in the Marketing LAN
. . . .	
120.32.01.29	DNS Server in the Corporate LAN
120.x.x.31 to 120.x.x.40	File and Print Servers Fall into the Range of .31 to .40
120.21.18.31	File Server in the Accounting LAN
120.101.02.32	File Server in the Marketing LAN
. . . . . .	
120.16.122.40	Print Server in the Corporate LAN
120.x.x.41 to 120.x.x.50	Switches Fall into the Range of .41 to .50
120.12.133.41	Switch in the Accounting LAN
120.84.03.42	Switch in the Marketing LAN
. . . .	
120.111.53.48	Switch in the Corporate LAN

Using the above guidelines, if an address ended in X.X.X.36, what kind of device might it be?

Within a specific LAN or intranet, host addressing should be well thought out and planned. Each host within a LAN must have a unique address. Network administrators should take care not to assign host addresses that are restricted, such as all 0s or all 1s. Using particular ranges of host addresses that identify specific types of devices can also be beneficial—for example, having servers fall within one range of host address values and routers within a different range. Table 6.5 provides an example of the use of address ranges to identify host devices. Using the guidelines in Table 6.5, if an address ended in X.X.X.36, what type of device might it be?

DEFINING A SUBNET MASK

When an organization has been officially assigned a network IP address or a range of IP addresses, it will likely be the case that the address or addresses assigned do not provide enough unique network identifiers to support the needs of the organization. Assume that a business has only one authorized ICANN IP address, yet it needs five networks in its enterprise. In order to get five unique network addresses from a single network address, the single network address must be subdivided, or subnetted. For the subnetting to function correctly, an additional element must be defined. That additional element is a subnet mask.

A subnet mask acts like a filter. When an IP address is compared with its associated subnet mask, what is revealed or filtered out is the network portion and value of the IP address, and the host portion and value of the IP address. This comparison process is done through a technique called ANDing. **ANDing** compares a host's IP address with a subnet mask and derives a result. ANDing an IP address to its subnet

Table 6.6 Default Subnet Masks for Class A, B, and C IP Addresses		
Class	Subnet Mask in Decimal	Subnet Mask in Binary
A	255.0.0.0	11111111.00000000.00000000.00000000
B	255.255.0.0	11111111.11111111.00000000.00000000
C	255.255.255.0	11111111.11111111.11111111.11111111

mask reveals network and host address values so that a sending host knows whether a receiving host is on the same or on a different network. If a receiver is on a different logical network from the sender, then routing must occur. A subnet mask helps reveal whether routing is needed. Let's find out how this works by looking at the subnet mask in greater depth.

A subnet mask, like an IP address, has 32 bits. The type of subnet mask used is based on the class of the IP address: Class A, B, or C. Each IP address class has a standard, or default subnet mask, defined. In the binary representation of the subnet mask, 1s indicate the network portions and 0s indicate the host portions of the IP address. Table 6.6 shows the default subnet masks used for Class A, B, and C addresses.

An organization is generally given one IP address to use as its network identifier. Given the current status of IPv4, public IP addresses are particularly expensive and difficult to come by. For this reason, organizations that require multiple networks take their single IPv4 network IP address and subdivide, or subnet, it. When businesses modify their allocated IP address, they must also modify its associated default subnet mask. Borrowing bits from the subnet's host portion allows for more network addresses to be accommodated. By extending the network portion of the subnet mask into the host portion, additional network or subnet identifiers can be created. However, this means that the default subnet mask will no longer work. When it is reconfigured or modified, the same subnet mask must be used throughout the organization's entire enterprise.

Subnet Addressing

Borrowing bits from the host portion of an IP address in order to use those bits as part of a network identifier creates a subnet. Each network in the enterprise requires a unique identifier. If an organization's enterprise is completely private—meaning that it is not connected to the public Internet—then subnetting is not an issue. This is because the organization could use the full range of class addresses defined in the IPv4 TCP/IP protocol suite. However, this is usually not the case for most enterprise networks. For this reason, some degree of subnetting is generally required in order for the organization to use its public IP address to connect to the Internet.

Organizations that connect their enterprise network to the Internet by means of a proxy server or firewall can also independently allocate IP addressing on the private portion of their networks. A proxy server or firewall hides the internal structure of the private portion of the enterprise and provides mapping of incoming and outgoing packets to internal hosts. Figure 6.9 illustrates how a proxy server might be positioned. Proxy servers and firewalls are described in detail in a later chapter. For now, you only need to understand that most organizations use some form of subnetting, because the number of public IP addresses they have available to identify their networks are very limited. The transition to IPv6 will eliminate this problem. With

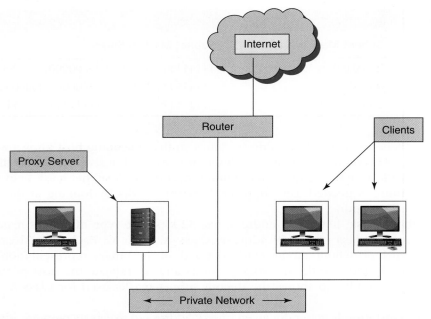

FIGURE 6.9 Use of a Proxy Server. In this example, the proxy servers functions as a layer between individual clients on a private network and the outside world. The proxy allows the clients to be hidden from those outside the network.

IPv6, your house or apartment or even your "smart" refrigerator could have its own public IP address.

Assume that ICANN has assigned an organization a Class B public network address of 156.101.0.0. However, the organization needs at least five network identifiers to support its current enterprise network configuration. Recall that the default subnet mask for a Class B address is 255.255.0.0, identifying the first two octets as network and the last two octets as host. The solution is to borrow high-order bits from the host portion of the standard subnet mask to create additional network identifier values. The number of high-order bits that will be borrowed depends on the number of network identifiers required.

The number of network identifiers available can be determined by a formula, 2^{n-2}, where n is the number of high-order bits borrowed. Therefore, if three bits are borrowed, the formula is 2^{3-2}, giving a result of 6, which in this example is one more network identifier than required (remember, 5 are needed). The reason 2 must be subtracted is that a network identifier cannot be all 0s or all 1s, which eliminates two values. If only two bits had been borrowed from the host, the formula (2^{2-2}) shows that there are only two usable network identifiers—too few for the organization's needs.

Borrowing high-order bits from the host requires that the subnet mask be modified to reflect the borrowed bits. Table 6.7 shows a standard Class B subnet mask and a Class B subnet mask with three high-order bits borrowed from the host. In this example, note that, rather than 16 – 2 bits being available for host addressing, only 13 – 2 bits are available. The 2 is subtracted because a host address of all 1s or all 0s is not allowed.

With the three bits borrowed from the host to make up network identifiers, the following bit network combinations are available: 000, 001, 010, 011, 100, 101, 110,

Table 6.7   Class B Subnet Mask with Three Bits Borrowed

Standard Class B Subnet Mask in Binary	The Same Standard Class B Subnet Mask in Decimal
11111111.11111111.00000000.00000000	255.255.0.0
Class B Subnet Mask with 3 Bits Borrowed in Binary	The Same Class B Subnet Mask with 3 Bits Borrowed in Decimal
11111111.11111111.11100000.00000000	255.255.224.0

and 111. There are only eight ways to put a combination of three binary 0s and 1s together. Of these eight, only six can be used because a network identifier of all 0s, 000, or all 1s, 111, is not allowed. Also, recall that the three bits borrowed were the high-order bits of the host octet, and these high-order bits will have corresponding high-order decimal values. Table 6.8 shows the range of network identifier values in binary and decimal that are available based on the new subnet mask configuration. Note that the high-order three bits in the byte are separated out to illustrate where they are located. Their high-order location determines their equivalent decimal value.

The following unique network identifier addresses are now available for use in the private portion of the enterprise: 156.101.32.0, 156.101.64.0, 156.101.96.0, 156.101.128.0, 156.101.160.0, and 156.101.192.0. Each of these addresses is now a potential subnet. Of course, these additional subnets were gained at the cost of having fewer host identifiers available. The new subnet mask must now also be configured for all hosts in the enterprise. Using this subnet mask, a TCP/IP host, by means of ANDing, can now determine whether the intended recipient of an IP packet is on the same logical network or on a remote network. By comparing a host address to the subnet mask, ANDing can determine whether two hosts are on the same local network. ANDing uses a comparative process and is a very interesting topic. For those who want to know more about ANDing and exactly how it works, see the "Topic in Focus" at the end of this chapter.

Setting up an IP addressing scheme by means of subnetting and subnet masking is crucial. One of your jobs as a network administrator may be to design just such an addressing scheme or to modify one already in place. Understanding why a business would want to subnet helps a great deal in understanding how to subnet. The reality is that while IPv4 is in widescale use, subnetting and subnet masking are going to be required.

Table 6.8   Network Identifiers Available with Three High-Order Bits Borrowed

Binary	Decimal	
001 00000	32	Original assigned address: 156.101.0.0
010 00000	64	
011 00000	96	Here we have separated out the high-order 3 bits in the byte simply to illustrate where they are located. Their high-order location determines their equivalent decimal value.
100 00000	128	
101 00000	160	
110 00000	192	

SUPERNETTING

Although many organizations choose to subnet their IP address, IP addresses can also be combined or aggregated in a process called supernetting. **Supernetting** borrows bits from the network rather than from the host (i.e., subnetting), in order to create additional networks. An organization might use supernetting when it has several Class C IP addresses, none of which allows a sufficient number of hosts for the desired network. Remember that a Class C address only allows for a maximum of 254 hosts in the network.

Assume you work for an organization that has four Class C addresses at its disposal. Also assume that your organization must have more than 254 hosts in its particular network. However, with a Class C address, you are limited to just 254 hosts. Do you give up and tell your boss the company is out of luck? No, you recommend supernetting, using supernet masking, and get that promotion you well deserve.

With supernetting, several IP addresses are in effect combined, or masked, to appear as one network that has a larger number of hosts. Rather than implementing supernetting with a subnet mask, a supernet mask can be used. A supernet mask works in just the opposite way of a subnet mask. Instead of borrowing bits from the host and making the borrowed bits ones, bits are borrowed from the network portion of the mask and made into 0s.

Supernetting is a function of **classless inter-domain routing (CIDR)**. The benefit of CIDR is that it reduces the size of the routing tables used by the routers on the Internet backbone. By reducing the size of the routing tables, faster review, and, in turn, access, can be achieved. By using a group of Class C addresses, CIDR provides for the aggregation of multiple routes to a particular organization. For example, consider an organization with four Class C addresses. All four addresses would have to be provided for in Internet backbone router tables. By using CIDR aggregation, only one entry in the router table would be required, not four. For one business, this may not seem like much, but what if this were done for 20,000 or more businesses? Suddenly the issue of routing table maintenance has become much more complicated. However, CIDR requires a contiguous set of network identifiers and does not work well with all routers, so caution should be used in its implementation.

Chapter Summary

TCP/IP has become a very popular networking model not only for WANs, but for LANs as well. With TCP/IP, both networks and devices, called hosts, have addresses. The use of these addresses enables communication within a LAN and across an enterprise, which is the collection of all the networks owned by a single organization. These addresses have a specific binary format that has a decimal equivalent. With IPv4, addresses are based on a 32-bit, 4-byte octet. Each octet contains 8 bits. When these 4 bytes, anchored with dots, are converted to decimal, the result is referred to as dotted-decimal notation.

Internet protocol addresses are categorized into five specific classes: A, B, C, D, and E. Of the five, Classes D and E are reserved for special use. Classes A, B, and C are used in public networks and for Internet connections. If an IP address will be used for public purposes, it must be officially authorized by ICANN, the managing body that controls the allocation of IP addresses and which also works with commercial vendors in fulfilling its responsibilities. Due to their scarcity, most businesses lease IP addresses from ISPs.

The type of IP address class determines the number of networks and hosts that can be supported on a network. Each class uses specific octets to identify the network and host portions of an IP address.

Subnet masks are used to filter the network and host components from an IP address. Each IP class has a standard default subnet mask: ones indicate network components, zeros indicate host components. Standard subnet masks are frequently modified to accommodate subnetting, which is the subdividing of a single IP address into multiple addresses.

Because most organizations require more than one unique network identifier for the enterprise, public IP addresses are often subnetted. With subnetting, an organization can subdivide one network address into multiple network addresses. Such subnetted addresses are used for internal communications within the enterprise. Subnetting uses a common sub-net mask for the entire organization. The subnet mask differs from the standard mask in that bits from the host portion of the subnet mask are borrowed to create additional network address identifiers. Based on organizational needs, the number of bits borrowed can vary, which in turn affects the number of network identifiers available. Borrowing bits from the host will result in fewer host addresses being available. These are among the considerations that should be understood when planning a subnetwork architecture.

In contrast to subnetting, supernetting aggregates network addresses. But, like a subnet, a supernet also requires a mask, called a supernet mask. The supernet mask borrows bits from the network, rather than the host.

Key Words

Address classes *110*
Address resolution protocol (ARP) *99*
ANDing *112*
Bit *108*
Byte *108*
Classless inter-domain routing (CIDR) *116*
Datagram *101*
Extranet *110*
Host *104*

Internet control message protocol (ICMP) *101*
Internet Corporation for Assigned Names and Number (ICANN) *109*
Internet group message protocol (IGMP) *102*
Intranet *109*
IP address *104*
Logical address *99*
Multicasting *102*

Network layer *99*
Octet *108*
Physical address *99*
Reverse address resolution protocol (RARP) *101*
Subnet mask *106*
Subnetting *106*
Supernetting *116*
Unicasting *102*

Chapter Questions

Short-Answer Questions

1. What is the function of ARP? Why is it used?
2. How does a host logical address differ from a network logical address?
3. What function does subnetting perform in an IPv4 network?
4. What purpose does a subnet mask serve?
5. What is the purpose for ICMP?
6. What is meant by multicasting?
7. Why are routers used?
8. What is the term for a combined network and host address?

Hands-On Projects

1. Specify the default binary and decimal values for IVv4 Class A, B, and C addresses.
2. Make up a Class B subnet address. Define its standard subnet mask in binary and decimal format.
3. From your worksite, college or university, or other public institution, investigate what IP addressing scheme is being deployed and if subnetting is implemented.
4. Assume you are given a single Class C address. Then define a modified subnet mask that will allow for a minimum of three additional networks. How many bits were borrowed? What ranges of values in binary and decimal might the new networks take?

Research in Brief

For one or more of the following questions, provide a one- or two-page report based on your findings.

1. Why might an organization choose to subnet? Provide an example.
2. Why might an organization choose supernetting? Provide an example.
3. Research IEEE. Report on one of its most current initiatives regarding Ethernet.
4. How can IPv4 class addresses be differentiated?

Case Study

Sheehan Marketing and Public Relations

The following network IP addresses have been authorized for use by SMPR:

> Los Angeles: 195.017.121.0
>
> New York: 201.162.24.0
>
> Chicago: 205.110.37.0

You have decided to develop an IP addressing scheme that will identify different types of devices: clients, servers, switches, printers, routers, and so on. Prepare a memo that outlines your addressing scheme for each branch office. Explain your reasoning for the scheme you have chosen.

You have also determined that the Los Angeles office could benefit by subnetting its single network into two networks. One network will host the organization's financial and business operations, such as payroll, accounts receivable, and the customer database. The second network will be used by the general staff. Provide an analysis that details such factors as the bits borrowed, the network addresses available, subnet masking, and so on.

Finally, over the past few weeks you have been working more closely with Karla. She is confused over how the subnetting process works and has asked you to explain it to her. In your own words, write a succinct narrative description for Karla on the subnetting process that describes why it is used and how it is implemented.

Topic in Focus

HOW ANDing WORKS

ANDing is a relatively simple mathematical process that compares a given host's IP address with its subnet mask in binary form. As a host initializes (i.e., when it is turned on), ANDing occurs. The result of the ANDing is stored in the host's memory.

Each of the 32 bits of a given IP address is compared with its corresponding bit in the subnet mask. If any two corresponding bits are both 1, the result is a 1; any other combination of corresponding bits, 0 and 1, 1 and 0, or 0 and 0, results in a 0.

Stored in the host computer's memory, the ANDed result can be used by the host to determine its own network identifier address. When the same host needs to send an IP packet to another host, the destination host's IP address is ANDed with the subnet mask. This result is then compared with the sending host's previously ANDed result that is still stored in memory. If the network identifier addresses are the same, the two hosts are on the same logical network; if not, the destination host is on a remote network, and the IP packet will need to be routed to its proper network.

The following example assumes a Class C network address of 224.16.128.0. The address is subnetted by borrowing three bits from the host octet, which gives six additional network subnet values:

224.16.128.32

224.16.128.64

224.16.128.96

224.16.128.128

224.16.128.160

224.16.128.192

So far, only the first three values are used: the network identifiers ending in 32, 64, and 96. A host with an IP address of 224.16.128.33 wants to send an IP packet first to host 224.16.128.60 and then to host 224.16.128.66. Are these hosts all on the same logical network? ANDing will reveal the answer. Table 6.9 contains the results of three ANDing processes: the initial host's ANDing and then the ANDing of the two hosts with which it wants to communicate.

Table 6.9 Three ANDing Results

	Decimal IP	Network Binary IP	Host Binary	Host Dec
IP Address of Sending Host	224.16.128.33	10100000.00010000.1000000.001	00001	1
Subnet Mask	255.255.255.224	11111111.11111111.11111111.111	00000	
Initial ANDing	224.16.128.32	10100000.00010000.1000000.001	00000	
	This is Host 1 on Network 224.16.128.32			
IP address of 1st Receiver	224.16.128.60	10100000.00010000.1000000.001	11100	28
Subnet Mask	255.255.255.224	11111111.11111111.11111111.111	00000	
Second ANDing	224.16.128.32	10100000.00010000.10000000.001	00000	
	This is Host 28 on Network 224.16.128.32—A local host			
IP address of 2nd Receiver	224.16.128.66	10100000.00010000.10000000.010	00010	2
Subnet Mask	255.255.255.224	11111111.11111111.11111111.111	00000	
Third ANDing	224.16.128.64	10100000.00010000.1000000.010	00000	
	This is Host 2 on Network 224.16.128.64—A remote host			

What some find confusing is that in IP subnet addressing, the address has both the network ID and the host ID embedded within it. In our example, because of how the subnet mask was set up, the IP address 224.16.128.33 reveals that this address is for network 224.16.128.32 and host 1. Thus, the last octet value of 33 really contains information on two things: the network and the host ID. The same is true, of course, for the other two addresses. For the first receiver, the last octet value of 60 after ANDing reveals network 32 and host 68. For the second receiver, the last octet value of 66 after ANDing reveals network 64 and host 2. At first it may not be clear whether two IP addresses are on the same network. By deriving the network address identifier, ANDing resolves that question.

7

Transport and Application Layer Services and IPv6

The Business Benefit

In 2011, AT&T conducted a survey of 2,246 small business owners. *Small* was defined as being a business with between 2 and 50 employees, including full-time and part-time workers. The intent, according to AT&T, was to achieve a better understanding of how small business owners viewed the importance of mobile technologies, and specifically mobile applications ("apps") to these businesses. The results were revealing.

Of the business surveyed, 70 percent were using mobile apps for daily business operations. Of these, 40 percent indicated that their business could not survive or would be extremely challenged without the use of these apps. At the top of their list, 49 percent selected mapping and GPS as the app tool of most importance. Other applications of most interest included social media marketing, document management, travel and expense reporting, and credit-card payment services. Forty percent further indicated that most of their employees were using wireless devices and technologies in order to continue work while away from the business location. Also reported from the survey was the growing importance to small business owners of social media outreach, through such applications as Facebook and Twitter.

Clearly, small businesses are beginning to take advantage of technologies that allow them to compete effectively with larger, more technology-equipped competitors. In this chapter we explore how transport and application layer services help make this possible.

Learning Objectives

After studying this chapter, you should be able to:

- Differentiate between transport and application layer services.
- Describe the key elements of transport services.
- Differentiate between connection-oriented and connectionless communications.
- Describe the key elements of application layer services.
- Define a well-known port.

■ Define a well-known service.

■ Identify ways of transitioning from IPv4 to IPv6.

■ Describe IPv6 addressing types and packet format.

In Chapter 8 you will find that a LAN is composed of both logical and physical components. These components work together so that resources can be shared and network devices can communicate. A business may, of course, have more than one LAN and need for its multiple LANs to be able to communicate and share resources. For such communication and sharing to occur, network devices require two critical pieces of information: the physical and logical addresses of the devices participating in the communication, as was presented in an earlier chapter.

TRANSPORT LAYER SERVICES

As with network layer services, the **transport layer**, which sits above the network layer and below the application layer, also uses protocols. The two key transport layer protocols are the transmission control protocol (TCP) and the user datagram protocol (UDP). The two protocols operate in very different ways.

Well-Known Ports, Well-Known Services, and Sockets

Before moving into our discussion of TCP and UDP, at this point we need to introduce the concepts of well-known ports, well-known services, and sockets.

We have seen that IP addresses are necessary for a sender and receiver to be able to communicate with each other. However, once the sender's packets arrive at the receiver's host device and begin to travel up the receiver's protocol layer stacks, at the final point these packets must be directed to the appropriate application running on that receiver's host device. This is where TCP and UDP are brought into play. Both protocols use "port numbers," included in every TCP and UDP header, to iden-tify specific processes and services running on the receiver's host device. The port number is used to identify the application-layer protocol that generates the packets being processed. (We look at a few of these application-layer protocols shortly.)

Simply stated, a **well-known port** on the Internet is an address number, specifically a port address, that is standardized or bound to a particular well-known service. The advantage to the user is that he or she does not need to specify such a port address when accessing a well-known service.

Like a well-known port, a **well-known service** on the Internet is a standardized Internet program that is associated with a well-known port address. As these well-known ports and services are standardized across the Internet, local client software will be able to access the needed service on any remote host.

These port numbers are assigned by the Internet Corporation for Assigned Names and Numbers (IANA; *www.icann.org*), a standard-setting body introduced in Chapter 1. Each TCP/IP-based system will have a "Services" file that holds a list or inventory of the most common well-known port numbers and the well-known services to which these port numbers are assigned.

A socket is the combination of an IP address and a port number. **Sockets** are notated by the IP address anchored at the end with a colon and the port number, such as 157.34.80.102:53. In this instance, the well-known port number 53 is associated with a **domain name service (DNS)**.

Something that must be made clear is that port-number assignments for TCP and UDP are separate, meaning it is possible for a given specific port number to be used

Protocol	Well-Known Port	Purpose
TCP	21	File Transfer Protocol – Control
TCP	23	Telnet – Terminal Network
TCP	25	Simple Mail Transfer Protocol
TCP	53	Domain Name Service
UDP	53	Domain Name Service
UDP	111	Remote Procedure Call
UDP	123	Network Time Protocol
UDP	161	Simple Network Management Protocol

Table 7.1 Examples of Standard TCP and UDP Well-Known Ports

for different services by TCP and UDP. Table 7.1 contains examples of well-known ports, and the protocol they are associated with for both TCP and UDP.

TRANSMISSION CONTROL PROTOCOL

Transmission control protocol (TCP) is a connection-oriented protocol; it is also called a *reliable stream transport layer service*. The term *connection-oriented* applies because the sender cannot send until the receiver is contacted and agrees to a communication. This agreement establishes the connection. To better understand the concept of a reliable stream, keep in mind that there are sending and receiving TCP hosts. Figure 7.1 illustrates a TCP transmission.

When used, the TCP on the sending host accepts a stream of data from the sending host's application layer and segments these data into packets. The packets are then sent, using reliable services, to a receiving TCP host. The TCP on the receiving host's end takes the incoming packets and delivers them as a steam of data to the receiving host's application layer. The TCP service is said to be reliable because before data transmission can begin between the sender and the receiver, a connection must be established. This implies that both the sender and the receiver are reliably prepared for and ready to begin communications with each other.

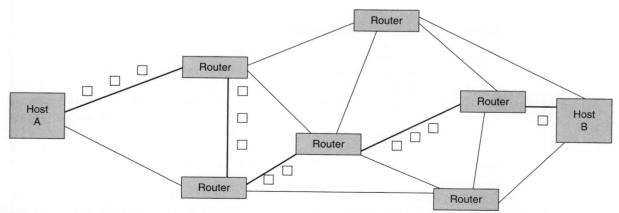

FIGURE 7.1 A TCP Transmission. In this example, there are many possible routes between Host A and Host B. The small boxes (□) represent multiple data packets required for one message. Note that all the data packets are following the same sequence of links on their way from Host A to Host B. With a TCP transmission, all packets that make up the same message follow the same sequence of links from sender to receiver.

Transmission control protocol has much more overhead than its counterpart, user datagram protocol (UDP). Indeed, TCP provides for packet acknowledgment, error detection and control, and flow control. Generally, the use of TCP as a delivery service is appropriate when larger data streams that cannot fit into a single packet need to be transmitted across the network. Also, for a message for which it is especially important that all the data packets arrive without loss and in the proper sequence, TCP is the delivery method of choice. With TCP, the data packets that make up the message all take the same route to their destination. For noncritical data or for data that can fit within a single packet, UDP is the more appropriate protocol.

TCP's Three-Step Approach to Establishing a Reliable Communication

First, from the transport layer of the sending device a request packet is transmitted to the receiving device's transport layer asking if a session can be established. Second, if available, the receiving device sends a packet back to the sending device indicating that it is available for communication. Then, in the third and final step, the sending device begins to send its data to the receiving device.

The information sent by the sender includes source and destination values, sequence numbers for data messages that may be broken into smaller segments for transmittal, and a checksum value that is used by the receiver to determine whether a transmission error has occurred. The information sent from the receiver back to the sender includes acknowledgment values for the packets received. The sender's TCP for flow control then uses the receiver's acknowledgment values. Transmission control protocol uses the sliding windows method of flow control.

In a previous chapter you learned that checksums can be used for error detection. That chapter also examined the benefits of sliding windows and how it works. You can now see how these two topics relate to the TCP/IP transport layer. The original "request for comments" 1981 document on TCP can be found at *www.faqs.org/rfcs/rfc793.html*. Request for comments (RFCs) are a series of formal documents that, since 1969, present technical and organizational notes about the Internet (originally the ARPANET). See *www.rfc-editor.org* to find out more about this important document series and how it is managed. Any standard that is eventually formally incorporated into the Internet or TCP/IP starts as a request for comment. As you might imagine, these comments can be very influential.

USER DATAGRAM PROTOCOL

Unlike TCP, **user datagram protocol (UDP)** is a connectionless, unreliable delivery service. **Connectionless service** means that the sender does not have to first establish a link to the receiver before beginning to transmit data. *Unreliable* does not mean worse or unacceptable. With UDP, **unreliable communication** simply means that the sender does not guarantee to the receiver that all the transmitted data packets will arrive. Also, if a message requires multiple packets, the packets may or may not take the same route to the receiver, and thus may arrive out of sequence. It is up to the receiver to verify that the data expected have in fact been received and to put the packets back in order, if needed.

Depending on the data being transmitted, UDP can be the better choice than TCP. Because UDP does not require the sender and receiver to establish a connection before sending data, time is saved, increasing efficiency. The sending host simple begins to transmit its UDP packets. If a message requires more than one datagram, the sent datagrams are treated independently. This means that the datagrams may take

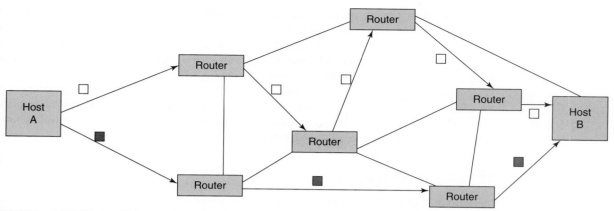

FIGURE 7.2 A UDP Transmission. In this example of a user datagram protocol transmission, the data packets have taken two different routes to get from Host A to Host B. The two packets could be part of the same message. If they are, it will be up to Host B's upper-layer services to put the packets back in proper order.

different routes to their ultimate destination and likely will not arrive in sequence. User datagram protocol leaves it to higher-level services on the receiving host's end to determine whether all packets have been received, determine whether any of the packets received have errors, and to place the packets back in order. As a result, at the transport layer, UDP can provide greater efficiency, but at the potential cost of high-layer services having to do more work. Figure 7.2 demonstrates a UDP transmission.

User datagram protocol does not provide for packet acknowledgment, error detection and control, or flow control. Because UDP does not support these services, it has far less overhead than TCP. With less overhead, UDP can be more efficient, assuming that all packets arrive with no errors at the receiving host. Also, because UDP packets are independent of each other, they can be routed through different links, unlike a TCP transmission. This means that if a UDP encounters a bad or congested link, it can be routed around the problem area. Under the right circumstances, then, UDP can be the preferred delivery option.

The use of how UDP is deployed has evolved over time. Although still mostly associated with small data files that require few packets, today UDP also is used for streaming audio and video. With a streaming audio or video file, it is usually not essential that every single byte be accounted for, as would be the case with traditional data, especially numeric data. Whether using TCP or UDP, the transport layer ultimately passes its data stream up to application layer services. Remember from Chapter 2 that the application layer sits at the top of the TCP/IP model. You should also recall that in the TCP/IP model the application layer includes the session, presentation, and application layer equivalents of the OSI model.

APPLICATION LAYER SERVICES

Many protocols are defined at the **application layer** of the TCP/IP model, and covering them all would be another textbook in itself. The application layer sits at the top of the TCP/IP layer stack, directly above the transport layer. The application layer provides the user an interface and a connection to the network. Many application layer protocols follow the client/server approach.

In the client/server model, a local host machine runs an application layer program called a *client*. The client application requests a resource from a remote host that is running a server-based application layer program. Server-based applications, assuming that the request is successfully authenticated and/or supported, fulfill requests for services. Note that a host can, if so configured, run both client- and server-based services. It may be a little confusing, but a device running server services is not necessarily a server. A formal server is a more specialized type of device. A later chapter looks at servers and how they are used.

The following presents a sampling of some of the more common protocols that you are likely to encounter. With each example, keep in mind that a client component is installed on the local host machine and that a server component is running on the remote device that is providing the service.

TERMINAL NETWORK

Terminal Network, or **Telnet**, is an application layer program that enables a user to remotely login and use the resources of a remote computer. To be successful, the remote computer must authenticate the user. Authentication is usually accomplished by means of a user ID and a password. Once authenticated, a user can use the processor, file system, drives, and other resources of the remote host.

Telnet was designed for use in time-sharing environments, whereby a large central computer, typically a mainframe, supported multiple users who logged in to the computer to access its resources. Network administrators also use Telnet to monitor, configure, and maintain remote devices.

File Transfer Protocol

Another popular application layer program is **file transfer protocol (FTP)**. In the TCP/IP environment, file transfer protocol is used to copy files from one host to another. On the client host side, FTP has three components: a user interface, a client control process, and a client transfer process. On the server host side, there are two components: a server control process and a server transfer process. Depending on the connection, user authentication may be required. See Figure 7.3 for further explanation.

Many FTP servers are set up for anonymous users, meaning that anyone with a FTP client can connect to the anonymous FTP server and use that server's resources. Other FTP servers have more stringent login requirements. Many free FTP clients are available over the Internet. One popular version is WS-FTP, which is provided

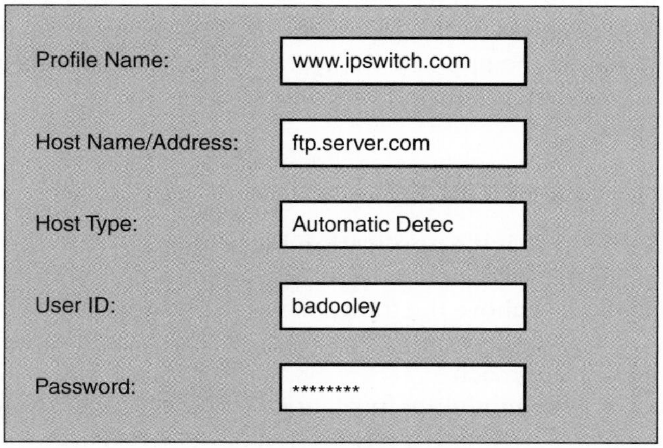

Profile Name:	www.ipswitch.com
Host Name/Address:	ftp.server.com
Host Type:	Automatic Detec
User ID:	badooley
Password:	********

FIGURE 7.3 Example of Data Required from a Typical FTP Client

The Ethical Perspective

Sharing? Or Something Else?

The Internet has come a long way from being a tool used mostly by scientists and researchers to exchange technical information. Now, hundreds of millions of people shop, play, communicate, and share resources over the Internet. The issue of sharing has become a major ethical issue. Web-based applications, primarily using peer-to-peer sharing protocols, enable a user to exchange and share files with other local computers. Many of these "shared" files are music, video, or other types of artistic- or entertainment-based materials.

To the businesses and artists who create these works, the rampant sharing of these materials has resulted in a loss of control over their works, as well as millions of dollars of lost income. Many users who "share" these works do not reimburse the artist or owner for use of the work. Some users claim such works should be free, and they see no problem with sharing technologies.

However, buying a single version of the content and then sharing that version with many others is very controversial. Many say that this action is illegal; others maintain that it is unethical. This type of file sharing, with no reimbursement to the original owner, was a key reason for the passage in 1998 of the Federal Digital Millennium Copyright Act (DMCA; *www.loc.gov/copyright/legislation/dmca.pdf*).

What do you think? Is it ethical to share copyrighted materials without reimbursing the creators or owners? Should there be laws for or against such sharing? Should file sharing be legislated? How would you argue for or against these sharing technologies? If you were a network administrator, would you define a policy on the sharing of files using corporate computers and networks? How would you enforce such a policy? Should a business be legally responsible for what an employee does, even if the organization has no knowledge of what the employee is doing? As you can see, this is a very complicated issue.

by Ipswitch (*www.ipswitch.com*). More fully featured versions, some of which are also offered by Ipswitch, are available for a fee. When you purchase an FTP client, documentation and technical support are often provided.

Simple Mail Transfer Protocol

Simple mail transfer protocol (SMTP) is a popular network protocol for providing e-mail services. This protocol makes use of two components: a user agent and a mail transfer agent. On the client end, the user agent (UA) prepares the message and puts it into a form that can be transmitted across a TCP/IP network. The mail transfer agent (MTA) transfers the mail across the network or over the Internet. On the server end, SMTP servers receive outgoing mail from clients and transmit mail to destination e-mail servers. Another type of SMTP server maintains the mailboxes from which e-mail clients retrieve their mail. Figure 7.4 shows a simplified diagram of how user agents and mail transfer agents might be configured.

Two common protocols that servers use to maintain e-mail mailboxes are *post office protocol version 3 (POP3)* and *Internet message access protocol (IMAP)*. One machine may run POP3 or IMAP in addition to SMTP. In that case, the servers are not separate physical devices, but one device running multiple logical server operations. Again, a later chapter looks more closely at the different types of servers used to integrate the enterprise. A basic discussion on e-mail and the use of SMTP and POP3 can be found at *www.howstuffworks.com/email.htm*.

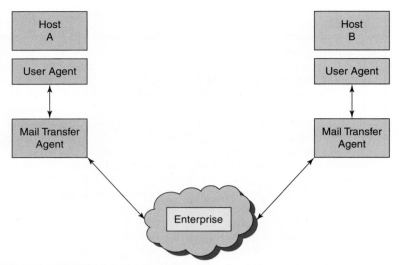

FIGURE 7.4 User and Mail Transfer Agents

Simple Network Management Protocol

Simple network management protocol (SNMP) provides a basic set of tools for managing a TCP/IP network. Because it uses UDP, SNMP is also connectionless. Generally, certain host devices that have a "manager" component control a group of devices, usually routers, that run an "agent" component. Simple network management protocol is sufficiently general so that hosts from different manufacturers and on different physical networks can be monitored. The manager receives information from agents and assembles it for presentation to network administrators.

Many networked devices—including routers, switches, and hubs—can serve as agents, reporting to the manager device regarding the status of the network. Each agent has a management information base (MIB) that it builds as it collects network statistics. The agent distributes its MIB to the manager. Based on the data received, a management station can cause an action to take place at an agent or it can change an agent's configuration setting.

Hypertext Transfer Protocol

Hypertext transfer protocol (HTTP) is used primarily to access information on the World Wide Web (WWW). This protocol enables data (text, hypertext, video, graphic, audio, or other medium) to be transferred from a server device to a client, meaning a webserver to a client browser. After a TCP/IP connection is established, the client browser and the webserver can begin to exchange data. Two message types are used by HTTP: requests and responses. Every HTTP message has a start line, an optional header, a blank line that identifies the end of the header section, and the body of the message, which is also optional. A formal Internet working group is devoted to HTTP. You can find out more about this interesting group at *ftp.ics.uci.edu/pub/ietf/http*.

There are a number of protocols associated with the application layer, as illustrated in Figure 7.5.

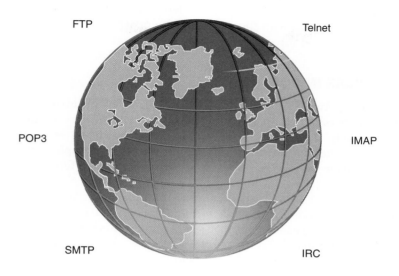

FIGURE 7.5   HTTP and Other Standard Internet Application Layer Protocols Used Worldwide

DOMAIN NAME SYSTEM

The domain name system (DNS) is an integral part of almost all TCP/IP networks. When a user connects to the Internet, she or he enters a DNS server or URL (uniform resource locator) into her or his web browser or other application to resolve the name of the system provided into an IP address. Most of us find entering a user-friendly DNS/URL name, such as *www.pearson.com*, easier to work with than a numeric IP address. The Internet's domain name system is often compared to a hierarchical directory tree, as illustrated in Figure 7.6.

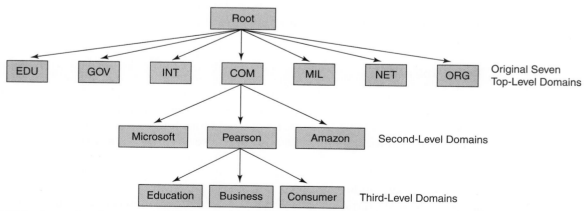

FIGURE 7.6   Comparing the Internet's Domain Name System to a Hierarchical Directory Tree with Multiple Levels of Organization

The user supplies the DNS/URL name for a desired server to a client application. The client application, in turn, initiates the process that ultimately resolves the provided name into an IP address. If the name provided cannot be resolved, for a variety of reasons, no communication with the server will be possible. To learn more about DNS, read the Topic in Focus at the end of this chapter.

THE TWO LAYERS IN CONTEXT

Let's place the top two TCP/IP layers in context. The application layer provides the enterprise network user an interface for connecting to and interacting with the network. Very likely, the user wants to communicate with either another user or a service offered by another network in the enterprise—for example, a database server. The destination user or service could be on the same or different network as the originating user.

When two hosts in a TCP/IP network communicate, it is critical, as with any other communication, that they be able to identify each other. In this communication, the transport layer manages the transmission of data between sender and receiver. The transmission provided may be connection-oriented or connectionless. The application and transport layers then depend on mid- and lower-level layers services to complete the communications process.

Before moving on to the networking implementations part of this text, some last additional information regarding the transition from IPv4 to IPv6 needs to addressed.

IPv6 AND THE NEW INTERNET

Technologies such as 4G, 802.11, and Bluetooth derive much of their appeal from providing all-time access to that network of all networks—the Internet. As connectivity technologies have evolved, it should be no surprise that the Internet also has had an evolutionary plan in place. The Internet we know and love, **IPv4**, has been around, at least in a very basic form, since the late 1960s. For a computer-based technology, this is truly ancient history. But the long life that IPv4 has enjoyed says a great deal about how well designed it was and how reliable and flexible a technology it is. However, "all good things must come to an end." To many, the end of the road for IPv4 is close at hand. Gradually replacing IPv4 is the new and improved Internet, **IPv6** (Internet protocol version 6), also known as **IPng** (Internetworking protocol, next generation). So, why is IPv4 being retired and how does IPv6 differ? Next, we consider these very questions.

IPv4 Limitations

The Internet was initially designed primarily as a tool for researchers, scientists, and engineers to more easily exchange data and information with each other. Who could have foreseen that their creation, IPv4, would turn into one of the most wildly popular communication technologies the world has ever seen? Also, at that time the types of data that IPv4 was created to carry were fairly simple: textual and numerical. Today, we require the IPv4 infrastructure to transmit much more complex types of data, including video, audio, graphics, and voice. IPv4 can do this, but not as efficiently as is desired or required in today's world of instant mass communications. The extraordinary popularity of IPv4 has also resulted in the rapid deletion of an essential element needed of any entity that wants an Internet presence—namely an IP address Internet Protocol version 4 uses a two-level, hierarchical, addressing scheme. Part of an IPv4's address is used as a host and part as a network, as we discovered in an earlier chapter. IPv4 address classes are A, B, C, D, and E. This type of addressing scheme is not efficient for the numbers and types of networks now in place. As an example of this inefficiency, you now know that a Class A IP address has one network identifier, but up to 16 million host addresses. On the other hand, a Class C IP address has only 254 usable host addresses. The first address Class, Class A, has far too many host addresses, and the second, Class C, for most organizations, far too few. Keep in mind, though, that what IPv4 was designed for and how it ended up being used are two very different things.

Internet Protocol version 4 can be used to carry multimedia types of data, such as video and audio, but not very well. Multimedia types of data were never provided for in the IPv4 architecture, because at that time such needs did not exist. Also, very importantly, IPv4 does not inherently provide for encryption and authentication—two technologies critical to securing the enterprise. Instead, encryption and authentication technologies had to be designed around the limitations of IPv4. It would, of course, be more efficient for such capabilities to have been designed into the architecture of IPv4, but that would have required a fortune teller.

The wireless revolution has been a resounding success. What is stalling this multi-billion-dollar wireless revolution in its tracks, however, is the lack of IPv4 addressing. Wireless devices and the wireless LANs they run on must have IP addressing availability in order to fulfill their promise. Without an IP address, there is no connectivity. So-called workarounds using techniques such as network address translation (NAT), subnetting, and supernetting have helped extend IP addresses, but such techniques can only take IPv4 so far. Many believe this limit has been reached. And finally, many countries outside of the United States and Europe were not part of the initial IP address giveaway. For these countries, the lack of IP addressing would mean literally having no Internet presence.

Fortunately, all of these problems have been apparent for some time. In response, the Internet engineering community began in the early 1990s to develop a solution. That solution is IPv6, which has been designed to take into careful consideration all the limitations of IPv4.

IPv6 Address Notation

A notable feature of an IPv4 address is that it is limited to a 32-bit, or 4-byte, value. The binary equivalent of an IPv4 address is often expressed in a dotted-decimal format, such as 192.37.113.12. IPv6 uses 128 bits, or 16 bytes. Because of the length of the IPv6 address, the dotted-decimal format has been dropped. Instead, IPv6 addresses are expressed in what is called a **hexadecimal colon notation**. Hexadecimal is the base-16 numbering system, and is more efficient for expressing large numbers.

Recall that a decimal 15 is expressed as F in hexadecimal, using one character instead of two, making hexadecimal more efficient. Thirty-two hexadecimal digits can represent the 128 binary bits of a 16-byte IPv6 address. The rule is that 2 binary bytes in hexadecimal notation require 4 hexadecimal digits to be expressed. So, 16 binary bytes can be expressed in 8 groups of 4 hexadecimal digits. A colon is used to separate each set of 4 hexadecimal digits from each other. Here is an example of what could be an IPv6 address:

DA3F:38C7:1934:EC8B:5671:0000:A690:21FD

In the IPv6 addressing scheme, each 128-bit address string uniquely identifies one single networked device on the worldwide Internet. As in IPv4, there is a network and a host portion embedded within the 128-bit address. But, unlike IPv4, with IPv6 there is much greater flexibility in assigning of network and host portions within the 128-bit string. Another difference that IPv6 makes in its addressing scheme is that only three address types are allowed: unicast, multicast, and anycast. Within these three address types an additional characteristic called the address *type prefix* is used. The type prefix specifies the purpose of the address.

IPv6 Addressing Types

A **unicast** address defines one specific, networked, or host, device. No two devices can use the same unicast address, with two exceptions: the unspecified address and the loopback address. The unspecified address, represented by two colon characters (::), is used by a device, as it powers up, if that device does not know its own IP address. The unspecified address is used by that device to send a message to attached routers on the local link, asking available routers for addressing information. In this way, the device that does not know its address can be updated as to what its address is. The unspecified address is composed entirely of 0s.

The second exception, the **loopback address**, is composed entirely of 0s, except for the final bit, which is set to 1. The loopback address is represented as two colons followed by a 1 (::1). A device uses the loopback address to test itself to determine whether it has been properly configured for communication, without going out into the network. In effect, the device uses the loopback address to make sure that its software layers have been correctly set up to allow for communications.

A **multicast address** is used when a message needs to be sent to a group of devices that may or may not be on the same type prefix. The use of the multicast and the anycast addresses in IPv6 does away with broadcast packets. This is an advantage, as broadcast packets, which go to all devices on a network, consume a lot of bandwidth and are therefore inefficient. In a multicast IPv6 world, devices have to "subscribe" or sign up to a multicast group in order to receive the multicast transmission. For devices not on the same physical network that participate in a multicast group, routers must be configured as subscribers to the multicast traffic in order to pass the multicast traffic on to its intended destination.

Unlike a multicast address, the **anycast** address is for a group of devices that are of the same type prefix. The anycast address is new to IPv6. A packet addressed to an anycast address is delivered to the closest device with that address's anycast type prefix.

IPv6 Packet Format

Internet Protocol version 6 packets have three potential components: a required header, an optional extension header, and the message or payload. The required header is fixed at 40 bytes. This header has been redesigned to make processing time faster for intermediate routers and any ultimate destination devices. Six fields from the old IPv4 header have been eliminated, three fields have been updated, and two fields have been added. Of the two added fields, the class field supports prioritization packets and the flow field has been left open for future interpretation. All packets are encapsulated at the data link layer.

The IPv6-required base header includes the IP version number and source and destination addresses, as well as such important values as class value and payload length. The class value, as mentioned earlier, allows for setting of prioritization. Prioritization values are especially important as they allow IPv6 to provide a quality of service (QoS) capability. A QoS component can be critical when network congestion is occurring and certain, higher priority, data must be transmitted before lower priority data. With IPv6, congestion-controlled and noncongestion-controlled traffic can be identified; IPv4 did not have this built-in capability.

With congestion-controlled traffic, it is understood that packets may be delayed, lost, or received out of sequence. This type of traffic is assigned a priority from 0 to 7, with 7 as the highest. For noncongestion-controlled traffic, important in such applications as real-time audio or video, priority numbers from 8 to 15 are assigned. Generally, data that can experience more packet loss, because the data contain more redundancy, might be assigned a lower priority value (e.g., 8), whereas less redundant data are given a higher number (e.g., 12). The idea here is that IPv6 allows the network administrator to fine-tune the delivery of data packets, so that what is important gets through first.

From IPv4 to IPv6

The full transition from IPv4 to IPv6 will not happen over one or two years; it will more likely be a decade in the doing. Considering the huge implementation base of the current IPv4 infrastructure, moving seamlessly into the IPv6 architecture continues to be a challenge. With this in mind, the IPv6 design team has put together a set of guidelines to assist in the transition to the new Internet. Their recommendations take three approaches: dual stack, tunneling, and header translation.

The **dual stack** scenario has IP devices running both IP stacks, meaning IPv4 and IPv6. Running dual stacks is seen as a transitional phase that assists networks in gradually moving from one platform to the other. It requires more processing overhead, but it also allows IPv4 devices to communicate through and with IPv6 devices. More than likely, the most important devices in the dual stack approach will be network routers. Dual stack routers are a common means of translating between the old and new Internet architectures. Essential to the dual stack approach is the domain name system. When a device sends or receives a packet, the DNS should be able to determine whether an IPv4 or an IPv6 packet is being processed.

Tunneling is recommended when two IPv6 devices want to communicate and yet must pass through an IPv4 network. In such a scenario, the IPv6 packets are encapsulated into an IPv4 format, traverse the IPv4 infrastructure, and then are ultimately translated back into their original IPv6 form. Two types of tunneling could be implemented: automatic and configured. For *automatic tunneling*, the receiving device already uses a compatible IPv6 address, so no reconfiguration is required. If the receiving device does not support IPv6, then *configured tunneling* is required. In this scenario, routers are used as the mechanism to translate between IPv6 and IPv4. In this way, the receiving device ultimately receives the packet in the format that it understands.

Finally, with **header translation**, the assumption is that the sender needs to send an IPv6 packet through an IPv6 infrastructure, but that the receiver is still on IPv4. This scenario assumes that most of the Internet has transitioned to IPv6. In this example, the header format is changed through header translation from IPv6 into an IPv4 header. In such a case, the IPv6 mapped address is changed to an IPv4 address by evaluating the right-most 32 bits from the originating IPv6 address. Recall that an IPv4 address is 32 bits in length. The receiving IPv4 device can then process the communication.

In this discussion of addressing it must be pointed out that the IETF (Internet Engineering Task Force) has defined two types of IPv6 addressing techniques that can embed IPv4 addresses: compatible and mapped. An IPv6 compatible address has its first 96 bits set to 0, followed by a 32-bit IPv4 address. A compatible address is used when an IPv6 device wants to communicate with another IPv6 device over an IPv4 region. An IPv6 mapped address sets its first 80 bits to 0, the next 16 bits to 1, and the final 32 bits contain the embedded IPv4 address. A mapped address travels through IPv6 networks to an ultimate IPv4 device. Compatible and mapped addresses travel through networks of the opposing sorts. Both will be required as we transition from IPv4 to IPv6.

Chapter Summary

The two essential transport layer protocols are the transmission control protocol (TCP) and the user datagram protocol (UDP). The two protocols operate in very different ways. A well-known port on the Internet is an address number—specifically a port address, which is standardized or bound to a particular well-known service. Like a well-known port, a well-known service on the Internet is a standardized Internet program that is associated with a well-known port address. Port numbers are assigned by the Internet Assigned Numbers Authority (IANA; *www.iana.org*).

Each TCP/IP-based system will include a "Services" file that holds a list or inventory of the most common well-known port numbers and the well-known services to which these port numbers are assigned. The combination of an IP address and a port number is what is known as a socket. Sockets are notated by the IP address anchored at the end with a colon and the port number.

Transmission control protocol (TCP) is a connection-oriented protocol; it is also called a reliable stream transport layer service. The term *connection-oriented* applies because the sender cannot send until the receiver is contacted and agrees to a communication. This agreement establishes the connection. Transmission control protocol has much more overhead than its counterpart, user datagram protocol (UDP). The former provides for packet acknowledgment, error detection and control, and flow control. Generally, the use of TCP as a delivery service is appropriate when larger data streams that cannot fit into a single packet need to be transmitted across the network. Transmission control protocol takes a three-step approach to establishing a reliable communication.

Unlike TCP, user datagram protocol (UDP) is a connectionless, unreliable delivery service. Connectionless means that the sender does not have first to establish a link to the receiver before beginning to transmit data. Depending on the data being transmitted, UDP can be the better choice than TCP. Because UDP does not require the sender and receiver to establish a connection before sending data, time is saved, increasing efficiency. The sending host simply begins to transmit its UDP packets. If a message requires more than one datagram, the sent datagrams are treated independently. User datagram protocol does not provide for packet acknowledgment, error detection and control, or flow control.

The application layer sits at the top of the TCP/IP layer stack, directly above the transport layer. The application layer provides the user an interface and a connection to the network. Many application layer protocols follow the client/server approach. In the client/server model, a local host machine runs an application layer program called a client. The client application requests a resource from a remote host that is running a server-based application layer program. Common application layer services include, but are not limited to, Telnet, FTP, SMTP, SNMP, HTTP, and DNS.

Gradually replacing IPv4 is the new and improved Internet, IPv6 (Internet Protocol version 6), also known as IPng (Internetworking Protocol, next generation). Internet Protocol version 6 uses 128 bits, or 16 bytes. It supports three address types: unicast, multicast, and anycast. Internet Protocol version 6 packets have three potential components: a required header, an optional extension header, and the message or payload. The full transition from IPv4 to IPv6 will not happen over one or two years; it will more likely be a decade in the doing. Considering the huge implementation base of the current IPv4 infrastructure, moving seamlessly into the IPv6 architecture continues to be a challenge.

Keywords

Anycast *132*
Application layer *125*
Connectionless service *124*
Connectionless communication *124*
Connection-oriented communication *123*
Domain name system (DNS) *129*
Dual stack *133*
File transfer protocol (FTP) *126*
Header translation *133*
Hexadecimal colon notation *131*

Hypertext transfer protocol (HTTP) *128*
IPng *130*
IPv4 *130*
IPv6 *130*
Loopback address *132*
Multicast address *132*
Reliable communication *123*
Simple mail transfer protocol (SMTP) *127*
Simple network management protocol (SNMP) *128*

Socket *122*
Telnet *126*
Terminal Network *126*
Transmission control protocol (TCP) *123*
Transport layer *122*
Tunneling *133*
Unicast *132*
Unreliable communication *124*
User datagram protocol (UDP) *124*
Well-known port *122*
Well-known service *122*

Chapter Questions

Short-Answer Questions

1. What is an example of a UDP protocol?
2. How does TCP differ from UDP?
3. Under what circumstances might UDP be preferred over TCP, if ever?
4. What is a socket?
5. What is one limitation of IPv4?
6. What is meant by tunneling in relation to an IPv6 transmission?
7. How many bits and bytes are there in an IPv6 address?
8. What is meant by a unicast address?

Hands-On Projects

1. Visit *www.selfseo.com* and use a tool available there to identify the IP address of at least three websites.
2. Compare and contrast two different FTP applications.
3. Determine the type of network statistics available to SNMP through a MIB.
4. Write out socket identifiers for at least two TCP and two UDP services. Specify what they are.

Research in Brief

For one or more of the following questions, provide a one- to two-page report based on your findings.

1. Why might an organization choose a connection-oriented service over a connectionless service?

2. Visit the ICANN website and report on any latest initiative, project, or research.
3. Research and report on an application layer protocol not discussed in this chapter.
4. Compare and contrast POP3 with IMAP.

Case Study

Sheehan Marketing and Public Relations

President Sheehan is very interested in knowing how mobile apps and social media can better leverage Sheehan Marketing and Public Relations against its competitors. He wants to know what strategic values or opportunities could be made available to the company. President Sheehan has asked you to prepare a PowerPoint, or similar, presentation on this topic. He has directed you to use as your model for discussion and presentation a businesses of similar size, background, and service/product offerings as Sheehan Marketing.

Topic in Focus

THE DOMAIN NAME SYSTEM (DNS)

The domain name system, or DNS, was initially put forward in 1983 by Peter Mockapetris as two IETF (Internet Engineering Task Force) documents. A "key" intent was to create a means for allowing ordinary users of the Internet, you and me, a way of accessing remote resources without needing to know the numeric IP address of the resource. Imagine having to keep track of and memorizing long strings of numbers as opposed to names. Instead, DNS allows users to supply character-based "user-friendly" names, such as *www.pearson.com*. These user-friendly names would then would then be resolved, or equated, to the true IP address of the resource.

The domain name system performs this task by using the client/server model previously presented in this text. A client makes a request, the server fulfills the request. Simply stated, domain names are resolved to IP addresses by use of "name servers." These name servers take the entered domain name, perform a database query, and then return the IP address for that domain name. This assumes, of course, that a valid domain name was entered. Many Internet service providers, and some organizations, maintain their own DNS servers. Changes made to these servers are then propagated throughout the Internet.

Mockapetris proposed three basic elements that would compose the DNS. First, a hierarchical name space will divide the host system database into components called *domains*. Second, domain name servers will provide information about host and subdomains within a domain. And finally third, resolvers will generate requests for information from configured domain name servers. Let's see if we can put this into clearer context.

The DNS name space is based on a concept of domains. A domain has a hierarchical structure similar to a directory tree, or tree structure, in a file system. At the top of the hierarchy is the foundational root, with domains and subdomains that flow down from the root. In this context a domain is equivalent to a directory that can have other subdirectories, or subdomains, that form the directory tree. You are likely very familiar with several top-level domains.

The original DNS name space assigned seven top-level domains:

com   for commercial use

edu   for educational institutions

gov   for formal governmental institutions

int   for international organizations

mil   for military applications

net   for networking organizations

org   for not-for-profit organizations

Since its inception, other top-level domains have been introduced.

In practice, if a local network server cannot resolve an address, the local server sends out a request to the next higher DNS server. If the next higher DNS server also cannot resolve the address, that server will send out a request to the next higher server. The process continues until the address is resolved. If the address cannot be resolved—perhaps it does not exist or was not entered correctly—the appropriate error message is returned.

DNS servers are essentially database servers that store and provide information about hosts, domains, and subdomains. The client host process that generates the request using a DNS query is called a *resolver*. Basically a resolver is a set of library routines in the client's operating system that generates and sends requests to a DNS server, evaluates the returned response from the server, and then hands the response to the originating application, perhaps a web browser, for example.

Chapter

8

Local Area Networks and Backbone Networks

The Business Benefit

"Time is money," particularly for a business considering the cost of professional staff time, including that of a network technologist. Such a technologist will need good, quality documentation, so that he or she can respond effectively in a timely manner to any network infrastructure problem that might arise.

All the steps in the design and implementation of the local area network should be well documented. Is the documentation current? Is it accurate? Comprehensive? Readily available? Easily understandable? Writing good documentation is an art, and skilled technical writers are well paid. Regardless of the field of data or telecommunications in which you may find yourself, there will be times when the quality of your documentation is the only thing between you and disaster.

When the LAN is in place, continuing the documentation process will be crucial. Assume you work for a large organization that has 20 database servers in different locations of the enterprise. You have been put in charge of upgrading all database servers with a software patch critical to their functioning. Without that patch, the servers might fail or be vulnerable to outside attack. How are you going to discover where these database servers are? If your documentation is well maintained, it should tell you exactly the type, location, and address of all the servers in the enterprise.

Your documentation needs to be current, accurate, and reliable. It should be able to tell you such things as what types of NICs you are using and where; the names, locations, and addresses of all your hubs, switches, routers, and servers; the status of your licensing for the server operating system and client applications; where and what types of printers you have; how users are granted or denied login user IDs and passwords; when and how backups are performed; who is responsible for administration of each part of the network; and more.

When a valuable resource on your network becomes unavailable, there will be a cost to pay.

Learning Objectives

After studying this chapter, you should be able to:

- Describe three major topologies: star, ring, and bus.
- Describe a client/server network model.
- Describe a peer-to-peer network model.
- Identify key LAN design considerations.
- Describe backbone networks.
- Identify two forms of backbone architecture: distributed and collapsed.
- Describe simple backbone design considerations.
- Differentiate between wiring closets and data centers.

This chapter starts a different direction, addressing network models and components rather than strictly the layers of the TCP/IP model. Networks can be classified into a number of different categories. The focus of this chapter is local area networks (LANs) and backbone networks (BNs). This chapter will demonstrate how a small, relatively simple LAN can grow into a larger, more complex system. Each type of network, whether small or large, has its own issues and topics of concern. It is not unusual for a networking professional to specialize in one of these areas, or even a subset of an area. Regardless of your intended area of specialization, it is to your benefit to know something about each type of network.

LAN COMPONENTS

Good LAN design is an art, and with the rise of pervasive computing, increasingly important. LAN components are either physical or logical. *Physical* components include NICs, client devices, servers, printers, cables, hubs, switches, and routers, to name just a few. These items can be seen and touched; they require installation, configuration, and maintenance. *Logical* components typically include device drivers, network operating systems, and desktop operating systems, as well as software that can be used to monitor, troubleshoot, and evaluate the performance of a LAN. The term **troubleshoot** refers to locating and evaluating a problem so that corrective action can be taken. Troubleshooting tools may be software based, but they can also be as simple as determining if a documented chain of procedures for accomplishing steps in a process was correctly followed. Logical components, like physical components, also need to be installed, configured, and maintained.

A LAN's physical and logical components are equally important. In fact, physical components could not work without their logical counterparts, and vice versa. Physical components are frequently referred to as *hardware*. Logical components are usually called *software*, but may also include procedures that define how a particular task should be accomplished. **Software** is a set of programmed instructions that tell a device how to perform its functions. Software is executed, or run, electronically, using some type of computer processor. Whether physical or logical, successfully working with both types of components is dependent on the quality of their documentation.

An additional element in a LAN that also has physical and logical characteristics is the LAN's topology. A **topology** refers to how the pieces of a network are connected. A topology has a physical layout, which may be wired, or wireless, as well as a logical mechanism that determines how devices access the physical layout. In fact, based on your knowledge from reading previous materials, you are already familiar with two ways that devices can get access: Ethernet and token ring. Ethernet and token ring are protocols. A third topology is the **star topology**, which is most often used in mini- and mainframe computer networks.

TOPOLOGIES

Topologies determine not only how devices are connected to each other but also how they access the media they use for communication. A topology is both physical and logical. However, a network's logical layout may differ from its physical layout. What you physically see may not represent what is logically happening in the LAN. Classic Ethernet is a bus topology. Ethernet and variations of it are by far the most commonly deployed topology in LANs today. There is some controversy with the advent of switching technology as to whether an Ethernet LAN that uses switches can still be called a bus. We discuss this in more detail later in this chapter. First, two other types of topologies are briefly explored, if only for historical interest: star and ring.

Star Topology

A traditional star topology is configured such that a central controlling device has other networked devices connected to it by point-to-point circuits. Each connected device typically has two point-to-point circuits, one for sending and one for receiving. The central controlling device is often a mini- or mainframe computer. Devices connected to the mini- or mainframe are usually referred to as *terminals*. For terminals to communicate with each other or with the mini- or mainframe, they must work through the central controlling device. This type of topology can be useful in certain wide area network (WAN) situations whereby applications in outlying offices must communicate with a central office. Figure 8.1 demonstrates a standard physical and

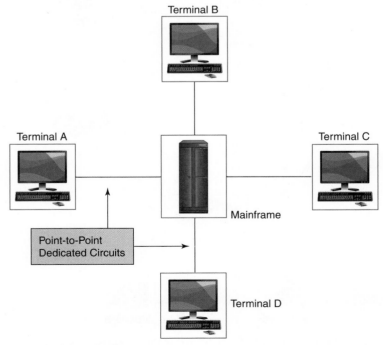

FIGURE 8.1 A Standard Star Topology

logical star topology. An advantage of the star topology is that it centralizes key network resources, such as data and applications. This centralization simplifies network management.

Ring Topology

IBM introduced the ring topology. It uses a single cable such that the cable ends meet and form a closed loop. IBM also introduced the token ring protocol, which is associated with the ring topology. This might seem confusing, but a topology and a protocol are not the same thing. Think of a *topology* as how devices are to be physically connected and the *protocol* as that which controls or manages the connection. Physically, a network using a ring topology looks somewhat like a star, because each networked device is connected directly to a central media access unit (MAU). The MAUs connect the devices to the ring. Logically, however, the cables connected through the MAUs function as a true ring. Figure 8.2 illustrates a ring topology using MAUs.

Bus Topology

The **bus topology**, like the ring, views its circuit as a single cable. Unlike the ring, the cable does not form a closed loop. Devices connect to the central cable, using it as a communications pipeline. The protocol most often associated with the bus topology is **Ethernet**. The IEEE has formalized the bus protocol as Ethernet 802.3. A bus topology uses a **broadcast** mechanism. With classic Ethernet, when a device puts its data packet on the bus, the packet is broadcasted, or sent, to all the devices on the bus.

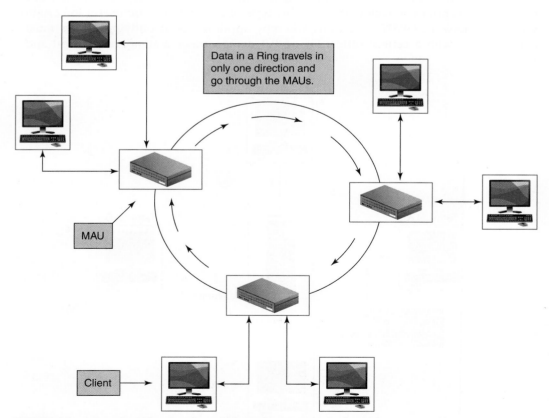

Data in a Ring travels in only one direction and go through the MAUs.

MAU

Client

FIGURE 8.2 A Standard Ring Topology with Media Access Units (MAUs)

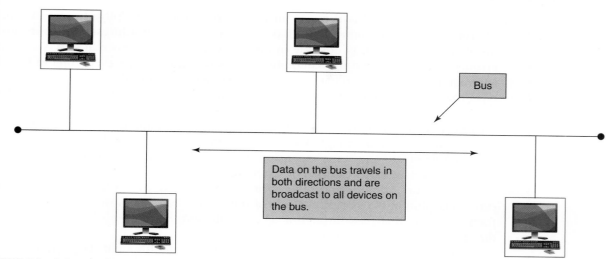

FIGURE 8.3   A Standard Bus Using a Broadcast

All devices evaluate the packet to determine whether it is addressed to them or not. Devices ignore packets not addressed to them and process those that are. In addition, only one device at a time can use the bus for communication.

The bus topology, using the 802.3 protocol, is a contention-based topology. Devices contend for access to the communication circuit by means of CSMA/CD (carrier sense multiple access/collision detection). It is theoretically possible in a classic 802.3 network with heavy traffic that some devices will never gain access to the communication circuit. In addition, overall network performance can rapidly degrade when too many devices attempt to use the shared circuit at one time. However, an 802.3 LAN is moderately easy to install and configure and uses relatively inexpensive cabling. Cost has made the 802.3 the king of choice in current LAN topologies. Figure 8.3 shows an example of a traditional bus topology using broadcasting.

Later in this chapter, you will learn how Ethernet has been modified to significantly improve performance and provide improved balance of access to all connected devices. Switching technology has transformed how Ethernet is configured. Regardless of the topology, a variety of physical hardware elements are used to make the LAN operational. The next section reviews some of these elements.

PHYSICAL ELEMENTS: HARDWARE

A LAN might use many different types of physical components, or **hardware**. It is not possible to describe them all in this text. Instead, this text identifies some of the most common LAN hardware elements, explaining their purpose and operation. Many of these elements were introduced in earlier chapters.

NETWORK INTERFACE CARDS

An essential hardware component that each device on a LAN must have in order to communicate is a network interface card, or NIC (pronounced "nick"). A NIC is also known as an **adapter card**. As you now know, each NIC has a physical MAC layer address. A physical address is an address that is specific, unique, and assigned to one and only one NIC.

A NIC's physical address is, in fact, part of the card's physical manufacture. Therefore, if two or more NICs have the same physical address, communication problems will occur. It is possible in the manufacturing process that two NICs could erroneously be assigned the same physical address. In such an event, one of the two NICs would have to be replaced. In a TCP/IP network, any device, regardless of its type, that is connected to the network is referred to as a *host*. A host might be a client machine, a server, a printer, or any other type of device connected to the network. That host, however, must have a NIC that allows it to communicate on the network.

Many NICs are internal to the host, meaning that on a typical microcomputer, the NIC is plugged into one of the expansion slots available on the computer's motherboard. Network interface cards can also be external, possibly connected to a computer's serial or parallel port. Laptops and other types of portable devices often make use of PC cards that plug into a slot. Regardless of the kind of NIC, its most important job is to frame the data that pass through it. The quality and capabilities of a NIC can have a direct effect on the performance of a LAN.

Choosing the most appropriate NIC requires some thought. Depending on the type of host, the capabilities of the NIC can be critical. For example, a file server that services many clients should have a NIC that is fast and has sufficient throughput so that the device it is connected to, in this case a file server, does not become a bottleneck, slowing the network down. So what factors should one consider when selecting a NIC?

First, what is the NIC's **bus width**? A bus is like a multilane highway, providing the circuitry paths along which data bits flow. The wider the bus, the more data bits the bus can transmit at one time. A 32-bit bus can handle four times the data bits of an 8-bit bus. For a high-end server, you would likely want a wide bus, perhaps 64-bit, whereas for a low-end device, a 16-bit bus may be sufficient. Second, how much memory, and of what type, does the NIC support? This memory is also called the NIC's *buffer,* or **cache**. A NIC's cache is used to temporarily hold data to be processed and assists in speeding up the performance of the LAN. Typically, the larger the cache, the better the performance of the NIC.

Two other NIC memory-related questions need to be addressed. First, does the NIC support direct memory access? **Direct memory access (DMA)** is the capability of the NIC to directly use the host device's memory. Second, does the NIC support **bus mastering**—a technique that incorporates a CPU (central processing unit) on the NIC? Through bus mastering, a NIC can process incoming data without having to wait for the host's CPU to do the job.

A NIC's bus width and memory capabilities have a direct impact on its throughput capability. Throughput for a NIC is a measure of how many bits it can process within one second. An Ethernet NIC can have a throughput of 10 or 100 Mbps. Gigabit Ethernet adapters can support up to 1 Gbps (billion bits per second) or 1,000 Mbps. Generally, the higher the throughput, the higher the cost of the NIC. Not all network devices require the highest level of throughput. Part of your analysis as a network administrator will be to determine what is cost-effective in terms of the NIC that you deploy in your organization. A NIC might cost $20 or $1,000, depending on its capabilities. In an organization with 5,000 hosts, you can see that cost becomes a major consideration.

An Ethernet bus is by far the most commonly deployed topology in LANs today due to its ease of installation and relatively low cost. Consequently, most NICs use Ethernet physical addressing. (NIC addresses, by the way, are assigned and allocated in blocks to card manufacturers by the IEEE.) An Ethernet NIC address consists of 48 bits composed of 12 hexadecimal digits. Hexadecimal, or hex, is the base-16 numbering system. Hex uses the values 0 through 9 and the capital letters

A through F. In hex, A is 10, B is 11, C is 12, D is 13, E is 14, and F is 15. For conversion then, a decimal 10 is a hex A, a decimal 11 is a hex B, and so on, for a maximum up to 15, or F. Ethernet MAC addresses are usually expressed in hex octets. An octet is equivalent to eight bits. An Ethernet MAC NIC address might then look like this:

08:00:5A:28:E4:F8

The first six hex digits specify the NIC's manufacturer. The last six hex digits specify the interface serial number. Note the use of the word *digit*, keeping in mind that in hex, the capital letter A is the hex-digit equivalent of the decimal 10; E is 14, and F is 15. Manufacturers of NIC are allocated specific numeric ranges. In our example, 08:00:5A identifies that the NIC was manufactured by IBM. The 48-bit Ethernet MAC numbering scheme allows for almost 300,000,000,000,000 unique addresses. As more devices (e.g., household appliances) become network aware and require a MAC address, this huge quantity of Ethernet NIC addresses will be quite useful.

Like most hardware devices, NICs also have a logical component—in this case, a device driver. **Device drivers** are software programs that control the NIC and allow it to work in association with the host device's network operating system. When purchasing a NIC, it is important to determine if that NIC's driver is compatible with the network operating system in use. It should never be assumed that a given NIC will function in all types of networks. Many NICs do support multiple protocols and can be configured to support differing network environments. However, you should always first consult the NIC's documentation to determine if multiple protocols are supported.

MEDIA

There are several forms of physical layer media that can be used in a data communications network. (*Media* is plural, providing for several types. *Medium* is singular, referring to one specific type.) An essential physical component of a LAN is the physical medium over which data are transmitted over the network. Today, the most common LAN medium is **unshielded twisted-wire pair (UTP)**. It is inexpensive and very flexible and can be made to fit into tight places. Newer buildings typically have UTP automatically installed.

Available in several categories, UTP Category 5, 5e, or 6 has become the most common medium found in LANs because of its low cost, ease of installation, and high transmission capacity. As Ethernet has evolved, the type and quality of cabling used to configure an Ethernet network has also evolved. Cat 5, or 5e, has over time mostly replaced Cat 3 as the UTP cable of choice. In due course, Cat 5 will gradually be replaced with Cat 6, a higher-quality UTP.

The UTP cable category classification determines the maximum number of bits that the cable can transmit. A higher cable category number represents a larger cable size. A larger cable size results in less resistance to the signal being carried on the cable. Reduced resistance translates into higher transmission speeds.

Cat 5 is used in segments no longer than 100 meters. Segments are connected by RJ-45 connectors. Typical Cat 5 speeds range from 10 to 100 Mbps. An enhanced version of Cat 5 is available if Gigabit Ethernet is being considered. For some LANs, Gigabit Ethernet provides more transmission capacity than is needed; consequently, it is not very cost-effective. Backbone networks, which demand much greater throughput capacity, can more adequately take advantage of a gigabit connection. Network wiring usually runs from all connected devices to a communications wiring closet.

Wiring closets should be physically secured and locked to prevent unauthorized access. Keep in mind that the length of a cable segment must include the full path from the networked device to the communications closet. In many cases, the signal in the closet is regenerated before it is sent to other areas of the network. When a signal is **regenerated**, it is in effect reissued or re-created at its original strength in order to send the signal to other parts of the network or enterprise.

SERVERS

Servers are critical to the enterprise. Because of their importance, an entire chapter of this text is devoted to servers. Servers are computers that fulfill specific, specialized functions. They allow LAN resources to be made available for multiple users to share and utilize. Local area network resources can include, among other things, printers, applications, data, information, files, databases, security services, directory services, modems, web hosting, and e-mail—basically anything that a group of users would need to have access to. Very popular are Blade servers, which are designed to fit into existing servers. Due to their modularity, blade servers are small and cost-efficient. Because blade servers are usually smaller, they also consume less power. Blade servers plug into a chassis in the housing unit. (A good website to look up unfamiliar technology terms is *www.webopedia.com*.)

Because servers can share resources, they provide significant cost savings to a business. For example, rather than purchasing individual printers for each user, users can access a pool of common printers managed by a print server. Or, for applications that are widely used, it is cheaper to buy a networkable version of an application and share it across the LAN using an application server instead of buying individual user licenses. Keep in mind that for such sharing to work, the resource must be capable of being accessed or distributed across a network.

Not all devices or applications are network compatible. In addition, for a resource that is mission critical—meaning that the resource must be available when the user requires it—redundant servers may be needed to manage that resource. A single server that manages an essential resource is also a potential single source for failure. If that server fails or crashes, for whatever reason, the resource it manages also becomes unavailable. This can be particularly troublesome for servers that authenticate users to the network. If that server fails, no one can login to the network. In such cases, redundant servers are essential. However, redundancy, although providing fault tolerance and improved security, is also an added expense.

The type of server chosen and its capabilities will be based on the tasks the server is expected to perform. Some resource-intensive services, such as managing and making databases available, require relatively powerful servers. In contrast, a print server that manages 10 or fewer printers can be an inexpensive low-end device. Servers also require controlling and managing software. Such software is called a *network operating system (NOS)* or *server operating system (SOS)*. Depending on the scale of the LAN, the choice of server operating system will be important. Some server operating systems are designed for very small LANs having 20 or fewer networked devices. Larger, more complicated LANs that have hundreds of users require more sophisticated server operating systems.

CLIENTS

Servers have become an essential LAN tool, but they are essential only because they provide access to resources required by users. Without users, there would be no need for servers, or even for the LAN itself. Users connect to the LAN and to server resources using **client** devices. Thus, LAN clients are another hardware component of the LAN architecture. Although client devices are usually associated with human users, this is not always the case. A LAN client can also be another machine, such as a printer. In a TCP/IP LAN, networked devices, like clients, are referred to as **hosts**. Each host has a physical address identified by its NIC as well as a logical network address. A client's logical network address in TCP/IP version 4 is based on a 32-bit binary number that has to be configured in order for that client to connect to the LAN. In TCP/IP version 6, a 128-bit binary number is used.

Today, clients encompass a wide array of devices. For example, a smart phone or a digital table could be a network client. The most common client device, though, is a microcomputer, or desktop, of some type. Based on the needs of the user, the client computer may be a standard, moderately scaled device, or a very powerful computer. Powerful user computers capable of performing complex and sophisticated applications are usually referred to as **workstations**.

Whether the client is a digital tablet, a simple $500 desktop, or a $10,000 workstation, it uses some type of user-oriented client operating system. Modern client operating systems are often already network aware. This means that the client operating system software contains the necessary functionalities that allow that client to recognize and be easily configured for common network layer protocols.

The TCP/IP incorporates protocols at the network layer as well as at the transport and application layers. Clients login to the network in order to access its resources. Typical login components include a user ID and a password. As part of the login process, clients are validated and authenticated. Assuming they pass this process, the clients are then able to use those resources for which they have been previously configured. This type of LAN—one that uses dedicated servers and independent clients—is called the **client/server model**.

Another type of model used in very small networks (those typically with 15 machines or fewer) is the **peer-to-peer model**. With a peer-to-peer LAN, a specialized server operating system is not required. Instead, the networking capabilities provided in client operating systems are used. In this type of network, a device, depending on how it is set up, can function as a client, as a server, or both. Since *peer* means "equal," in a peer-to-peer network, computers are equal in what they may be configured to do. If a user's computer is attached to a printer, the user can use the client operating system's networking ability to share that printer with other users. To do so, the administrator would have to set up an account for each user who wants to access the printer over the network. For a few users, this is not too complicated.

However, if a network grows beyond a certain point, again approximately 15 user stations, then setting up and maintaining user accounts on a peer-to-peer network begins to get complicated and unmanageable. Very likely, other users on the smaller LAN will also have resources that they need to share. User accounts have to be set up on each of these machines as well. If the network grows, and the number of resources to share also increases, the peer-to-peer model no longer functions very well. At that point the administrator would likely move to a client/server model, which provides greater control for larger groups of users.

Ethernet is the most common LAN architecture. Over time, Ethernet has evolved into several flavors. Standard 10-Mbps Ethernet LANs use traditional hubs and bridges, maintaining the classic bus architecture. Then there are Ethernet LANs—including Standard, Fast, and Gigabit Ethernet—that use switches rather than hubs. Today, most Ethernet LANs are more likely to use switches than hubs. This makes for a significant difference in how an Ethernet circuit is shared.

Because of how switches function, contention and collision—the defining characteristics of an Ethernet bus—are no longer a factor. The question then becomes, if an Ethernet network is no longer limited or defined by the need for collision detection, is it still an Ethernet network, or is it something else? We defer that decision to the various standards-setting bodies, particularly the IEEE, and present here that switched Ethernet is still Ethernet. The point is that newer forms of Ethernet differ from the older, traditional bus topology and result in faster, more efficient transmission capacity. To learn more about the different forms that Ethernet can take, read the Topic in Focus at the end of this chapter.

SWITCHES AND ROUTERS

As a LAN grows, it may be necessary to begin to segment the LAN in order to keep performance at adequate levels. A critical indicator of performance is the response time necessary to fulfill a request. When there are too many users on the same segment of a LAN, traffic can cause the network to slow to an unacceptable pace. In that case, different types of hardware devices can be used to segment the network. Two devices in particular have become very prominent in LAN architectures: switches and routers. As you now know, switches are often associated with the data link layer, or layer 2. Routers are associated with the network layer, or layer 3. Certain switches called *multilayer switches* can function at either layer 2 or layer 3.

Multilayer switches are more complicated, sophisticated, intelligent, and expensive than single-layer switches. The choice of going with multilayer switches, then, should be evaluated based on a cost-benefit analysis. One option is to use multilayer switches only in select circumstances and to use layer 2 switches in all other cases. Switches in general cost far less than routers. As switching capabilities continue to improve, especially with layer 2 switches becoming more intelligent, switches are increasingly being implemented where routers were once used. Routers are now more commonly being deployed as devices at the edge of the network. Much more expensive than switches, routers are also more complicated to configure and manage. However, routers perform functions that switches cannot, hence their continued importance. For an organization that has many networks, routers are required for the networks to be able to communicate with each other. Every network has its own logical identifier.

If a host on network A wants to send a packet to a host on network B, a layer 2 switch will not be able to route the packet to its correct destination. A layer 2 switch recognizes only its own network. A router, however, recognizes different networks by their addresses. Routers use tables that contain addresses of networks that they can reach and addresses of other routers that they may need to send a packet to in order for that packet to reach its final destination. A router's address table may be manually or dynamically updated based on the router type.

Because a router uses addressing tables, it does not broadcast packets. A broadcast sends a packet to all hosts on a network. Through addressing, a router determines exactly where to send the packet. Based on the network layer address attached to the packet, a router recognizes the next step the packet should take on its journey. Because packets are not broadcast, traffic is reduced. A router can also connect networks that use different topologies or architectures; for example, it can connect a token ring with an Ethernet network. Hubs and switches connect networks of the same architecture. Routers act like hosts on a network, but unlike an ordinary host, a router has addresses on, and links to, multiple networks at the same time. Put simply, routers accept packets from one logical network and pass them forward to a second connected logical network. A backbone network connects the many networks of a single enterprise.

NETWORK/SERVER OPERATING SYSTEMS

Today, most LANs are of the client/server model and use some form of server software. Server software makes up the bulk of a **network operating system (NOS)**. The NOS controls and manages the servers. Because of this server focus, some networking professionals refer to a NOS as a **server operating system (SOS)**. The TCP/IP protocol suite has become the platform of choice for many common SOSs.

Older, legacy network operating systems had an additional client component that had to be installed on each client in order for that client to connect to the network. Today, most modern client operating systems automatically provide networking capability, especially for TCP/IP, thus the client element is usually no longer be required. The server operating system controls the means by which client hosts connect to the LAN in order to access server resources. Depending on the NOS, many types of server resources can be managed. One essential aspect of a NOS is its ability to authenticate and validate users who are attempting to login to the network. Login usually requires the user to have both a user ID and a password. How complex the user ID and password are, how frequently user passwords must be changed, and how user IDs and passwords are created, maintained, and distributed are based on network administration policies. The more important security is, the tighter and more defined network administration policies are, or at least should be.

Something to keep in mind is that server operating systems are not applications in the sense of user tools such as word processors and spreadsheets. Rather, a server operating system is used to interface with user applications and make those applications available to the user. It is fairly common for application software to be installed and managed on application servers. Cost savings usually result when a business is able to put a networkable version of an application on a server and then have the server manage and distribute the application across the network. In this way, the business does not need to buy individual user licenses for each client, but instead achieves economies of scale by purchasing either a metered or site license for application products.

LICENSING

A **metered license** is one whereby the server is programmed to count how many users are currently using a given product. When a certain number has been reached, a number determined by the metered-license agreement, the server prevents new users from accessing the product. Once the metered value has been reached, a current user has to log out of the application for a new user to access it. An analysis should be performed to determine what the most effective metered value should be. If it is too small, users will become frustrated because they will not be able to access the application. If the value is too large, the business will be paying for licenses that it is not using. A balance has to be determined.

In contrast, a **site license** covers the entire site so that anyone validated by the network can access the application as needed. Typically, a site license costs more than a metered license, but it is still less than purchasing an individual license for everybody. The size of the site will depend on the business, which may have, say, as few as 50 or as many as 10,000 users. Metered and site licensing are similar in that they are both used to determine how many copies of a software program or application an organization is legally authorized to use.

LAN DESIGN CONSIDERATIONS

Having identified the physical and hardware components of a LAN, the question becomes one of how to put these elements together when designing the network. No two businesses are exactly alike, so network needs will vary. Several factors can guide the design of a LAN. The factors listed in this section are not the only ones, of course, but they are likely ones that most network designers would address when designing a LAN. Figure 8.4 illustrates that LAN design is a cyclical process, meaning that once a LAN is implemented, it must continually be evaluated and improved.

Perhaps one of the most important items to consider is the budget. Businesses want the best technology, the fastest throughput, and the highest level of security, but many may not be able to afford them. Realistic budget data are needed in order to determine the type of network that can be configured. The budget will affect the number and type of servers that are installed, the quality of the NICs used on all host devices, the number of clients and servers, the server operating system, software licensing, the type of cabling, staffing for installation and maintenance, and whether hubs, switches, or routers are used.

The list could go on, but you probably get the point. You cannot know what you can build until you know how much you can afford. A budget gives you a baseline from which the best alternative solutions can be pursued. Part of this decision process may involve the solicitation of **request for purchase (RFP)** proposals from various networking vendors. It is usually good to have competing bids, but you need to be very clear as to what it is you are requesting bids for. Good systems analysis skills are essential.

Local area network design must address the types of applications that the LAN is expected to support. Applications such as digital/video editing are resource and bandwidth intensive and require an infrastructure that can support such needs. However, if the business primarily makes use of low-end, text-driven types of data applications, then bandwidth and throughput requirements will be far less demanding. For the applications used, how, where, and when are they to be distributed? Do users expect 24/7 remote and local access or is the business run along the lines of a more traditional 9-to-5, five-days-a-week operation?

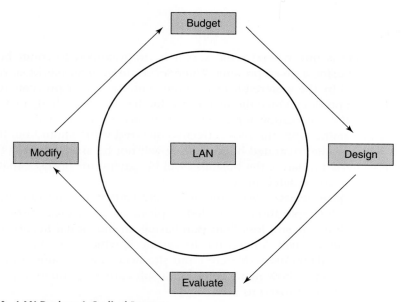

FIGURE 8.4 LAN Design: A Cyclical Process

In addition, you should ask yourself the following questions: In what type of facility is the network to be installed? Is there appropriate air conditioning and/or air filtration for sensitive equipment, if such equipment is required? Are server rooms and wiring closets expected? If so, are they available? If wiring closets are required, but not currently available, is there space for their construction? Does the facility accommodate the types of cabling your network may demand? Will walls, floors, or ceilings be affected by wiring needs? If your approach is wireless, do any walls or other obstructions prevent line-of-sight access? Is the facility on a factory floor where powerful electrical and/or magnetic equipment may be used? If so, the installation of your network must take that into consideration.

The LAN design should also address the scale of the network. Is the network for a small business of 10 employees or will it need to support 1,000? Scale will also impact your level of staffing. Very small networks may have only one person who performs all tasks: installation, configuration, maintenance, troubleshooting, user and technical support, and so on. Larger networks will likely require dedicated staff with specific and identified responsibilities. Is there sufficient staff to support the network proposed? If not, is such staff available for hire? If so, at what cost? Also, for future reference, how do you plan to keep your technical and user staff trained as your network evolves with changing technologies?

As businesses of all sizes depend on networking technologies, and as access to these technologies has become universally prevalent, the importance of network security has also increased significantly. How does your LAN design account for securing the network? What procedures determine who has access to the network? Are critical pieces of equipment—such as servers, switches, and routers—protected and secured from unauthorized access? What policies are in place that protect against intrusion into the network by unauthorized individuals? Does your LAN design need to make use of such technologies as firewalls, encryption, or multiple layers of login authentication? What areas of the network are most vulnerable? What applications and data are critical to the business, such that if they were lost, stolen, or corrupted, lasting damage would result? In that event, does your LAN design include backup and recovery procedures? Have those procedures been tested? How frequently are they tested? As you can see, many questions will need to be answered.

BACKBONE NETWORKS

A small organization might have only one LAN; larger organizations might have dozens or hundreds. Organizations with multiple LANs will want these LANs to communicate with each other, not only to share physical resources, such as printers, but also data, information, authentication, and software. Connecting all of the LANs of an organization entails another type of network—a **backbone** network (BN). When properly designed, a BN provides a high-speed circuit that serves as the central conduit across which the LANs of an organization can communicate.

Not surprisingly, backbone networks have their own issues and topics of interest. They can be used to connect LANs within a building, across a campus, and, increasingly, across much greater distances. An organization might also utilize a metropolitan area network (MAN). A MAN spans a city and is often used to connect remote BNs. In a very real sense, a MAN is a citywide backbone. In fact, as backbone technologies have evolved, and as the geographic distances they cover have increased, especially with the use of fiber-optics, it is becoming increasing difficult to determine whether a particular network is a BN, a MAN, or even a WAN. Today, backbone networks connect networks between floors of a building, across a city, or between states and countries. Because of the importance of BNs to data communications, this chapter emphasizes backbone networks. However, much of the information presented holds true for a MAN as well. The terms *BN* and *MAN* are sometimes used interchangeably, based on the scope of the BN.

NETWORK SEGMENTS

Each individual LAN owned by an organization is a network segment. A moderate- or large-scale organization might have a network segment on each floor of a multistory building. Because each network segment, or LAN, typically occupies its own floor, this type of network segment is often referred to as a **horizontal network**. For example, assume that a business occupies three floors of a building. On each floor is a separate LAN, or horizontal network segment. In addition, each of these LANs could, and probably would, be connected to each other by a vertical BN. This type of multifloor connection is an example of a vertical BN, whereby multiple LANs on separate floors of a multistory building are connected vertically to each other by a backbone network. The BN in this instance is the central connecting cable running vertically from floor to floor that enables the horizontal networks to communicate with each other. Figure 8.5 compares a horizontal network with a vertical one.

As indicated by its name, a BN is a network of its own. Besides connecting the various network segments, the backbone may have its own devices that can be accessed by other network segments. Later in the chapter you will see how this might work.

SIMPLE HORIZONTAL NETWORK VERSUS A VERTICAL NETWORK

Horizontal LANs on different floors of a building being connected vertically to a BN is fairly common. However, it may be the case that the network segments are housed in a large, single-story warehouse such that each network segment is on the same horizontal plane. In this case, the BN that connects the LANs, rather than being vertical, is also horizontal, as illustrated in Figure 8.6. The physical facility in which the networks are housed determines how the BN is or can be configured.

Part of configuration analysis includes determining how each network segment connects to the backbone network. Generally, each network segment is connected to the BN using either a switch or a router. Switches and routers enable a host on one LAN to communicate with a host on any other LAN that is connected to the backbone. The choice of which connecting device to use—switch or router—depends on how the network is to be used. Because routers are typically more expensive than switches, part of the BN configuration analysis includes determining whether the right device is in the most effective location. However, one of the first decisions to be made regarding a BN is deciding which type of BN protocol to use.

BACKBONE PROTOCOLS

Of the many factors that will influence your decision as to which BN protocol to use, one key factor stands out: What are the traffic demands of the network segments to be supported? For example, are the various LANs connected to the backbone in constant communication with each other? Or, do the individual network segments work mostly independently of each other?

In the first case, the BN needs to support high traffic demand. This means that the BN protocol selected should support higher throughput than the protocol used by the LANs. Assume that all the network segments connected to the backbone use Fast Ethernet and that the network segments communicate extensively with each other.

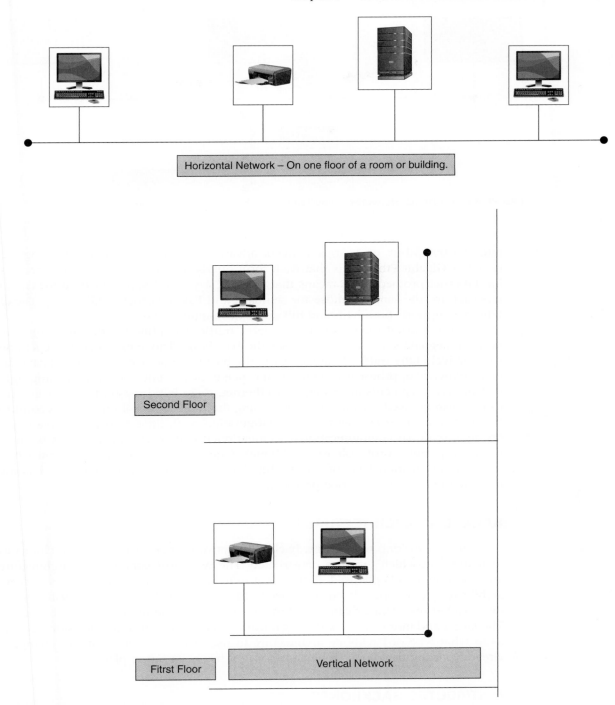

Horizontal Network – On one floor of a room or building.

Second Floor

Fitrst Floor

Vertical Network

FIGURE 8.5   A Simple Horizontal versus Vertical Network

If the backbone is going to adequately support this amount of traffic, it will need a protocol that offers a faster throughput than Fast Ethernet. A logical choice would be to run the BN using Gigabit Ethernet.

In fact, Gigabit Ethernet is a very popular choice for BNs. The IEEE's initial standard for Gigabit Ethernet is the 802.3z standard. Gigabit Ethernet allows for a data

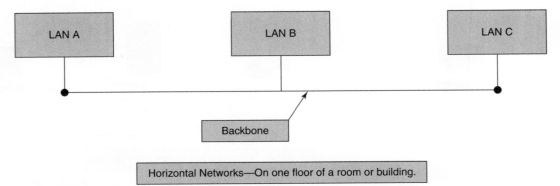

FIGURE 8.6 Horizontal Networks Connected by a Backbone on a Single Floor

rate of 1,000 Mbps, or 1 Gbps. A major advantage of all of the officially recognized forms of Gigabit Ethernet is that each form builds on the standards of the preexisting Ethernet protocol. This means that the MAC layer and access method for Gigabit Ethernet are the same as those for standard and Fast Ethernet. Additionally, Gigabit Ethernet supports both half- and full-duplex communications.

In the second case, assume that most traffic is confined within the individual network segments and rarely traverses the backbone. This means that the backbone has relatively little traffic. In such a case, the backbone does not require a faster, and more expensive, protocol to support the needs of the enterprise. Supposing again that the LAN segments are using Fast Ethernet, there is no reason that Fast Ethernet cannot also be used for the backbone. Using the same protocol for the LANs and the BN results in lower cost and easier configuration, with little, if any, negative impact on organizational communications. As mentioned earlier, Gigabit Ethernet is one of the most popular protocols for backbones. One of the reasons for its popularity is the wide installation base of standard and Fast Ethernet. Gigabit Ethernet has thus become the leading backbone protocol.

BACKBONE ARCHITECTURES

Like any networking technology, backbone networks have a backbone architecture, or manner in which they are constructed. The two most common BN architectures are distributed and collapsed. Factors that influence a business's decision as to which architecture to use include business needs, the condition of the physical facility (sometimes called the plant or campus), how users need to communicate, and the budget. The larger and more complex the organization, the more critical the decision becomes as to what type of backbone architecture to use. It can be very costly to change an already existing backbone architecture once it has been put in place.

DISTRIBUTED BACKBONES

The word *distributed* means "in more than one location." A **distributed backbone** is one that runs throughout the entire enterprise. This type of backbone uses a central cable to which the network segments are connected. The central cable, which is the backbone, requires its own protocol, such as Gigabit Ethernet; it is also its own network. The backbone is considered to be distributed because each network segment has its own cabled connection to the backbone. The backbone is distributed to the LANs by connecting the LANs to the backbone.

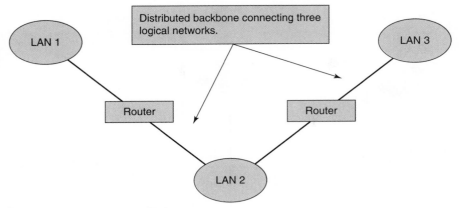

FIGURE 8.7   A Simple Distributed Backbone

Local area networks may be connected to the backbone by either switches or routers. Other devices, such as servers, can also be attached to the backbone. A server connected directly to a backbone is part of that backbone's network; it is not part of one of the LANs connected to the backbone. Shortly you will see why having certain types of servers, or other devices, directly connected to the distributed backbone cable can be a good idea. Figure 8.7 illustrates a simple distributed backbone.

A distributed backbone typically has separate routers that connect each logical network to the backbone. Because separate routers are used, internetwork traffic may have to pass through several routers to reach its destination. The more routers a packet has to pass through, and the greater the internetwork traffic, the more likely communications will be delayed. Additionally, because each network segment has its own cabling and connecting device to the backbone, distributed networks can be costly. Security, maintenance, and monitoring of a distributed backbone are also complicated because the connecting resources are distributed.

However, depending on the layout of the enterprise, a distributed backbone may be the only practical solution. For example, it may be that the distance of the network segments from the backbone to which they must be connected is too great for a copper cable to support. In this case, a collapsed backbone, discussed shortly, is not possible, and a distributed one will have to be deployed.

One advantage of a distributed backbone is that it allows resources required by most, if not all, internetworking users to be placed directly on the BN. Assume that an organization has a customer database server located on LAN A that is to be used by all of the other network segments. If for some reason LAN A becomes unavailable—perhaps the room in which LAN A is housed has a power failure—then the customer database server is unavailable to the entire organization. Even if LAN A remains available, because it has the database server, all internetwork traffic for that database server goes to LAN A, which may become overwhelmed by the resulting traffic. The result is that no one gets access to the server.

A better solution would be to put resources required by most network segments on the backbone network itself, as shown in Figure 8.8. In this example, the database server is placed directly on the backbone. Usually, the backbone has a higher bandwidth capacity than the networks connected to it, allowing for a faster and more reliable response. Such a scenario is possible on a distributed backbone, but not on a collapsed one. The following discussion describes why this is so.

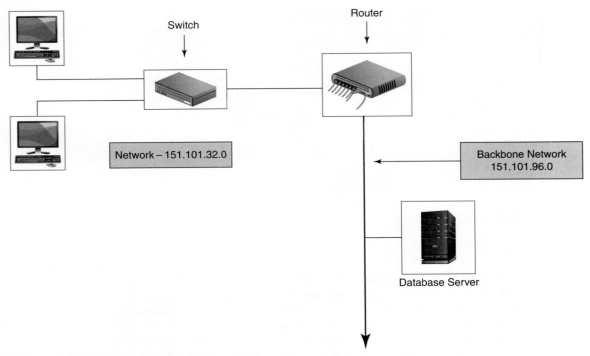

FIGURE 8.8   Database Server Directly Connected to Backbone

COLLAPSED BACKBONES

Essentially, a **collapsed backbone** connects all network segments to a central, single router or switch. This central device is, in effect, the backbone. The network segments typically connect to the central backbone device by means of a hub, switch, or router. Because only a single, central backbone device is used, cabling is greatly reduced. Furthermore, additional connecting devices are not required. A collapsed backbone can result in significant cost savings. Also, because the collapsed backbone is a device and does not use a central cable, as does a distributed backbone, a separate protocol for the backbone is not required. This means, for example, that a collection of Fast Ethernet network segments could connect to a Fast Ethernet-based switch or router. A collapsed backbone's central connecting router or switch makes use of something called a *backplane*.

A backplane is an internal, high-speed communications bus that is used in place of the connecting cables found in a distributed backbone. A communication bus is like a highway that enables components and devices to transmit data between themselves, and thereby communicate. The hubs, switches, and routers of the organization's network segments plug directly into the collapsed backbone's backplane. In a typical configuration, the hubs and switches of a collection of 100Base-TX copper-based network segments are connected to a 100Base-FX switch or router by fiber-optic cabling. The switch or router then routes the traffic between the various network segments. Figure 8.9 shows a simple collapsed backbone. Because fiber-optic cabling is used to connect network segments to the collapsed backbone's backplane, long distances are possible. With fiber-optic cabling, network segments may be widely scattered across a building or even a campus.

Legacy Ethernet networks, however, may not be able to utilize a collapsed backbone architecture. Remember that the term *legacy* describes older technologies that

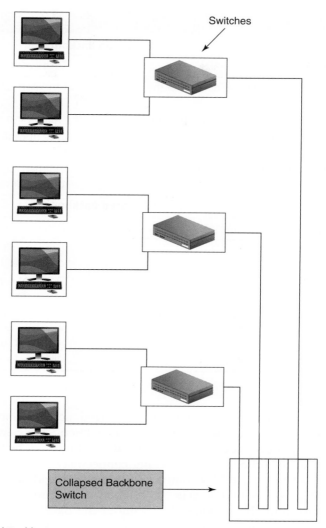

FIGURE 8.9 A Simple Collapsed Backbone

are still in use and that must still be supported. An organization may have legacy Ethernet 10-Mbps networks that use older media such as Category 3 UTP or Thin Ethernet cabling. These types of media cannot support long cable runs to a distantly located collapsed backbone device. If the legacy network segments are in different buildings, the problem of connecting to a central collapsed backbone only increases. One solution to this problem would be to upgrade legacy networks to current standards. An alternative solution would be to use a distributed backbone. Either option should be evaluated with a cost-benefit analysis. A factor in this analysis should be the future needs of the organization. Keep in mind that the wiring, configuration, and installation of network cabling are some of the most significant costs a business incurs. However, this cost can be depreciated over time. Different options will afford different break-even timelines.

A major advantage of a collapsed backbone configuration is that internetwork traffic has to pass through only one device, usually a router, on its way to its final destination. However, each hub or switch for each network segment must be able to span the distance to the central router, or collapsed backbone. Another benefit is that

Table 8.1 Advantages/Disadvantages of Distributed and Collapsed Backbones	

Distributed Backbones

Advantages	Disadvantages
Allows places of devices directly on the backbone	Increased cabling costs
Usually offers a higher bandwidth capacity	Complex to manage due to distribution
Can support Legacy Ethernet Networks	Type of cabling used may not support long distances between networks and backbone
Well suited for networks that may be widely separated from each other	Internetwork traffic may need to pass through several intermediary devices

Collapsed Backbones

Advantages	Disadvantages
Reduced cabling costs	Does not allow for placing devices directly on the backbone
Easier to manage due to centralization	Does not support Legacy Ethernet Networks
Fiber-optic cabling allows for long distances between networks and backbone	Not well suited for networks that are widely separated from each other
Internetwork traffic only needs to pass through one intermediary device	Hubs and switches must be able to span distance to a distant backbone

because a collapsed backbone is centralized, security, monitoring, and maintenance are much easier than with a distributed backbone. For newer networks, or those with few, if any, legacy segments, a collapsed backbone can be a cost-effective and efficient means of providing internetworking connectivity. Table 8.1 compares the advantages and disadvantages of distributed and collapsed backbones.

Regardless of the type of backbone architecture selected, backbone fault tolerance must be provided for. Without the backbone, network segments have no means of communicating and sharing resources with each other. The following material considers fault tolerance and how the enterprise can be secured against a potential backbone failure.

BACKBONE FAULT TOLERANCE

An organization's backbone allows the various segments of the enterprise to communicate and share resources with each other. Should the backbone fail for some reason, internetworking might no longer be possible. In such an event, business could come to a standstill and, depending on the recovery time, irreparable damage may occur. However, if fault tolerance has been built into the backbone, internetworking will likely still be possible. **Fault tolerance** is the capability of a technology to recover in the event of error, failure, or some other unexpected event that disrupts organizational communications and functions. Part of a network administrator's job is to prepare for future network catastrophes. When designing backbone architectures, a network administrator can do several things to ensure adequate fault tolerance.

Many network administrators provide a level of fault tolerance by allowing for redundancy of critical resources in their network design. Duplicating a networked resource creates redundancy. Such a resource may be either software or hardware.

By duplicating a resource, should one of them fail, the other is probably still going to be available. The more critical the resource to the business, the more redundancy should be implemented. For example, if a given network segment is particularly critical for internetworking communications, the network administrator may decide to use two routers on that network segment to connect it to the backbone. In that way, should one router fail, the functioning router can still route data to and from that segment. In addition to routers and switches, important servers may also be duplicated. If all the network segments use e-mail, the network administrator may place the e-mail server on the distributed backbone, and also provide two or more such e-mail servers in the event that one should fail. Redundancy is a simple way of providing for fault tolerance; however, it does result in higher costs and maintenance.

For those organizations in which the backbone is particularly critical—meaning that failure of the backbone for any length of time would result in severe damage to users, customers, or the business—a redundant backbone is probably required. Should one backbone become unavailable, the other can still be used for internetworking traffic. Furthermore, using a redundant backbone also allows for the load balancing of internetworking traffic. By placing half the network segments on each backbone, internetworking traffic is shared, or balanced, across the backbones, resulting in improved communications performance. Of course, duplicating the entire backbone is much more expensive than simply duplicating one or more key devices. Figure 8.10 shows what a redundant backbone architecture might look like.

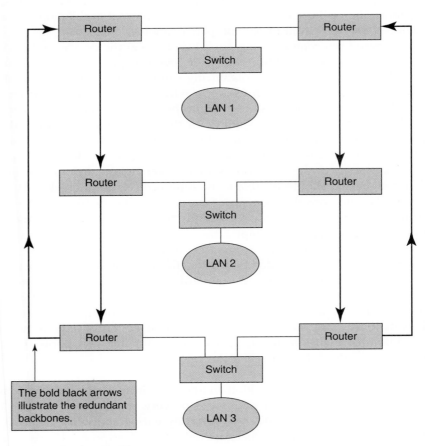

FIGURE 8.10 A Redundant Backbone

Fault tolerance is more than just a technology; it is also the use of good procedures and documentation. Recall that a technology's degree of fault tolerance will determine its ability to survive an error, damage, or some other unforeseen circumstance. As you design and implement your backbone, part of your implementation will be the defining, documenting, and testing of procedures to follow in the event of component failure. Your documentation should include a written history of the network and diagrams of important details such as where routers and switches are located, what their addresses are, where and how the backbone cabling has been deployed, what network segments are supported and their location, the personnel responsible for corrective measures should problems occur, and any other information that will help you in recovering your network and backbone as quickly as possible.

Once the documentation is created, it is equally important that it be maintained and kept as up-to-date as possible. Documentation that does not reflect the current status of the enterprise's environment is not very useful, and it may do more harm than good. Procedures should be in place that describes how the documentation is to be maintained and by whom.

BACKBONE DESIGN CONSIDERATIONS

Backbones connect other network segments. Therefore, when designing network segments, you must also consider how they fit into the design of the backbone. How the network segments are connected to the backbone is critical. When connecting network segments to the backbone, will the cabling be internal; in other words, behind the walls, above the ceilings, or beneath the floors? Internal installations usually connect network segments to wall plates and patch panels.

A **patch panel** is a central wiring point located near the devices to be connected to it. The patch panel is not a hub, switch, or router; it provides no communication of its own. It is simply a means of organizing cables so that they can be efficiently maintained. The network designer must know where all the devices for each network are located and how these devices are going to be cabled to run to their central connecting hub, switch, or router. Depending on the size of the enterprise, there may be hundreds of identical wires running through walls, ceilings, and floors, which makes planning and documentation essential. Knowing the cable routing path from the network segments to the backbone should never be a matter of guesswork, but rather information that should be able to be retrieved relatively quickly. The internal design must take into consideration such factors as media susceptibility to the external environment, local building code regulations, fire and safety hazards, and data link layer protocol capabilities. For example, the various forms of Ethernet have collision domain parameters that have to be accounted for in a backbone design.

A collision domain is bounded by the length of the cable for a particular implementation of an Ethernet network. A standard Ethernet segment may measure up to 2,500 meters, whereas a Fast Ethernet segment can be no more than 250 meters. This length is the *collision domain*. An enterprise with multiple types of Ethernet networks (Standard, Fast, and/or Gigabit) may consequently have networks with differently bounded collision domains. It is important that you know the collision domain of each of the Ethernet networks within an enterprise as you design and build your backbone.

As you might expect, implementing an internal wiring design—encompassing the wiring within ceilings, floors, and walls—can be very complicated. It is not unusual for businesses to contract such work to a facility-wiring specialist. External wiring, although unattractive, is far simpler, because the cabling is exposed. However, exposed wires are more susceptible to damage and have fire and safety code issues as well.

The Ethical Perspective

Assume that ACME Corporation has requested that you present a bid to install the wiring for its entire enterprise network. You have visited several of ACME's facilities and have noted that many of the networks do not comply with current fire and safety regulations. ACME has made it clear that it wants the work done for the lowest possible cost. After completing your analysis, you provide your estimate.

Later, one of ACME's managers informally, not in writing, tells you that you can have the job if your bid were lower, perhaps through the use of lower-quality materials that may not meet minimum requirements. This is a job that you and your employees would really like to have, because it could lead to other jobs. What would you do in this scenario? If you do not accept the job at ACME, should you alert a government agency about ACME's lack of compliance? What if other firms will not hire you should they discover that you reported ACME for lack of compliance? Does this situation involve business ethics?

WIRING CLOSETS

Many network configurations require the use of one or more wiring closets. In fact, patch panels are usually housed in wiring closets. The wiring closet may also contain servers that provide resources across the enterprise. In a multifloor design, wiring closets are usually placed one above the other. Placing the wiring closets in vertical alignment greatly facilitates their connection. Figure 8.11 shows three wiring closets in vertical alignment. Although wiring closets tend to be relatively small, because they

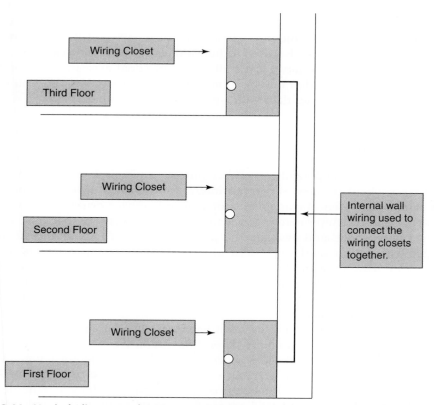

FIGURE 8.11 Vertical Alignment of Wiring Closets. Closets contain essential equipment to connect networks together.

house only the essential equipment to support the backbone, they are usually well lit and tightly secured.

The wiring closet should be environmentally friendly to the equipment it houses; for example, it should have adequate air conditioning, heating, and air filtration, as needed. Specialized electronic circuitry can be particularly susceptible to heat, cold, dust, and humidity. Fortunately, administrative tools running on routers, switches, servers, and other devices have made it increasingly possible for network administrators to monitor and fine-tune their wiring closet equipment without having to physically be in the room itself. This makes remote administration, from a different city, state, or even country, possible.

DATA CENTERS

For horizontal backbone architectures that use a distributed environment, wiring closets are fairly common. A collapsed backbone architecture, however, is more likely to make use of what is commonly referred to as a **data center**. Wiring closets tend to be small rooms housing minimal, but essential, backbone networking equipment. In contrast, data centers are usually moderately to largely spaced and house all the necessary networking equipment for the entire enterprise in a central location. As with wiring closets, data centers should be tightly secured and environmentally appropriate for the equipment they house. The data center may contain routers, switches, servers, and even network segment hubs that connect individual devices to their network segment.

For organization and ease of access, equipment in a data center is usually mounted on racks that may reach from floor to ceiling. Racks are at least 19 inches wide, and hubs, switches, routers, and servers can be stacked and bolted into them. Various types of racks, available through such vendors as Server Racks Online (*www.server-rack-online.com*), are also used to house multiple servers. Racks also allow for centralized wiring. Because most, if not all, of the essential networking equipment of the enterprise is centralized in one location, maintaining, servicing, and troubleshooting equipment is much easier than with a distributed environment.

Chapter Summary

Local area network components are either physical or logical. Physical components include NICs, client devices, servers, printers, cables, hubs, switches, and routers, just to name a few. Logical components may include device drivers, network operating systems, and desktop operating systems, as well as software that can be used to monitor, troubleshoot, and evaluate the performance of a LAN. Device drivers are associated with peripheral devices, network operating systems with servers, and desktop operating systems with clients. Logical components, like physical components, also need to be installed, configured, and maintained. Whether physical or logical, successfully working with both types of components is critically dependent on the quality of their documentation.

An additional element in a LAN that has both physical and logical characteristics is the LAN's topology. Topologies determine not only how devices are connected to each other but also how devices access the media they use for communication. Three types of topologies are the star, ring, and bus. Of the three, the bus is the most commonly used. The IEEE has formalized the bus topology as Ethernet 802.3. A classic bus topology uses a broadcast mechanism when packets are placed on the bus. The bus topology is a **contention-based topology**. Devices contend for access to the communication circuit using CSMA/CD. An 802.3 LAN is relatively easy to install and configure and uses inexpensive cabling.

Use of switching technology has especially transformed how Ethernet is configured. A LAN may use many types of physical components, or hardware. An essential hardware component that each device on a LAN must have in order to communicate is a NIC, which provides a physical layer MAC address. These cards are also called adapters. Factors to consider when choosing a NIC include its bus width and memory capabilities.

Another essential physical component of a LAN is the physical medium over which data are transmitted over the network. The most common form of LAN medium installed today is unshielded twisted-wire pair, or UTP. A UTP's cable category classification determines the maximum number of bits that it can transmit. A higher cable category number represents a larger cable size. A larger cable size results in less resistance to the signal being carried on the cable. Reduced resistance translates into higher transmission speeds.

Server and client devices also make up part of the physical LAN. Servers are computers that fulfill specific, specialized functions. Servers allow LAN resources to be made available for multiple users to share and utilize. These resources can include, among other things, printers, applications, data, information, files, databases, security services, directory services, modems, web hosting, e-mail, or almost anything that a group of users would need to have access to. When configuring a server, several factors should be considered, including the server's processor, hard drive speed, primary memory, and cache. A server also has a network, or server, operating system. Users connect to the LAN and to server resources through client devices. In a TCP/IP LAN, client devices are referred to as hosts.

As a LAN grows, it may be necessary to segment it in order to maximize performance. Two popular LAN segmentation devices are switches and routers. Switches are often associated with the data link layer, or layer 2. Routers are associated with the network layer, or layer 3. Today, the use of switches has pushed routers to the edge of the network. A number of issues must be considered when designing a LAN. Design considerations include the budget, the types of applications the LAN should support, the scale of the LAN, the facility the LAN is to be housed in, security needs, and staffing requirements. All elements of the LAN should be well documented. Documentation should also be a continuing process as the LAN evolves.

A backbone network is used to connect all of an organization's LANs. When properly designed, BNs provide a high-speed circuit that serves as a central conduit over which all the organization's LANs can communicate. The terms *BN* and *MAN* are sometimes used interchangeably, depending on the scope of the backbone. Each of an organization's individual LANs is a network segment. An organization might have a network segment on each floor of a multistory building. Because each network segment, or LAN, is on its own floor, this type of network segment is often referred to as a *horizontal network*. The BN links the network segments together. Devices accessible to other network segments may reside directly on the BN.

Two common types of backbone architectures are distributed and collapsed. A distributed backbone is one that runs throughout the entire enterprise. This type of backbone uses a central cable to which the network segments, or LANs, are connected. A collapsed backbone connects all the network segments to a central, single router or switch. This central device is, in effect, the backbone. Because the collapsed backbone uses a single, central backbone device, cabling is greatly reduced.

Fault tolerance is the capability of a technology to recover in the event of error, failure, or some other unexpected event that disrupts smooth organizational communications. Many network administrators provide for backbone fault tolerance by duplicating critical network resources. This duplication is called *redundancy.* Documentation is also important to network design. Documentation should include such important details as where routers and switches are located, what their addresses are, where and how the backbone cabling has been deployed, what network segments are supported and their location, and the personnel responsible for corrective measures should problems occur.

When designing network segments, consideration should also be given to how the segments fit into the design of the backbone. With internal installations, network segments are connected to wall plates and patch panels. External installations are simpler, but exposed wires are more susceptible to damage and have fire and safety issues. In a usual configuration, especially for horizontal networks housed on multiple floors, organizations use one or more wiring closets that provide a centralized location for network cabling. Data centers, which are usually associated with collapsed back-bones, are moderately to largely spaced and provide for a centralized location to house all the necessary networking equipment for the entire enterprise. As with wiring closets, data centers should be tightly secured and environmentally appropriate for the equipment they house.

Keywords

Adapter card *143*	Device driver *145*	Regenerated *146*
Autosensing *169*	Direct memory access	Request for purchase
Backbone *151*	(DMA) *144*	(RFP) *150*
Broadcast *142*	Distributed backbone *154*	Server operating system
Bus mastering *144*	Ethernet *142*	(SOS) *149*
Bus typology *142*	Fault tolerance *158*	Site license *149*
Bus width *144*	Hardware *143*	Software *140*
Cache *144*	Horizontal network *152*	Star topology *141*
Client *147*	Host *147*	Topology *140*
Client/server model *147*	Metered license *149*	Troubleshoot *140*
Collapsed backbone *156*	Network interface card	Unshielded twisted-wire
Contention-based	(NIC) *143*	pair (UTP) *145*
topology *162*	Patch panel *160*	Wiring closet *146*
Data center *162*	Peer-to-peer model *147*	Workstation *147*

Chapter Questions

Short-Answer Questions

1. What is the purpose of a NIC? What are three factors that might influence your selection of a NIC?
2. Briefly describe how a server differs from a client.
3. What differences, if any, are there between how switches function versus hubs?
4. How do metered and site licensing differ? Are they in any way the same?
5. When would Gigabit Ethernet be a good choice for a BN?
6. What is a Blade server?
7. In regard to a NIC, what is meant by direct memory access?
8. How and why are wiring closets used?

Hands-On Projects

1. Using an online retailer or a physical business, compare and contrast the cost, capabilities, and functions of a low-end versus a high-end NIC.
2. On paper, design a small Ethernet network of 10 devices. Specify the purpose for each device. Include at least one server and switch.
3. What specifications are associated with CAT 5 versus CAT 6 UTP cable?
4. At your college, university, or place of employment, determine what type(s) of backbone network(s) are implemented and describe.

Research in Brief

For one or more of the following questions, provide a one- or two-page report based on your findings.

1. Research and contrast Linux-based software for servers and Windows 2008 server. How are they similar? How are they different? What are their relative advantages and disadvantages?
2. Explain whether the choice of NICs can affect the performance of a network for both clients and servers. When choosing NICs for clients and servers, what characteristics should you consider and why? Use a Fast Ethernet network with a Gigabit Ethernet backbone as your basis for NIC selection.
3. Visit the website for the IEEE (*www.ieee.org*). Search the site and report on three current topics related to LANs.
4. What are "server farms"? Investigate how server farms are being used today. What types of computers are used in server farms? What is their cost? How are they connected? In what industries are server farms more prevalent?

Case Study

Sheehan Marketing and Public Relations

You have visited all three of SMPR's locations: Los Angeles, Chicago, and New York. Based on your analysis, you see an important need for SMPR to move from a peer-to-peer network infrastructure to a client/server network infrastructure. President Sheehan has asked you to prepare a report identifying the advantages and disadvantages of using either a Linux- or a Microsoft-based solution for both client and server machines. He wants your report to include such information as cost, ease of use, staff training, and any other areas you think might be relevant.

Part of your analysis should be recommendations on what might need to be done with the current hardware being used by SMPR. All the offices have computers that are at least 5 years old running on Windows Vista. The only new computers are five up-to-date Intel machines in the L.A. office that are running Windows 7. President Sheehan wants to know what issues might be involved in upgrading all of SMPR's technology.

In addition, President Sheehan would like to know, in general, how servers differ from ordinary computers and what benefits SMPR might get from using a server technology. Would security be improved? Would staff be better able to share resources? Would the use of servers make managing the three regional office networks easier? If so, how? Your report is due in a week and is expected to include a narrative description, a cost analysis of the two proposed solutions (Linux or Windows), and a final recommendation.

Topic in Focus

FORMS OF ETHERNET

Standard Ethernet

Understanding standard Ethernet emphasizes the benefits gained from newer Ethernet forms. Standard Ethernet is a bus topology that uses hubs to extend the network. On a bus, when a host transmits, all other hosts on the shared circuit receive the transmission whether it is addressed to them or not. With a bus, only one host at a time can use the circuit. Hubs broadcast all frames that go through them. Filtering is not performed. As far as all the devices connected to a hub are concerned, they are on the same, shared, single circuit. The hub is simply a means of extending the diameter, or distance, of the LAN.

By evaluating the destination address, receiving hosts are able to determine if the packet is for them or not. The bus topology uses CSMA/CD as its MAC mechanism. In bus networks that have many hosts on the same circuit or where traffic is heavy, contention and collision of packets is a problem. Ultimately, network performance degrades to the point where no communication, or work, is being performed. For the end user, this is a frustrating situation. As the network administrator, your business-networked smart phone will begin to ring—often and noisily—from your many annoyed users.

Common standard Ethernet LANs transmit at 10 Mbps using two pairs of either Category 3, 4, or 5 UTP. This type of Ethernet LAN is referred to as *10BaseT*. The *10* stands for 10 Mbps, the *Base* represents baseband, and the *T* is for twisted-wire pair. 10BaseT LANs use Manchester encoding, which was previously introduced in an earlier chapter. The maximum end-to-end LAN diameter of 10BaseT Ethernet is 2,500 meters. The 2,500-meter limitation is based on physics. CSMA/CD requires that a transmitting device be able to sense a collision before an entire frame is sent out onto the transmission medium—in this example, the UTP cable. For standard hub-wired 10BaseT, before the last bit of the frame is sent, the sender must be able to determine if a collision has occurred. If all bits of the entire frame are sent and the sending device has not detected a collision, it assumes that all is well. If the LAN's total diameter were too long, which for 10BaseT is more than 2,500 meters, the sender would not have enough time to be able to determine that a collision has occurred. Here's why.

The smallest Ethernet frame possible is 64 bytes, or 512 bits. Let's assume a frame of 64 bytes needs to be transmitted. At 10 Mbps, sending 512 bits takes 51.2 microseconds. According to CSMA/CD, before the last bit of the 512 bits is sent from the sending host, the first bit must have reached the farthest end of the LAN's diameter. Because this example uses a standard bus having a broadcast mechanism, all devices on the shared, single circuit must get the frame, even those at the far end of the network.

In this way, if a collision occurs at the far end of the network, before the sender has sent that last bit, there will be time for the sender to get back, or receive, a signal that indicates that a collision has occurred. Without that collision signal, the sender assumes that all is well once that last bit is sent. Once all bits of a frame are sent, the sender clears that frame from its buffer, making retransmission of the frame, in the event of a collision, impossible.

If the segment length is too long, the sender could send the last bit of its frame and not be aware that a collision had occurred at the other end of the network because the collision signal had not returned in time. For this reason, a standard 10BaseT Ethernet LAN can have an end-to-end diameter of no more than 2,500 meters.

Switched Ethernet

Hubs can extend the diameter, or distance, of a LAN. They do not, however, create independent, dedicated circuits for the devices that are attached to them. This means that if eight devices are connected to a hub, they still only share one circuit, not eight. In a bus topology, contention for the circuit is not improved by using a hub. Switches, however, are different. Switches, like hubs, have ports that host devices plug into. Switched Ethernet LANs use switches in place of hubs. Depending on the switch, switch ports can be configured for different speeds. Each device that connects to a switch has a dedicated circuit to that switch. Because the circuit between the host and switch is dedicated, there is no competition, or contention, for use of that circuit. When a device needs to transmit or receive, its circuit to the switch is always available. Like hubs, switches can also extend the diameter of the LAN, with the added benefit of not broadcasting the data frames that pass through them because switches are capable of recognizing addresses.

Another major difference between hubs and switches is that whereas hubs cannot overcome the maximum distance limitation that a 10BaseT LAN can span (2,500 meters), switches can. Because switches eliminate collisions, collision detection between the two farthest hosts in the network is not a factor. A host can send its entire frame without having to wait for the first bit of the frame to get to the farthest host on the network. The sending host only needs to use its dedicated circuit to the switch, send its entire frame to the switch, and have the switch handle it from there. Thus, switched Ethernet does not have a maximum-distance limitation. A switched Ethernet LAN might be 2,500 or 25,000 meters. Naturally, good network planning and design should determine how big the eventual LAN should be. Simply being able to create a 25,000 meter LAN does not mean you should!

Be aware, however, that although switched Ethernet does not have a maximum-distance limitation for the entire network, there is a distance limitation between each pair of switches. When using UTP, the distance limitation between switches is 100 meters. However, there is no limit to the number of switches deployed between the farthest two hosts. When using fiber, the limitation is much higher, from 1 to 5 kilometers between switches. Fiber, though, is a technology usually implemented for BNs, MANs, or WANs, not the typical LAN.

Whether UTP or fiber, switches are configured in a hierarchy, with no loops among the switches. If loops were allowed, a frame could circle a network endlessly. Because a hierarchy is used, frames can take only one possible path among the hosts. Ethernet switches use address-forwarding tables that are relatively simple. Depending on the switch and how it is used, the forwarding table can be manually or automatically maintained. The larger the network, the more efficient automatic table addressing becomes. Switches have the capability of learning which port is associated or assigned to each connected device's MAC address. Each MAC address of a device connected to a switch has only one switch port number assigned to it. When a frame needs to be transmitted, the switch reads the MAC destination address of the frame to be sent. Then the switch, using its forward addressing table, looks up the MAC port address for the frame. Finally, the switch forwards the frame to that assigned port, and only that assigned port. Figure 8.12 demonstrates a possible switched Ethernet LAN.

Automatic table addressing makes for efficient, and fast, switch-path decisions. In addition, as already mentioned, switches of different capacities can be configured in a hierarchy. The result is that a central or backbone root switch may support gigabit capacity. Switches connected to servers, directly below the root switch, could be 100 Mbps, and those farther below, connected to clients, only 10 Mbps. Not everyone,

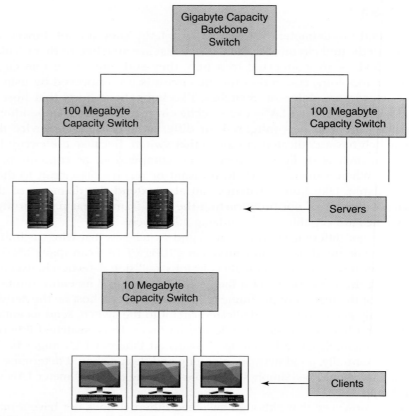

FIGURE 8.12   An Ethernet Switching Hierarchy

or every connection, needs a gigabit or even a 100-Mbps switch. Businesses can leverage their switching cost based on the transmission capacity needed at different levels of the hierarchy. Figure 8.12 illustrates a switching hierarchy.

Switches vary significantly in capability and price. Some switches are strictly layer 2 devices. Others, costing more, can also operate at layer 3 of the OSI and TCP/IP networking models. Today, growth in switching technology has exploded. A factor that has made such technology particularly attractive is that when moving to a switched environment, the existing network cabling, NICs, server operating system, topology, protocols, and other infrastructure elements may require no change. The hub, bridge, or router is simply swapped out for a switch. Although switches cost more than hubs, for most organizations their performance gain has outweighed the added expense. Also, switches will require more configuration and monitoring then simple hubs or bridges. Costing far less than routers, switches have caused routers to be pushed to the edge of the network.

Fast Ethernet

Using switches is one way to improve Ethernet performance. Another way of increasing data rate, without changing the minimum size of the Ethernet frame, is to decrease the round-trip time it takes for a collision signal to get back to a sender. To decrease round-trip time, the length of the Ethernet LAN diameter is shortened from 2,500 to 250 meters. This decrease in LAN diameter does not require a change in frame format, or access method, so the Ethernet standard remains intact. Fast Ethernet is based on

LAN diameters of 250 meters when hubs are used. When used with switches, as with Standard Ethernet, the LAN diameter is only limited by the network design. The IEEE has designated two categories of Fast Ethernet: 100BaseX and 100BaseT4. Of the two, 100BaseX has been the clear market winner.

There are two types of 100BaseX: 100BaseTX and 100BaseFX. As with the 10BaseT label, important Fast Ethernet characteristics can be determined from the standard's name. For *100BaseTX, 100* represents 100-Mbps capacity; *base* is, again, baseband; and *TX* designates, at a minimum, two pair of either Cat 5 UTP or STP cables that connect a host to a hub. One wire pair carries frames from the host to the hub. The second wire pair carries frames from the hub to the host. The maximum segment length of a 100BaseTX cable, as with 10BaseT, remains 100 meters. An important difference between the two is that 10BaseT can use less expensive Cat 3 or 4 level cable. 100BaseTX, though, must use, as a minimum, the more expensive Cat 5 cable. For Gigabit Ethernet using UTP, enhanced Cat 5 cable or better should be used, which is an additional expense. For optimal Gigabit Ethernet, fiber-optic cabling is recommended, an even higher additional expense.

100BaseFX is fiber-optic-based Fast Ethernet; it is more likely found in BNs. Significantly, the maximum segment length of fiber Fast Ethernet is 412 meters to 2 kilometers, depending on the type of fiber medium used. Gigabit Ethernet is examined more closely in Chapter 6 during the discussion of BNs. Fast Ethernet also includes 100BaseT4, another IEEE standard. Designed to avoid the need for rewiring to achieve a higher data rate capacity, 100BaseT4 has proven unsuccessful in the networking market. 100BaseT4 requires four pairs of Cat 3 UTP. Most modern buildings already have this wiring available. Even so, 100BaseT4 has been mostly ignored.

Network interface cards for Fast Ethernet are sometimes called *10/100-Mbps adapters*. These types of NICs, unlike those for a standard 10BaseT Ethernet LAN, often have the ability to perform autosensing. **Autosensing** enables Fast Ethernet NICs to automatically sense, and adjust, to speed capabilities of 10 or 100 Mbps. In an enterprise that has a mix of 10- and 100-Mbps devices, the faster device must communicate at the slower device's capacity. If a 100-Mbps host device with an autosensing NIC senses that it is communicating with a 10-Mbps hub, the faster host device will slow down to accommodate the hub's slower speed. Slower NICs cannot speed their capacity to match the faster device. A good website for additional information on Fast Ethernet is *www.ethermanage.com*. This site also has a graphic showing the first hand drawing of Standard Ethernet by Dr. Robert M. Metcalfe in 1976.

Gigabit Ethernet

As organizations began to transition from Standard (10 Mbps) Ethernet to Fast (100 Mbps) Ethernet, the IEEE saw the need for a faster backbone protocol. The result was the development of Gigabit Ethernet and the 802.3z standard. Gigabit Ethernet allows for a data rate of 1,000 Mbps, or 1 Gbps. A major advantage of all of the officially recognized forms of Gigabit Ethernet is that they are all built on the standards of the preexisting Ethernet protocol. This means that the MAC layer and access method for Gigabit Ethernet are the same as for Standard and Fast Ethernet. Additionally, Gigabit Ethernet is backward-compatible with existing media, which makes it easy to upgrade from Standard or Fast Ethernet. Finally, Gigabit Ethernet supports both full-duplex and half-duplex operations.

One major difference with Gigabit Ethernet, however, is that the collision domain, or diameter of the network, is reduced. Because of the reduced collision domain, additional planning is required when connecting network segments to the backbone. Network segments must be able to reach the backbone, thus an important consideration is the type of cabling used. It is not unusual for a Gigabit Ethernet backbone to be connected to Fast Ethernet networks. (The Gigabit Ethernet Alliance, a nonprofit organization, provides additional information on Gigabit Ethernet at *www.10gea.org*.)

Forms of Gigabit Ethernet

Gigabit Ethernet comes in several forms. The original IEEE 1000Base-X standard (802.3z) allowed for three physical layer cable options: 1000BaseLX and 1000Base-SX, both using fiber-optic, and 1000Base-CX, using copper. Of the three, 1000Base-CX never became a market success, and virtually no products were available for it. A fourth form of Gigabit Ethernet, 1000Base-T, ratified by the IEEE in June of 1999, uses UTP cable. Gigabit Ethernet, besides being used for backbones, is also a popular option for server farm configurations and for networks using applications that have high bandwidth requirements (e.g., graphics programs). Increasingly, MAN service providers are offering Gigabit Ethernet as a lower-cost option to businesses that need metrowide data communications capabilities.

Gigabit Ethernet also has other advantages. Because Gigabit Ethernet is based on Standard Ethernet, technical personnel are probably familiar with the technology, so retraining is likely minimal. When upgrading to Gigabit Ethernet, because cabling and adapter cards may not need to be upgraded for most devices, disruption to the network is usually low. Gigabit Ethernet offers full-duplex data flow. Also, Gigabit Ethernet provides for Quality of Service (QoS) services, such as traffic prioritization. Also, QoS allows data to be transported without packet loss, offering predictable end-to-end delay and real-time delivery of data once a connection is completed.

Resource Reservation Protocol (RSVP), which is the capability to call for a service level from the network to support a particular application, can be implemented using Gigabit Ethernet. Essentially, RSVP enables network bandwidth to be reserved and supported on intermediate devices such as routers. This allows network administrators to fine-tune traffic demand and throughput.

Because it is based on Standard Ethernet, Gigabit Ethernet is fully compatible with networks configured for Standard and Fast Ethernet hosts, which allows for scalability. A technology is scalable when it allows for easy expansion or contraction as growth and transaction volume demand. Vendors commonly reference the scalability of their hardware and software products as a competitive advantage. Businesses that buy into a technology want that technology to be flexible so that it can, at a reasonable cost, grow or shrink with business needs.

1000Base-LX

As a fiber-based physical layer implementation, 1000Base-LX is used for backbones that span relatively long distances. If using single-mode cable, the maximum segment length is 5,000 meters. This is the longest segment length for any of the forms of Gigabit Ethernet presented in this chapter. (As an interesting side note, 1000Base-LH [for Long Haul] is a form of Gigabit Ethernet not approved by the IEEE that allows for distances of 1 to 100 kilometers, depending on the form of 1000Base-LH used.) A single-mode 1000Base-LX fiber core is 9 microns in diameter. Do you recall microns from Chapter 2?

Microns are measured in millionths of a meter. Single-mode cable, because it can span relatively long distances, is best for long-distance applications, such as connecting networks across a city. Multimode 1000Base-LX uses segment lengths of 550 meters. Thus, it is better suited for short-distance applications, such as connecting networks across a campus. With multimode, the core diameter is either 50 or 62.5 microns.

1000Base-LX uses long-wavelength laser transmissions that range from 1,270 to 1,355 nanometers. Single-mode fiber is more expensive than multimode, but it spans greater distances.

1000Base-SX

Usually, 1000Base-SX is used for shorter backbones or in horizontal wiring. Unlike 1000Base-LX, 1000Base-SX uses only multimode fiber-optic cable. Segment lengths usually are 220, 275, 500, or 550 meters. Segment lengths of 220 and 275 meters have core diameters of 62.5 microns; 500 and 550 meter lengths have core diameters of 50 microns. 1000Base-SX uses short-wavelength laser transmissions that range from 770 to 860 nanometers. Note that these short-wavelength transmissions are the same as those used in CD and CD-ROM players.

9

Wide Area Networks

The Business Benefit

For businesses, inefficiency usually translates into lost income. Businesses typically seek out the most efficient means of accomplishing a task in order to maximize resources and revenue. If a business is shipping inventory, or having inventory delivered, that business likely wants to have its shipment and/or delivery accomplished in the most cost-effective manner as possible. If delays hold up merchandize delivery, or errors occur in transit of the merchandize, or parts of the shipment never arrive, it might prove costly to the organization to correct these problems.

Business organizations want to have their data "shipped" or "delivered" in a conceptually very similar manner. They seek a network data delivery infrastructure that is timely, as much as is possible reduces or eliminates errors, and does not result in data loss in transit.

As with physical inventory or merchandize that is delayed, damaged, or lost, resulting in unwanted expenses, the same holds true for data that are delayed, delivered with errors, or lost. This chapter explores wide area networking infrastructures that attempt to ensure the timely and accurate delivery of data in as efficient and cost-effective manner as possible.

Learning Objectives

After studying this chapter, you should be able to:

- Understand the need for varying types of WAN connectivity options.
- Explain switching services.
- Define circuit-switching services.
- Define packet-switching services.
- Describe frame relay.
- Describe asynchronous transfer mode.
- Describe multi-protocol label switching.

In Chapter 8, you learned that an organization's enterprise might include local area networks (LANs), backbone networks (BNs), and metro area networks (MANs). The scope of an organization's data communications needs may be multistate or global. Large enterprises and home users connecting to the Internet require **wide area network (WAN)** services. These services facilitate electronic payments, make information available to clients wherever they may reside, enable employees to access data and software from remote distances, and permit a host of other services. This chapter explores some of the major architectures that make up WAN technologies.

CONNECTING TO A WAN

Depending on the enterprise's needs, WAN connections can be established in several ways. Usually, because of cost, organizations make use of common carrier infrastructures, such as those provided by AT&T, MCI, and Sprint, to make their WAN connections. Common carriers are essential to the North American telecommunications infrastructure. The Institute for Telecommunication Sciences has an interesting website that provides detailed information about the U.S. telecommunications infrastructure (*www.its.bldrdoc.gov*).

The type of carrier service that a business uses has varying expenses and requirements. A WAN connection, for example, may be as simple as a home user connecting to the Internet, or as complicated as a business utilizing elaborate packet-switching or cell relay technologies. *Frame relay (FR)* is a popular packet-switching implementation. *Asynchronous transfer mode (ATM)* is the leading cell relay technology. Overtaking both FR and ATM is yet another more current technology: *multiple layer protocol switching (MPLS)*. All three of these WAN connectivity options, among other topics, will be explored in this chapter.

SWITCHING SERVICES

For data communications, various devices need to communicate with each other, whether across a room or across a continent. For this communication to occur, some type of physical connection must be established. If the devices were in the same room, the creation of a direct point-to-point connection, whereby each device would have a direct physical connection to all of the other devices, might be a realistic solution. This is called a *mesh topology.* However, if the scope is larger than a single room or if there are more than 10 devices, a mesh topology can quickly become impractical and extremely expensive to implement. The larger the network infrastructure, the more links are required to connect those devices to each other, and the more devices there are that need to communicate. An infrastructure with too many links becomes overly complicated and costly to support. Figure 9.1 shows how complicated a mesh topology of only six devices can be. The solution to this problem is a technology called *switching*.

In a **switched network**, interlinked devices called switches are used to create temporary connections between two communicating devices. Switches may be hardware, software, or a combination. Switches can be connected to form multiple links, providing for alternative pathways through a networking infrastructure. Communicating devices use switches to create a link without concern as to how the route is established. The advantage of this strategy is that a permanent link is not required between any two communicating devices. Instead, communicating devices use the switching infrastructure as a means of establishing and creating a link when one is needed. This switching infrastructure is often referred to and graphically illustrated as a *cloud,* as shown in Figure 9.2.

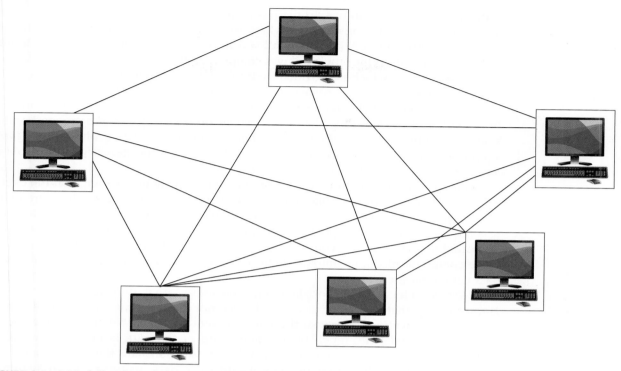

FIGURE 9.1 A Mesh Topology of Six Devices. Even in this simple network of six devices, the cabling within a mesh topology begins to get complicated. Each device has a point-to-point connection to all other devices.

FIGURE 9.2 A Switching Cloud. Whether circuit or packet switching, a business needs only to be concerned with its local connection to the cloud. Within the cloud, the services of the carrier take over.

Two common switching technologies are circuit switching and packet switching. Switches reside in and make up the so-called cloud, whereas external devices connect to the cloud in order to communicate. The external devices that connect to the cloud are often referred to as **edge switches** or *edge routers*, because they are on the "edge," or outer boundary, of the cloud. Once the data arrive at the cloud, the cloud's switching network takes over and assumes control in getting the data from the sender to the receiver.

CIRCUIT SWITCHING

An important characteristic of **circuit switching** is that it creates a direct connection, or path, between two communicating devices. The term **path** is used with circuit switching; the term **link** is used with packet switching. When a circuit is established, no other devices can use that circuit path to communicate. In this sense, the circuit is dedicated when it is in use. In the past, one of the most common communications that used circuit switching occurred when two people shared a standard "land-based" telephone conversation. While their call was in progress, they had a direct, dedicated circuit to each other. Once their call was completed, the circuit was terminated. In fact, **circuit switching**, which is provided by Public Switched Telephone Network (PSTN) providers, was designed for voice communications.

Throughout this chapter, as in previous chapters, new terms will be introduced. In an earlier chapter, Webopedia (*www.webopedia.com*) was noted as a good online source for defining technical terms. Another good reference site is offered by Novell, a vendor of networking software solutions. Novell's online glossary is available at *www.novell.com/info/glossary/glossary.html*.

Circuit-switched paths may be temporary, or permanent, meaning that the circuit is leased and is always available to the user leasing the line. Permanent lines are much more expensive, but they guarantee the user that the line will be available whenever it is required. Whether temporary or permanent, while the circuit is being used, it is dedicated to that particular communication. Although this is well suited for traditional voice communications, circuit-switching networks are not efficient for most types of data communication.

A basic characteristic of data transmissions is that they tend to be bursty. **Bursty** means that the data are sent in bursts, not as a continuous stream, like most voice communications. Because the data are sent in bursts, when a business uses a circuit-switched path, much of the bandwidth of the path is not used, which is inefficient. As noted earlier, inefficiency in businesses translates into lost income.

In addition, when two devices establish a path using a circuit-switched connection, their link will be at one constant rate, and the rate will be determined by the slower of the two devices. Faster devices will have to transmit at slower speeds to accommodate slower devices, which again is inefficient for data transmissions. Also, for a circuit-switched service that does not use permanently leased lines, it is possible for calls to be denied due to lack of circuit availability.

Finally, circuit switching treats all requested transmissions in the same manner, meaning that whoever requests an open circuit first can have it. This may sound fair, but in many cases certain data transmissions are likely to be regarded as more critical than others. In such a scenario, it would make sense for there to be a way to prioritize communications so that the most critical data transmissions are assured of getting the circuit first. For these reasons, packet switching is preferred for data communications.

PACKET SWITCHING

With **packet switching**, the data are broken into units called *packets*. Individual packets are sent though the packet-switching cloud from the sender to the receiver. Between the sender and the receiver, and within the cloud, are many packet-switching devices. The connection between each packet-switching device is referred to as a *link*, rather than a path. Packet switching significantly improves line efficiency because packet streams from different communications can use the same links between packet-switching nodes. Links are not dedicated to one single communication, but can be used by many communications. In this way, packet-switched services do not use a dedicated path between the sender and the receiver, as with circuit-switched services, but instead have a series of shared links between packet-switching nodes.

Because links are used, data-rate link conversion between packet-switching nodes can be performed, which is a considerable advantage. This means that the data transmission rate between the originating sender and ultimate receiver is not determined by the slower of the two devices. Instead, link transmission rates between each

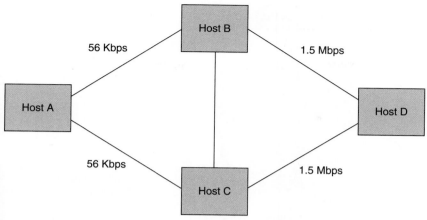

FIGURE 9.3 Packet Switching with Varied Link Rates. Host A can only transmit at 56 Kbps to either Host B or C. But both Host B and C can transmit at the faster rate of 1.5 Mbps without regard to Host A's slower rate.

packet-switching node can be negotiated and used to maximum efficiency. Thus, if the link between packet-switching nodes A and B is slow, A and B will transmit at that rate. However, if the link between B and C is fast, the faster rate of B and C can be used without regard to A and B's slower rate. Figure 9.3 illustrates this point.

With circuit-switched services that do not use expensive leased lines, such as standard dial-up services, it is possible that some communications can be denied access when "all circuits are busy." In the past, traditional telephone service users experienced this when making a phone call during an event of national significance taking place and millions of users were trying to place calls at the same time. An advantage of packet-switched services is that such communications may be delayed, but they will not be denied. Another advantage of packet-switched services is that communications can be prioritized. This means that packets can be tagged for high-priority delivery. Prioritization provides much greater control over organizational communication needs. With circuit-switched services, there is a distinct difference between temporary dial-up and permanent services. Packet-switched services also vary.

The network implementation determines the size that a packet can take. Regardless of the packet size, a **packet** contains not only user data, but also control information, such as source and destination addresses, that is used by the packet-switching network. Packets are sent through the cloud, from one packet-switching device to the next. Along the way, the packet is temporarily stored and then routed, depending on the control information contained in the packet. Based on the type of packet-switched service used, how the packets are sent will differ. Packet-switching services are based on datagrams or virtual circuits. As you might guess, the two methods differ greatly as to how packets are delivered through the packet-switching cloud. A datagram approach works well for transmitting a simple e-mail message, for example, but not so well for a file containing critical financial data. For data files in which every bit of every byte is critical, a virtual-circuit approach is preferred.

DATAGRAM PACKET SWITCHING

When a packet-switching network makes use of datagrams, a sender's initial message is broken into individual and independent units called **datagrams**. A critical characteristic of this method is that each packet, or datagram, that makes up the message is treated independently. A small message may be contained within one datagram, but

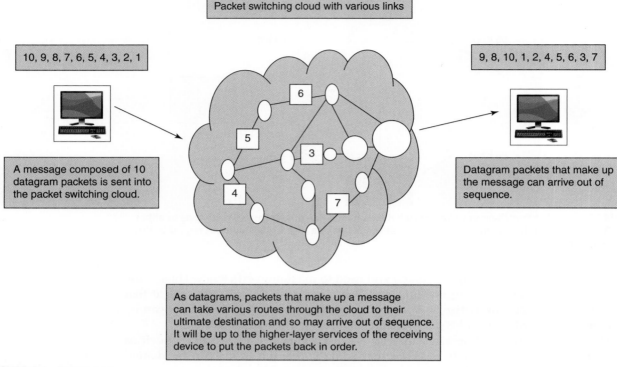

Packet switching cloud with various links

10, 9, 8, 7, 6, 5, 4, 3, 2, 1

9, 8, 10, 1, 2, 4, 5, 6, 3, 7

A message composed of 10 datagram packets is sent into the packet switching cloud.

Datagram packets that make up the message can arrive out of sequence.

As datagrams, packets that make up a message can take various routes through the cloud to their ultimate destination and so may arrive out of sequence. It will be up to the higher-layer services of the receiving device to put the packets back in order.

FIGURE 9.4 Datagrams

a larger message may require several datagrams. Because each datagram is treated independently, each datagram may take a completely different route through the packet-switching cloud. Furthermore, there is no guarantee that all the packets that make up a message will arrive in proper sequential order at the receiver's end, and in fact it is likely that they will not.

For a message of 10 packets that are sent as datagrams through the packet-switching cloud, packet 7 could arrive first, followed by packets, 3, 6, 5, 4, 2, 1, 10, 8, and finally 9, as illustrated in Figure 9.4. When using a datagram service, the receiver's higher-level layer services must put the packets back in order. The receiver's higher-level layer services must also determine if any packets are missing, and if so, request retransmission of the message.

One advantage of the datagram method is that, as there is no predetermined route, datagrams require little overhead, therefore the routing information does not have to be maintained for the stream of packets that make up a message. A second advantage is that datagrams are flexible in that they can take alternative routes to reach their destination. If a link within a cloud is bad, congested, or unavailable for some reason, a datagram can be routed around it. Because datagrams can be routed through alternative links, should one or more links fail, datagrams are more consistent in terms of delivery. Also, because datagrams do not require any set-up procedures between the sender and the receiver, the datagram method of service is faster than virtual-circuit packet services. A disadvantage of datagram delivery, however, is that routing decisions, which require time, must be made at each link that a datagram traverses through.

VIRTUAL-CIRCUIT PACKET SWITCHING

Datagram circuits are one type of packet-switched service. The other major type of packet-switched service is the virtual circuit. **Virtual circuits (VCs)** come in two forms: switched and permanent. Both switched and permanent virtual circuits set up a single route of links between the sender and the receiver. Keep in mind that the links are shared by multiple communications, meaning that multiple senders and receivers can use the same link. However, because a single route of links is established, both forms require a set-up procedure before communication can begin. Any time set-up procedures are required, time is involved, which is one of the disadvantages of VCs as compared with datagrams. Datagrams do not require any special setup between senders and receivers.

Switched virtual circuits (SVCs) are similar to standard dial-up, circuit-switched connections in that the route of links a circuit takes is established only temporarily for the duration of the communication. After a communication concludes, SVCs are dissolved, as with a circuit-switched, dial-up connection. Because SVCs are temporary, a set-up procedure is required for every established communication.

In contrast, permanent virtual circuits are more like a leased-line, circuit-switched connection. **Permanent virtual circuits (PVCs)** are continuous and, once defined, do not require an additional set-up procedure because they are permanent. The user of a PVC is guaranteed use of that circuit. All the communications that use a PVC take the same route each time. Whether using an SVC or a PVC, all of the packets that make up a single message are sent in sequence along the same route of links. This is very different from a datagram service in which each packet can take an independent route between the sender and the receiver and the packets likely arrive out of sequence.

Virtual circuits are less flexible than datagrams in that if a problem occurs along the route, the packets cannot simply be routed around the problem area. Instead, a new virtual circuit must be established. Recall that with a datagram, if a link is bad or congested, the datagram can simply take a different route. In order to use a single route, virtual circuits also require that packets carry, besides sequence numbers, additional identification information. This identification information includes the address of the virtual circuit being used as well as the address of the specific communication on the virtual circuit. An address for the specific communication is required because multiple communications share the virtual circuit links and the packet-switching cloud needs a way to differentiate one communication from another. Figure 9.5 illustrates this concept.

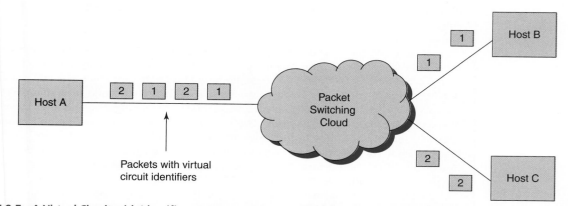

FIGURE 9.5 A Virtual Circuit with Identifiers. Between one device and another, a logical virtual circuit connection is established. Packets that make up a message are tagged with a virtual circuit identification numbers. These numbers in turn identify the series of links that packets will take to get from one packet switching device to another. In the example below, Host A is sending packets to Host B using virtual circuit number 1. Host A will use virtual circuit number 2 in sending packets to Host C.

Four forms of packet-switched services are X.25, frame relay (FR), asynchronous transfer mode (ATM; also called a *cell relay packet-switching service*), and multiple-protocol label switching (MPLS). The X.25 is the oldest packet-switched service and is virtually obsolete. The MPLS form is the most recent and is gaining in use and popularity.

X.25

In 1976, the **X.25** packet-switching model was accepted by the International Telecommunications Union-Telecommunication Standards Sector (ITU-T), introduced in Chapter 1. The X.25 model used data terminal equipment (DTE) and data circuit-terminating equipment (DCE) to transfer packets through the X.25 cloud. Also, X.25 used virtual circuits and statistical time-division multiplexing to transfer packets. Like the OSI and TCP/IP models, X.25 was also a layered design. X.25 defined three layers, from bottom to top: physical, frame, and packet.

The amount of error checking provided by X.25 was once an advantage due to the lower- quality transmission media that were used in the past. As media quality

The Ethical Perspective

WAN Technology, Employees, and Privacy

Many businesses rely on wide area network technologies to provide services to various groups of users. The WAN infrastructure enables project data to be shared among staff members, product information to be made available to customers, and partnering vendors to more efficiently exchange financial data. Within these three groups—employees, customers, and vendors—much discussion is taking place, particularly as to what defines appropriate use of the corporate WAN. For example, is sending an e-mail on company time to a family member using company networking technology an ethical use of that technology? Or, if an employee is accused of harassing another employee using the same corporate e-mail system, is the business also at fault if the harassed employee seeks legal damages? Wide area networks, and particularly the Internet, have transformed the boundaries between private and business communications. Today, it is not unusual for businesses and universities to have written policies on ethical behavior regarding the WAN. The San Joaquin County (California) Office of Education has a detailed employee Internet ethics and acceptable user policy that guides employee behavior (*www.sjcoe.net/InformationTechnology/ Employee.pdf*).

Businesses also expect employees to be responsible in their use, management, and protection of corporate information resources. Assume a sales representative loses her digital tablet device (DTD) and does not report the loss to her manager. The DTD had been purchased for the employee by the business. The DTD is later found by a stranger. Using information stored on the sales representative's DTD, the stranger is able to electronically break into the business's databases. The stranger succeeds in corrupting and damaging data that ultimately results in lost sales and jeopardized customer confidence. Once the break-in is discovered, the sales representative is dismissed for not having reported her loss of the DTD. The business blames the representative for not doing enough to protect the privacy of the business's customer and financial data.

Situations like this have occurred. Do you think the sales representative should have been dismissed? Do you think the sales representative had an ethical duty to report the loss of her DTD? Finally, do you think that policies such as those defined by the San Joaquin County Office of Education should bind employees to an ethical agreement? What would you include in or omit from such a policy?

improved, X.25's error-checking processes became a major disadvantage. Much of the bandwidth capacity of an X.25 network was taken up by traffic related to error control. In addition, newer types of data communications needs—specifically those related to graphics, video, multimedia, and voice—showed that X.25 was inadequate because of its limited data rate capacity.

Frame Relay

Although an older technology, **frame relay** is still in use. As a packet-switching alternative, frame relay became popular due to its relatively high-speed transmission capability, even though there are issues with its flexibility and cost. Unlike X.25, frame relay does much of its work at the data link layer of the OSI and TCP/IP models. Like X.25, frame relay uses variable-length data packets. For delivery purposes, a data link connection identifier (DLCI) identifies the virtual circuit between the sender and the receiver.

With frame relay, a subscriber negotiates a **committed information rate (CIR)** from a carrier that guarantees a specific level of bandwidth. Based on the subscriber's needs, the carrier can also dynamically provide, usually at an additional cost, more bandwidth for those occasions when network demand exceeds normal usage. This temporary need for higher bandwidth is referred to as a *burst*. The user negotiates with the carrier a price for a **committed burst rate (CBR)**, which specifies a maximum bandwidth that will be available during such temporary increases in traffic.

When connecting to a frame relay cloud, the user site makes use of a **frame relay access device (FRAD)**. The FRAD is the interface between the local user site and the frame relay cloud. Whereas frame relay does much of its work at the data link layer, the FRAD functions at the network layer. On the sending end, a FRAD takes data from the local network and repackages it for transport through the cloud. On the receiving end, another FRAD does just the opposite, repackaging the data into a form required by the local network. A FRAD can assemble and disassemble frames from other protocols, such as SNA, IP, and ATM. The frame relay access device provides no routing services, but simply forwards data packets from the local network to an edge switch at a carrier's local **point of presence (POP)**. A POP is an access point to a WAN infrastructure that is provided by a common carrier.

A leased line is the most common way that frame relay users connect to their carrier's POP. Because the cost of a leased line is usually directly related to the length of the line, the location(s) of a carrier's POP is an important consideration. Businesses choosing frame relay as a WAN solution should evaluate how many POPs a carrier has and their location when selecting a solution provider.

Another important consideration is the number of virtual circuits that run from the FRAD's leased line to other business network sites. For example, if a business has six remote sites that need to be connected through a frame relay WAN, the leased lines at each of the six sites should be capable of handling the virtual circuit traffic demands coming from the five other locations. If a leased line cannot adequately support all of the traffic coming through, an additional leased line might be required. Alternative solutions will be based on business needs. Frame relay uses only two layers—the physical layer and data link layer—thereby making it inherently more efficient than its predecessor, X.25.

At the physical layer, frame relay supports any protocol defined by ANSI (the standards-setting body identified in Chapter 1). At the data link layer, frame relay uses a simplified form of HDLC called core **link access procedure function (LAPF)**. Only a minimum level of data link control functions is provided by LAPF. This means that frame relay has far less overhead than the X.25. Another significant difference between

FIGURE 9.6 Congestion Control. This figure illustrates the concept of congestion control by using a traffic officer managing a too-busy roadway.

frame relay and X.25 is that in a frame relay network, virtually no flow and error control are supplied between links or by end-to-end routing. Instead, frame relay leaves it up to higher-level services to provide these functions. However, because frame relay does not support flow control, traffic congestion can be a significant problem.

Congestion control in frame relay has two basic characteristics: avoidance and recovery. Figure 9.6 uses the image of a traffic officer to demonstrate the concept of congestion control. Frame relay has a fairly primitive mechanism that it uses to address these two elements. It makes use of two bits in a frame to notify the sender and/or receiver of congestion on the network. Frame Relay uses a **backward-explicit congestion notification (BECN)** bit signal to alert the sender of network congestion. A **forward-explicit congestion notification (FECN)** bit signal is used to alert the receiver of network congestion. If either of these signals is detected, the network should initiate congestion-avoidance procedures.

Congestion avoidance implies that the sender or the receiver will begin to reduce, or throttle down, its transmission in recognition of the network's congested status. Here is a practical comparison. Imagine that you are driving on a superhighway whose speed limit is 70 miles per hour. Also imagine that initially there is little traffic, so it is possible to drive the maximum speed limit. Now assume you begin to encounter heavy traffic, such that you are required to throttle down your speed to 5 miles an hour. You are performing a type of congestion avoidance.

In a frame relay network, if for some reason congestion-avoidance procedures are not initiated, then congestion-recovery procedures are started. With **congestion recovery**, a "discard eligibility" bit signal is used on frames that are considered less important. If a frame's discard eligibility bit is turned on, then that frame can be discarded in the event of network congestion. Again, it will be up to higher-level network services to request retransmission of any frames discarded due to network congestion. In the superhighway example, congestion recovery would be similar to highway patrol officers directing cars off of the superhighway until traffic had a chance to clear up and return to normal.

Various vendors provide frame relay solutions. Compared with X.25, frame relay provides better transmission capacity and flexibility at a reduced cost. Still, frame relay is not a perfect solution. For the integration of voice, data, and video, frame relay has proven to be inadequate. Another WAN solution is asynchronous transfer mode.

Asynchronous Transfer Mode

The promise of **asynchronous transfer mode (ATM)** was that it could be a universal, integrated carrier of voice, data, video, and any other resource-intensive type of data. These are real advantages. However, two significant disadvantages of ATM are its high cost and high level of complexity. These two disadvantages have limited the widespread acceptance of ATM as a WAN connectivity solution. Like frame relay, ATM operates at two levels: the physical layer and data link layer. Unlike frame relay, ATM uses fixed-length packets called **cells** to transmit data. Asynchronous transfer mode cells are fixed at 53 bytes. These 53 bytes are divided into 5 bytes of header and 48 bytes of data, as shown in Figure 9.7. The 5 bytes of header may not sound like a lot, but these 5 bytes account for almost 10 percent of the total cell, a relatively large amount of cell consumption. In comparison, a full-sized Ethernet frame has less than 2 percent of its frame taken up by control information.

Because ATM cells are fixed, it is much easier to measure and regulate their bandwidth usage over a connection. The fixed cell length also makes ATM easier to manage and predict than variable-length delivery systems such as frame relay. Another feature that makes ATM so appealing is that a quality-of-service feature has been built into the protocol, making it easy to implement prioritization of data transmission. Communications considered critical can be flagged and be granted priority access to circuit capacity. As a protocol, ATM has been more successful as a backbone technology, primarily due to its cost and complexity. With desktop LAN speeds of 25.6 Mbps, ATM is at a disadvantage compared with Fast Ethernet, with its speeds of up to 100 Mbps. As a backbone, however, ATM can run up to 2.46 Gbps.

Asynchronous transfer mode is a **point-to-point protocol** solution. For this reason, ATM networks use switches rather than routers. However, ATM switches, as well as NICs, are typically more expensive than those found in a comparable Ethernet network—another disadvantage. By definition, ATM is a connection-oriented protocol that does not have broadcasting capabilities. Consequently, without complicated software interfaces, protocols such as Ethernet cannot directly detect an ATM network. The fact that setting up and maintaining an ATM network is so complicated also means that finding qualified staff can be difficult, and when found, likely expensive.

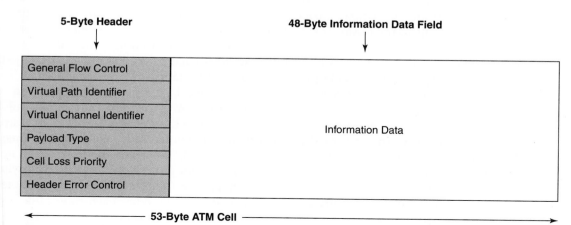

FIGURE 9.7 A Simple ATM Cell

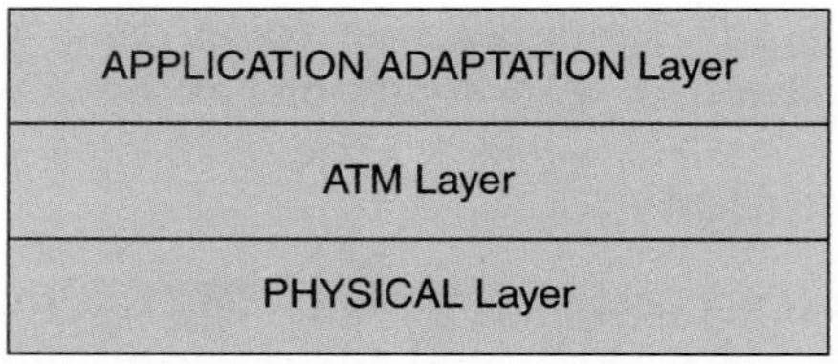

```
┌─────────────────────────────────────┐
│     APPLICATION ADAPTATION Layer      │
├─────────────────────────────────────┤
│             ATM Layer                 │
├─────────────────────────────────────┤
│           PHYSICAL Layer              │
└─────────────────────────────────────┘
```

FIGURE 9.8 The ATM Layers

Although it functions at the physical and data link layers, ATM defines three layers, as shown in Figure 9.8. From the bottom to top, these layers are the physical, the asynchronous transfer mode (ATM), and the application adaptation layers. At the physical layer, the transmission medium can be twisted-wire pair, coaxial cable, or fiber-optic. The ATM layer is responsible for delivery, traffic control, and switching and multiplexing services. For delivery, the ATM layer makes use of a **virtual path identifier (VPI)** and a **virtual channel identifier (VCI)** between the sender and the receiver. A VPI and a VCI are carried in each cell and are important for identifying the destination device. The application adaptation layer permits existing networks to connect to ATM services.

Application adaptation is responsible at the sender's end for disassembling upper-layer data into ATM's fixed 53-byte cells and at the receiver's end for reassembling the data back into its original format. A significant advantage of ATM is that it can easily handle all data types, including voice, graphics, data, audio, and video. However, for organizations that do not have high-bandwidth applications, such as videoconferencing, Gigabit Ethernet is probably a more cost-effective and more easily managed backbone solution.

Another WAN solution that has proven more popular than frame relay or ATM, and thus more widely deployed, is multi-protocol label switching. We look at that solution next.

Multi-Protocol Label Switching

Multi-protocol label switching (MPLS) works by means of what is referred to as *label* or *tag switching*. It is a solution developed by a private vendor, Cisco, and then later formalized by the Internet Engineering Task Force (IETF). A major advantage of MPLS is its ability to transfer any type of protocol data over any type of transport medium over any WAN technology. Also, MPLS has been developed such that it can accommodate mechanisms for varying classes of service. These classes of service are used to identify whether packets should be given preference in their routing. What this means to the business is that higher priority data can be labeled or tagged in such a way that this data receives preferred services and routing across the WAN. Being able to prioritize packets is definitely an advantage given that not all data needing to be transported by an enterprise is of equal importance.

Often, MPLS networks are privately owned by large telecommunication service providers. The providers, in turn, make their WAN MPLS infrastructure available to other businesses for a cost. These businesses can then utilize the MPLS infrastructure without concern for how the infrastructure is configured, maintained, or managed. This brings us back to the concept of the "cloud," by which the user of the network need not be concerned as to how data gets from point A to point B, even when the distance covered between A and B is hundreds or thousands of miles or kilometers.

With other packet-based services, such as frame relay, each router that a packet would be passed through would have to analyze the packet in some depth in order to determine the link or route that that packet should take. This is a time-consuming

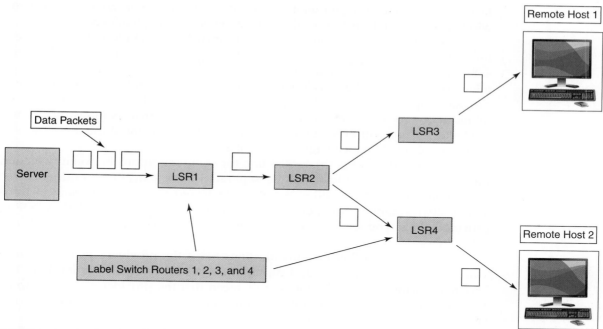

FIGURE 9.9 The MPLS Process. Data packets sent from the server below are evaluated by label switch routers (LSRs). The LSRs determine the best path for the packets based on packet destination IP address. The LSR attaches a path label to the packet and sends the packet on to its next LSR. That LSR in turn also evaluates, attaches an appropriate path label, and sends the packet onward. Label switch routers at the end of the process remove the attached labels and deliver the packets to their ultimate host devices.

process. Multi-protocol label switching does not use this method for delivering packets to their ultimate destination. Instead, packets passing through an MPLS network will have "labels" attached to them that **label edge routers** briefly evaluate. The MPLS label attached to the packet identifies that packet's next destination along its route, as well as the class of service that packet should receive. The MPLS labels that are attached to the packet are ultimately removed as the packet exits the MPLS cloud once that packet reaches its ultimate destination. Figure 9.9 illustrates this process.

TRUNK CARRIER SERVICES

Although point-to-point protocols (PPP) connections are inexpensive, widely offered, and easy to implement, they also suffer from seriously limited bandwidth capacity. A PPP provides for a direct connection between two networked devices. For many users and businesses, higher-capacity WAN links are required. Like PPP links, other options supplied by PSTN providers also include various forms of leased lines. The most commonly used forms are referred to as *T-1, T-3,* and *fractional T-1 services,* although there are others. The *T* in these names stands for **trunk carrier service**. Organizations that lease these lines are referred to as *subscribers.* T-1 lines are among the most common trunk lines for businesses and universities due to their lower cost.

Leased lines provide, at a significant cost, a dedicated and permanent connection between two sites linked by a telephone network. The line is dedicated in that it is available to the subscriber 24 hours a day, 7 days a week. The line is permanent in that it is not necessary to dial in to establish a connection. However, it is also not possible to call a different location without changing the line's hardware installation. Of course, a service provider will be happy to do whatever the business wants—for a price.

Realistically, when an organization sets up its leased line connections, it needs to plan wisely and accurately as to how the installation is to be implemented.

The cost of a leased line includes an initial installation fee, the hardware costs for connecting devices, and an ongoing monthly subscription fee. For this cost, the subscriber gets a guaranteed, specified bandwidth and quality of service, both determined by how much the subscriber is willing to pay. Within the quality of service, the provider stipulates a guaranteed percent of service availability and error-free communications. For example, the provider may guarantee that its infrastructure will be available 99.7 percent of the time and error-free 99.8 percent of the time. These types of quality of service percentages are negotiated.

The subscriber uses the leased line for communications between two connecting points. The two points may be separated by a state or a continent. For the subscriber, the PSTN provider installs a dedicated link between each of the subscriber's two communicating end points and the PSTN's own local POP. A POP is the provider's local connecting point or facility for establishing local physical links to subscribers.

Once the subscriber's communications reach the provider's POP, the provider's switching facilities take over and supply the rest of the communication link. Thus, a leased, permanent line does not literally mean that the provider gives the subscriber a single physical wire connecting two end points. Instead, the provider's switching facilities, or cloud, are being leased.

The subscriber does not need to be concerned with what happens to communications once they reach the provider's POP. From the POP, the cloud takes care of end-to-end communications. The advantage to subscribers is that they do not need to concern themselves with how the cloud is configured or maintained. The disadvantage is that subscribers have no control over how the cloud implements and secures communications.

Leased lines can be analog or digital; most leased WAN connections are digital. Digital leased lines have a range of bandwidth capacities that are referred to as **digital signal (DS)** speeds. The digital signal speeds are used to categorize the various trunk-carrier levels: T-1, T-2, T-3, and T-4. A given trunk-carrier level is capable of supporting a given number of 64-Kbps, voice-grade communication channels. The higher the trunk-carrier-level designation, the greater the number of communication channels possible, and the higher the bandwidth capacity. Table 9.1 identifies the various trunk-carrier levels and their associated characteristics.

Within a trunk-carrier level, each 64-Kbps channel can be used for voice or data traffic. One potential problem with leasing a trunk carrier is that the organization's voice and data demands may not fully utilize the amount of bandwidth available. Costs will depend on whether the T-1 line is one that spans a city or a country. Organizations that do not require a dedicated, always available T-1 connection may instead lease

Table 9.1 T-Carrier Level Characteristics

DS Level	T-Carrier Level	Bandwidth Capacity	Number of 64 Kbps Channels
DS-0	DS-0	64 Kbps	1
DS-1	T-1	1.54 Mbps	24
DS-2	T-2	6.31 Mbps	96 (4 T-1's)
DS-3	T-3	44.74 Mbps	672 (28 T-1's)
DS-4	T-4	274.18 Mbps	4,032 (168 T-1's)

a fractional T-1 connection. Fractional T-1 lines are shared by multiple subscribers and provide a more cost-effective solution for businesses whose data communication needs do not require the capacity of a private T-1 connection. However, a dedicated T-1 line might be cost-effective for an organization that has hundreds of users who need frequent, reliable, and secure access to such resources as Web and e-mail services.

CHANNEL AND DATA SERVICE UNITS

To establish a T-1 connection, each end of a digital leased line requires two devices that are usually combined into one unit: a channel service unit and a data service unit. The **channel service unit (CSU)** is the end point of the digital link; it keeps the link open and active even when the communication device connected to it—a bridge, router, or private branch exchange—is not using the link. A *private branch exchange (PBX)* is an on-site switching facility that connects the telephones of a site and provides access to a public switched telephone network (PSTN). For large organizations, T-1 lines are commonly used to support PBX operations.

The job of the **data service unit (DSU)** is to convert signals from the connecting device, again, usually a bridge, router, or PBX, into the type of digital signal, usually bipolar, required by the leased line. The CSU/DSU can be configured to provide channeled or unchanneled services. A channeled service breaks up the leased line into multiple channels for multiple uses. Multiple channels require that a multiplexer be placed between the CSU/DSU and the connection to the local network. Recall that with multiplexing, multiple devices can share a single high-speed circuit. An unchanneled service simply uses the leased line as a single-channel pipeline for transmitting communications.

At one time, T-1 lines were just about the only game in town for organizations requiring reliable, secure, and relatively high-capacity bandwidth WAN connections. Today, other solutions are available that offer cost-effective WAN services.

Chapter Summary

Wide area network connections can be established in various ways. For example, a WAN connection might be created by means of a home user connecting to the Internet or by use of elaborate packet-switching or cell relay technologies. Forms of packet-switching and cell relay technologies include frame relay (FR), asynchronous transfer mode (ATM), and multi-protocol label switching (MPLS).

A switched network is one in which a series of interlinked devices, called switches, are used to create temporary connections between two communicating devices. Switches can be hardware, software, or a combination of both. Switches can be connected to multiple links, providing for multiple pathways through a networking infrastructure. This switching infrastructure is often referred to and graphically illustrated as a cloud. Two common switching technologies are circuit and packet switching. A key characteristic of a circuit-switching service is that it creates a direct connection, or path, between two communicating devices. The term *path* is used for circuit switching; *link* is used for packet switching. Circuit-switched paths may be temporary, such as a standard dial-up connection, or permanent, meaning that the circuit is leased and is always available to the user leasing the line.

With a packet-switched network, rather than treating the data or communication as one flowing, continuous stream, similar to a voice transmission, the data are broken into units called packets. Packet switching significantly improves line efficiency because packet streams from differing communications can use the same links between packet-switching nodes. Packet-switching services may be datagram or virtual-circuit based. When a packet-switching network uses datagrams, a sender's initial message is broken into individual, independent units called datagrams. Virtual circuits (VCs) are either switched virtual circuits (SVCs) or permanent virtual circuits (PVCs).

The X.25 is a packet-switching model that was developed by the ITU-T in 1976, and is mostly obsolete. Frame relay (FR) does much of its work at the data link layer of the OSI and TCP/IP models. Frame relay uses a data link connection identifier (DLCI) that identifies virtual circuits. When connecting to a FR cloud, the user site makes use of a frame relay access device (FRAD). Like FR, asynchronous transfer mode operates at two levels—the physical layer and the data link layer. Unlike FR, ATM uses fixed-length packets, called cells, to transmit data. As a protocol, ATM has been more successful as a backbone technology, primarily due to its cost and complexity. Multi-protocol label switching (MPLS) has increasingly become the packet-switching WAN connectivity solution of first choice.

Although point-to-point protocols (PPP) connections are inexpensive, widely offered, and easy to implement, they also suffer from seriously limited bandwidth capacity. The most commonly used forms are referred to as T-1, T-3, and fractional T-1 services, although there are others. The *T* in these names stands for *trunk carrier service*.

Keywords

Asynchronous transfer mode (ATM) *183*

Backward-explicit congestion notification (BECN) *182*

Bursty *176*

Cell *183*

Circuit switching *175*

Channel service unit (CSU) *187*

Committed burst rate (CBR) *181*

Committed information rate (CIR) *181*

Congestion avoidance *182*

Congestion control *182*

Congestion recovery *182*

Datagram *177*

Data service unit (DSU) *187*

Digital signal *186*

Edge switch *175*

Forward-explicit congestion notification (FECN) *182*

Frame relay (FR) *181*

Frame relay access device (FRAD) *181*

Label edge router *185*

Link *175*

Link access procedure-function (LAPF) *181*

Multi-protocol label switching *184*

Packet *177*

Packet switching *176*

Path *175*

Permanent virtual circuit (PVC) *179*

Point of presence (POP) *181*

Point-to-point protocol (PPP) *183*

Switched network *174*

Switched virtual circuit (SVC) *179*

Trunk carrier services *185*

Virtual channel identifier (VCI) *184*

Virtual circuit (VC) *179*

Virtual circuit identifier (VCI) *179*

Virtual path identifier (VPI) *184*

Wide area network (WAN) *174*

X.25 *180*

Chapter Questions

Short-Answer Questions

1. Describe two ways in which circuit switching differs from packing switching.
2. What is meant by a switching "cloud"?
3. In what ways does frame relay differ from ATM?

4. What advantages are provided by MPLS?
5. When might a static IP address be used or preferred?
6. What is a label edge router?
7. What is meant by congestion control?
8. Where would an edge switch be placed within the context of a network design?

Hands-On Projects

1. In what key way does a datagram packet-switched service differ from a virtual circuit packet-switched service?
2. What advantages to a business are there, if any, in selecting a network provider with many POPs?
3. How does BECN differ from FECN and when are they utilized or activated?
4. What characteristics or features would you consider before purchasing or recommending a label edge router utilized in a MPLS network?

Research in Brief

For one or more of the following questions, provide a one- or two-page report based on your findings.

1. This chapter introduced packet switching services. Research the evolution of this technology. How has it changed over the last decade? What professional forums address packet switching?
2. This chapter has presented material on frame relay as a WAN connectivity solution. Visit the following website: *www.broadband-forum.org*. What types of information does the site provide? Sample and evaluate one or more of the tutorials on the site. How does this site promote the use of frame relay?
3. Investigate in greater detail how datagram packet switching differs from virtual circuit packet switching. Identify situations when one or the other may be more appropriate. Explain the relative advantages and disadvantages of each technology.
4. Multi-protocol label switching is a popular WAN connectivity solution. Research and report on the history and development of MPLS. What bodies were involved in its evolution? What benefits does an MPLS network provide? Why has MPLS become a preferred WAN connectivity solution?

Case Study

Sheehan Marketing and Public Relations

Two additional branches, one in Miami and the other in Nashville, have finally joined the three original SMPR offices. The growth of SMPR means that more networking staff must be hired. You are working closely with President Sheehan and with Karla to plan for SMPR's WAN and staffing needs.

President Sheehan has asked you to present and prepare a report identifying the different WAN connectivity options that can be used to connect the five branch offices. He wants to know the relative advantages and disadvantages of each and which one you recommend for SMPR use and why. Because of the nature of SMPR's business, very large audio and video files need to be shared by project teams who may be located at two or more remote branches. Video conferencing is not required. President Sheehan wants fast and reliable bandwidth capacity to support the type of data that SMPR's clients provide. Furthermore, he wants your solution to provide for any multiplexing that might be required across the sites. He also wants to know the costs that such a solution would entail.

You have been approved to hire three additional networking staff. Working with Human Resources, you have been asked to provide job descriptions for two intermediate networking technicians and one senior networking administrator. The vice president of Human Resources is unfamiliar with the skills required for these types of positions. He has asked you to research classified advertisements, professional organizations, and local employment agencies to develop accurate job descriptions with salary profiles.

Privately, you have some concerns that Karla may be anxious about the new hires. Over the past year, you have developed an excellent working relationship with Karla and have assisted her in getting the technical training that she needed. In fact, she has become a valuable asset, and you worry that she may be looking for another position. Do you plan to share this concern with either President Sheehan or the vice president of Human Resources? Why or why not? Would this news put Karla in an awkward position? How would you deal with Karla's unease with the new staffing positions?

Topic in Focus

DIGITAL SUBSCRIBER LINE

Digital subscriber line (DSL) has become a popular choice in the U.S. market, especially for the home user connecting to the Internet. Two factors have made DSL competitive: its relatively low cost and high transmission speeds. Digital subscriber line can support simultaneous voice and data communications based on the type of DSL service selected. Because there are different types of DSL services, DSL is not a single service type, but rather an umbrella of service types. Technically, DSL is referred to as *xDSL*, with the *x* used to indicate the type of DSL service provided, as shown in the following list:

- Asymmetrical digital subscriber line—ADSL
- Asymmetrical digital subscriber line lite—ADSL Lite
- High-bit-rate digital subscriber line—HDSL
- ISDN digital subscriber line—IDSL
- Rate-adaptive digital subscriber line—RADSL
- Symmetric digital subscriber line—SDSL
- Very-high-bit-rate digital subscriber line—VDSL

Table 9.2 provides a snapshot view of the various DSL service options and lists some of their characteristics. The characteristics of each DSL service option are described in greater detail in the following sections.

Notice in Table 8.2 that shorter segment lengths are associated with higher bandwidth capacity, and that not all forms of DSL simultaneously support voice and data communications. Notice also that depending on the type of DSL service selected, the terms *downstream* and *upstream* are used. Let's take a moment to describe what these terms mean and how they might affect a subscriber's decision as to what DSL service to choose.

Symmetric and Asymmetric DSL Services

When a user of a DSL service pulls data, meaning that the data are coming from a remote location to the local device, the term *downstream* is used. When a user pushes data from the local device to a remote device, the term *upstream* is used. When the

Table 9.2	Types of DSL Service		
Type of xDSL Service	**Segment Length**	**Simultaneous Voice Support**	**Bandwidth**
ADSL	10,000 to 18,000 feet	Yes	1.544 to 8.448 Mbps downstream 640 Kbps to 1.544 Mbps upstream
ADSL Lite	18,000 feet	Yes	Up to 1 Mbps downstream Up to 51k Kbps upstream
HDSL	12,000 to 15,000 feet	No	1.544 Mbps to 2.048 Mbps
IDSL	18,000 feet	No	Up to 144 Kbps
RADSL	10,000 to 18,000 feet	Yes	1.544 to 8.448 Mbps downstream 640 Kbps to 1.544 Mbps upstream
SDSL	10,000 feet	Yes	1.544 Mbps to 2.048 Mbps
VDSL	1,000 to 4,500 feet	Yes	12.96 to 51.84 Mbps downstream 1.6 to 2.3 Mbps upstream

DSL downstream and upstream bandwidth capacities, or speeds, are equivalent, the type of service is *symmetric*. When the two rates vary, with the downstream speed generally being greater than the upstream speed, the service is *asymmetric*. For most users, especially those at home using DSL as an Internet connectivity solution, most traffic is generated downstream, pulling data rather than pushing data upstream. For this reason, asymmetric digital subscriber line (ADSL) is among the most popular of the DSL services offered.

The typical traditional telephone line that connects a home or business to a telephone provider's local point of presence uses only a small amount of the line's bandwidth for voice communications. Standard voice communications do not require much in terms of transmission capacity. This leaves much of the bandwidth available for other services, such as DSL. Standard voice telephone bandwidth frequencies are in the range of 0 to 4,000 Hz (hertz). DSL uses frequencies above this range, up to 1.1 MHz, to carry data traffic. Critical, however, to the ability of DSL to work is the distance of the user from the telephone provider's local point of presence. Users beyond 18,000 feet of a local provider's point of presence are not able to use DSL. The greater the distance the user's local site is from the point of presence, the slower the transmission rate.

Asymmetric services are less costly than symmetric services. As it happens, when data travel upstream from the user's machine to the telephone provider's local point of presence, the wiring at the point of presence is more susceptible to near-end cross-talk, which can result in signal loss. Because signal loss is more likely to occur upstream than downstream, asymmetric services compensate by using slower upstream speeds than downstream speeds. Because most DSL users are more interested in downstream data, offering ADSL has worked out well for service providers. For businesses that require faster or equivalent upstream and downstream rates, services such as HDSL are available, but cost more because the lines used must be configured to support faster upstream rates.

Asymmetric digital subscriber line offers an "always on" connection, assuming that the devices using the connection are powered on. The data portion of an ADSL circuit functions in many ways like a leased line, but at far less cost. Because the connection is always on, there is no need for a session set-up procedure. Devices that are always on and connected to the Internet are useful in that content is always available to customers, employees, or other service users. [vendors, too?]Of course, devices that are always on and connected to the Internet are also much more vulnerable to security attacks and attempts by unauthorized users to break in. (We explore how to secure the enterprise against this type of unauthorized access in a later chapter.)

Digital subscriber line services have been positioned not only as a consumer solution for high-speed Internet access but also as a cost-effective business solution. Unlike the typical consumer, a business owner will very likely require e-mail and web hosting, an electronic payment system, online catalogs and product information, or other customer-focused services. For these reason, business DSL services generally cost more.

A business also needs to consider whether to lease a static or a dynamic IP address. Static IP addresses are fixed and unchanging. Dynamic IP addresses may change each time a connection is established. You may recall from an earlier chapter that all devices connected to the Internet must have an IP address. Static IP addresses usually cost more but have several advantages. For example, for a corporate web server that is accessed by employees and customers, a static IP address is desirable. Also, with a static IP address, the business will be able to associate and register an Internet domain name for that address. Static addresses also work well when the business needs to frequently transfer files. However, static IP addresses also pose a greater security risk, due to the fact that they are unchanging. Dynamically assigned IP addresses are like a moving target and are less susceptible to hackers. An organization should evaluate with its DSL provider whether a static or dynamic IP address is better for its business needs.

Chapter

10

Servers in the Enterprise

The Business Benefit

Choosing the right tool for the task at hand, whether that tool be a hammer, a calculator, a user-friendly product software interface, or a networked computer, is an objective that all businesses seek to implement. Without the proper tool, or technology, projects may not be completed, customer service could suffer, inventories might not be delivered or shipped, and competitors will likely step in to take your market share. For these reasons, and more, businesses try to ensure that their staff and customers have all the right tools they need to provide services and/or products or to gain easy access to services and/or products.

When configuring a network, a network designer and/or network administrator also wants to ensure that the right tools or technologies are deployed and implemented. Part of this analysis will include identifying critical hardware components that offer the right blend of quality, capability, and cost. In a computer network, having the most powerful, capable, and expensive server or client device may not make for a good business decision when a lower-end, less costly, more bare-bones device might be perfectly adequate.

Part of what this chapter discusses is precisely this type of business-based evaluation that a network administrator should consider when selecting and implementing networked devices. The business goal is simple: the right tool, for the right job, at the right cost.

Learning Objectives

After studying this chapter, you should be able to:

- Differentiate between clients and servers.
- Describe five physical components that can affect server performance.
- Identify the major types of servers.
- Understand the basic functionalities of the major types of servers.
- Describe how well-known ports are used in a TCP/IP environment.
- Explain server clustering and its advantages.
- Understand the concept of system area networks (SANs).

Up to now, you have learned about different data communications networking models, including LANs, BNs, MANs, and WANs. In the next three chapters of this text we'll begin to consider ways in which these models can be integrated, supported, and secured. Various hardware devices and their associated software are critical to the seamless integration of these networking models.

SERVERS AND CLIENTS

Servers have become a critical component at all levels of the enterprise. This chapter explores how and why servers differ from clients. The chapter also presents several types of commonly used servers. How servers were used in the past and how they are used today are in some ways the same, but in other ways quite different. Let's begin by defining servers and clients.

At its simplest level, a **server** is a device that provides services and resources to other devices, called clients. A **client** is a device that requests services and resources from servers. In the distant past, the late 1980s, the distinction between servers and clients was very clear. Servers were dedicated; they only provided resources to clients, they were never used as clients themselves. Similarly, clients never functioned as servers, meaning that clients did not share resources or services with other clients. Servers and clients had specific, limited roles, as conceptualized in Figure 10.1. Servers and clients also had distinctly different types of operating systems.

This all changed with the introduction of network-aware client desktop operating systems. Client desktop operating systems that are network aware are capable of sharing their local resources (e.g., printers or files on a hard drive of the devices on which they run). One of the earliest examples of this type of network-aware desktop operating system was Microsoft's Windows for Workgroups, introduced in 1992. Desktop operating systems that are network aware can be fairly easily configured to run in a peer-to-peer networking model. A peer-to-peer network allows a device to function as both a server and/or a client based on how that device is configured.

Virtually all current client desktop operating systems are able to run in a peer-to-peer network. For very small networks, this works well; however, for medium- to large-scale networks, the peer-to-peer model is inefficient and difficult to manage. Also, for very small networks, it is possible to run server services on standard desktop computers. However, more robust and demanding networks require specialized servers running specialized software.

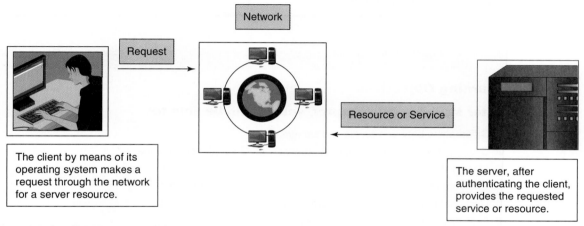

The client by means of its operating system makes a request through the network for a server resource.

The server, after authenticating the client, provides the requested service or resource.

FIGURE 10.1 The Client/Server Model

Today, servers normally run some type of **server operating system (SOS)** that provides services and resources to clients. In the past, an SOS was also referred to as a **network operating system (NOS)**. Although servers using modern SOSs can function as clients, this is not common. Instead, most servers are, for all practical purposes, dedicated machines that do not perform such client-based tasks as word processing, payroll, or inventory analysis. Typically, servers are physically secured in such a way that only certain authorized personnel can access them. Because of how servers are used, they have specific physical considerations that make them different from clients.

SERVER CHARACTERISTICS

Because servers are not used in the same way that client machines are used, servers differ physically from clients. For example, servers do not normally need to offer audio features. Therefore, servers are not usually provided with speakers or advanced audio/sound features. Considering that servers are frequently locked away in secured rooms or closets, it makes sense that a high-end sound system would not be deemed very significant or cost-effective. Other physical characteristics, however, are significant. This section considers five physical features that differentiate a server from a client: the physical case, the memory, the processor, the drive interface, and NIC support.

The Physical Case

Client machines are usually placed on top of or very near a user's physical desk, hence the term *desktop computer*. Because other items occupy the space on or near a user's work area, the footprint of client machines is usually kept to a minimum. This means that the physical case that houses the components that make up the user's computer is also kept to a minimum. If you have ever opened up a standard desktop computer, you know that inside the case there is generally not much room. Circuitry and components are positioned very tightly in order to make the case, and its footprint, as small as practically possible. With a server, however, small footprints are not as critical an issue.

In most enterprises, servers are not left in public or open areas where they are vulnerable to unauthorized access. Instead, whenever possible, servers are placed in secured rooms or closets. Because servers are isolated and infrequently accessed by staff, footprint considerations are not as critical as with a client machine. The result is that servers generally have larger and more rugged physical cases than do client machines. A server case is frequently referred to as a **chassis**. Larger physical cases also make it easier to upgrade a server because there is more space for expansion bays and slots and because there is more room to work within the case.

Larger cases also allow for more components to be installed within the server. With more components, more electrical power is required. This means that servers, because of the quantity of components within a case, also tend to have larger, more robust power supplies. Not only will a server have a stronger power supply but it will also have redundant power supplies, depending on how critical the server is in the event of a power failure. Because power surges can also negatively affect a computer's circuitry, a server might also have an internal surge protector. Of course, such redundant and additional features also have additional costs.

The Memory and the Processor

At the time of this writing, standard client machines typically come configured with 2 to 4 GB of memory called **random access memory (RAM)**. The RAM modules, or sticks, plug into slots housed on a computer's motherboard. A **motherboard** is the key circuitry component that all internal devices connect to within a computer's case. Servers generally accommodate much higher RAM capacities than do clients, supporting anywhere from a very low end of 4 to 32 GB or more. Furthermore, although a server's motherboard may not have more RAM slots than a typical desktop computer, the server's RAM slots are usually able to support much higher-capacity sticks of RAM.

Another key difference between a server's motherboard and a client's is the number of processor slots on the motherboard. A processor is also referred to as a **central processing unit (CPU)**. The CPU is the workhorse of the computer and is critical to the processing of instructions and data. A standard client machine may have one, or perhaps two, CPU slots on its motherboard. However, a server might have 4, 8, 16, 32, or more CPUs. Of course, the more CPUs that are supported and used, the higher the cost of the server. Also, servers with multiple CPUs require SOSs that support this functionality. If a server has eight CPUs but its SOS only supports four, then half of that server's processing power will go [or goes] unused.

Operating systems that can simultaneously control two or more physical CPUs are said to be SMP **symmetric multiprocessing (SMP)** capable. The processors being controlled are given equal access to input/output devices. Today, SMP CPUs for LAN servers are fairly common. The advantage of using multiple CPUs within a server is that processing tasks can be shared by the CPUs. Symmetric multiprocessing CPUs share a common memory pool and input/output (I/O) bus. A motherboard has several types of buses. A **bus** is the circuitry on the motherboard that allows data to be moved from one location of the computer to another.

One problem with servers using multiple SMP CPUs is that although the CPUs share a common memory pool, they do not share cache memory. **Cache memory** is a very high-speed memory, faster than ordinary RAM, that is used for recently or frequently accessed data and instructions. Each CPU has its own cache. Data or instructions needed by one CPU might be stored in the cache of a different CPU. Motherboards that provide for multiple SMP CPUs are hardwired to allow CPUs to reference each other's cache, but this referencing results in additional processing overhead. Beyond eight CPUs, the overhead needed to support cache referencing, as well as memory and I/O bus sharing, can result in contention problems that will cause server responsiveness to degrade. Also, for a server running multiple CPUs, should one of the CPUs fail, it may be necessary to stop, repair, or remove the failing CPU and then restart the server. Bringing down a server, even for a short period of time, is something network administrators try to avoid.

The Drive Interface: IDE, SATA, and SCSI

Servers typically need to support more drives than a standard desktop machine. Because servers provide resources to potentially hundreds, if not thousands, of users concurrently, they have to support varied and highly capable drive systems. Three common **drive interfaces** are IDE (integrated drive electronics), SATA (serial advanced technology attachment), and SCSI (small computer system interface). **Integrated drive electronics** is an older technology and has largely been replaced with SATA. In general, IDE and **serial advanced technology attachment** drives are used for user desktop workstations, and **small computer system interface** is used for servers or high-performance computers. The combined IDE/SATA is more often used in client devices for a number of reasons, with cost being the most significant. An enterprise will generally have many more clients than servers, and because IDE/SATA drives are relatively inexpensive, it makes economic sense to configure most clients with IDE/SATA technology.

Because IDE/SATA is limited in the number of devices it can support, it may not a good choice for data-intensive services. Rather, SCSI is commonly found in servers that support large numbers of clients. Small computer system interface can support up to 15 internal and/or external devices. Those SCI devices also require, like IDE/SATA devices, a controller. A SCSI controller is commonly referred to as a *host adapter*. The SCSI host adapter may be part of the server's motherboard or it may be an expansion card that plugs into an available motherboard slot, with the latter being more common. The SCSI devices also use their own specific types of cables.

The SCSI host adapter uses a parallel bus to communicate with the devices attached to it. Each device on the parallel bus has its own unique SCSI identifier number. The SCSI devices plug into each other in a daisy-chain manner, forming what looks and functions like a mini-network of SCSI devices. Because of their parallel bus, SCSI devices can work independently of each other and are not restricted to a shared channel as IDE devices are. Especially for frequently accessed hard drives shared across a network, SCSI provides much better performance. Also, SCSI supports device types that IDE/SAT may not be able to do. The downside to all of this is that SCSI is a more complicated and expensive technology than IDE/SATA. However, the benefits of SCSI as a server technology sufficiently outweigh its cost and complexity, making SCSI a drive interface of choice for servers.

Network Interface Cards (NICs)

Drives, and hard drives in particular, can be a critical bottleneck in a network when demand from clients exceeds the ability of the server to respond in a timely manner. Because of this type of demand, servers commonly use SCSI devices. Another component that can result in a network performance bottleneck is the server's network interface card. Whether the device is a client or server, devices connected to the network must have a NIC. Before data can enter or exit a networked machine, the data must pass through that device's NIC. The speed, or throughput, at which the NIC is capable of passing data becomes a significant factor in how responsive that NIC-connected device can be. For a server that has a lot of traffic passing to and through it, having a fast NIC is a necessity.

All of the devices in the network do not have to have NICs of the same throughput capacity. Faster and more capable NICs cost more. In a network, the NICs used by clients do not have to be of the same capability as those used by the servers. Using less expensive and less capable NICs for clients helps keep network costs down. For example, clients may use standard Ethernet NICs, whereas servers on the backbone may use Fast or Gigabit Ethernet NICs. Additionally, because NICs can support either half- or full-duplex communications, it may be worth the cost to purchase server NICs that are capable of full-duplex communications. Servers that experience significant throughput traffic should have full-duplex NICs.

Server NICs can also support **direct memory access (DMA)**, which allows the server to move data directly from the NIC's memory buffer to server RAM without the direct intervention of the server's processor. A server NIC might also use bus mastering. **Bus mastering** enables the NIC to take temporary control of the bus into which it is plugged to move data directly into the server's system RAM. In addition, NICs may have their own RAM, called buffers. With larger buffers, the NIC can store data that it cannot immediately process. The NIC can then process the data later, with later being mere fractions of a second, thereby preventing the NIC from becoming a bottleneck. Finally, NICs can incorporate their own processors. By having a processor on the NIC, the NIC puts less work on the server's processor, thereby improving network performance.

As physical and logical devices, servers are regularly monitored to ensure that they are running correctly and at optimal performance. Many monitoring tools are available to network administrators to help them keep their servers running in top form. See the "Topic in Focus" at the end of this chapter for information on just a few such tools.

TYPES OF SERVERS

Now that you have learned how servers differ physically from clients, let's examine a few of the different types of servers that an enterprise might use. If a resource can be networked, a server can probably be configured to manage it. Networked resources may include data, software, hardware, information, e-mail, or directory services or anything else that needs to be shared and managed. Depending on what the server does, how many users it services, and the complexity of the resource or resources that it manages, the server will need to be more or less capable. Also keep in mind that a single physical device can run more than one logical server. Servers are logical as well as physical. One physical device may be an e-mail server, a file server, and a web server, all at the same time. However, if one device runs too many types of server services, network performance begins to degrade. As performance degrades, thought should be given to dividing out server services to other physical server devices.

File and Application Servers

Files and applications are two commonly accessed resources needed by multiple users in an enterprise. Keeping duplicate copies of frequently used files on each user's local hard drive very quickly proves unmanageable and confusing. Who has the most current version of the file? When was the file last updated and by whom? If a file is copied across multiple locations, how can it be secured? How many copies of the file have been distributed? As you can see, such a system would be quite problematic. File servers that control, manage, and make commonly used files available by request are a better solution for networked environments.

File servers control access to file and disk resources. These servers also are usually configured to authenticate users before they can access a file resource, thereby providing a level of security. Not only can users be authenticated, but access to files can be synchronized. Synchronization of access can be critical when two or more users are attempting to modify the same file. In such a scenario, without controls, it is possible for one user's changes to overwrite those made by a different user. A well-run file server ensures that file or data locking occurs so that files do not become corrupted.

A file server must be fast and reliable and have sufficient storage to accommodate users' needs. File server services are often implemented through software that runs on a physical device. One potential problem with file servers is that when users log in to the server to request a file, the server must send the entire file across the network to the user's local machine. If the file is small, the traffic and time needed to send it across the network is not likely to be significant. But for very large files, the traffic generated by sending copies across the network may result in a file server bottleneck. Fast hard drive access is essential and is one reason, as discussed earlier, that SCSI drives are a popular choice for servers.

Like frequently used files, applications can also benefit from server management. Businesses usually find that they save money by using site or metered licensing for commonly used applications rather than giving users their own individual licensed copy. Maintaining one version of an application that everyone uses is much simpler than trying to maintain multiple versions across multiple workstations. Also, when applications are stored and accessed from a central application server, upgrading the application becomes much easier.

Applications that are controlled and run from a server have two parts. One part, called the **front end**, runs on the client machine. The front end allows the user from his or her local machine to request and give commands necessary to the **application server**. The second part, the **back end**, runs on the application server, and, depending on the application, much of the work can be performed there. To the user, it appears as if the application is running on his or her local machine. This front-end/back-end structure typifies a client/server architecture. Be aware that not all applications can be networked, which may be a business factor when selecting applications.

Database Servers

Database servers provide management access control software that makes database records available to users across the network. Based on a user's request for data, the database server retrieves the data record, processes the data according to the user's request, and sends the result of the process to the requesting user. This means that, unlike a file server, much of the work is done on the database server, not on the user's local device. Like application servers, database servers have a front end on the client and a back end on the server.

For very large databases, servers can be configured to manage a portion of the database, which results in a distributed database environment. Databases can be distributed in a number of different ways. For example, one database server may host customer accounts A through M, whereas a second server, in a different physical location, hosts accounts N through Z. Another distribution could be by geographical location or by functionality. However the database is distributed, to the user it appears as if the database is at one physical location. Figure 10.2 illustrates the distributed database concept.

Database servers can also be configured so that they replicate the database across several locations. In such a situation, as the master version of the database is modified, the modifications are replicated to copies of the database that are maintained in other locations. In this discussion, replication means that a master or original version of the database is copied and/or updated to other database servers. Replication of databases can be very handy when user groups are scattered across remote distances.

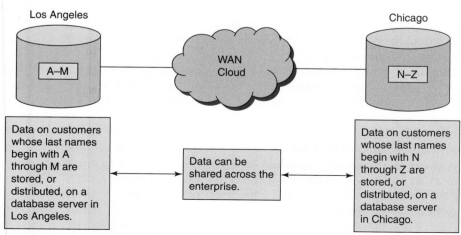

FIGURE 10.2 Distributed Database

For example, a business with a branch office in Los Angeles and another in Chicago could benefit from replicated database technology. If there were two database servers, one in Chicago and one in Los Angeles, each user group would have faster access to the database because a copy of the database is geographically close to it and its applications.

Web, E-mail, and FTP Servers

Many organizations rely on web-based services to support their clients and staff. A business may want to make an online catalog available to customers or allow staff to remotely login to project files hosted on a web server. Simply put, **web servers** run software that enables clients to make requests for services. For web services to function, the client must also have a component called a **browser** in order to make requests.

A web server runs application layer TCP/IP protocols. One such protocol is **hypertext transfer protocol (HTTP)**. Another commonly used protocol is **file transfer protocol (FTP)**. Webpages hosted on a web server are expressed, or programmed, in **hypertext markup language (HTML)**—referred to as a "tag-based" programming language because it uses "tags" to indicate what function or operation to perform when displaying a webpage. Web servers, based on what they need to do, do not necessarily have to be powerful machines. However, the more clients that are expected to access the web server, the more capable the web server needs to be. Another option, typical with e-mail servers, is to have more than one server of a particular type available for client access. For organizations that support moderate- to large-scale e-mail, FTP, or website hosting, multiple web servers are usually configured to provide the needed resources.

A web server is a program. Windows- and UNIX-based web servers have been the most common. That may change with the advent of Linux. In the UNIX world, the Apache server is highly popular. Apache is an open-source technology that supports not only UNIX but Windows and Macintosh platforms as well. Regardless of its origination, a web server program running on its host computer "listens" for incoming client browser TCP requests.

Requests come to the web server over ports. **Ports** are logical designations that represent a particular type of requested service. *Port values,* referred to as **well-known ports,** are assigned by the Internet Assigned Numbers Authority, or IANA. The most common port used by client browsers when requesting a HTTP service is port 80; it is the standard port for an HTTP server. (Port 80, in fact, is one of the most targeted ports assaulted by hackers attempting to break into a network. Why? Because port 80 is used extensively in HTTP for access by a web client browser. Chapter 12 explores port security in more detail.)

Different types of service requests are made using different logical port designators. Many such application layer service requests have been standardized to use particular logical, well-known ports. Although web-based services use many well-known port identifiers, depending on the network, nonstandard ports also can be specified. However, if a client uses something other than the standard port for a particular service, the nonstandard port number must be specified in the request.

A client request is accomplished through what is known as a **uniform resource locator (URL)**. For most users of a web server, a URL takes the form of a World Wide Web (WWW) address—for example, *http://www.pearson.com.*

A URL may have four parts. First, a protocol is specified. In the example address, the protocol is HTTP. For a FTP server, the protocol is ftp://. Second, either the server's IP address or the server's domain name system (DNS) is provided. Third, a port number may be provided. If the port number is the standard logical port for the requested service, then the number does not have to be provided. For example, an HTTP request using standard logical port 80 would not have to include 80 in the request URL. Finally, the directory and/or file being requested needs to be specified. Thus, a URL has the following format: protocol://server-identifier:port-identifier/directory/file.htm.

For the address provided in the example, a complete URL would look like *http://www.pearson.com:80/index.html*. In this example, it is not necessary to specify port 80 because that is the default well-known port for this URL request. However, if the URL were not available at standard port 80, the nonstandard port would have to be included in the URL request.

Simple mail transfer protocol (SMTP) is another application layer protocol used by TCP/IP. When TCP is used as the transport protocol, SMTP uses well-known port 25 at the server. SMTP servers receive outgoing e-mail from clients and transmit e-mail to destination e-mail servers. Another type of e-mail server works with SMTP to maintain the mailboxes from which clients access their e-mail. The two most common installations of this type of server are **post office protocol version 3 (POP3)** and **Internet message access protocol (IMAP)**. Both POP3 and IMAP often run on the same physical device as the SMTP server. More sophisticated e-mail server products are available from such vendors as Microsoft, Novell, and IBM, among others.

A POP3 server provides basic mailbox services. A client needs a service such as a POP3 server because clients, in general, are not always connected to the Internet or to the network that provides their e-mail. Because clients are not always connected, they are not always available to receive incoming e-mail from an SMTP server. This is where POP3 comes in. A POP3 server is, or at least should be, always connected to the network so that it is always available to receive e-mail from an SMTP server. It can temporarily store the client's e-mail in a mailbox so that the client can eventually access and download his or her mail. The POP3 uses well-known port 110.

Whereas POP3 provides for only temporary storage of a client's e-mail, IMAP stores e-mail on its server for as long as required, even permanently. Thus, IMAP is a more sophisticated mailbox service protocol and offers more ways for clients to access and control their e-mail. It allows clients to create folders in their mailboxes in order to file their messages. Also, IMAP allows clients to view their mail in a list format by header only, so that clients can more easily select which messages they want to download. Finally, IMAP allows for search capabilities not provided by POP3, so a client can search messages based on the header, subject, or body of the message itself. The benefits of IMAP, though, come at a cost. For instance, IMAP requires much more in terms of network and system resources. The choice between POP3 and IMAP may depend on how critically important the organization views its e-mail capabilities.

File transfer protocol is also a widely used application layer service that requires an FTP server and client. An FTP server enables authenticated clients to transfer files from one host machine to another. As a service, FTP is fairly basic, having just a few file-management commands. Unlike HTTP, which uses a single well-known port, FTP uses two ports to perform its job. Well-known port 21 is used by an FTP client to create a connection to an FTP server. If successful, this connection remains intact and open for the duration of the communication. Using the port 21 connection, the FTP client and server can exchange command and reply information. For the file transfer itself, the FTP server creates a second connection over well-known port 20. After the file has been transferred, the port 20 connection is terminated. Table 10.1 summarizes some of the most commonly used well-known ports.

Table 10.1	Common Well-Known Ports
Port	**Service**
8	Ping requests
20	FTP file transfer
21	FTP client/server command exchange
25	E-mail
67	DHCP server
68	DHCP client
80	HTTP webpage transfers
135	Microsoft distributed computing environment locator service for remote service management
139	Windows file and print services
445	Microsoft transport service for server message block over TCP
1433	Microsoft SQL server
3128	Proxy services
8080	HTTP and proxy servers

Keep in mind that whether using web, e-mail, or FTP services, both a server and a client must be involved for the service to be successful. Many free programs are available for each of these services for both the client and the server. Many other programs are available for a fee. Fee-based programs usually have more features, a better user interface, and documentation and/or support.

The Ethical Perspective

Using Web Server Technology to Track Employees

Web servers enable a business to have a global presence. Using web servers, a business can market, sell, and track products and services to customers who are geographically distant from the business. Web servers, however, can also be used by a business to track and observe its own employees. Many employees may not be aware that web servers are configured to maintain activity logs. These activity logs are like electronic diaries that keep track of every activity an employee performs while using web-based services. As an example, the following list identifies just a few of the types of information that a web server can record and track:

- The name, domain, and Internet address of the host computer from which the employee accesses a website
- The date, time, and duration that an employee spends at a particular website
- The specific webpage accessed within a website; the number of times a particular page was accessed; and whether any data, text, audio, or graphic files were downloaded

Most businesses require employees to log in to their workstations using a unique user ID and password. Yet, it is possible that an employee could step away from his or her desk, perhaps for a coffee or tea break, without logging out of his or her workstation.

In the employee's absence, someone else could then use that workstation in a manner that violates company policies. For example, a business policy on sexual harassment may state that employee workstations may not be used to view pornographic websites and that employees who violate this policy will be terminated.

If such a scenario were to occur, do you think that the business has an ethical duty to verify that the employee being dismissed was in fact the policy-violating employee? What if the innocent employee claims that he or she had no knowledge of the policy violation and did not even know about such a policy because the policy had not been openly and visibly published for all employees to read? How do you think such a situation should be handled? Software application monitoring products are available that can invisibly record a user's e-mail, chat, instant message sessions, websites visited, and keystrokes entered and then place this information in a hidden location on a user's computer. A manager could then later review this recorded data.

Do you think this type of recording would engender a sense of trust among employees? Do you think a business and/or manager is ethically correct in installing such recording software on a worker's computer? Are there arguments for and against this type of employer tracking of employee activities? On its website (*www.ethix.org*), the Institute for Business, Technology, and Ethics (IBTE) provides commentary and articles for an ethically run business.

What do you think are the ethical boundaries a business should follow in tracking its employees?

Domain Name System Servers

Another type of server of particular importance in a TCP/IP environment is a **domain name system (DNS) server**. To understand this type of server, you must first understand what is meant by DNS. Recall that in the TCP/IP model, there are several types of addresses. For example, the data link layer has a MAC physical address. The network layer has a logical IP addresses. The application layer has a type of address called a domain name. Domain names are used at the application level because they are much easier for mere mortals to understand and work with than data link or network layer addresses. Thus, DNS has evolved and is in place so that people can understand and more easily recognize the devices in a TCP/IP world.

Simply stated, the DNS matches a web host's IP address with a more English-type domain name address if that host is going to be accessed by other hosts for such services as web hosting, FTP, e-mail, and so on. Such a host is usually a server of some type. The DNS allows for an IP address to be associated with its domain name address. Like HTTP, FTP, and TCP, DNS is a protocol. To resolve an IP logical address to a DNS address, a sequence of steps is followed. These steps are illustrated in Figure 10.3.

A DNS is based on a hierarchy of domains. A domain is similar to a directory. Like a directory on a computer's hard drive that can have subdirectories, a domain can have subdomains. This structure of domains with associated subdomains is how the DNS hierarchy is constructed. There are top-level domains and second-level domains. The best known, and original, top-level domains include .com, .edu, .gov, .int, .mil, .net, and .org. The Internet organization that controls assignment of top-level domains (ICANN) has since considered and accepted other top-level domain names as shown in Figure 10.4, which charts the domain hierarchy.

Domain name system servers resolve a domain name, such as *www.pearson.com*, to its equivalent IP address. A **domain name** is resolved when the DNS server matches a client's IP address with a domain name address. In a TCP/IP network, client devices are configured to point to one or more DNS servers.

1. A client browser sends a request to its local, primary, DNS server for resolving a domain name address—for example, What is the IP address of http://www.pearson.com.?

2. If the local DNS server does not have this information, the local DNS server sends a request to the root domain server for the required information.

3. The root domain server responds by sending to the local DNS server the IP address of the remote, secondary, DNS server responsible for the domain being requested.

4. The local DNS server then contacts by the secondary, remote DNS server.

5. The remote DNS server gives to the local DNS server the requested IP address information—for example, 201.14.101.0.

6. The local DNS server then gives this IP address information to its local client.

7. The local client with the required IP address information can now directly request, through its browser, information from the web server hosting the information for http://www.pearson.com.

8. The web server hosting information for http://www.pearson.com sends to the requesting client browser the requested information.

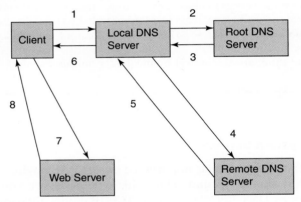

FIGURE 10.3   Steps in the DNS Resolution Process

This process is pretty much invisible to the user. The user enters a URL in a web browser on the client device. The client device then issues a request to its associated DNS server to resolve, or discover, what IP address is associated with the URL that the user entered. The DNS server may or may not have that information stored in its own local table held in its memory. If the information is available, the DNS server provides the requested information to the client. If it is not available, the DNS server issues its own request to other DNS servers to see if they have the required information. In the event that a bad URL has been entered or if the desired host is not available for some reason, the client is eventually so informed. If the URL is good and the desired host is available, other protocols, such as HTTP or FTP, take over and deliver the data.

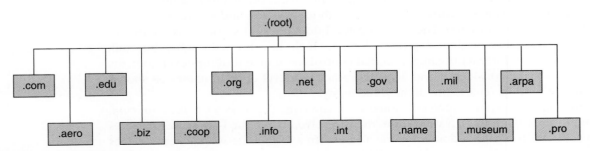

FIGURE 10.4   The DNS Hierarchy

It is not unusual for organizations to have more than one device configured as a DNS server. If an organization has only one DNS server, then clients would not be able to have their URLs resolved if that server were to fail. In simple terms, a failed server would mean no Internet access. Also, in a network with a lot of web-based requests, having only one DNS server can result in bottlenecks because all clients have to go through that single DNS server for address resolution.

Dynamic Host Configuration Protocol Servers

Clients in a TCP/IP network have to be configured so that they can identify their DNS servers. Clients also must have their own IP addresses. Without an IP address, a TCP/IP client cannot function in a TCP/IP network. For very small networks, it is possible for network technicians to manually configure and maintain each client's IP address. In this scenario, the IP addresses are usually fixed, meaning that they can be changed only by a networking technician. This type of unchanging address is called a **static IP address**. However, if the network contains hundreds or thousands of clients, it becomes very complicated and difficult to manually configure and maintain static IP addresses. To address the problem of assigning and maintaining many static client IP addresses, another protocol was developed: dynamic host configuration protocol (DHCP).

The term *dynamic* implies that the service is automated. By being automated, network administrators are relieved from having to manually configure and maintain client IP addresses in their enterprise. **Dynamic host configuration protocol** is a service that runs on a designated DHCP server. Clients interact with the DHCP server to retrieve and determine their IP addresses. A client configured to use a DHCP server does not have a static IP address. Instead, the client will use dynamic addressing through a DHCP server. To access a DHCP server, clients must be configured with the address or addresses of their DHCP servers. A client configured to function in a DHCP environment will, as it boots or powers up, issue a request based on its configuration information to a local DHCP server.

The primary job of the DHCP server is to assign IP addresses, although DHCP servers can perform other related tasks. How a DHCP server assigns an address can vary. For example, some DHCP servers can be configured to assign a specific, fixed IP address to particular clients. This may be useful for host machines that need a stable and unchanging IP address value—for example, routers, web servers, or FTP servers. In a more typical scenario, a DHCP server is configured to have a pool of IP addresses available to it. This type of DHCP server allocates IP addresses from its pool to client machines as clients power up and request addresses. Usually, clients assigned IP addresses in this way are only given a "lease" on the address, meaning at some point the client has to reissue a request to renew its lease on its "temporary" IP address. In such a case, the leased address may or may not be renewed depending on other network variables.

Using port 67 at the server and port 68 at the client, DHCP servers can also be set up to provide information to clients on subnet masking. Most modern client desktop operating systems are capable of functioning as a DHCP client. As with e-mail and FTP servers, open-source code for DHCP is widely available.

Proxy Servers

Like many of the other types of servers presented thus far, a **proxy server** is a program or service that can run on a physical device hosting other types of services or servers. The intent of a proxy server is to provide a measure of security. A proxy server provides security by functioning as an intermediary between a client and a server. This fact should be clearer after the term *proxy* is defined.

Being a *proxy* literally means having the authority to act for another. Thus, a person who is a proxy has another person's authority to act on his or her behalf. For example, let's say that a public figure was concerned for her privacy or safety and did not want to meet with a group of reporters. She might designate a proxy to meet with the reporters. The proxy would then communicate back to the public figure what the reporters wanted her to know. Thus, the proxy acts as a layer between the public figure and the reporters. A proxy server functions in a similar manner.

Proxy servers are commonly used in situations where filtering is desirable. In the case of a network, if a client on the inside of a firewall (a protective program discussed in Chapter 12) wants to communicate with a device outside the firewall, a proxy server could be used. The proxy server takes the client's request from inside the firewall and passes this communication to the device outside the firewall. To the device outside the firewall, the proxy server is the originating communicating device. The original, or true, communicating device is hidden from the receiver. The type of filtering provided by a proxy gives a great deal of assistance to the firewall. In fact, a firewall may have a separate proxy server for each application used by client devices.

Used primarily for web-based communications, client browsers can be configured to send all of their outgoing requests to a proxy server rather than directly to an Internet server. The proxy server, using its own IP address, not the originating client's address, acts on the client's behalf and passes the client's request to the Internet server. Keep in mind that many clients can go through the proxy. The internal IP addresses of these clients are also hidden. Thus, by using a proxy server's IP address, outsiders are limited in what they can discover about a network's internal architecture. This is a real benefit to security. As with the other server types discussed thus far, both the client and the server must be configured for the proxy service.

SERVER CLUSTERS

Very small organizations may have only one or two servers, whereas large organizations might have hundreds. One way to take advantage of multiple servers in the enterprise is to connect them into a group called a *server cluster.* To a client device accessing a server cluster, the servers in the cluster appear to be a single server. A key advantage of having servers participate in a cluster is that the servers can now share their workload, resulting in the load balancing of network traffic. Another advantage of server clusters is that they provide improved fault tolerance. Should one of the servers in the cluster fail, other servers in the cluster can be configured to take over the failing server's responsibilities. This process is referred to as **failover capability**.

Servers participating in a cluster are connected not only physically but logically as well through their SOS. Depending on the type of server operator system, server behavior within the cluster can vary. In a network load-balancing cluster, each server has its own resources (i.e., its own hard drives and applications). Each server in a load-balancing cluster can function as an independent unit, although the servers may share applications and storage. Additionally, servers in the cluster provide each other with updated status information. This means that clustered servers share with each other their current workload demands and other relevant information.

Clients connect to what they see as a single server. Once connected, they can be directed to the server in the cluster that has the smallest workload. In this sense, the clients see a virtual server. A **virtual server** is highly scalable because it is built

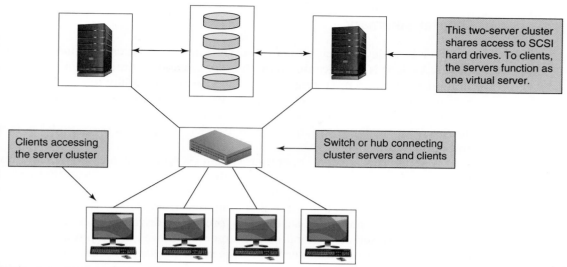

This two-server cluster shares access to SCSI hard drives. To clients, the servers function as one virtual server.

Clients accessing the server cluster

Switch or hub connecting cluster servers and clients

FIGURE 10.5   Servers in a Server Cluster

on a cluster of real servers. The fact that the virtual server is scalable means that servers in the cluster can be added or removed as network demands require. The makeup of the virtual server cluster is transparent to the clients using it. Clients see only a single virtual server. Figure 10.5 illustrates the concept of a virtual server in a two-server cluster environment.

SYSTEM AREA NETWORKS

The success of server clusters has resulted in the development of a technology called **system area networks (SANs)**. As with most other technologies we have discussed, standards for SANs are still evolving. A SAN is a local network designed for high-speed interconnection (server to server) in cluster environments using multiprocessing systems and storage area networks. These SANs almost exclusively use what is called a *switched fabric*. A switched fabric refers to how ports within a switch are linked so that they can communicate and transfer data. In this instance, a switched fabric refers to the physical ports that enable devices to connect to a switch, not the logical well-known ports that were presented earlier.

An Ethernet switch has physical ports that devices can plug into or connect to. Within the switch, hardware circuitry connects the physical ports. This interconnection creates what vendors call a switching fabric. This switching fabric can then provide for high data-transfer rates. **Fibre channel** is an implementation of a switched fabric that is usually associated with a system area network. A fibre channel can utilize a half-duplex or full-duplex. To differentiate fibre channel from fiber-optic, note that the differing spelling of *fibre*. Fibre channel provides a high-speed switched environment in which any device on the network can connect with any other device and then communicate over a dedicated high-speed link. It at the physical and data link layers of the OSI and TCP/IP models. Using standard networking hardware elements, fibre channel implements much of its functionality in the hardware that it uses rather than programmatically.

Chapter Summary

A server is a device that provides services and resources to other devices called clients. A client is a device that requests services and resources from servers. Virtually all modern desktop operating systems incorporate the ability to run in a peer-to-peer network. In a peer-to-peer network, a device can function as a client, a server, or both, depending on how the client is configured. For very small networks this works well; however, for medium- to large-scale networks, the peer-to-peer model is inefficient and difficult to manage.

A server runs a server operating system (SOS) to provide services and resources to clients. Typically, servers are physically secured in such a way that only certain authorized personnel can access them. Because of how servers are used, they have specific physical attributes that make them different from clients. These attributes include differences in the physical case, memory, processor, drive interface, and NIC support.

Generally, servers generally have larger and more rugged physical cases than client machines. Because a server has a large physical case, it is easy to upgrade because there is room for expansion bays and slots and more room to work within the case. Servers can support higher RAM capacities than clients. A server's motherboard may have more processor slots than a client motherboard. Whereas a client machine may have only one, or at the most two, CPU slots on its motherboard, a server can have 4, 8, 16, 32, or more CPUs.

Most servers typically need to support more drives than a standard desktop machine does. Three common drive interfaces are integrated drive electronics (IDE), serial advanced technology attachment (SATA), and small computer system interface (SCSI). In general, IDE and SATA drives are used for user desktop workstations, and SCSI is used for servers or high-performance computers. A SCSI host adapter uses a parallel bus to communicate with the devices attached to it. Each device on the parallel bus has its own unique SCSI identifier number.

The type of NIC card installed on a server can cause or prevent network bottlenecks. If a server has a lot of traffic passing to and through it, it should have a fast, full-duplex NIC. If the NIC card is not adequate for the traffic, a bottleneck will result. Network performance can also be improved by having a processor on the NIC. When the NIC has a processor, the NIC puts less work on the server's processor, thereby improving network performance.

If a resource can be networked, a server can probably be configured to manage it. Servers are logical as well as physical. A single device can be configured to run more than one server service. As performance degrades, thought should be given to dividing out server services to separate, physical devices.

File servers control access to file and disk resources. These servers are usually configured to authenticate users before they can access a resource, thereby providing a level of security. To be effective, a file server must be fast and reliable and have sufficient storage to accommodate user needs. Application servers, which require a front end on the client and a back end on the server, are useful for managing user applications that can be shared across the network. Database servers provide management access control software that makes database records available to users across the network. Database servers can also be configured so that they replicate the database across several locations.

Web servers run software that enables clients to make requests for services from the server. A web server runs application layer TCP/IP protocols. One such protocol is hypertext transfer protocol (HTTP). Another commonly used protocol is file transfer protocol (FTP). Webpages and sites hosted on a web server are expressed in hypertext markup language (HTML). A web server is a program. Windows, UNIX, and Linux-based web servers are all available. For Windows, Microsoft provides Internet information server (IIS) free with its server products. In the UNIX world, the Apache server is quite popular.

Simple mail transfer protocol (SMTP) is an application layer protocol used by TCP/IP. An SMTP server receives outgoing e-mail from clients and transmits it to destination servers. The two most common types of servers used with SMTP are post office protocol version 3 (POP3) and Internet message access protocol (IMAP). A POP3 server provides basic mailbox services, whereas an IMAP is a more sophisticated mailbox service protocol and offers more ways for clients to access and control their e-mail.

Another type of server of particular importance in a TCP/IP environment is a domain name system (DNS) server. It provides a host's IP address with a more English-type domain name address if that host is going to be accessed by other hosts for such services as web hosting, FTP, e-mail, and so on. A DNS allows for an IP address to be associated with its domain name address. It is not unusual for organizations to have more than one device set up to operate as a DNS server.

Clients in a TCP/IP network have to be configured to identify their DNS servers. These clients also have to be configured with their own IP addresses. Without an IP address, a TCP/IP client cannot function in a TCP/IP network. For large networks, manual configuration of IP addresses is too complicated. Dynamic host configuration protocol (DHCP) solves this problem; the job of the DHCP server is to assign IP addresses.

A proxy server provides security by functioning as an intermediary between a client and a server. Proxy servers are commonly used in situations where filtering is desirable. With web-based communications, client browsers are configured to send all of their outgoing requests to a proxy server rather than directly to an Internet server. The proxy server, using its own IP address, not the originating client's address, acts on the client's behalf and passes the client's request to the Internet server.

One way to take advantage of multiple servers in the enterprise is to group them into server clusters. To a client device accessing a **server cluster**, the servers in the cluster appear to be a single server. Servers participating in a cluster are connected not only physically but also logically through their SOS. When clients connect to what they see as a single server, they can be directed to the server in the cluster with the smallest workload. In this sense, what the clients see is a virtual server. A virtual server is highly scalable because it is built on a cluster of real servers.

The success of server clusters has led to the development of a technology called system area networks (SANs). A SAN is a local network designed for high-speed interconnection in cluster environments (server to server) using multiprocessing systems and storage area networks. Standards for SANs are still evolving.

Keywords

Application server *199*
Back end *199*
Bus *196*
Bus mastering *197*
Buffers *197*
Cache memory *196*
Central processing
 unit (CPU) *196*
Chassis *195*

Client *194*
Database server *199*
Direct memory access
 (DMA) *197*
Domain name *203*
Domain name
 system (DNS)
 server *203*
Drive interface *196*

Dynamic host
 configuration protocol
 (DHCP) *205*
Failover capability *206*
Fibre channel *207*
File server *198*
File transfer protocol
 (FTP) *200*
Front end *199*

Chapter Questions

Short-Answer Questions

1. In general, how does a server differ from a client?
2. How might a server's hard drive affect its performance?
3. How does a file server differ from a database server?
4. What is meant by a "virtual server" with regard to server clustering?
5. What is bus mastering?
6. What is the purpose of a drive interface?
7. How might a proxy server be used?
8. What are well-known ports?

Hands-On Projects

1. If your college or university has the requisite resources, configure and connect two client devices such that they recognize each other in a peer-to-peer network.
2. If your college or university has the requisite resources, install and configure a device to function as a simple server.
3. If your college or university has the requisite resources, using the server configured in item 2 above, connect two client devices to the server such that they are recognized by the server.
4. Visit the online store of a server hardware vendor such as Dell, Intel, or HP (Hewlett Packard) and compare and contrast the capabilities and components of a low-end/low-cost versus a high-end/high-cost server. Pick a particular server type, such as a blade server, web server, application server, and so on.

Research in Brief

For one or more of the following questions, provide a one- or two-page report based on your findings.

1. This chapter presented the concept of well-known ports in relation to certain TCP/IP functionalities. Research and report on other types of well-known ports. What are the benefits of using well-known ports? Are there any problems associated with well-known ports? If so, what are they and how can these problems be addressed? In what ways can a network administrator take advantage of well-known ports for supporting network services?

2. Investigate where current research in SAN architecture is going. How might SANs transform data communications? What hurdles must be overcome to implement this technology? What organizations or industries are involved in developing standards for SANs? In your investigation, make sure you do not confuse storage area networks with system area networks; the two are related but different.

3. Many FTP client and server products are available. Select two FTP client and server products. Compare and contrast them. How do they differ? How are they similar? What advantages and disadvantages do each offer? When and where would you recommend one over the other and why?

4. Research server-clustering solutions from such providers as IBM, Compaq, Dell, or other server vendors. How do their solutions differ? In what ways are they the same? What costs are involved for different scales of clusters? Compare and contrast the solutions of at least three different providers.

Case Study

Sheehan Marketing and Public Relations

President Sheehan has asked you to prepare a report on what would be required for SMPR to host its own website and web server for client and staff access. He wants to know what products are available and which would be best for SMPR. The president also wants to know what hardware and connectivity issues would be involved in hosting a website. Should it be hosted in-house or would it be better to use the services of an ISP?

In addition, SMPR needs a more sophisticated e-mail system. You have been asked to evaluate and recommend e-mail server solutions from IBM and Microsoft. You need to evaluate and explain the advantages and disadvantages of their respective products and make a final recommendation. As always, President Sheehan expects a cost-benefit analysis in your recommendations.

Topic in Focus

MONITORING SERVER PERFORMANCE

Servers are a critical component in today's enterprise systems. Because servers are often used to share and/or distribute resources, they can become a significant bottleneck, negatively affecting enterprise performance, if they are not running properly. Due to their importance, network administrators constantly monitor server performance. Many network monitoring tools are available to network administrators that enable them to monitor server performance.

Reasons for Monitoring a Server

Let's first explore a few reasons why a server needs to be monitored. The following list presents a few of the more important reasons for server monitoring:

- *Hardware failure.* Servers run on computers; computers are machines. Like all machines, computers can suffer from hardware failure. When a server goes down, its resources or the resources that it manages will likely no longer be available. To your user and customer groups, an unavailable server can cause much frustration.
- *Unauthorized access.* Hackers recognize that servers are critical components in the enterprise. Because of their importance, servers are a prime target for hacker

intrusion. Network administrators should closely monitor who is accessing server resources.

- *Software failure.* Servers frequently run essential business applications. Should one or more of those applications fail, staff and customers could be negatively affected. When applications are unavailable, the business may be unable to accomplish its work, resulting in financial losses.
- *Other security issues.* Besides unauthorized access, other security issues come into play with server technologies. Servers maintain passwords, contain resources that must be secured, provide directory services, authenticate users, and so on.
- *Port monitoring.* Administrators need to know whether an application or service running on a given IP address and port is running.
- *Content monitoring.* Administrators need to know if content has been altered and if the content delivery mechanism is working properly.
- *Database monitoring.* Administrators need to know if the database server is running and if it is accessible. As you can see, monitoring server performance is essential. Many tools are available to the network administrator that enables him or her to perform such monitoring.

Network Monitoring Tools

One popular server monitoring tool is the simple network management protocol, or SNMP. Devices running SMNP use a file called a MIB (management information base). This MIB can be used to "trap" information, such as a device's functionality and status, unauthorized access attempts, reboots, and other activities that a device might encounter. The information recorded in the MIB can be relayed to a network administrator either through a log file or a paging mechanism. Simple network management protocol traps can issue "send" and "get" commands that make this report monitoring possible. Used mostly to monitor hardware, SNMP can also be used to report on the status of applications.

For SNMP-enabled networks, products are available that enable administrators to monitor traffic flow through network servers. Paessler (*www.paessler.com*) offers a free, although limited, edition of its router graphics software that can report on such things as server CPU utilization and hard drive usage. The Paessler Router Traffic Grapher software is used in Windows environments. For a fee, Paessler offers more sophisticated tracking and monitoring products. Other vendors offer tools and applications that can remotely monitor a business's servers.

Another type of useful tool provides server-change detection capability. Tripwire (*www.tripwire.com*) is an industry leader in the change-detection software market. Change-detection software enables a network administrator to determine, for example, if employees are installing unauthorized software or are viewing files they should not be accessing, if rogue programs (worms and viruses) have been activated, and other such changes to a system. The Tripwire software is designed to alert network administrators of additions, deletions, and changes to files, applications, and systems. In addition, the software can produce reports of what it is monitoring, and, if properly configured, it can reverse changes that have been detected. Tripwire's products provide coverage for many different platforms, real-time alerts, automatic rollbacks, and web-based management.

The scale of the enterprise will of course guide the server-monitoring solutions that you pursue. Although free monitoring tools are available, many of the tools are not free. However, before investing money in a product, you should take advantage of the free-trial test periods that many vendors offer for their products. Public domain tools can function very well, although they usually do not come with documentation and/ or service support.

Integrating the Enterprise

The Business Benefit

THE ECONOMIC VALUE OF DATA AND INFORMATION

Businesses rely on their data and information resources to provide a vital competitive advantage. Not only must these resources be current and accurate but they must also be readily available to staff, suppliers, business partners, and customers. The need to access data and information across the enterprise has transformed how businesses implement storage technologies and how these data and information resources are processed and delivered once they are accessed. Data and information that are freely and easily available to users across the enterprise can give a business a strong competitive edge.

In a global economy connected through an international infrastructure, an enterprise must be prepared to compete for customers not only from its local industry but also around the world. Organizations that are not competitive eventually disappear from the business scene. This chapter examines various enterprise solutions that enable businesses to leverage their data and information resources.

Competition among businesses often drives technology in new directions; data communications technology is no exception. Information is a business tool and a competitive weapon. The tremendous growth of data-intensive applications such as e-commerce and web-based services has driven the development of better enterprise solutions.

Learning Objectives

After studying this chapter, you should be able to:

- Define cloud computing.
- Explain server and desktop virtualization.
- Define voice-over IP (VoIP).
- Describe direct attached storage (DAS).
- Describe storage area networks (SANs).
- Describe Network-Attached Storage (NAS).
- Understand virtual private networks (VPNs).
- Explain the advantages of web services.

In Chapter 10 you learned that businesses rely on server technology to meet their networking needs. However, servers and their associated software, hardware, and staffing are not without costs. Ideally, businesses recover these costs from the services and efficiencies that server technologies provide. These services and efficiencies are very often tightly coupled with enterprise solutions. Enterprise solutions are designed to allow a business to run its enterprise more efficiently and effectively with regards to cost, service, and security. This chapter explores just a few of these enterprise-level solutions.

CLOUD COMPUTING

Cloud computing essentially virtualizes the networking infrastructure such that the user of cloud services and resources does not need to be concerned with, or even aware of, how the cloud is configured, maintained, or implemented. If all three of these elements are properly managed—configuration, maintenance, and implementation—the user of the cloud will have a seamless and successful experience. Ideally, for the user, services and resources should be easily pushed to the cloud or pulled from the cloud as needed, in such a way that these services and resources are readily accessible, secure, and timely.

Cloud computing is, of course, ultimately hardware based. However, through software, the hardware (servers, switches, routers, media, etc.) becomes virtualized to the user. Three significant reasons for the popularity of cloud computing are cost, accessibility, and flexibility.

For the typical user of the cloud infrastructure, the user does not have to hire staff, purchase hardware and/or software, or maintain the infrastructure, resulting in cost savings. Instead, all of these elements are the responsibility of the cloud service provider. The cloud service provider, in turn, charges the user a fee for use of the cloud infrastructure. Even so, the user saves money, as the user only pays for those services needed.

Cloud computing applications can be widely varied and often include such services as software as a service (SaaS), file storage, data backup, customer relationship management (CRM), among others. Because the cloud is "virtualized," the physicality of the cloud is not of concern to the user. What this means is that the user can store (push) or retrieve (pull) data, applications, files, and so on, from the cloud from virtually anywhere that the user happens to be. This results in a high degree of accessibility.

Users of a cloud may also want to have use of and access to various types of servers, disk drives for storage and/or backup, high-speed bandwidth channels, databases, or other resources. Resources available in the cloud can be configured by the cloud service provider in such a manner that the user of the service can scale the service up or down as the user's need demands. In this manner the cloud frees the user from the limitation of having to be concerned about physical platforms and hiring staff. This, in turn, for the user, results in a high degree of flexibility.

Three types of cloud services include (1) software as a service, (2) platform as a service, and (3) infrastructure as a service. For **software as a service (SaaS)**, the cloud service provider offers various types of applications that free the user from having to purchase and maintain the applications. Instead, the user pays a fee for access to the needed software. As you may guess, with **platform as a service (PaaS)**, users pay a fee for access to and use of such hardware platforms as storage devices, servers for hosting applications, or platforms that can be used to build, test, and develop applications and products. With **infrastructure as a service (IaaS)**, the user is paying the cloud service provider for use of that provider's networking infrastructure. The cloud provider is responsible for setting up and maintaining the infrastructure, and the use then pays a fee to access and use it.

Besides types of services, clouds can also vary by model. Three common cloud models are (1) public, (2) private, and (3) hybrid. *Public clouds* offer services and resources to all who are willing to pay a negotiated fee to the service providers. The user does not own, maintain, configure, or secure any part of the "public" cloud. Instead, these responsibilities all belong to the cloud service provider. Although the public cloud may provide the most flexible model, of concern to many users is the security of such public cloud infrastructures.

Primarily due to security some organizations prefer to create and maintain their own *private cloud*. Such a "private" cloud is only available to those authorized by the enterprise. If data and/or applications are particularly sensitive or highly classified in nature, a private cloud affords an organization better security and higher confidence of access. A *hybrid cloud* model permits an organization to place certain services and resources within the confines of a smaller private cloud, and still allows the greater organization to make use of public cloud services.

SERVER AND CLIENT VIRTUALIZATION

The use of cloud computing has transformed how businesses, large and small, and even individual users, utilize resources. Of particular importance to organizations has been the ability to use cloud computing concepts, specifically their use of **virtualization**, and apply those concepts to server and client desktops. It has become increasingly common for enterprises to deploy virtual server and virtual client operating systems, applications, and data. In such a scenario, the user of a server or client device may not be accessing resources that are local to that user. Instead, the resource is remotely maintained and managed. Driving the push in this direction of virtualization is the need to economize.

As devices such as servers and clients become virtualized, a number of benefits to the enterprise can be realized. First, applications, whether server or client oriented, can be installed, maintained, and updated without having to touch a user's individual desktop. This means that hundreds, even thousands, of users can have their applications maintained from a single resource, resulting in a significant savings in technical support staff time. Also, should a problem arise with a virtualized resource, the patch or fix need only be applied to potentially one device. Further, data needed by staff can be remotely stored in a single location, making backup and securing of the data easier. Finally, users of the virtualized resources who are not at the physical location of the enterprise or who are outside of the business's firewall can still gain access to these resources remotely.

VOICE-OVER INTERNET PROTOCOL

Voice-over Internet protocol (VoIP) is a technology designed to carry voice communications over digital, packet-switched networks. As an enterprise solution, it has received considerable attention over the last few years. The technology of VoIP can be combined with a virtual private network (VPN) for a more complete enterprise solution. Major vendors who provide VoIP solutions include Avaya (*www.avaya.com*), Nortel (*www.nortel.com*), Siemens (*www.siemens.com*), and Cisco (*www.cisco.com*). To some, VoIP offers long-desired benefits; to others, VoIP offers more problems than it resolves. So, is VoIP a blessing or a curse?

Voice-over Internet protocol, which is a data service, requires us to remember that voice functionalities must still be supported. These functionalities include supervision, signaling, dialing, voice transmission, call routing, ringing, billing, and administration, among others. Standard voice transmission differs from VoIP in several ways. For example, standard voice is carried as direct current over copper wiring, whereas VoIP sends a bit stream, also over copper wiring. Standard voice is analog; VoIP is digital. Standard voice transmission is continuous; VoIP uses packets.

Because voice communication is analog, when you speak and hear a voice communication you hear a smooth flow of sound without the annoyance of dropped sound bites along the way, which can happen when voice is converted into data packets. You may be wondering why anyone would want to convert voice transmission from analog to digital. This transition is being driven by a term you will likely hear much more of in the near future: *convergence*. In this instance, the convergence is between voice and data infrastructures.

Another important factor driving the transition to VoIP is cost. It promises to provide voice-level services at a significant cost savings. The financial advantages of VoIP have proven irresistible. But how many times have consumers been promised something, particularly involving a technology, that did not live up to expectation? What is the current status of VoIP?

Traditional analog voice communications use TDM (time-division multiplexing) with private branch exchange hardware. A **private branch exchange (PBX)** functions like a miniature telephone system within the enterprise. The PBX, which is owned by the enterprise, switches calls between enterprise users on lines within the enterprise to a limited number of external phone lines to the common carrier. The common carrier is often a **public switched telephone network (PSTN)** provider. The PBX connects users to the common carrier's telecommunications infrastructure. The key advantage of a PBX is that it saves the cost of requiring the enterprise to implement individual lines for each user to the telephone company's central office. Also, the PBX gives the organization control and security over its internal voice communications. The PBX sits between the telephone company's technology and the enterprise. In general, layers between the outside world and the enterprise's internal operations provide the organization more control and security over the enterprise.

A PBX functions like a physically isolated network through which all enterprise voice communications must pass. In addition, the PBX box is housed in a specific physical location. This means that call centers that run from a PBX are tied to a specific geographic location. Traditionally, PBX has been highly proprietary, meaning that an organization has to buy into a specific vendor's PBX implementation, which many view as a disadvantage.

However, another significant benefit of the PBX approach is the high level of security provided. To hack into or secretly record voice conversations carried through a PBX, unauthorized users must have physical access to the PBX box, which is usually physically secured. Or, the unauthorized user must find a way to splice into the phone lines that feed into the PBX.

A disadvantage of the PBX approach is that it requires a separate infrastructure in addition to the one that carries the data of the enterprise. Because voice and data are carried on separate networks, a cost is involved. If voice and data could be transported over a single technology, in this case IP, substantial cost savings can be realized. Recall that IP is a data-based technology. Imagine the following scenario.

Your organization's call center is no longer controlled from a central, physical location. Because IP is used as the voice-delivery mechanism, calls can be managed, accessed, and routed to and from virtually any point that can access the Internet. In addition, because both the voice and data infrastructure are based on IP, a client can seamlessly contact the enterprise by using voice, fax, e-mail, chat, or any other web-based service. This integration of messaging services is called **unified messaging (UM)**. Because voice and data resources are integrated over the same IP-based network, significant cost advantages are realized. All communications and data pass through the same terminals in the form of integrated voice/data client workstations. In addition, the organization's customer resource management (CRM) software can now use computer-telephone integration technology to link to customer database servers and their applications. This may sound good—but for this scenario to happen, several factors must be considered.

First, what is the current network utilization? It is critical for the organization to know current network bandwidth maximums, minimums, and averages, because voice communications can suffer significantly from latency, jitter, and packet loss when carried over an IP infrastructure. Second, network infrastructure elements need to be evaluated to see if they can even be configured to support VoIP. For example, are the Ethernet switches currently in place capable of supporting VoIP traffic?

Does the current network support IP-based quality of service (QoS)? (QoS, as you may recall, enables a network administrator to prioritize packets). In the case of VoIP, it may be necessary to ensure that voice packets have a higher priority than more delay-tolerant traffic. Dropped sound bites are very irritating in a voice conversation!

An organization considering VoIP must know its current and future voice-bandwidth requirements. For example, does the business need to support 100 voice lines or 10,000? Voice traffic, both incoming and outgoing, must be analyzed to determine what level of traffic a VoIP network needs to support. Most PBX-based systems provide statistical information on voice utilization. Traditional PBX voice services that a VoIP solution must provide include call forwarding, call waiting, call return, call hold, call back, call block, and other similar functions.

Security is a particularly sensitive topic with regard to VoIP. Private branch exchange-based solutions do not suffer from viruses or denial-of-service attacks, problems associated with IP-based networks running servers. Firewalls, intrusion detection technology, and security practices are critical in protecting the enterprise's voice communications over an IP network. However, VoIP and PBX do not have to be mutually exclusive. In fact, many organizations deploy both. Figure 11.1 illustrates a VoIP network with a PBX configuration.

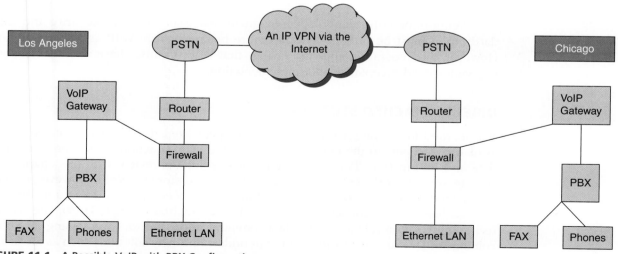

FIGURE 11.1   A Possible VoIP with PBX Configuration

The Ethical Perspective

Whose Data Is It Anyway?

Businesses have always maintained data on their customers, even if only on paper. With the advent of technologies such as **storage area networks (SANs)** and **network-attached storage (NAS)** appliances, businesses are finding that the quantity of data that they can capture, access, and utilize has grown exponentially. This vast quantity of customer data can drive such applications as data mining, data warehousing, knowledge management, and trend analysis. Using database technologies linked by web services and supported by WAN infrastructures, businesses can access their data from virtually anywhere.

In the past, the extent to which businesses collected data on customers was not a controversial issue. Times have changed. Increasingly, customers are becoming concerned, and in some cases alarmed, at the degree of data recording that is taking place. Much of the data captured by businesses is sensitive and personal in nature: financial, medical, job location and pay, addresses, telephone numbers, driver's license numbers, credit/debit account numbers, and so on. After a business captures such data, is it strictly up to the business as to how those data are used? Can the data, for example, be sold or shared with other businesses? In many cases, at least in the past, the answer has been yes, to the anger and frustration of many consumers. For this reason, consumers have turned to legislative bodies to restrict what businesses may do with the data they capture.

In the United States, the Health Insurance Portability and Accountability Act (HIPPA) of 1996 greatly restricts how, when, where, and to whom a patient's medical history, paper and electronic, can be released. Amazingly, prior to the passage of this act, a patient could have been denied access to his or her own medical records. In July 2003, the state of California began to enforce a personal privacy act, Senate Bill 1386. This legislation requires a business to inform a customer when his or her name, in conjunction with a Social Security number, driver's license number, or credit/debit card number, has been accessed by an unauthorized person. Many businesses believe that legislation of this type places an unfair economic burden on them.

What do you think? Is a business ethically bound to notify customers if the business shares or sells customer data? Should government bodies regulate and mandate such compliance? Should a business be required to give a customer of that business full or limited access to the data that the business maintains on that customer?

Details of HIPPA can be found at *www.hhs.gov/ocr/hipaa*. Other states and nations are implementing similar measures.

Vendors of VoIP technology recognize that issues such as security and standardization must be fully addressed before businesses see VoIP as a total solution. However, the integration and cost savings that VoIP promises have won this technology widespread acceptance and implementation.

DIRECT ATTACHED STORAGE

You learned in Chapter 10 that servers are specialized devices that make resources available to clients in the enterprise. One of the main functions of servers is to store data and information. Two storage enterprise solutions reviewed in this chapter are storage area networks (SANs) and network-attached storage (NAS). However, to truly understand the benefits of these two solutions, you need to know about a technology that has been around for several decades: **direct attached storage (DAS)**. This mature technology plays a role in today's data communications world. By assessing the shortcomings of DAS as a server tool, you will understand why solutions such as SANs and NAS are being pursued.

Usually DAS is used by organizations for backing up data and for the off-line storage of data that are not frequently referenced. **Off-line** refers to resources that are not immediately available but that could be made available in a reasonable amount of time (i.e., less than a minute). Data that are immediately available are said to be **online**. Direct attached storage devices, such as a hard drive, are connected by cable to a computer's processor inside a computer's case. This direct connection means that a DAS device is attached to a single computer and, in this discussion, to a single server. As a storage technology, DAS is optimized for single, isolated processors and thereby provides for a lower initial cost.

Regardless of the type of storage device, **input/output (I/O) requests** read and write data from and to the storage device. Storage devices can use a variety of I/O protocols. For a DAS server, the protocol of choice is small computer systems interface (SCSI), discussed in Chapter 10. An SCSI command can tell a hard drive to retrieve data from a specific location, or block, on the drive or to mount a specific tape cartridge. Small computer systems interface is known as a block-level I/O protocol because it specifies block locations on the drives that it accesses. It is possible for SCSI commands to be issued over Ethernet media, fibre channel, serial storage architecture (SSA), and standard SCSI parallel cables. Most implementations of DAS devices use standard SCSI cables.

A standard SCSI parallel cable should be no longer than 25 meters, which limits how far an external storage device can be from its direct-connect server. You may recall from Chapter 10 that SCSI supports both internal and external devices. A DAS server does not permit a second server to directly or simultaneously access its storage drives. This limits a DAS device's ability to perform capacity sharing. With capacity sharing, a storage device pools storage space or tape drives with other processors. The ability of a storage technology to pool storage space makes a technology scalable, or able to dynamically expand or contract based on network needs. Direct attached storage devices do not provide flexible capacity sharing. Additionally, DAS devices do not support data sharing. Data sharing is the capability of a storage device to share data and files concurrently with other storage devices. Capacity sharing and data sharing are not the same thing.

Think of **capacity sharing** as the ability of multiple servers to share and pool their multiple storage resources in such a way that a client or user views these resources as a single resource. By appearing as a single resource, capacity sharing in effect creates a virtualization of server storage. The term *virtualization* here means that several physical devices—multiple server hard drives, for example—appear as one logical hard drive. In contrast to capacity sharing, think of **data sharing** as the ability of a single server to allow its stored data files and applications to be simultaneously used by other servers.

Generally, because of its built-in limitations, DAS is best for organizations that have a small number of servers or that have fairly low I/O demands. For a long time, DAS was the only solution available for this type of storage requirement. However, more flexible, though more costly, storage solutions are now available. One such solution is a storage area network.

STORAGE AREA NETWORKS

As its name implies, a storage area network (SAN) is itself a network, which is both its advantage and disadvantage. The advantage comes from the efficiencies that a SAN, as a separate network, can bring to storage access and retrieval. The disadvantage comes primarily from the initial cost and complexity of setting up the SAN infrastructure. As with any business solution, the decision of whether to use a SAN will be based on how cost-effective and efficient a SAN would be for the organization.

A SAN is a network of storage devices that other computers, servers, and/or clients can access. This means that enterprise resources such as files, databases, applications, e-mail, or anything else that needs to be stored and retrieved can be removed from the LAN and stored on the SAN. By putting these resources on a SAN, traffic on the LAN is significantly reduced and access to stored data is improved. A LAN in a SAN-configured enterprise has clients and servers as well as an interface, or connection, to the SAN. The connection is typically from the servers to the SAN. Thus, servers are connected to the data network, the LAN, and to the storage network, the SAN. Figure 11.2 illustrates this type of SAN.

Storage area networks are usually implemented with fibre channel, although other connecting networking technologies, such as gigabit Ethernet, are possible. In theory, SANs are independent of the underlying network topology. Recall that a *topology* defines how a network is physically cabled together. Fibre channel is a high-speed (100 million bytes per second) switched-fabric technology capable of connecting hundreds or even thousands of devices. A SAN might be as simple as a single server connected to a single storage array using fibre channel or as complicated as hundreds of servers connected to hundreds of storage arrays. Optimized for storage

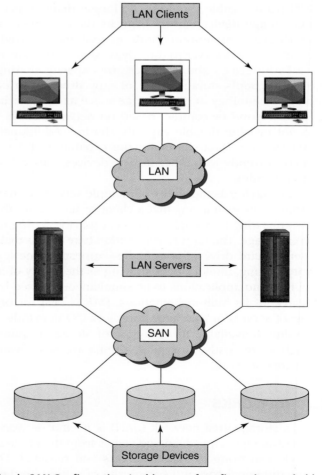

FIGURE 11.2 A Simple SAN Configuration. In this type of configuration, probably using fibre channel, storage resides on a separate network rather than on the LAN. Servers access the SAN on behalf of their clients and each other.

traffic, SANs manage multiple drives and storage devices as a shared pool, provide a single point of control, and offer specialized backup facilities that reduce server and LAN utilization.

Using technologies such as fibre channel, SANs can be far away from the computers or processors that use the stored data. This means that servers do not have to be physically close to the SAN, as they would be with a DAS device in a SCSI setup. Furthermore, because SANs offload I/O traffic from the LAN, higher data availability and improved performance result. As a SAN solution, fibre channel is faster than most LAN media, which is another advantage. Importantly, large numbers of computers, servers, or clients can be connected to the same storage device residing on the SAN, which is not possible in a DAS device configuration.

Note that devices do not have their own separate, physical connection to the SAN. Instead, most devices connect to a server that is connected to the SAN. The result is the virtualization of the SAN to the devices that use it. This means that the devices view the storage area network as a single pool of storage resources. Because a SAN appears to be a single pool of storage resources, capacity sharing is possible.

Storage area networks are not just hardware, they also require management software. The SAN management software component must do two things. First, any network topology selected to support the SAN, most probably fibre channel, must itself be managed. Managing the topology includes monitoring the storage network, remote maintenance and diagnostics, security management that could involve authentication or encryption, and performance management and fine-tuning. Second, a SAN management component has to provide for management of the stored data itself. Capacity analysis, load balancing, file sharing, data movement, and data backup and restoration are just a few examples of what a SAN software manager must do. Providers of SAN management software include IBM (*www.ibm.com*), Sun Microsystems (*www.sun.com*), Hewlett-Packard (*www.hp.com*), and Fujistu (*www.fujistu.com*), among others.

There are several scenarios in which SANs may be appropriate. For example, SANs are likely to achieve their best performance in large organizations that have substantial I/O traffic of any type. Organizations that have heavy database activity also are probably good candidates for a SAN. Also, organizations with multiple departments that have cross-dependent data needs may be well suited for a SAN solution. Note that storage area networks do not have to be implemented across the entire corporation but can be targeted for specific areas of concern. Because SANs can be costly to implement and may require significant staff training in their use, organizations usually consider several factors in determining whether a SAN is the right solution for them. An organization may want to consider the following questions before deciding on a SAN solution:

- What applications now in use would justify the implementation of a SAN?
- How is the enterprise currently utilizing its storage and server capacities?
- How many departments and/or locations might be part of or able to take advantage of a SAN?
- If multiple departments and/or locations are expected to participate in the SAN, what are their current storage and connection requirements?
- What business objectives—short-, medium-, or long-term—support the choice of a SAN solution?
- How is the business expected to grow over the short and long term with regard to both the market and geographically?
- What technical staffing resources are available for a SAN implementation, and are other personnel issues involved?
- How have server and storage technologies been budgeted in the past and how will this budget be impacted by a SAN solution?

NETWORK-ATTACHED STORAGE

Like SANs, network-attached storage (NAS) is a technology that addresses enterprise storage needs. In some ways, NAS technology is like teaching an old dog to do new tricks—in this case, teaching an old-style file server how to do more, and better, tricks than what file servers of the past were able to perform. Network-attached storage can be implemented in conjunction with a SAN, but it can also be a stand-alone solution. Figure 11.3 shows a standalone NAS LAN configuration. At times, NAS devices are also referred to as *network-attached storage appliances* (NAS appliances). In general, a NAS appliance is a high-performance storage device that provides shared data and file serving to clients and servers in a LAN. Several factors are driving this push for more, and superior, networked storage solutions.

As mentioned earlier, businesses need to capitalize on their information resources to gain a market advantage over their competitors. A NAS appliance, and a SAN, by providing faster and more reliable access to data and information, allows these resources to be more efficiently utilized. Better and faster storage of data have provided businesses alternative ways to competitively leverage existing data for applications such as data mining, data warehousing, knowledge management, and trend analysis. For such applications, NAS and SANs are very useful. **Data mining** is used to find hidden patterns in data that may be useful for predicting future behavior. Businesses that can predict the future behavior of their market base have a strong competitive edge. For a more detailed look at data mining, be sure to read the "Topic in Focus" at the end of this chapter. **Data warehousing** is a means of viewing a wide variety of data that can offer a comprehensive view of business conditions at a given point in time.

Knowledge management is a process that businesses follow to generate value from their intellectual property and knowledge-based assets. It involves the creation,

FIGURE 11.3
A Standard NAS Configuration. In this configuration, the NAS appliance with its integrated processor is attached to a TCP/IP LAN. The NAS appliances are accessed using specialized file access and sharing protocols.

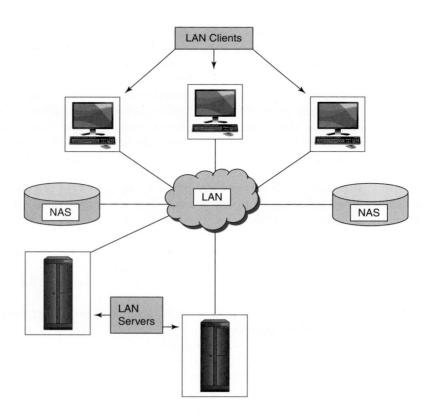

dissemination, and utilization of corporate knowledge. **Trend analysis** enables businesses to anticipate where their industry is going. Technologies, such as the ones identified above, can play a significant role in e-commerce.

Networked-attached storage appliances have internal, integrated processors that are optimized to manage disk storage. Using a hub or a switch, a NAS appliance is ordinarily attached to a TCP/IP network, either a LAN or a WAN. However, a NAS appliance must be attached to a network that supports IP-based protocols.

Using a stripped-down and proprietary operating system, a NAS appliance's only function is to provide file services to clients or servers. Using specialized file-sharing protocols, typically the Network File System (NFS) or the Common Internet File System (CIFS; pronounced "siffs"), networked devices request file services from the NAS appliance. The NAS appliance's internal processor then translates and processes these requests. The NFS and the CIFS are file-level I/O protocols. SCSI, which is also an I/O protocol, is, however, a block-level protocol. Both NFS and CIFS are device-independent protocols, meaning that they are not limited to a specific vendor's hardware implementation. The NFS's origins are in the UNIX world, whereas CIFS originates from Microsoft's NT operating systems.

Network-attached storage appliances can be connected directly to a LAN or WAN or placed on a separate dedicated storage network. The choice depends on how the accessed files are used. For example, if the NAS appliance will house a database or other commonly shared application, it may be preferable to have the appliance on its own network. In that way, servers on the LAN, on behalf of their clients, can interact with the NAS appliance, thereby reducing traffic on the LAN itself. However, if the NAS appliance is used to store individual client files, it may be best to directly connect the NAS appliance to the LAN. Another option is to use a network-attached storage gateway (NAS gateway). With a NAS gateway, the NAS appliance has an internal processor but does not have its own integrated storage. Instead, the NAS gateway appliance is in most cases connected to a SAN. Figure 11.4 illustrates the NAS gateway concept.

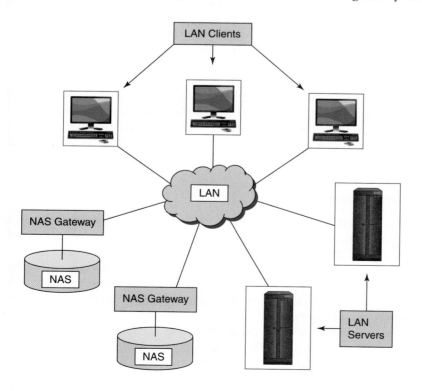

FIGURE 11.4 A NAS Configuration Utilizing a NAS Gateway. In this configuration, the NAS Gateway is a device without integrated storage. Instead, the NAS Gateway connects to external storage either directly, as in this example, or through a SAN.

VIRTUAL PRIVATE NETWORKS

Storage technologies play a critical part in enterprise networking solutions. However, businesses today are looking for ways to leverage existing technologies, such as those provided by the public telecommunications infrastructure. One data communication technology that has proven of great interest to many organizations because of its relatively low cost and ease of implementation is virtual private networking.

A **virtual private network (VPN)** is a private data network that uses a common carrier's public telecommunications infrastructure, at a cost, for private organizational purposes. A VPN can implement privacy through various tunneling and security procedures. **Tunneling** refers to a technique that allows packets from one protocol to be wrapped, or encapsulated, within a second protocol. At the sender's end, the sender's protocol packets are wrapped (encapsulated) in the protocol used by the transmitting infrastructure. The wrapped packets can then be transported over this different packet networking infrastructure. At the receiving end, the packets are unwrapped back into their native, or original, protocol.

Physical private networks are owned, in general, by one organization and used only by that organization. A virtual private network is very different. Many organizations can concurrently use a common carrier's telecommunications infrastructure for their VPNs. Hundreds, or even thousands, of VPNs, with each VPN completely unaware of the others, can share the carrier's infrastructure. Virtual private networks provide the same capabilities as private leased lines, but at much lower cost. A VPN is in some ways a type of outsourcing. Outsourcing refers to one business paying a different business for services rendered. (Many types of services today are outsourced, including manufacturing, call center assistance, payroll services, and even software engineering.)

Businesses that use VPNs have, in effect, outsourced their networking infrastructure. This means that the business paying for the VPN is not responsible for the staffing, management, maintenance, configuration, or security of the VPN's infrastructure. Those issues are left to the common carrier. Of course, that is both an advantage and a disadvantage. For many organizations, having no control over the networking infrastructure can be a problem. A business must carefully weigh the pros and cons of whether to use a VPN.

The popularity of VPNs suggests that for many organizations the advantages outweigh the disadvantages. Selecting a VPN, however, requires some analysis in order to select the most appropriate type of virtual private network: trusted, secure, or hybrid. Each type of VPN has its own particular characteristics and requirements.

Trusted Virtual Private Networks

Trusted VPNs preceded secure and hybrid VPNs. Originally, VPNs were circuits that a business leased from a communications carrier. The business had to rely on the carrier's assurances that the carrier's infrastructure was reliable and secure. At first, businesses were slow to adopt VPN. Because few businesses initially utilized VPNs, security was not considered a critical issue. Instead, businesses simply "trusted" the carrier to provide protected and reliable services. This arrangement constituted a **trusted virtual private network**.

For a trusted VPN, no one other than the carrier can affect the creation or modification of the VPN's path. The path is the series of links between the sender and the receiver that the data traffic flows through. This series of links appears to the

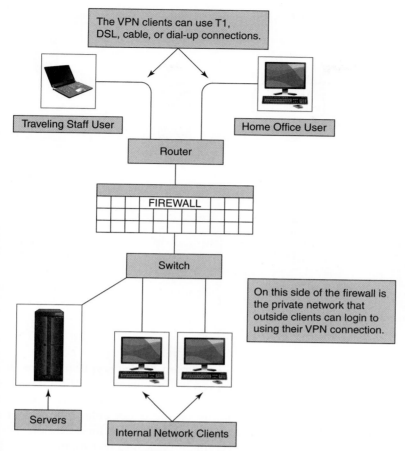

FIGURE 11.5   A Typical Trusted VPN Configuration

business as a cloud. With a trusted VPN, many customers can, and are, using the same links within a path. The value of a trusted VPN is that the carrier can be relied on to provide a secure and reliable path. Businesses that use VPN technology should understand that common carriers share each other's infrastructures; therefore a VPN might span the infrastructure of more than one carrier.

Besides having a path, a trusted VPN also carries data. An additional requirement of a trusted VPN is that no one other than the trusted VPN carrier can change, add, or delete data on the trusted VPN. Any change to the data on the path would affect the characteristics of the path itself. Finally, before a trusted VPN path can be established, routing and addressing have to be defined between the sender and the receiver. Figure 11.5 shows a configuration of a possible trusted VPN.

Secure Virtual Private Networks

Over time, trusted VPNs gained in popularity because they were relatively low in cost and easy to implement. As a result, more businesses began using common carrier infrastructures for transporting more data. Increasingly, businesses using trusted VPNs grew concerned about the security of their data, especially because they had virtually no control over the carrier's infrastructure. To address security concerns, carriers began to incorporate encryption technology into their VPN services. With such VPN

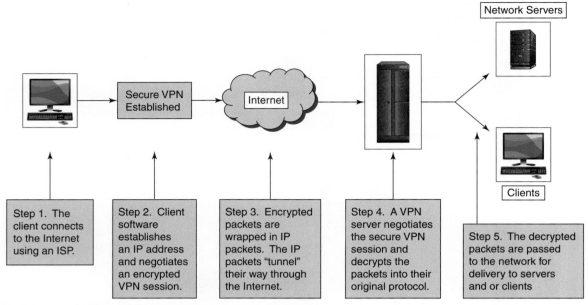

FIGURE 11.6 A Typical Secure VPN Process

services, the data at the sender's end is encrypted. The encryption can be done by the customer or by the carrier. As the encrypted traffic passes over the VPN, it behaves as though it were in a tunnel that connects the sender and the receiver. If an unauthorized user intercepts the encrypted data, he or she is not able to read it or change it without the receiver being made aware of the intrusion or modification. The receiver, upon receipt of the encrypted data, decrypts it back into its original form. This use of tunneled encryption creates what is called a **secure VPN**. (Chapter 12 examines the topic of encryption in more detail as a means of securing the enterprise.) Figure 11.6 shows the steps in a typical secure VPN transmittal.

By definition, all traffic on a secure VPN must be encrypted and authenticated. Also, all parties must agree on the security characteristics of the VPN. For example, are the security features automated? Are they available 24 hours a day, 7 days a week? Are the security features transparent to the user such that the user is not inconvenienced? Will the security features slow network performance? If so, will this slowdown be acceptable to users?

A secure VPN has one or more tunnels. Each tunnel has two end points, one at the sender and the other at the receiver. The administrators of each of the two end points must agree on the characteristics of the tunnel's security properties. Finally, no one outside the VPN should be able to affect the security properties of the VPN.

A trusted VPN and a secure VPN are not mutually exclusive. This means that a secure VPN can run as part of a trusted VPN. Between a sender and a receiver, a portion of a communication may be either trusted or secure. Such a pairing creates the third type of VPN technology: the **hybrid VPN**. The secure part of the hybrid VPN can be controlled by the user through secure VPN equipment on site or through the provider of the trusted VPN connection.

Because a hybrid VPN is a combination of trusted and secure VPNs, the boundaries between the two types of VPNs must be well defined. This means that within a hybrid VPN communication, the administrator must be able to determine whether the traffic between a sender and a receiver is part of the secure VPN. The ability to differentiate the traffic is important, because trusted VPN traffic does not use encryption, and secure VPN traffic must be encrypted. The type of VPN used will depend on the business, the nature of the data, and the capabilities of the provider.

Using a Virtual Private Network

This section considers three ways that a virtual private network might be used. Depending on the enterprise, VPNs can provide secure remote access, intranet access, extranet access, or Internet access. Secure remote access is usually offered to staff who are on the road and who need to remotely, but securely, log in to a network and access needed resources such as databases, project management files, and documents.

To access the VPN, the remote user must have a **VPN client** installed on his or her connecting device. The VPN client may perform several functions, such as negotiate tunnel properties and establish the tunnel. Because the connection is secure, the client authenticates the user and establishes what the user's rights are to the requested resource. The client also establishes security keys for encryption and decryption. Beyond establishing encryption and decryption rules, the data itself must be encrypted and decrypted by the client.

An **intranet**, which is based on the same technology as the Internet, is the internal portion of the enterprise that is primarily for staff access. Intranet access can be useful for connecting remote offices, whether across a city, state, or country. For this type of secure VPN, it is not unusual for intranet access to be filtered first through a firewall or server. The firewall or server can then perform the secure VPN functionalities of tunneling, authentication, and encryption.

An **extranet** is the portion of an enterprise's network that is meant to be shared and accessed by selected customers, suppliers, and/or business partners. This type of VPN access is particularly sensitive because the business is granting access to portions of its network to users who are not formally part of the business. In such a scenario, great care must be taken to ensure that all necessary firewall and security measures are in place. The intent is to precisely limit the resources that are made available through the extranet and to ensure that those using the extranet are in fact authorized to do so.

As you have already read, a VPN requires a tunneling procedure. This tunneling, which is a form of wrapping, or encapsulation, is performed by protocols. The four most common VPN tunneling protocols are Point-to-Point Tunneling Protocol, Layer-2 Tunneling Protocol, Multi-Protocol Label Switching, and Internet Protocol Security. The tunneling protocol used depends on the enterprise's networking protocols; the tunneling protocol must be supported by the networking protocols.

Internet protocol security (IPSec), which was standardized by the IETF, is usually associated with secure VPNs. **Point-to-point tunneling protocol (PPTP)** is widely installed because it enables PPP to be tunneled through an IP network. Point-to-point tunneling protocol does not change PPP, but is simply a means of carrying PPP communications. Most Windows-based clients automatically support PPTP. **Multi-protocol label switching (MPLS)** is associated with frame relay and ATM networks. **Layer-2 Tunneling Protocol (L2TP)** is a Cisco-sponsored protocol that combines the Layer-2 Forwarding Protocol (L2F) with PPTP. L2TP is also an emerging IETF standard. Cisco views L2TP as a key building block for supporting mobile workforce access to VPNs. A detailed discussion of these tunneling protocols is beyond the scope of this text.

Many businesses have found VPNs to be an attractive and effective data communications option. Because of their low cost and benefits, VPNs have a receptive market.

WEB SERVICES

Web services is an umbrella term used to describe technologies that, utilizing the Internet and particularly the WWW, provide access to a host of services for customers, employees, and business partners. Like VPNs and VoIP, web services are viewed as an enterprise technology capable of affecting such areas as business process integration, application integration, and web-based application development. As an umbrella term, web services refer to a collection of software components designed to dynamically interact with each other using Internet standards.

Internet standards are formulated by several organizations. For web services, three standards organizations in particular must be noted: the **World Wide Web Consortium (W3C)**, the **Organization for the Advancement of Structured Information Standards (OASIS)**, and the **Distributed Management Task Force (DMTF)**. Their respective websites are *www.w3.org*, *www.oasis-open.org*, and *www.dmtf.org*.

Web services are enterprise applications that use languages and protocols to enable devices, software, and people to better communicate and collaborate with each other, ultimately to provide better service. The trend today is toward a higher integration of data and applications. Integrating data with applications achieves cost efficiencies. Web services can be used to integrate data and applications as well as to access data and applications.

As envisioned by enterprise application technology developers, web services offer superior access by allowing different interfaces to interact with enterprise resources, particularly data and applications. Web services can be accessed through a client application, such as a browser, or through wireless devices, voice-activated interfaces, web portals, or other mechanisms. Using web services, customer database information could be updated through a wireless device, a webpage, or another type of web service. Also, devices using web services can communicate with each other, potentially leading to a highly adaptable enterprise infrastructure. Because web services are based on components, they can be implemented incrementally. Moving to a web services infrastructure does not have to be an all-or-nothing proposition. But what are web services based on?

Web service components are based on protocols and service platforms. The key web service protocol is **Extensible markup language (XML)**. The two key service platforms are Sun Microsystems' **Java 2 Enterprise Edition (J2EE)** and Microsoft's **C#** (pronounced "C sharp"), a programming language within .Net (pronounced "dot net"). "Dot net" is Microsoft's application development platform. In addition, web services are typically tied to a relational database from which data and information are pulled or pushed.

Extensible markup language is a structured data definition language that was formalized by the W3C for describing webpage content. A number of XML-based languages are used expressly for web services. Two frequently used XML-based languages are Web services description language and simple object access protocol. **Web services description language (WSDL)** is used to describe a web service. **Simple object access protocol (SOAP)** is used to transport data to and from a web service. Used by programmers to create automated web-based services, SOAP requests resources from remote software objects using XML over the Internet. Also, SOAP encapsulates its data in an envelope, as shown in Figure 11.7.

Like XML, SOAP is a standard maintained by the W3C. A key advantage of SOAP is that it uses two widely implemented protocols: XML and HTTP. Because SOAP automatically supports these two protocols, it enables existing web-based programs to be more accessible to a greater range of users. It is worth noting that Microsoft's Internet

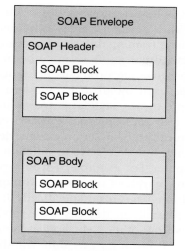

SOAP defines an XML-based structure for transmitting messages. The SOAP envelop structure includes a header with block and a body with blocks.

The SOAP header encapsulates the message and specifies the delivery process. The SOAP body contains the message data, also sometimes referred to as the payload.

FIGURE 11.7 The SOAP Envelope

information server (IIS) and the open-source Apache web server, which together direct over half of the world's Internet traffic, are already SOAP enabled.

Simple object access protocol is a lightweight protocol that provides for the exchange of structured information in a decentralized, distributed environment. (The term *lightweight* is used in association with protocols whose functionalities are relatively simple and straightforward.) Web services, by nature, tend to be highly decentralized and distributed. Simple object access protocol uses a call/response mechanism, which performs well in a client/server environment. This means that a client application makes a call to a web server that is somewhere on the Internet. In its call, the client also passes parameters within its request to the web server. When the web server receives the client's call, it then provides a response. The request and response are transmitted in the form of XML documents. Figure 11.8 demonstrates this request/response scenario.

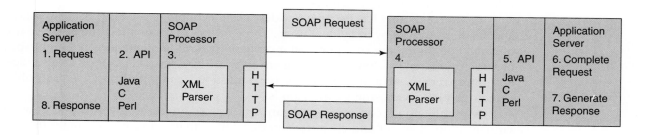

In Step 1, a user issues a request to an application server. The request is passed to an Application Programming Interface (API) that uses a programming language such as Java, C, or Perl. Next, the API hands the request to the SOAP processor, which in turn generates SOAP envelopes. The SOAP envelopes are passed over the Internet using the HTTP protocol. On the receiver's end, a response is generate and ultimately sent back to the requestor, in Step 8.

FIGURE 11.8 A Simplified SOAP Request and Response Process

Another significant advantage of SOAP is that it allows a device running one kind of operating system to communicate with a device running a different kind of operating system. Because the two devices can be running different operating systems, and yet have a seamless communication, the communication is said to be *transparent*. This transparent communication can occur because the protocols being used, HTTP and XML, are widely implemented standards used by all major modern operating system platforms. Here we see another example of why standards are so important.

Keep in mind that web services are not web applications. Web services are used by web applications. A **web application** is typically a browser on a client device, such as a personal computer. A web service does not, however, have to function through a browser or through a standard desktop computer. For example, a web service might be a request coming from a cell phone using **wireless markup language (WML)**. Wireless markup language is an XML-based language used specifically for creating applications capable of running on mobile, handheld devices with small viewing screens. Also, web services can make requests from other web services. Simple object access protocol makes these service-to-service requests possible. Another important characteristic of a web service is that the point where a requested transaction begins may not be the point where the interaction ends. This situation is very different from the standard client/server model, where a requested resource is returned to the requesting device.

The intent behind web services is to bring integration, interoperability, and flexibility to enterprise applications. Vendors are designing tools, devices, and applications with this in mind—in many cases making XML a built-in part of their technology solution. Breaking away from the traditional client/server model in determining how, when, and where resources can be delivered, web services represent an evolutionary step in enterprise solution development.

Chapter Summary

Businesses rely on their data and information resources for competitive advantage. Data and information that are not freely and easily available to users across the enterprise can put a business at an economic disadvantage. The tremendous growth of e-commerce and web-based services has driven the pursuit of better enterprise solutions in data communications.

Cloud computing has become a widely used technology used by businesses large and small, as well as by individual users. Three factors that can affect the effective use of cloud computing are configuration, maintenance, and implementation. Three types of services offered by cloud computing are software as a service, platform as a service, and infrastructure as a service. Three types of cloud computing models are public clouds, private clouds, and hybrid clouds.

As with cloud computing, organizations are increasingly looking toward virtualization of server and client resources. Such virtualized resources might include operating systems, applications, and data. Also, as with cloud computing, cost savings are playing a significant role in an organization's decision to move toward virtualized servers and clients.

Direct attached storage (DAS) is a mature technology that continues to have an important role in the data communications world. Usually, DAS is associated with magnetic tape and hard drives. Direct attached storage devices, such as a hard drive, are directly connected by cable to a computer's processor inside a computer's case. As a storage technology, DAS is optimized for single, isolated processors, thereby providing for a lower initial cost. However, DAS devices do not support data sharing.

Data sharing is the capability of a storage device to share data and files concurrently with other storage devices.

A storage area network (SAN) is a network of storage devices that other computers, servers, and/or clients can access. A LAN in a SAN-configured enterprise will have clients and servers and an interface, or connection, to the SAN. Storage area networks are usually implemented with fibre channel, although other networking connection technologies, such as gigabit Ethernet, are possible. In themselves, SANs are independent of the underlying network topology. Recall that a topology is how a network is cabled together. Storage area networks allow for greater distances between the computers that use the stored data and the data themselves. Storage area networks are not just hardware, they also require a software-based management component. Providers of SAN management software include IBM, Sun Microsystems, Hewlett-Packard, Computer Associates, and Fujitsu. Storage area networks are best for large organizations that have substantial I/O traffic of any type.

Network-attached storage (NAS) is another recent technology. It can be implemented in conjunction with a SAN, but it can also be a stand-alone solution. Network-attached storage appliances have an internal, integrated processor optimized to manage disk storage. Using either a hub or a switch, a NAS appliance is ordinarily attached to a TCP/IP network, either a LAN or a WAN. A NAS appliance must be attached to a network that supports IP-based protocols. Network devices use the network file system (NFS) or the common Internet file system (CIFS) protocol to make requests from NAS appliances. Network-attached storage is good storage technology for small businesses or for workgroups or departments within a large organization.

A virtual private network is a private data network that uses a common carrier's public telecommunications infrastructure. A VPN implements privacy through various tunneling and security procedures. Tunneling is a technique whereby packets from one protocol are wrapped, or encapsulated, within a second protocol. Three types of VPN technologies are trusted VPNs, secure VPNs, and hybrid VPNs. Each type of VPN has its own particular characteristics and requirements.

For a trusted VPN, no one other than the carrier can affect the creation or modification of the VPN's path. No one other than the trusted carrier can change, add, or delete data on the trusted VPN. Before a trusted VPN path can be established, the routing and addressing have to be defined between the sender and the receiver. The use of tunneled encryption creates what is called a secure VPN. By definition, all traffic on a secure VPN must be encrypted and authenticated. Also, all parties must agree to the security characteristics of the VPN. A hybrid VPN can be a combination of trusted and secure VPNs. The boundaries between the two VPNs must be well defined. The type of VPN implemented will depend on the business, the nature of the data, and the capabilities of the provider. Virtual private networks can be used to provide secure remote access, intranet, extranet, and Internet access.

Voice-over Internet protocol (VoIP) is a data service that is used to carry voice communications. It promises to provide voice-level services at a significant cost savings. Traditional voice communications use time-division multiplexing with private branch exchange (PBX) hardware. A PBX functions like a physically isolated network through which all enterprise voice communications pass. It offers a high level of security. Voice-over Internet protocol allows voice and data to be transported over the same networking infrastructure, which is a strong advantage. An organization considering VoIP needs to know its current, and future, voice bandwidth requirements.

Web services are an enterprise technology that can be used to provide business process integration, application integration, and web-based application development. As an umbrella term, *web services* are software components designed to dynamically interact with each other using Internet standards. Web services integrate data with applications. Because web services are based on components, they can be implemented incrementally. Web service components are based on protocols and service platforms. The leading web service protocol is XML (extensible markup language). Two primary web service platforms are Sun Microsystems's J2EE (Java 2 Enterprise Edition) and Microsoft's C#. Web services are typically tied to a relational database. Web services are not web applications, but they can be used by web applications. The goal of web services is to bring integration, interoperability, and flexibility to enterprise applications.

Keywords

Capacity sharing *219*
Cloud computing *214*
Common Internet File System (CIFS) *231*
C# *228*
Data mining *222*
Data sharing *219*
Data warehousing *222*
Direct attached storage (DAS) *218*
Distributed Management Task Force (DMTF) *228*
Extensible markup language (XML) *228*
Extranet *227*
File-level I/O protocol *223*
Hybrid VPN *226*
Infrastructure as a Service (IaaS) *214*
Input/output (I/O) request *219*
Internet protocol security (IPSec) *227*
Intranet *227*

Java 2 Enterprise Edition (J2EE) *228*
Knowledge management *222*
Layer-2 tunneling protocol (L2TP) *227*
Multi-protocol label switching (MPLS) *227*
Network-attached storage (NAS) *218*
Off-line *219*
Online *219*
Organization for the Advancement of Structured Information Standards (OASIS) *228*
Platform as a service (PaaS) *214*
Point-to-point tunneling protocol (PPTP) *227*
Private branch exchange (PBX) *216*
Public switched telephone network (PSTN) *216*
Secure VPN *226*

Simple object access protocol (SOAP) *228*
Software as a service (SaaS) *214*
Storage area network (SAN) *218*
Trend analysis *223*
Trusted VPN *224*
Tunneling *224*
Unified messaging (UM) *217*
Virtual private network (VPN) *224*
Virtualization *215*
Voice-over internet protocol (VoIP) *215*
VPN client *227*
Web application *230*
Web services *228*
Web services description language (WSDL) *228*
Wireless markup language (WML) *230*
World Wide Web Consortium (W3C) *228*

Chapter Questions

Short-Answer Questions

1. In what ways does a DAS solution differ from a SAN solution?
2. How does a standard NAS differ from a NAS with a gateway?
3. What advantages do web services offer?
4. What factors should a business examine when considering a VoIP solution?
5. Describe cloud computing.
6. What is an extranet?
7. Where would in intranet most likely be used?
8. What is a characteristic of secure VPN?

Hands-On Projects

1. List the factors that might influence a business to select a SAN solution.
2. Investigate and detail the steps necessary to set up a VPN connection.
3. From the World Wide Web Consortium website (*www.wc3.org*), identify and detail a recent project or workgroup involving SOAP.
4. Identity three of the Oasis standards group's (*www.oasis-open.org*) standing committees and briefly state the purpose for each committee.

Research in Brief

For one or more of the following questions, provide a one- or two-page report based on your findings.

1. Three organizations in particular are associated with web service protocol standards: the World Wide Web Consortium (W3C, *www.w3c.org*), the Organization for the Advancement of Structured Information Standards (OASIS, *www.oasis-open.org*), and the Distributed Management Task Force (DMTF, *www.dmtf.org*). Investigate the DMTF. Who makes up the organization's membership? What standards does the organization set? What current projects is the group actively working on? What are the goals and objectives of the organization? Report your findings.
2. Many organizations use VPNs. When secure VPNs are used, IPSec is the tunneling protocol of choice for encrypting communications. The Virtual Private Network Consortium represents an organization of interested parties who work on and discuss VPNs. Their website, *www.vpnc.org*, has much information on IPSec. Visit this organization's website and investigate and report your findings regarding IPSec. What issues are currently being discussed? Who is participating in the discussion? How is this organization related to standards-setting bodies that affect the Internet and the World Wide Web?
3. Many organizations still use DAS devices, particularly small businesses that have data storage needs. Investigate the storage offerings provided by local retail businesses or by online providers and report on the types of SCSI-based DAS solutions for both hard disk drives and magnetic tape. What are the typical costs? What are the installation and configuration issues? What functionalities and capabilities do various DAS devices support? What types of services and warranties do different vendors provide? What types of networks do these devices support?
4. Many believe that XML is the key protocol that web services and networking integration continue to be built on. As with any other technology, XML has both advantages and disadvantages. Investigate how XML is currently used. In what ways is XML being positioned for future technologies? What are its advantages and disadvantages? How are vendors such as IBM, Microsoft, and Sun, among others, incorporating XML into their technology solutions? Many technologists have expressed concerns about the security of XML as a delivery platform. How are vendors addressing this issue? Based on your research, where and how do you see XML being used five years from now?

Case Study

Sheehan Marketing and Public Relations

You have approached SMPR's president with a suggestion that SMPR deploy a SAN at each branch office. Each office uses data, audio, video, and graphic files that are shared by staff at each location. The SAN may incorporate NAS devices, but you have not yet evaluated the solutions provided by various vendors. During your meeting, Mr. Sheehan, the president of SMPR, stated that he agreed with your recommendation. Your next step is to research and provide more detailed specifications on SAN and NAS solutions. What is required to implement a SAN and/or NAS? Which vendor or vendors should be used and why? What are the costs involved? How can SMPR benefit from these technologies?

At each branch location, SMPR has public relations (PR) account executives who increasingly work outside the office. In fact, these PR executives are finding that they often need access to network resources at more than one branch location. You have recommended that PR executives and other remote-access staff be provided with laptops or other mobile technologies that will allow them to use a secure remote access VPN to dial in to SMPR's intranets. President Sheehan has directed you to provide him a report that explains, in simple English, what a secure remote access VPN is. He wants to know how this technology can help agents in the field with their access problems. He is also concerned about the security of client project files and wants to know how you plan to address security.

Topic in Focus

DATA MINING

This chapter examined technologies, particularly SANs and NAS, that increasingly enable businesses to store vast quantities of data. Having a mountain of data, however, does not necessarily translate into having useful data. Raw data are not considered information. For data to become information, the data must be transformed. Advances in hardware, software, storage, and database technologies have given businesses a new tool that better allows them to competitively use their mountains of data. This tool is data mining.

For many, data mining is a confusing topic. For example, how does data mining differ from such technologies as data warehousing, data marts, and online analytical processing (OLAP)? Data mining complements these other technologies. To better understand data mining, let's first examine these three technologies, beginning with OLAP.

Each of the technologies just mentioned has a particular focus and strength. That is why these technologies complement, and do not replace, each other. Online analytical processing, which is tied to server technologies, focuses on events that have happened in the past. To paraphrase a famous philosopher, only by understanding the past can we prepare for the future. The same holds true for businesses as well. Businesses evaluate and analyze the past behavior of their customers, industry competitors, B2B partners, and staff to make strategic decisions. This is where OLAP comes in. Using software tools, OLAP enables businesses to gain insight about outcomes from data patterns. Online analytical processing tools do not predict behavior, but instead try to understand past behavior. By understanding data patterns, businesses can determine how the patterns affect them.

Online analytical processing tools help a business to better understand enterprise data prior to the process of data mining. Whereas OLAP uses data to create a theoretical hypothesis, data mining uses the data to identify patterns that may relate to a potential business problem. Data mining then, helps a business uncover hidden patterns and relationships that can consequently be used to validate a theoretical hypothesis developed by an OLAP tool.

The term *data warehouse* is fairly flexible; depending on whom you ask, you may get a variety of answers as to what one is. Many consider a data warehouse to be a collection of summarized data that has been cleansed, structured, and optimized for access by such technologies as data marts, OLAP, and data mining. To say that data have been "cleansed" means that the data have been checked for missing values, incorrect values, and other syntactical problems. Syntactics deals with formal relationships—in this case, the relationship between data fields. Thus, a data warehouse becomes a collection, storage, and staging area for enterprise data. The quantity of warehoused data, however, can be vast. Because data warehouses can be too extensive in the amount of data they offer, data marts have been developed.

A *data mart* is a segment or category of data that has been extracted from a data warehouse. The data mart groups the data together into a form more specific to, say, a department or workgroup. Departments, using a data mart, can then better customize the data they use. This means that a given department can summarize, sort, select, and structure its data, within its data mart, without having to consider data from other departments. In fact, other departments will have their own data marts. Data marts also enable decision support system (DSS) software to reach down to the department level. Significantly, the unit cost of the device that houses the data mart is generally far less than the servers or computers that maintain the potentially huge, centralized data warehouse. A data mart enables a business manager to focus on his or her department when analyzing business problems.

In this discussion, the essential element that differentiates data mining from the other tools mentioned is that data mining looks for hidden patterns in data that might otherwise have gone unnoticed. A variety of data mining models is available. The type of data mining model used depends on the business problem to be resolved. For example, an inferential data mining tool attempts to explain relationships among data, draw inferences from the data, and relate data objects to one other so that a conclusion can be drawn. An associative data mining tool seeks correlations between data attributes. A comparative data mining tool provides comparisons of similarities and differences between data sets. Other models are possible, and different models can be combined to mine the data. The following are just a few of the many vendors that provide data mining solutions:

- IBM Intelligent Miner (*www.ibm.com*)
- Megaputer Intelligence PolyAnalyst (*www.megaputer.com*)
- Oracle 11i Data Mining (*www.oracle.com*)
- SAS Institute Enterprise Miner (*www.sas.com*)
- SPSS Clementine (*www.spss.com*)

Regardless of the data mining tool selected, a business should explore several questions prior to deciding whether data mining is the right solution. For example, Is the tool scalable? Is the data mining tool designed for a single or a multiprocessor environment? Are data mining activities restricted by such factors as server hardware memory, processor, and disk storage? These factors will affect scalability. Is the tool being considered compatible with other third-party tools? Very likely, the data mining tool selected will need to work with a business's OLAP, data warehousing, and data mart solutions. Each of these tools may be from a different vendor, hence the importance of compatibility.

Does the business's current infrastructure support the data mining tool being considered? If not, what hardware and software, including licensing, issues need to addressed? How large a budget has been allocated? Is the tool one that is appropriate for the business's particular industry? Also, how will the data mining tool be administered? Are staff trained in the use of the tool? For whom within the organization is the tool intended:top, middle, or operational managers, or all three? As you can see, many questions must be asked before a decision can be made.

12

Securing the Enterprise

The Business Benefit

A reality for today's consumers worldwide is that in order to find, purchase, and have goods and services delivered, they will more often than not need to surrender sensitive personal information to a vendor. Such information can include addresses, driver license number, phone numbers, credit card numbers and security codes, marketing preferences, and a host of other data. These data are captured and used by vendors to provide services. But once captured, what guarantees does the consumer receive that his or her information will be secured and not used for purposes that the consumer did not intend?

Technologies such as cloud computing have transformed consumer expectations of what is possible as regards storing, accessing, and retrieving many types of data and services. But such technologies have also put consumers on alert as to privacy, security, and business integrity.

Businesses often make it a key marketing tool to assure their customers that any data the business captures will not be used for unwanted purposes, and that the data and information will be secured. When businesses breach that promise, or are found to have used customer data in a manner to which the consumer did not agree, that business may find itself not only in legal jeopardy but also without a significant portion of its former market base.

For the business that can effectively demonstrate reliable, capable, secure, and ethical use of sensitive customer data, a competitive advantage can be achieved.

Learning Objectives

After studying this chapter, you should be able to:

- Understand the importance for security in the enterprise.
- Identify four components of security.
- Understand the purpose for and use of cryptography.
- Describe asymmetric and symmetric ciphers.
- Explain how firewalls and proxy servers are used in security.
- Comprehend the importance of physical security.
- Explain the benefits of a disaster recovery plan.
- Define an integrated security system.

THE NEED FOR SECURITY

Building an enterprise network may require networking models of various sizes, from local area networks to wide area networks. With the enterprise network in place, a critical concern becomes how to secure the infrastructure. To many, security means simply preventing unauthorized access to enterprise resources. In practice, however, securing the enterprise means several things. For example, can the enterprise recover in the event of a disaster? Is the network protected against data tampering? For servers that maintain or access essential data, is recovery planned for in the event of storage failure? What policies are in place to assure that enterprise security measures are being followed? Are security policies, in fact, defined? How can customers and staff be confident that data and information concerning them are reliable, accurate, and confidential? Table 12.1 identifies some of the types of security policies that a business should address.

THE COMPONENTS OF SECURITY

All the preceding questions, and more, highlight the types of issues that must be addressed in securing the enterprise. Four key components that can define security are confidentiality, access, integrity, and nonrepudiation, sometimes referred to as the CAIN principles. First we take a moment to define what each of these components represents. Following that, the remainder of our chapter is a discussion of technologies that address one or more of these four components of security.

Confidentiality

Simply stated, **confidentiality** requires that uninvited others not be able to observe our communications. In a secure enterprise, data, information, and communications are only revealed to those who are authorized to review them. Many users of data communication infrastructures worry that those who should not officially have access to the infrastructure could view sensitive data. There are various ways that confidentiality can be enforced in the enterprise. File- and object-level controls can be applied, for example, through such server operating systems as Novell's Netware and Microsoft's Windows Server products. Transmission confidentiality can be implemented using various encryption technologies. **Encryption** is a means of disguising or altering data in such a way that it cannot easily, if at all, be understood by those without an encryption key. Confidentiality is an essential component of security.

Table 12.1	Types of Security Policies
Policy	**Description**
Computer Use	Appropriate use of organizational computers
Information	Who has access to what information
Backup	Timing and type of backups performed
Staff Management	Security policies that restrict employee access to appropriate resources
Disaster Recovery	Procedures to follow in the event of a natural or human-made disaster
Incident Handling	Steps to follow when unanticipated incidents occur
Account Management	Adding, deleting, and modifying systems and users
E-Mail	Appropriate uses of organizational email systems

Access

As a security component, **access** must address two factors. First, access means that information and other enterprise resources are available to authorized users when needed. Availability, however, is only half of the equation. A second important characteristic of access must be that those who do access enterprise resources are authenticated for such access. **Authentication** confirms that the user attempting to use a networked resource has been granted appropriate rights and privileges to that resource. One way to assure availability of data is to implement forms of redundancy for fault tolerance.

Fault tolerance allows for a degree of fault or failure so that a service or resource remains available in some form or capacity. Redundant systems, or resources, are inherently fault tolerant. Something that is "inherent" to an object is inseparable or part of a given object. A common means of authentication is a requirement that each user of the enterprise has an authorized login, user ID, and password. This user ID and password are then directly associated with certain rights, privileges, and restrictions. This type of login requirement is one kind of security policy.

Integrity

In relation to enterprise security, **integrity** means that only those who have the right to do so can modify data and information. By applying integrity constraints to data and information, the enterprise attempts to ensure that these resources are not tampered with or changed. Making data available as needed is one thing. The enterprise must also make sure that those who access the data are appropriately limited as to what they can do with the data once they access it. Limiting what can be done to the data or application makes up the integrity component of security. As an example, you would not expect your bank to allow just anyone to withdraw funds from your checking account. Such an action—the withdrawing of funds from your account without your approval—would lack integrity, besides being very annoying.

Nonrepudiation

Every data communication has a sender and a receiver. In a secure enterprise we want to be certain that data and information received are in fact from the person who claims to have sent it. Additionally, we must assure that any data or information in transit has not been altered. **Nonrepudiation** means that we are assured that whoever we are communicating with is indeed who he or she represents himself or herself to be. A customer paying for a commodity over the Internet using a credit card wants to be certain that the vendor is who he or she claims to be, and furthermore that sensitive financial data are not tampered with in the process.

Nonrepudiation also means that someone who has received your communication can be verified as having done so. For example, a customer claims that payment was sent for a product using secured technologies, and yet no record of that payment is found. With the proper security technology in place, you would be able to verify that what the customer is claiming is in fact accurate.

These four components of enterprise security, confidentiality, access, integrity, and non repudiation can be implemented in various ways. An enterprise that takes its security seriously will make use of several mechanisms and technologies that address one, if not all, of these components. Something to keep in mind, however, is that no technology is perfect. Used in combination, though, multiple security measures can make it much more difficult for an enterprise to be attacked and exposed to security vulnerabilities. Next we examine some of the technologies that can be implemented for this purpose.

BASICS OF CRYPTOGRAPHY

Storing data in a manner that makes it easily and reliably accessible, as well as recoverable in the event of hardware failure, is essential. Also essential is the need to verify that those who are accessing enterprise data are authorized to do so. Authentication and digital certificates are a common means of providing for verification of such authorization. In addition, when data are transported across the enterprise, it may be desirable, especially if the data are sensitive, to scramble or jumble the data. In scrambling the data, the hope is to render it useless to anyone who may intercept it. These types of issues—authentication, certification, and scrambling—touch directly on all four components of security previously identified: confidentiality, the authentication element of access, integrity, and nonrepudiation.

One technology in particular, **cryptography**, plays a major role in securing the enterprise. Cryptography is, in fact, central to many security-based applications. Although by themselves, cryptographic methods cannot guarantee total security, but then no technology does, cryptographic methods are elemental in adequately protecting the enterprise. Simply put, cryptography is the science of ensuring that data and information cannot be easily understood or modified by unauthorized individuals. Some of the security functions cryptographic methods address are authentication, nonrepudiation, privacy, assurance of message integrity, and provisions for digital signatures.

The field of cryptography is a study unto itself, a science with its own history, methodologies, and, important to our discussion, vocabulary. In order to understand how a cryptographic method works, a few of its basic terms must be presented.

THE VOCABULARY OF CRYPTOGRAPHY

A cryptographic method makes use of an **alphabet**—the set of symbols used in either an input or an output message. The alphabet may be the same for both, or not, depending on the cryptographic method. The alphabet can be based on numbers or characters (such as English or some other language). Using its alphabet, a cryptographic method is applied against data in its raw form. Data in its raw form are referred to as being **plaintext** or **cleartext**. In order to transform the data from cleartext to a scrambled or "encrypted" form, a cipher is used. A **cipher** is a coding or mapping system used to translate cleartext data, based on the cryptographic method's alphabet, into ciphertext. **Ciphertext** is the encrypted form of the original data. Table 12.2 includes a list of cryptographic terms.

After the cryptographic method is applied, the cleartext data is encrypted and is no longer in its original form. In combination with the cipher, a "key" is used to encode and decode the data. The sender and receiver of the data must both have access to the key in order to encode and decode the data. The purpose of this encoding and decoding is to address the probability of an attack against the data. An **attack** is the systematic attempt by an unauthorized individual to discover the cleartext form of the data from its encrypted form.

At the heart of the cryptographic method is the cipher. A good cipher, or mapping system, should meet two criteria. First, the cipher should make it difficult for an encrypted message to be viewed in its cleartext form, without the use of the cryptographic key. As you can imagine, the key is, and must be, a controlled secret. Second, the cipher should produce ciphertext that appears random in format to a casual user, or to anyone without the key. This means that within the encrypted ciphertext, no ascertainable patterns should be apparent. Also, the alphabetic symbols that appear in the ciphertext, should appear with equal frequency. These two criteria, if met, make

Table 12.2	Cryptography and Encryption Terms
Term	**Definition**
Alphabet	The set of symbols used in either an input or an output message
Asymmetric Cipher	A cryptographic method that uses a key pair, one key to encode data and a second different key to decode
Certificate Authority	A trusted third party that manages digital certificates
Cipher	The mapping scheme used to encode data
Ciphertext	Encrypted data
Cleartext	Data and/or information in their raw and unencrypted form
Cryptanalysis	The process of evaluating cryptographic algorithms to discover their flaws
Cryptanalyst	Someone who uses cryptanalysis to find flaws in cryptographic algorithms
Cryptography	The science of encrypting and decrypting information
Cryptographer	Someone trained in the science of cryptography
Digital Certificate	A method used to validate a digital signature
Digital Signature	A means of encrypting data using a specific user's private key
Key	The algorithm used to encode and decode data
Public Key Infrastructure	A technology that allows for the digital certification of communications
Session Key	A key pair that is changed or renewed periodically
Symmetric Cipher	A cryptographic method that uses the same key to encode and decode

it very difficult for someone to statistically attack the data to discover the cipher's mapping mechanism. Using a cryptographic method, the sender encrypts and the receiver decrypts.

As a point of interest, one of the earlier and more famous ciphers used was the **Caesar cipher**, named for Julius Caesar, who used it for encrypting his messages. The Caesar cipher, or mapping, used Latin as the alphabet. Recall that a cipher works in combination with a key. The key used with the Caesar cipher works by replacing each letter in a message with the corresponding letter three positions following in the cipher's alphabet. Although Julius Caesar used Latin as the cipher, we can easily use his key but with English as the cipher. For example, the cleartext data "Allen Dooley," using the Caesar key, with English as the cipher, encodes to Doohq Grrohb. Doohq Grrohb is the ciphertext, encrypted form, of the cleartext data. Because you know the key, you can easily convert Doohq Grrohb back into its original, cleartext form. What does your name map to using the Caesar key with an English alphabet cipher?

TYPES OF CRYPTOGRAPHIC CIPHERS

There are two major branches of cryptography into which ciphers generally fall: symmetric and asymmetric. Sender and receiver may be using one or both, based on how enterprise security is configured. With *symmetric ciphers*, the sender and receiver of the communication must be using the same key for encryption and decryption. With *asymmetric ciphers*, the sender and receiver use different keys for encryption and decryption; however, both the sender and the receiver must agree as to the keys used. Each category of ciphers has its advantages and disadvantages, which we now explore.

Symmetric Ciphers

Symmetric ciphers require that the sender and receiver share information on the key used for encoding and decoding data. The simple act of sharing the key inherently means that symmetric ciphers have a greater security risk because multiple parties have access to the key. Also, when the sender and receiver in a communication are physically distant from each other, a secure exchange of the secret key becomes more difficult. Here, distance is itself a problem because greater physical distances between sender and receiver allow more opportunities for intrusion or attack.

A famous proverb by the Chinese philosopher Sun Tzu holds that if two people share a secret, then you no longer have a secret. With symmetric ciphers each party using the cipher must share and maintain the secrecy of the key. The advantage of symmetric ciphers is that they are normally faster to compute than asymmetric ciphers. Where speed is critical, as in real-time applications, symmetric ciphers provide an edge.

Asymmetric Ciphers

With **asymmetric ciphers**, two separate keys are used—a public key and a private key. One of the keys is used for encryption, the other for decryption. The **public key**, as its name implies, is made public for anyone to use. The **private key** is known only to its owner, and can be managed locally by that owner. Both the sender and receiver have public keys and private keys.

When the sender, Jack, wants to send a message to Jill, Jack encrypts his message using Jill's public key. Jill's public key is available, or published, for anyone to use. Jack sends his encrypted message to Jill. When Jill receives the message, she uses her private key to decrypt the message. Only Jill has her private key, so only she can decrypt the message. The situation is reversed when Jill sends a message to Jack. Figure 12.1 describes a communication between Jack and Jill using asymmetric encryption. In Figure 12.1, when the sender, Jack, wants to send a message to Jill, Jack encrypts his message using Jill's public key.

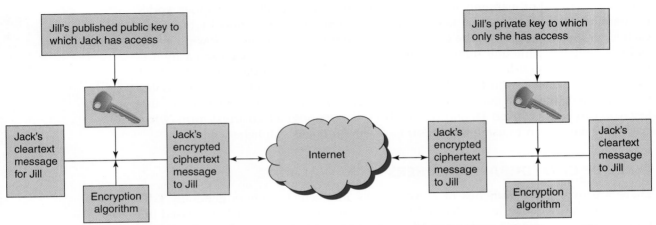

FIGURE 12.1   Jack and Jill using Public and Private Key Encryption. Using Jill's published public key with his encryption algorithm, Jack encrypts his message to Jill and sends it over the Internet. On her end, Jill uses her private key to decrypt the message that Jack has sent her.

Jack and Jill can both change, and republish, their public keys for anyone to use whenever they want. Jack and Jill can also change their own private keys whenever they want. Changing private keys frequently is one way to improve security, because your private key becomes a moving target, and harder for someone to discover. Public keys can be freely distributed without compromising security. Secure communication with multiple parties only requires the exchange of public keys. One concern with asymmetric ciphers is authenticating the user of a public key. Is that user who he or she claims to be? Also, asymmetric ciphers take longer to process, and therefore may not be suitable for time-sensitive applications.

Session Keys

One way to combine the benefits of both symmetric and asymmetric ciphers is to create what is referred to as a **session key**, which is a key pair that is renewed, or changed, periodically. When a sender and receiver establish a connection for communication, a **session** is established. In a session key approach, the message, which is the largest part of the communication, is carried using a symmetric cipher, which makes for faster processing. To maintain security, an asymmetric cipher is used to pass and/or update the shared keys for the symmetric process. During the communication, data is encrypted and decrypted using this one-time session key pair. When the communication terminates, the session key pair is also terminated.

Public Key Infrastructure

This discussion of cryptography is important because it is the basis of a technology that is critically relied on to authenticate and allow for digital certification of communications: **public key infrastructure (PKI)**. This technology creates key pairs that establish confidential communications. In doing so, PKI uses **digital certificates** that attempt to enforce two criteria. First, only the owner of the digital certificate may possess the private key that corresponds to a certified public key. Second, an unauthorized user who may intercept the digital certificate cannot use it to discover the private key. Public key infrastructure is based on asymmetric ciphers using public and private keys. Server operating systems such as Windows 2008 incorporate PKI as part of their functionality.

A **digital signature** is a means of encrypting data using a specific user's private key. This digital signature is used to determine if the sender of a message is in fact who he or she says he or she is. The receiver of a message with a digital signature can validate that message using the sender's public key. If the data in the message have been changed in any way, the digital signature will fail, and the receiver will know that the message is not valid. A third party called a **certificate authority**, or CA, usually manages digital certificates, and the ability to use them. The CA binds private keys to public keys and guarantees between sender and receiver that the digital signature used in a secure communication is valid. VeriSign (*www.VeriSign.com*) is one of the best-known CAs today.

Technologies such as PKI support not only confidentiality and authentication but nonrepudiation as well. A highly secure, cryptographic PKI process can, for example, verify whether an event claimed to have happened, or not, by a client or staff did occur. In a maximum cryptographic scenario, it is possible to determine, based on digital signatures, whether an event indeed took place, at what date and time, and by which device. Such technology provides evidence that a user of the enterprise infrastructure did, or did not, explicitly request a specific action. With financial applications especially, such electronic evidence is necessary. Figure 12.2 shows where a certificate authority would be positioned in a secure communication.

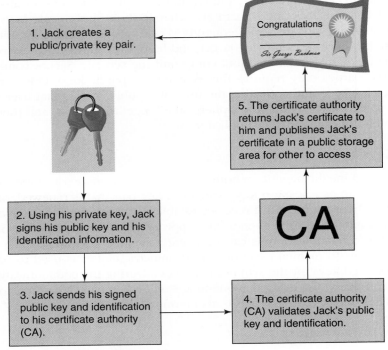

FIGURE 12.2   The Certificate Authority Process

The Ethical Perspective

Identity Theft and You

Identify theft occurs when someone obtains key data about another person and then uses that data to impersonate that person. The most common types of data that identity thieves try to obtain are Social Security numbers, driver license numbers, credit and/or debit card numbers, bank account numbers, and other financial information. After enough data have been compiled, it is relatively easy for someone you do not know to take over your identity and turn into your evil twin. For many, having one's financial identify stolen is traumatic enough. In some cases, the identify thieves may also commit crimes that then become part of "your" criminal history.

According to a September 2003 report (*www.ftc.gov/os/2003/09/synovatereport.pdf*) written for the Federal Trade Commission (FTC), 3.23 million consumers, or 1.5 percent of the population, discovered that new accounts had been opened or that other frauds, such as renting an apartment or home and obtaining medical care or employment, had been committed using their name. In addition, 6.6 million consumers had their existing accounts compromised by identity theft. On its website, the FTC provides useful information on how to guard against identify theft. The Privacy Rights Clearinghouse (*www.privacyrights.org*), a nonprofit organization, also provides reports, guidelines, education, and research on securing your personal information. Following are just a few of the security steps recommended by the FTC and the Privacy Rights Clearinghouse:

- Check your credit report at least twice a year.
- Keep your mailbox locked.

- Shred all legal documents and any documents that contain any type of account number that you plan to throw away.
- Place outgoing mail in secure mailboxes.
- Check with your post office if you have not received mail within four days.
- Destroy preapproved credit card offers and checks and other preapproved documents.
- Avoid using important identification numbers such as a Social Security number whenever possible.

Given the increased risk of identity theft, what measures do you think businesses should follow to protect consumer's identities? In what ways can organizations better secure, inform, and help consumers who have experienced identity theft? What role should the government play?

FIREWALLS AND PROXY SERVERS

With the use of Redundant Arrays of Independent Devices, our Topic in Focus at the end of this chapter, storage of essential data can be better protected. Using cryptographic methods such as public key infrastructure, can improve confidentiality and authentication. Additional technologies used to secure the enterprise against attack or intrusions are firewalls and proxy servers. Sometimes firewalls and proxy servers are implemented in combination with each other. Keep in mind that no intrusion security technology is perfect. Even so, firewalls and proxy servers are an important security component used by many organizations today.

Firewalls primarily serve as a barrier. A firewall can be a barrier between the outside world and the enterprise, or a barrier between networks within the enterprise. As a barrier between the outside world and the enterprise, a firewall is configured to keep out unauthorized individuals who are attempting to attack or penetrate the enterprise. A firewall placed between networks within the enterprise helps to isolate sensitive or critical data and applications from internal enterprise staff access. For example, an organization may keep its financial services, such as payroll and/or accounts receivable, on a separate network. A firewall can be placed between the financial network and other networks of the enterprise to protect the financial network's resources from unauthorized internal access. Figure 12.3 demonstrates how a firewall might be positioned.

Do you wonder how the term *firewall* was coined? In building construction, it is not unusual to erect an interior or exterior wall of fire-resistant materials. This fire-resistant wall becomes a "firewall" or a barrier. The intent for this wall is to prevent a

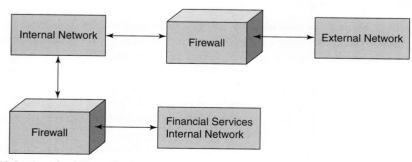

FIGURE 12.3 Standard Firewall

fire from spreading to other areas of the building. Our networking firewalls perform a similar service, but in this instance the fire we are attempting to control is the unauthorized access to a networked resource. Inside the firewall is the protected network, more often referred to as the **trusted network**. Outside the firewall is the **untrusted network**. Portions of the untrusted network are also sometimes referred to as the *demilitarized zone (DMZ)*. To be effective, a firewall needs to meet three essential characteristics.

First, all traffic to and from a trusted and untrusted network must pass through a firewall. Second, the firewall must be configured so as to allow only authorized traffic to pass through it. By passing all traffic through the firewall, trusted and untrusted, traffic is filtered. A successful firewall prevents unauthorized traffic from reaching the trusted network. Third, and finally, a firewall must be able to protect itself from attack and penetration. Those trying to break into a modern network know that firewalls are in place to protect that network. Because firewalls are a first line of defense, they themselves are targets of attack. If the firewall is successfully attacked, network resources become vulnerable.

Firewalls may be hardware-based, software-based, or, more commonly, a combination of the two. Two broad approaches can be followed in determining how firewalls should be configured. The stricter, and more secure, approach is that anything not specifically permitted is denied. The second, more open, approach is that anything not specifically denied should be permitted. These are two very different ways of allowing traffic into the trusted network. In a large enterprise a combination of the two approaches can be utilized.

With the first approach, an enterprise starts from a totally secure environment and gradually opens access as access needs are discovered. This approach can take time to fully implement and may annoy users of the enterprise who do not get immediate access to resources they require until the firewall has been properly configured. Such an approach emphasizes security over access. With the second, more open approach, the enterprise's firewalls are configured to prevent certain types of traffic as intrusions or attacks are encountered, not before. This technique is more of a wait-and-see approach and puts ease of access over security. For portions of the enterprise that are critical or particularly sensitive, starting from an open access model and gradually restricting access is probably not a good idea.

We now know that firewalls filter traffic. The next question, then, is How? There are four general ways that a firewall can be configured to perform its filtering. These four methods are not mutually exclusive, meaning that a particular firewall might incorporate more than one filtering methodology. The four types of filtering a firewall might perform are packet, application, circuit-level, and stateful packet inspection. Next we examine briefly each of these four types of firewall filtering.

Packet-Filtering Firewalls

Basic, low-level, filtering is provided by packet-filtering firewalls. This type of firewall drops or passes packets based on their destination and source addresses or ports. Routers can provide this type of **packet filtering**. A packet-filtering firewall inspects the header of each packet that passes through it. Based on that packet's header information, the packet is either passed to its next hop along its network path, or the packet is rejected and dropped. Generally, this type of firewall is relatively easy and inexpensive to set-up, but is limited in its filtering capabilities. Figure 12.4 illustrates the concept of a packet-filtering firewall.

With a packet-filtering firewall, one port of the firewall accepts outside traffic. Another port passes accepted packets unto their next destination. Before a packet is

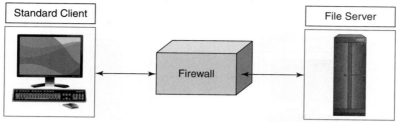

FIGURE 12.4 Packet-Filtering Firewall. A packet-filtering firewall evaluates packets that filter through it. Then, based on packet-filtering policy rules, it denies or allows access.

allowed to traverse the accepting and passing ports, a set of packet-filtering policy rules is applied to that packet. These policy rules can be based on a range of source or destination addresses, types of network protocols (TCP, UDP, or ICMP, for example), or port numbers being used in the communication. In previous chapters we found that in a TCP/IP network well-known ports are associated with various types of network requests.

Packet-filtering firewalls are usually able to handle greater amounts of network traffic because they have little overhead. They have less overhead because, unlike other firewalls, packet-filtering firewalls do not rely on proxies or require extra connection setups. However, a packet-filtering firewall will fail if its internal table of valid and invalid ports and/or addresses is incorrect. Also, packet-filtering firewalls are susceptible to an attack called **address spoofing**. This occurs when a filter is tricked into believing a packet is coming from an addressed device different from its true originating source. In such a scenario, the originator's true address has been forged or "spoofed." Because proxies are not used, traffic from a client is sent directly to a server, should that client's traffic pass the firewall. This direct communication between a client and server leaves the server exposed and vulnerable to attack.

Application-Filtering Firewalls

Application-filtering firewalls are also called *proxy firewalls* and *application-layer gateways*. This type of firewall provides for higher-level screening of traffic from specific applications, such as FTP and e-mail. An application firewall can perform more sophisticated evaluation and authentication of the packets that it filters. As with a packet-filtering firewall, policy rules must be configured that inform the application firewall how to perform. Policy rules are implemented by use of proxies. (You may recall our discussion of proxy servers in a previous chapter.) Each protocol filtered by an application firewall must have its own proxy. Several commonly used protocols that proxies will need to be configured for if using an application firewall include FTP, HTTP, SMTP, and telnet. Figure 12.5 illustrates the concept of an application-filtering firewall.

The necessity for proxies makes application-filtering firewalls more complex to set-up and manage. Application-filtering firewalls are also susceptible to SYN and Ping packet flooding. The abbreviation *SYN* stands for "synchronized" and is a type of packet used by a requesting device to establish a session with a receiving device. These *SYN packets* initiate a TCP connection. The receiver of such a packet is supposed to respond with a SYN ACK (acknowledgment) using the source address contained in the originating SYN request packet. However, in a SYN attack, the SYN source address is usually forged with a nonexistent or fake address. Typically, the attacker floods the receiving device, often a server, with a continuous stream of forged SYN requests. The targeted device, flooded with unanswerable packets, no longer is capable of fulfilling requests from legitimate users.

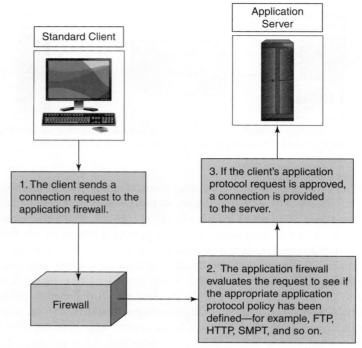

FIGURE 12.5 Application Filtering Firewall

Ping attacks are somewhat similar to SYN attacks in what they are attempting to do, which is flood the network with bogus communication traffic. As you may recall, ping is often used as a diagnostic tool. When one device pings another, the receiving device, if available, responds. In a ping flooding attack, thousands, even millions, of *ping packets*, using a forged source address as with SYN flooding, overwhelm a receiving device, again often a server of some type. Network bandwidth might be entirely consumed by attack traffic as the attacker and the targeted device exchange responses to millions of bogus packets.

Circuit-Filtering Firewalls

A **circuit-filtering** firewall, also called a *circuit-level gateway,* evaluates not only a packet's source and destination addresses but also the circuits that have been established for the packet's communication. This type of firewall is useful for connection-oriented TCP communications, but not with connection-less UDP communications. A proxy server is a common example of a circuit-filtering firewall. In this example, the circuit gateway relays TCP connection information from a trusted network device to an untrusted network device. To the untrusted device, the source address at the other end of the connection is the circuit gateway, not the true communicating, trusted device.

In this way, by supplying its own address, the circuit gateway functions as a proxy for the trusted communicating device on the inside of the firewall. After connections are established, the circuit-level gateway typically passes TCP packets from one connected device to the other without examining packet contents. Security comes from allowing the connection to be established in the first place. Also, when circuit-level gateways are used, communications are outbound, meaning from a trusted internal device to an outside untrusted device. Communications are not inbound, which can be a disadvantage.

Stateful Packet Inspection Firewalls

A **stateful packet inspection (SPI)** firewall combines the advantages of packet filtering with the advantages of application filtering, resulting in compromise between the two. Stateful packet inspection firewalls are not as fast as packet-filtering firewalls or as secure as application layer firewalls, but they provide some of the benefits of both.

A standard packet-filtering firewall examines each packet in a communication stream, evaluating that packet's header information, but not its content, and either passes or drops the packet based on filtering rules. On the other hand, SPI firewalls can examine packet contents as well. Also, SPI firewalls continuously evaluate packets to determine if a valid connection has been opened for them from inside of the network. If there is a valid connection for the packet or packet stream, the SPI firewall lets the packet through; otherwise, the packet is dropped.

In effect, the SPI firewall evaluates source and destination IP addresses, source and destination ports, and packet sequence numbers to decide if the packet belongs to a currently opened connection. While the SPI firewall monitors the communication, it also compiles information about the communication in a packet state table. For added security, a SPI firewall can close off ports used in a communication until connection to the specific port is requested. This is important, as many attacks come through open, well-known ports through a process called port scanning.

Port scanning is an application that searches out Internet-connected devices looking for open well-known port service accesses. Recall that with TCP/IP, there are thousands of well-known ports used for particular types of services. A malicious program can hide its intent by making a request through an innocent port service identifier. Although software-driven port scanning is not illegal, attackers searching for an open or weak part of a network's infrastructure often use such a technique. Closing these ports when not in use can significantly improve a networked organization's internal security.

PHYSICAL SECURITY

Tools such as cryptography and firewalls are useful in securing the enterprise, but **physical security** in terms of restricting physical access to sensitive network components is also important. Having a critical server, for example, out in an open area where it could easily be accessed, damaged, or stolen, is ill-advised. A network is not only logically vulnerable, but physically at risk as well. Additionally, damage or theft may not come from someone outside the organization, but from within. A few common-sense guidelines can go a long way toward providing adequate physical security to the enterprise.

For example, specialized devices such as servers, routers, and switches should be housed in appropriate wiring closets. These closets should themselves be secured by locks, or other physically restricting mechanisms, and only accessible to technicians and staff whose job functions require such access, as conceptualized in Figure 12.6. A policy should be in place to identify who has access, by what means, when access was granted, and for what purpose. When physical keys or badges are issued to permit entry to secured rooms, this information must be accurately documented and maintained. Intruder detection systems that work by alarm or other notification means can also be installed.

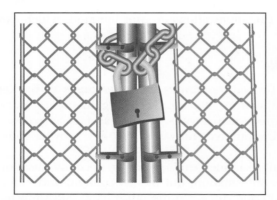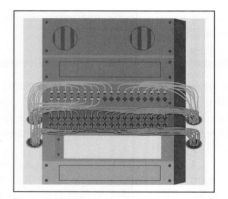

FIGURE 12.6 Securing a Wiring Closet. Wiring closets contain sensitive servers and other hardware. As such, they should be secured so that only authorized personnel can enter and access the technology.

If possible, expensive equipment should be physically secured in place so that it cannot be easily moved. Any media that can possibly contain sensitive data must be closely monitored, and should be wiped clean of all data before being openly released. In situations whereby any storage media used by the enterprise is either sold or donated, such media should have all its contents physically erased and tested for deletion prior to being released. Similar deletion or cleaning of content should occur with user workstations that are moved or assigned from one user to another, or when a user leaves the organization. Once again, events such as these must be documented.

It is essential to have a set of network security policies and procedures that explicitly defines guidelines for protecting network resources and that addresses organizational vulnerabilities. Part of this document should clearly specify job responsibilities, by title and functionally, for all areas of enterprise security. Such a document should describe how access is given, to whom, under whose authority, and under what conditions. Also specified should be how access is either denied or taken away. Security should be determined by such factors as who you are, what you do, what resources you require, and why.

Physically securing the enterprise is a topic that likely seems obvious and yet is an area that can easily be overlooked. Clear and thoroughly defined security policies and procedures with well-maintained documentation are an invaluable asset to a network administrator.

DISASTER RECOVERY PLANNING

Physical security is important to the day-to-day operations of the enterprise. When designing physical security implementations, the enterprise can exercise a degree of control over such factors as unauthorized access or damage and theft to network resources. What cannot be controlled, though, are events such as disasters, whether this be power blackouts, fire, flood, earthquake, tornado, or some other catastrophe, natural or humanmade. However, it is possible to prepare the enterprise to withstand, or at least survive, a disaster. A **disaster recovery plan (DRP)** must be an integral part of enterprise network planning. Having a DRP in place is only half the solution. You must also be confident that the plan works. Businesses should periodically put their DRPs into action by performing the procedures defined in the plan in order to determine whether they work or not. Finding a flaw in the DRP after the disaster has occurred is too late. Table 12.3 highlights steps in developing an effective disaster recovery plan.

Step	Description
Table 12.3 The Disaster Recovery Planning (DRP) Process	
1. Define planning groups	Planning groups must include key users from each business unit or operational area.
2. Establish priorities	The DRP must address essential business processes, technology, networks, systems, and services, and determine what functions are mission critical, important, or minor.
3. Develop a recovery strategy	The recovery strategy should cover the facts of surviving a disaster. The DRP should identify the following: people, facilities, network services, communication equipment, applications, clients and servers, and support and maintenance contracts required for the business to survive.
4. Verify measures and procedures	Does the DRP work? Measures should be identified and carried out that prove the disaster recovery strategy meets its goals and objectives.
5. Implement the plan	The DRP should be documented and communicated to all essential to its success. Periodically, the DRP should be tested by performing its defined procedures to determine that it works.

A first step in creating a DRP is determining the degree of recovery essential for the business to continue as a functioning entity. For some enterprises, full-scale redundancy may be needed, although such a scenario is relatively rare. More likely is that only selected business-critical data, applications, and services will need to be functioning within hours, if not sooner, after a disaster occurs. Many organizations make use of facilities called hot spots. A **hot spot** is an alternative facility where an organization can restore all or a portion of its business-critical systems within a short amount of time. The hot spot could be a branch office, or a separate organization that has entered into a DRP agreement with the affected enterprise. For example, two enterprises in the same industry, say manufacturing of auto parts, in different cities may have an agreement to be a hot spot for each other in the event of a natural disaster. The advantage of partnering with an enterprise in the same industry is that each is likely to have similar data communication infrastructures.

In order for a DRP to work, some degree of **redundancy** is required. Critical data, information, and applications must be backed up and shipped to secure locations, usually off-site. Backups are best shipped off-site, preferably to a different city, in order that they may be available for recovery at another location. Keeping backups at the same facility where the disaster occurs is self-defeating. If the facility is destroyed, very likely any backups they contained will also be destroyed or inaccessible. Backups may be incremental, meaning only files or data that have changed since the last backup are copied. Or, backups may be full, meaning all files and data are completely and fully copied. **Incremental backups** take less time to create, but more time to restore. **Full backups** take more time to create but less time to restore. Consider the following scenario.

On Monday morning at 6 A.M., the customer database is given a full backup. This means that all data on the customer database are saved and stored. The backup in this case is a full copy of the original customer database at that point in time. Beginning at 8 A.M., transactions begin to be applied to the original customer database. Customers are added or deleted or existing data are modified, such as customer phone numbers, addresses, or balance changes.

Assume that 1,000 such transactions take place each day of the week. By the following Monday, 7,000 changes have been made to the original customer database. If another full backup is made, those changes are then captured and stored on this latest copy of the customer database. In this scenario, if a problem occurred in the middle of the week—for example, Wednesday—and the customer database had to be restored from the previous Monday's backup, potentially 3,000 transactions would be lost because the backup was not current. The business could, to address this problem, make a full backup of the customer database at the end of each day. In this way, all transactions could be fully recovered. However, making a full backup takes time.

If a business used an incremental backup approach, the scenario would be different. Again, assume a full backup is made at 6 A.M. on Monday. At the end of Monday's business processing day, an incremental backup is performed. This incremental backup would backup only the data on those customers who had changes applied against their accounts for that Monday.

On Tuesday, another incremental backup is made, and again, only changes made on that Tuesday are captured and stored. On Wednesday, a third incremental backup is made. Then, say a disaster strikes and the database has to be recovered and restored. The business would first restore the full backup from Monday and then the incremental backups from Monday, Tuesday, and Wednesday, in that order. The transactions for those days would be recovered. The ability to recover transactions is critical to a business. Figure 12.7 illustrates the full-backup scenario and Figure 12.8 illustrates an incremental backup.

The timing of the backups also has to be considered. Two different sets of data may require two different backup timing cycles. Depending on the resource and how it is used, backup creation may be on a daily, weekly, monthly, or other time-framed basis. Knowing how your organization uses its data and applications is essential for planning the timing of backup cycles.

With more redundancy, greater expense is usually involved. But, with greater redundancy, the potential for fuller recovery is also improved. Balancing expense with

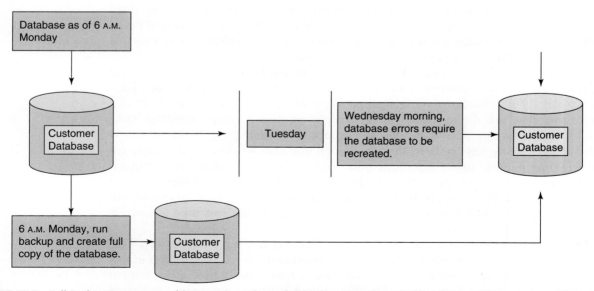

FIGURE 12.7 Full Backup Recovery. In this scenario, unless a full backup is made each day, all transactions are lost that were placed between Monday, 6 A.M., and the time of Wednesday's database recovery. Full backups take longer to create, but shorter to recover if done frequently. In this particular example, two days of missing data are probably not tolerable.

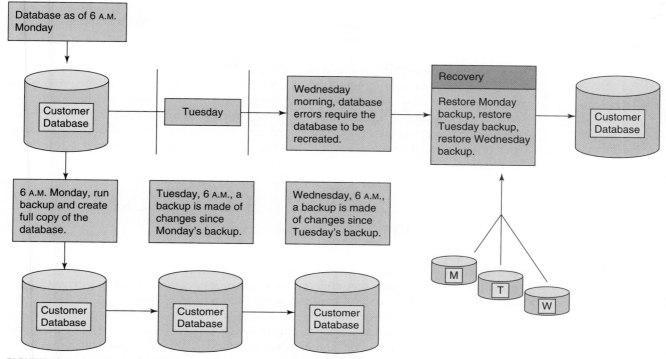

FIGURE 12.8 Incremental Backup Recovery. In this scenario, all transactions between Monday and Wednesday's last incremental backup are recovered. Some transactions may still have been lost, but far fewer than in our full backup example in Figure 12.7. Incremental backups are faster to create, but longer to recover.

recovery is why thorough analysis is needed to determine what functionalities truly are essential for the business to survive.

This text has repeatedly emphasized the need for, and usefulness of, good documentation. In the event of a disaster, good documentation can make the difference between survival or death for a business. In the DRP, instructions must outline who does what, where, when, and how in the event of a disaster. A disaster is not the time for guesswork, or for determining how and where key organizational functions and staff are to respond. Some organizations contract out the design of their DRP to vendors who specialize in this field. Disaster recovery plan vendors perform risk analysis and auditing of enterprise functionalities in order to determine what functions and data are essential to enterprise survival.

INTEGRATED SECURITY SYSTEMS

Securing the enterprise depends on a combination of technologies, tools, and planning. These components must work together in an integrated manner in order to be effective. The larger and more complex the organization, the more likely the organization will have a staff of experts whose job is to design, implement, and maintain an integrated security system. An integrated security system should incorporate preventive, detective, and reactive measures that are internal and external to the enterprise. Such a system is not a DRP, but includes a DRP within it.

Successful integrated security systems are adaptive, meaning the enterprise must establish an environment of continually educating itself on changing security threats.

Integrated security systems can include such elements as logical perimeter security gates using firewalls and proxies, surveillance systems to facility access control, close cable television, fire and intrusion detection, and other systems. As with a DRP, vendors are available for hire to design and implement integrated security systems.

Creating a security plan is a balancing act: Too much security gets in the way of doing business, yet too little leaves the enterprise vulnerable to attack. The goals of an **integrated security system** should be directly linked to the goals of the enterprise. Such a system should identify and prioritize critical enterprise assets and the level of protection these assets require. Integrated security systems should allow for detection and response to threats, and yet be flexible enough for users of enterprise resources to function. Perfect security is not possible, and probably not practical, but good security is a must.

Chapter Summary

Four critical components that define security are confidentiality, access, integrity, and nonrepudiation. These four components are sometimes referred to as the CAIN principles. Technologies that address these components make it more difficult for an enterprise to be attacked and exposed to security vulnerabilities.

Cryptography plays a major role in securing the enterprise and is central to many security-based applications. Cryptography is the science of ensuring that data and information cannot be easily understood or modified by unauthorized individuals. Cryptographic methods address several security features: authentication, nonrepudiation, privacy, assurance of message integrity, and provisions for digital signatures.

At the heart of the cryptographic method is the cipher. A successful cipher must make it difficult for an encrypted message to be viewed in its cleartext form, without the use of the cryptographic key. Also, a cipher must produce ciphertext that appears random in format to a casual user, or to anyone without the key. Two major branches of cryptography into which ciphers generally fall are symmetric and asymmetric. One way to combine the benefits of both symmetric and asymmetric ciphers is to create what is referred to as a "session" key, which is a key pair that is renewed, or changed, periodically.

Firewalls primarily serve as a barrier. A firewall can be a barrier between the outside world and the enterprise, or a barrier between networks within the enterprise. As a barrier between the outside world and the enterprise, a firewall is configured to keep out unauthorized individuals who are attempting to attack or penetrate the enterprise. A firewall placed between networks within the enterprise helps isolate sensitive or critical data and applications from internal enterprise staff access. Firewalls may be hardware-based, software-based, or a combination of the two. The four types of filtering a firewall can perform include packet, application, circuit-level, and stateful packet inspection.

A network is not only logically vulnerable but is also physically at risk Physical security addresses the day-to-day security of the enterprise. A set of network security policies and procedures need to be defined that explicitly contain guidelines for protecting network resources and that addresses organizational vulnerabilities. Security access is to be determined by such factors as who you are, what you do, what resources you require, and why.

A disaster recovery plan must be an integral part of enterprise network planning. Businesses should periodically put their DRPs into action by performing the procedures defined in the plan in order to determine whether they work or not. A first step in creating a DRP is determining the degree of recovery essential for the business to continue as a functioning entity. In order for a DRP to work, some degree of redundancy is required. In the DRP plan should be instructions that outline who does what, where, when, and how in the event of a disaster.

An integrated security system should incorporate preventive, detective, and reactive measures that are internal and external to the enterprise. Successful security systems are also adaptive. The goals of an integrated security system should be directly linked to the goals of the enterprise.

Keywords

Access *239*
Address spoofing *247*
Alphabet *240*
Application filtering *247*
Asymmetric cipher *242*
Attack *240*
Authentication *239*
Caesar cipher *241*
Certificate authority *243*
Circuit filtering *248*
Cipher *240*
Ciphertext *240*
Cleartext *240*
Confidentiality *238*
Cryptography *240*

Digital certificate *243*
Digital signature *243*
Disaster recovery
  plan *250*
Encryption *238*
Firewall *245*
Full backup *251*
Hot spot *251*
Incremental
  backup *251*
Integrated security
  system *254*
Integrity *239*
Nonrepudiation *239*
Packet filtering *246*

Physical security *249*
Plaintext *240*
Port scanning *249*
Private key *242*
Public key *242*
Public key
  infrastructure *243*
Redundancy *251*
Session *243*
Session key *243*
Stateful packet
  inspection *249*
Symmetric cipher *242*
Trusted network *246*
Untrusted network *246*

Chapter Questions

Short-Answer Questions

1. Identify the four components of security.
2. How do asymmetric and symmetric ciphers differ?
3. What is meant by encryption and why would it be used?
4. How does an incremental backup differ from a full backup?
5. What is a trusted network?
6. Define the term *hot spot*.
7. What is the purpose of a firewall?
8. What is application filtering?

Hands-On Projects

1. Compare and contrast two home-user vendor products that provide for virus protection.
2. Interview a network administrator at your college or university, or place of work, and determine the types of disaster recovery measures that are in place for that institution or place of business.
3. List and detail at least five elements that would make for a good disaster recovery plan.
4. Draft a policy statement that addresses how servers should be physically secured.

Research in Brief

Research a vendor that provides for disaster recovery planning. Report on the types of services it offers, the cost, the features provided, and the types of businesses it serves.

1. The use of cryptography is an essential tool of applications such as e-commerce, whereby assurances of financial security are crucial. There has been much political controversy over whether cryptography technology should be sold outside of the United States, meaning the techniques on which cryptographic technologies are based. For some time, selling cryptographic technologies outside the country was illegal. Investigate and report on the arguments for and against the for-profit sale of cryptographic methods to the world at large. Based on your findings, what would you recommend and why?

2. Research and select at least two cryptographic applications that could be useful for the small business user. Compare and contrast the functionalities, costs, benefits, and/or disadvantages of the two products. Which of the two products would you recommend and why.

3. More and more home users are using "always on" connections to the Internet. These types of connections leave the user vulnerable to external attack. Investigate and compare at least two firewall products targeted for the home user. Report on their functionalities, costs, benefits, and any disadvantages. Which of the two products would you recommend and why?

Case Study

Sheehan Marketing and Public Relations

You have not been surprised to discover that SMPR has no disaster recovery plan in place for any of its offices. You realize that this lack of planning for a possible disaster is a critical issue that must be addressed as soon as possible. Although you have not addressed this topic specifically with company president Sheehan, you believe the time is now right to present this problem to him.

In order to fully inform Mr. Sheehan on the options available to SMPR regarding disaster recovery you have decided to prepare a detailed report on disaster recovery planning's "best practices." This report will require that you seek out and investigate what experts in disaster recovery recommend being included in such a plan. Besides this general report that details what must be included in disaster recovery planning, and why, you want to include a brief section that highlights potential vendor-based solutions from two businesses in this area of expertise.

In addition to the written report, you have also decided to make an oral presentation with simple visual elements to SMPR management on your findings.

Topic in Focus

REDUNDANT ARRAY OF INEXPENSIVE DEVICES

Especially for medium- to large-scale enterprises, storage of data, and its access and recoverability, are issues of serious concern. Recoverability relates directly to fault tolerance. One of the most commonly used storage technologies used for improved performance, reliability, and recoverability is called a *redundant array of inexpensive devices (RAID)*, and it is also sometimes referred to as a *redundant array of independent devices*, or simply as a *drive array*. Regardless, RAID comes in six standardized forms numbered from 0 to 5, and addresses the access component of security. These numbers are used to identify the different levels each RAID solution stores and treats data. Higher RAID-level numbers do not necessarily imply increased power or speed.

As a storage security solution, RAID can be implemented as hardware, software, or a combination of the two. In general, hardware RAID solutions are faster but more expensive, whereas software solutions are slower but cheaper. Frequently, RAID-levels 3 and higher are implemented using hardware, due to performance requirements. If based on hardware, either a RAID controller card is used or an independent RAID drive array is implemented. If a controller card is used, the card, which is connected by cable to the RAID hard drives, is plugged into an available server's expansion slot. The advantage of a separate RAID controller card is that the card has its own processor and memory. Because the RAID card has its own resources, it does not have to utilize the server's processor or memory to perform its functions, improving overall server performance.

If, instead, an independent RAID drive array is used, it will also have its own processor and memory. In addition, the drive array unit will contain bays into which the RAID hard drives can be placed. Usually, an independent RAID drive array allows for easier expandability and greater storage capacity due to the number of drives the array can potentially hold. The drive array unit is then connected to a server. The RAID drive arrays are often based on SCSI (small computer system interface) technology. More expensive RAID drive arrays have a "backplane."

This backplane provides power to the hard drives, and also connects the drives directly to the unit's SCSI bus, such that separate cables are not required. For an added expense, RAID drive arrays can also support "hot swappable" drives. The advantage of a hot swappable drive is that it can be removed or inserted without powering down the RAID unit. This means that if one of the hard drives in the array fails, the failing drive can be replaced without taking down the entire array. The type of RAID level implemented determines whether such hot swappable drives can be utilized. Following is a brief discussion of the six standardized RAID levels, 0 through 5.

RAID Level 0

RAID Level 0, referred to as *simple disk stripping*, usually uses block-level stripping but can also be configured for byte-level stripping. A block is generally composed of 512 bytes. A byte is composed of 8 bits. Block-level stripping is preferred with data files containing small data records, as a data block, when it is retrieved, might contain the entire record. Byte-level stripping is preferred for large data records, because multiple drives can be read in parallel if a large record spans more than one drive. Assuming a three-drive RAID 0 array, block A is written to the first drive, block B to the second, block C to the third. Block D then writes again to the first drive, block E to the second drive, and so on.

The interesting thing about RAID 0 is that, in reality, it provides no redundancy, and therefore no fault tolerance, making it a potentially dangerous RAID choice. The advantage, however, of RAID 0 is that it offers the best performance in terms of data access as no overhead is involved for data recovery. Overhead is not involved because error checking is not performed. Also, drives can be accessed in parallel for read and write operations. On the other hand, for the multiple drives in a RAID 0 array, should one of the drives fail, the entire array fails. Consequently, this means that data on all the drives that make up the array becomes unusable should one drive fail. The result of this type of failure is absence of fault tolerance. Because there is no fault tolerance, when implementing RAID 0 an enterprise must make sure that regular backups are performed so that data can be recovered if the array fails.

RAID Level 1

RAID 1 can be implemented with disk mirroring or disk duplexing. Both provide a level of fault tolerance, with disk duplexing being superior. In a mirrored RAID 1, a single hard drive controller is used to manage two hard drives. As data are written to one drive, the data are copied, or mirrored, to the second drive as well. Should one drive fail, the second drive is available for data recovery. However, should the hard drive controller fail, then both drives in the array become unavailable.

Also, although two drives are used in the array, the enterprise does not get double performance access, or double the storage. Two 20 GB (gigabyte) drives that are mirrored or duplexed store the same set of 10 GB data, so disk utilization is very inefficient. Furthermore, when a write operation is performed, both drives are written to simultaneously, resulting in single drive speed performance. On the other hand, when a read operation is performed, the array can alternate between the two drives, improving read access performance.

Unlike a mirrored RAID 1, a duplexed RAID 1 has separate hard drive controllers for each hard drive. Should one drive fail, the second drive is still available. In addition, should one of the hard drive controllers fail, the second hard drive controller remains available, so a single hard drive controller failure does not bring the array down. Disk duplexing provides better fault tolerance because failure of both a hard disk drive and a hard disk drive controller can be experienced, yet data can still be accessed on the array. Of course, should both drives or both controllers fail, then the array fails, but such duplicated failure is less likely to occur in a duplexed RAID 1.

RAID Level 2

RAID level 2 uses some of its arrayed drives only for data and a portion only for error correcting codes (ECC). Error correction codes allow data to be reconstructed in the event of a data drive failure. But multiple ECC drives also put the array at greater risk, because if one of the ECC drives fails, all of them fail. Such a scenario is not secure. In practice, RAID 2 is rarely implemented because it is slow, disk-intensive, and unreliable in the manner in which the ECC disks are configured.

RAID Level 3

RAID 3 uses data striping at the byte level, but with the addition of parity checking. Unlike RAID 1, which has no automated error correcting mechanism, RAID 3 uses parity for data recovery. And unlike RAID 2, RAID 3 uses only one of the drives in its array for parity checking, not several. At a minimum, RAID 3 requires three drives, two for data and one for parity. More than two data drives can be supported. Should a data drive in the array fail, the parity drive can be used to rebuild that failed drive's data. But the single parity drive is itself a weakness. If the single parity drive fails, data drives cannot be reconstructed.

RAID Level 4

RAID 4 closely resembles RAID 3, except that RAID 4 uses block-level data striping instead of byte-level data striping. As with RAID 3, one drive is used for parity, and two or more drives are used for data. Like RAID 2, RAID 4 is not often implemented because RAID 5 is faster and more reliable. Graphically, RAID 4 looks just like RAID 3, except that the parity drive is block-based rather than byte-based.

RAID Level 5

RAID 5 also uses data striping at the block-level, but unlike RAID 3 or 4, parity or ECC information is distributed among the disks that make up the array. Because RAID 3 and 4 use a single parity drive, that drive becomes a bottleneck in terms of access performance, meaning that each write operation has to wait its turn for its parity data to be written to the parity drive. With RAID 5, distributed parity writing removes the single parity drive bottleneck, resulting in improved write performance. RAID 5's distributed parity also results in better rebuild of lost or damaged data, when required. Read performance, however, in a RAID 5 array can suffer because drives in a RAID 5 array contain both data and parity information. When the array is accessed for a read operation, drive heads have to bypass, or jump over, parity information maintained on the drive. Bypassing the parity information takes time, and, as the saying goes, time is money.

Of the various forms of standardized RAIDs we have considered, RAIDs 1 and 5 are the most commonly implemented. RAID 1 serves well for smaller organizations. RAID 5 is better suited for medium- to large-scale enterprises. Other, nonstandardized and proprietary forms of RAID also exist.

Chapter

13

Wireless Technologies

The Business Benefit

One of the basic concepts in economics is the concept of supply and demand. This principle concludes that the price of a product or service varies on whether the supply of the product or service (quantity) is equal to the demand for that product or service. When the quantity available of a good matches the demand for that good, supply and demand are in equilibrium—a perfect, if rare, balance.

However, if the supply for a good is not sufficient to meet the demand for that good, the price for that good rises. Conversely, if the supply for a good exceeds the demand for that good, the price falls. Several factors can affect supply, including production costs, prices of related goods, and the number of suppliers for those goods. Likewise, several factors can affect demand, including incomes of potential buyers, market preferences, and number of potential customers.

In this chapter we look at various wireless technologies. How, you may be asking, does that relate to the economics of supply and demand? Wireless technologies of all types depend on radio frequency bands for delivery and receipt of data. In this example the data might be voice, audio, video, textual, graphics, or some other choice. Depending on the radio frequency band used, service and quality can vary greatly. Consider these two options.

Option 1: Your data are delivered instantaneously, are always available, and have low latency and little if any introduction of error. *Option 2:* Your data are delivered slowly and are only intermittently available, with high delay and a great deal of possible error. If you were in the market for wireless delivery and receipt of essential business data for your organization, which of the two scenarios would you prefer? It's highly likely the demand for high-speed, always on, error-free data delivery will be greater than for low-speed, intermittent, error-prone data delivery. Would you be willing to pay a higher price for Option 1? What if the business demand for Option 1 were greater than the bandwidth supply available?

Recognizing that there is a huge market for services provided with Option 1 characteristics, major corporations are willing to spend vast amounts to control the supply of high bandwidth wireless radio spectrum frequencies. In its December 23, 2011, online edition, *The Wall Street Journal* (*www.wsj.com*) reported that the Federal Communications Commission (FCC) authorized telecom provider AT&T to purchase for almost $2 billion a block of 700 MHz spectrum. This is a block of prime radio frequency spectrum that could accommodate up to 300 million users. One may suppose that AT&T was willing to pay such a high cost for this supply of wireless bandwidth with the assumption that demand for that bandwidth would be equally high, if not higher.

Learning Objectives

After studying this chapter, you should be able to:

- Identify wireless LAN media.
- Show familiarity with 802.11 protocols.
- List five steps for configuring a small wireless LAN.
- Describe Bluetooth.
- Differentiate between Wi-Fi and Wi-Max.
- Describe 4G.

WIRELESS LOCAL AREA NETWORK STANDARDS (WLAN)

From previous chapters you now know that the IEEE composed a series of local area network standards under the umbrella of various 802 protocols—for example, token ring (802.5) and Ethernet (802.3). In 1990, the IEEE formed another committee to develop protocols for wireless LANS under an **802.11** working group. This working group proposed protocols for both the physical and the data link layers. The core function of the *physical layer* is to serve as a conduit for transfer of data from a given sender to a given receiver. In a wireless implementation, the physical layer also concerns itself with data rate, radio frequency band, and encoding techniques. For the *data link layer*, framing the data and assigning physical addressing to those frames are critical functions. In each case, the physical and data link layers were each further subdivided into two components each. Figure 13.1 illustrates these layers and their sublayer components.

For the physical layer, the defined subdivisions are the **physical medium dependent (PMD)** and the **physical layer convergence procedure (PLCP)** sublayers. The PMD sublayer defines standards for the characteristics of the wireless medium, which we discuss shortly. The PLCP sublayer reformats data received from the data link layer into a form that the PMD can transmit. In addition, the PLCP continuously evaluates the medium to determine when data can be transmitted.

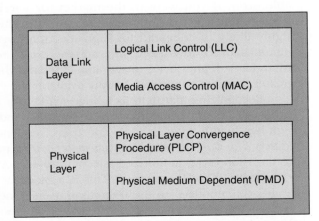

FIGURE 13.1 Physical and Data Link Layer Components. The PLC reformats data received from the MAC sublayer into a form the PMD can transmit.

At the data link layer, the sublayers are the **logical link control (LLC)** and the **media access control (MAC)**. The LLC is responsible for providing a common interface, flow control, and reliability. The MAC sublayer concerns itself with attaching an address to the frame to be transmitted. Together the functions of these two sublayers permit high-level protocols to work without concern for underlying physical layer specifications.

WIRELESS LAN MEDIA

The IEEE in its initial creation of the 802.11 standard allowed for three types of physical wireless media: (1) infrared, (2) frequency hopping spread spectrum (FHSS), and (3) direct sequence spread spectrum (DSSS). Of the three, infrared has proven unpopular due to two major constraints. First, successful infrared transmission requires an unobstructed line-of-sight capability between the sender and receiver, meaning that walls and partitions can prevent a communication from occurring. Second, infrared is limited in terms of the data rates that it can support, making it inefficient for such bandwidth intensive data as video.

Both FHSS and DSSS are a type of **spread spectrum** radio frequency transmission, as opposed to a **narrowband** transmission. Most of us are familiar with narrowband radio transmission as a means of listening to music or news on a typical AM or FM radio station—for example, AM 1650 or FM 94.1. In each of these cases, a specific, narrow frequency radio band, again FM 94.1 for example, is used to transmit data for one specific radio station signal. Narrowband transmissions typically require more power than spread spectrum transmissions because narrowband transmissions are more vulnerable to signal interference. You may have experienced this type of signal interference when you hear one AM or FM radio station intruding or bleeding into the delivery of another station on a similar or close frequency. Primarily for this reason, noise intrusion, the Federal Communications Commission (FCC) permits narrowband radio stations to transmit within a given geographic area only on a specific narrowband radio frequency. Table 13.1 identifies common radio frequency ranges and how they are designated.

In contrast, spread spectrum transmissions take a signal and "spread" it over a broader range of a given radio frequency band. This spreading characteristic inherently provides for greater security and improved capability for tolerating signals from other transmissions or systems. Narrowband transmissions typically ignore spread spectrum transmissions as a type of white noise. As you may suppose, FHSS and DSSS take different approaches to the "spreading" of a signal over a wider radio frequency band.

Table 13.1   Well-Known Allocated Frequency Ranges

Purpose	Frequency Band
AM Radio	535 KHz to 1.7 MHz
Short Wave Radio	5.9 MHz to 26.1 MHz
Citizens Band (CB) Radio	26.96 MHz to 27.41 MHz
Television Stations—Channels 2 through 6	54 MHz to 88 MHz
FM Radio	88 MHz to 108 MHz
Television Stations—Channels 7 through 13	174 MHz to 220 MHz

For **frequency hopping spread spectrum**, the frequency spectrum is divided into channels. In the United States, the number of channels available is 70. On these channels a data packet is split up, spread, and transmitted using a pseudo-random pattern that is known only to the transmitter and the receiver. **Pseudo-random** here means that although the changes in frequency appear random, there is in fact a method used to select frequency hops. During transmission, the radio frequency used changes rapidly, hence the term frequency *hopping*. In this manner, a short burst of data is sent first on one given frequency, then a second short burst at another frequency, then a third short burst at yet another frequency, and so on. The time spent at given frequency is referred to as **dwell time**. The process of changing frequencies, from one short burst to another, is the **hopping code**. Frequency hopping spread spectrum was targeted by the IEEE 802.11 workgroup to use the 2.4 GHz ISM (industrial, scientific, medical) radio frequency band and operate with a 1 or 2 Mbps data rate.

Ultimately, FHSS works by repeatedly hopping from one carrier frequency to another during a given transmission. An advantage of FHSS is that wireless networks that may be in close proximity to each other can use their own different pseudo-random pattern frequency sequences without interfering with each other. Also, during transmission of a given message, if interference is encountered on one channel, the transmitter and receiver can "hop" to another channel and the transmitter can simply retransmit its data packets on the new channel. Frequency hopping spread spectrum can work well for small data packets in an area where high interference may be an issue. Figure 13.2 illustrates the concept of FHSS.

Direct sequence spread spectrum was also designed to work at the 2.4 GHz ISM radio frequency band range. However, DSSS uses a different technique to spread its spectrum. For DSSS, the transmitter using a mathematical key spreads the data across a wide range of radio frequencies. The receiver has access to the same mathematical key so that the receiver can then decode the message once received. In its implementation, DSSS maps each single data bit into a string of bits, using one string

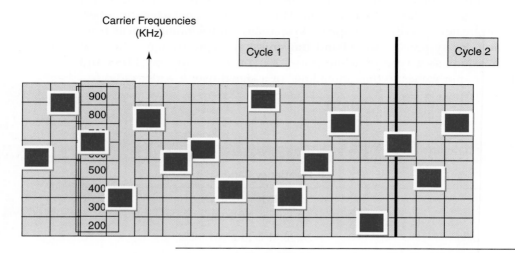

FIGURE 13.2 Conceptual Implementation of Frequency Hopping Spread Spectrum. In this conceptual illustration, the data packets are split up and transmitted on different frequency channels in a pseudo-random hopping known only to the sender and receiver.

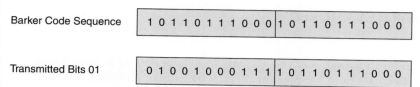

FIGURE 13.3 The Barker Code. Assume data bits 01 to be transmitted via direct sequence spread spectrum using the 11-bit Barker Code sequence.

for a binary 1 and another different string for a binary 0. These sequence strings are pseudo-randomly generated by means of the mathematical key used between the sender and receiver. The intent is to reduce the possible effects of interference and data degradation by spreading each data bit out over time.

The spreading signal mechanism used by DSSS results in a pseudo-random sequence of positive and negative values with a very high repetition rate. In fact, the spreading signal has a much higher bandwidth than the embedded data or informational signal. The base data signal is multiplied by the spreading signal algorithm at the transmitter's end, converted to 2.4 GHz, and then transmitted. The receiver, using the same spread signal algorithm, applies a "de-spreading" code to the transmission received, and converts the transmission back into the originating base data. Specifically associated with the DSSS implementation is the **Barker spreading code**. This code utilizes an 11-bit spreading mechanism. Figure 13.3 illustrates how an 11-bit Barker spreading code is applied against a single binary 1 and a single binary 0.

Under the 802.11 umbrella, a number of workgroup variants have been developed. Table 13.2 identifies these variants. We now take a brief look at five of these 802.11 specifications. Each of these standards is associated with a technology referred to as **Wi-Fi**, or wireless fidelity.

Table 13.2	802.11 Standards
Standard	**General Purpose**
802.11a	Wireless Networking
802.11b	Wireless Networking
802.11c	Bridge Operation
802.11d	Regulatory
802.11e	MAC Layer QoS (Quality of Service)
802.11f	Access Point Interoperability
802.11g	Wireless Networking
802.11h	Spectrum and Power Management
802.11i	Wireless Security and Authentication
802.11j	4.9/5 GHz Operation in Japan
802.11k	Wireless LAN Management and Maintenance
802.11m	Editorial and Technical Issues Related to the 802.11 Standard
802.11n	Enhancements to Wireless LAN Performance and Throughput

WI-FI: WIRELESS FIDELITY

802.11a

First, in an odd manner, 802.11a actually followed, and so is newer than, the 802.11b standard. Even so, here we present these standards in alphabetical order.

The **802.11a** IEEE specification utilizes the 5 GHz spectrum band. A key feature of this standard was to allow users within the United States to take advantage of the **Unlicensed National Information Infrastructure (UNII)**—yet another acronym to add to your vocabulary. Table 13.3 provides additional information on UNII. The intent behind the UNII was to encourage manufacturers to develop high-speed wireless network applications and appliances. It must be noted that unlike the 2.4 GHz spread spectrum specifications described later, 802.11a uses **optical frequency division multiplexing (OFDM)**. This technique makes use of multiple carrier signals at different frequencies. It is somewhat like frequency division multiplexing (FDM). Possible data rates per OFDM channel are 6, 9, 12, 18, 24, 36, 48, and 54 Mbps.

The PLCP sublayer of the 802.11a, used to format data for transmission, generates packets that are composed of a preamble, a header, and, of course, the data. The *preamble* is used for synchronization between the sender and receiver. The *header* is composed of six fields: the data rate field specifies the transmission rate; a reserved field for future use; a length file that contains the length value of the data; the data field itself; a parity field used for error checking; and a tail field that indicates the end of the header.

The 802.11a standard allows for increased channel allocation. Within the 802.11a framework, up to eight frequency channels can overlap and be simultaneously functioning in the UNII 1 and UNII 2 bands. Because transmissions can be sent over differing parallel subchannels, minimizing radio interference from external sources, transmission error is reduced.

802.11b

The **802.11b** specification extended the original DSSS scheme by extending data rates from 1 and 2 Mbps to 5.5 and 11 Mbps. To achieve this higher data rate in the same bandwidth, a modulation scheme referred to as *complementary code keying* is utilized. The 802.11b proved to be a commercial success.

The 802.11b PLCP (physical layer convergence procedure) is based on DSSS transmission criteria. In this scenario, the PLCP takes the data received from the MAC layer and reformats it into a frame that can be utilized by the adjoining PDM (physical medium dependent) sublayer for transmission. The frame delivered to the PDM has three key parts.

First, a preamble is used to prepare the receiver for the rest of the frame to be delivered. This preamble has a synchronization field and then a start of frame delimiter. The synchronization field is in place to allow the receiving device time to prepare for the incoming message. The start of frame delimiter filed denotes the beginning of the frame.

Table 13.3   UNII General Characteristics

Band	Frequency Range	Maximum Power Output
UNII I—Low Band	5.15 GHz to 5.25 GHz	50 mW
UNII II—Middle Band	5.25 GHz to 5.35 GHz	250 mW
UNII—Unnamed	5.46 GHz to 5.72 GHz	1000 MHz
UNII III—High Band	5.72 GHz to 5.82 GHz	

Second, a header is provided that contains information about the frame itself. The header has four parts. First the signal data rate is provided that designates the speed of the signal. Next a reserved service field for future use is appended. Following the reserved field is a length component that provides the length of the frame. Then a header error check field is provided that contains data that can be used to verify errors upon receipt of the frame.

Last, the data or payload portion of the frame follows, which contains the data actually being sent.

802.11g

Both 802.11a and 802.11b have proven successful in varying degrees. With the intent of developing a standard that would incorporate the best aspects of 802.11a and 802.11b, the IEEE created a workgroup referenced as standard **802.11g**, released by the IEEE in June of 2003. Able to utilize either OFDM or DSSS, there were two other key advantages designed into 802.11g. First, 802.11g extends data rate transmissions from 12 to 54 Mbps per channel. Second, 802.11g is backward compatible with 802.11b networks. Devices on an 802.11b network can converse with devices on an 802.11g network, and vice versa. However, should this occur, meaning an 802.11b network conversing with an 802.11g network, data passing through the 802.11b access point coming from an 802.11g network will use the lower 802.11b data rate.

802.11i

In this chapter, and in others, we will be touching on the issue of security. Wireless LANs (WLANs) bring many advantages to the enterprise and to users of the WLAN. However, one area in particular in which WLANs are more vulnerable than their wired counterparts is security. Wireless LANs bring with them a different set of security issues and problems as compared to wired LANs. Aware of this, the IEEE has created a wireless security workgroup under the **802.11i** standard. This standard defines security and authentication mechanisms at the MAC sublayer. Three important security features that 802.11i addresses include authentication, key management, and data transfer privacy.

When devices connect to a WLAN, they should be *authenticated* to verify that they are indeed authorized to access and utilize the resources of the network. This authentication will make use of virtual "keys" between sender and receiver, as was discussed in our previous chapter on security. After successful authentication and *key management, transfer of data* may begin, and, depending on the nature of the data being transmitted, encryption may be required to provide for necessary privacy.

802.11n

Wireless networks have proven to be extremely popular in both large and small businesses and organizations. Recognizing this, the IEEE continues to develop standards under the 802.11 umbrella that seek to enhance wireless network performance, access, reliability, and security. The **802.11n** standard was brought forward to address further improvements to the physical layer and MAC sublayer with the intent to enhance throughput. A main goal of the 801.11n standard is to provide for data rates of up to 100 Mbps. Other objectives for the 802.11n standard are to increase the range or distance for wireless communications between devices, to offer wireless communications that are more resistant to external interferences, and to take advantage of improved technologies related to the use of multiple and/or smart antennas.

When WLANs were first introduced under 802.11, the security mechanism provided for utilized a technique called **wired equivalent privacy (WEP)**. It was quickly demonstrated that as a security tool WEP was highly inadequate and could easily be

Table 13.4 Wireless LAN 802.11 Standards

Standard	Date Issued	Bandwidth (MHz)	Unlicensed Frequency Range (MHz)	Data Rate per Channel (Mbps)
802.11	1997	83.5	2.4 to 2.4835, DSSS, FHSS	1, 2
802.11a	1999	300	5.15 to 5.35 OFDM, 5.725 to 5.825 OFDM	6, 9, 12, 18, 24, 36, 48, 54
802.11b	1999	83.5	2.4 to 2.4835 DSSS	1, 2, 5.5, 11
802.11g	2003	83.5	2.4 to 2.4835 DSSS, OFDM	1, 2, 5.5, 6, 9, 11, 12, 18, 24, 36, 48, 54

broken or hacked. A major weakness of WEP is that it depended on a 40-bit key for security. In response, **Wi-Fi protected access (WPA)** was developed and put forward as a replacement, and major improvement, over WEP. Table 13.4 summarizes the 802.11 standards reviewed.

WIRELESS LAN MANAGEMENT

As with a wired LAN, planning and management are essential elements in configuring and deploying a WLAN. Wireless local area networks, by their nature, will have issues and concerns that need to be addressed differently from a wired LAN. But WLANs also offer significant benefits, including mobility, flexibility, scalability, a wide array of products and services that support wireless technologies, and interoperability.

In particular, interoperability is an important concept and of great interest to organizations, large and small, that plan to deploy WLANs. As mentioned earlier, there are many vendors that provide a wide range of products specifically with WLANs in mind. For organizations that do not want to be locked into one product provider, it becomes essential that devices and products from various WLAN vendors be able to interoperate. This concern for interoperability between different vendor products was so significant that an organization was formed to address interoperability, along with other related topics: the Wireless Ethernet Compatibility Alliance, or the **Wi-Fi Alliance** (*www.wi-fi.org*). With the explosive growth of WLANs, the Wi-Fi Alliance has proven a valuable organization. Their mission statement identifies the following goals of this organization:

- Provide a highly effective collaboration forum.
- Grow the Wi-Fi industry.
- Lead industry growth with new technology specifications and programs.
- Support industry-agreed standards.
- Deliver great product connectivity through testing and certification.

A core task of the Wi-Fi Alliance is to provide WLAN vendors an authoritative body that can test and then verify as to the interoperability of a vendor's product. The Wi-Fi Alliance certification process began in earnest in 2000. Since then, over 14,000 products have been officially certified. Ideally, the product being tested and verified would provide 100 percent interoperability with other vendor products. Initially focused on the 802.11b standard, the Wi-Fi Alliance now offers certifications for 802.11a and 802.11g products.

This stamp of approval from an authoritative body such as the Wi-Fi Alliance makes it easier for planners and designers of wireless networks to have confidence in the certified products and services they select. Of course selecting products and services is only one step in managing and securing a WLAN. Here we identify five general steps that a networking administrator, or business owner, might take in configuring a small WLAN: (1) planning, (2) acquiring, (3) configuring, (4) testing, and (5) securing.

Planning

First, an in-depth planning process must be initiated. Building the right solution requires that we first understand user networking requirements. For example, with a small WLAN the choice might be between designing for a peer-to-peer network or a WLAN that utilizes a *base station,* sometimes also referred to as an *access point* or *gateway.* You might recall from an earlier chapter that in a peer-to-peer network, devices operate in such a manner that allows them to share resources with no one device being a controlling or central managing device. Peer-to-peer networks, whether wired or wireless, work best in small-scale environments, say six devices or less. For wireless networks that have numerous devices that need to communicate or share resources, a peer-to-peer configuration will likely prove inefficient.

Wireless LANs that use a base station, or central access point, utilize the base station as a means of connecting the other wireless devices that make up the network. These types of base stations come with a range of features and performance capabilities. Typically, the more features and functionalities supported by the base station, the more expensive the base station. That is why when planning for the network, the designer must take into consideration how that network will be used, the types of resources to be shared, the number of users supported, the type of applications essential to the business, and other pertinent network characteristics.

The more uses that are expected to connect through the base station, the more critical it becomes to provide an access point with greater bandwidth capacity, or even to provide multiple access points. Once you have determined the type of WLAN best suited for your organization's purposes, the next step is the acquisition of devices and components.

Acquisition

Whether a peer-to-peer solution or access point designed, what types of user devices will be required? Laptops? Standard desktops? Printers? Servers? Are the applications and data that need to be supported by the network resource intensive, as with certain database applications or video/audio data? Or will the users for the network be using "lightweight" resources—for example, word processing and e-mail?

Many computing devices today come preconfigured in terms of their hardware for wireless access. Such devices have built-in Wi-Fi radio capability and need no additional hardware components for recognizing Wi-Fi signals. However, depending on the organization, there may be older legacy devices still in use and functioning that do not inherently recognize wireless communications. For these legacy devices there are hardware component solutions that allow these devices to participate in a WLAN. For example, PCI and ISA bus adapters, or adapter cards that can be plugged into an external port, or USB adapters serve the same purpose.

For networks that will depend on base stations or access points, how many and of what capability will be required? Whether base station, access point, or gateway, these devices can also typically provide services beyond being a connection point. For example, these devices might perform security functions, manage and track network communications and traffic, serve as a firewall, or other related tasks. Something that one has to be careful about is that the terms *base station, access point,* and *gateway* may mean different things to different people, or in our discussion, to vendor providers. In your acquisition process, be certain that the vocabulary used is clearly understood by all those involved.

Configuring

Devices that are built or manufactured with wireless capability are designed to automatically recognize Wi-Fi signals. However, even these devices will likely need to be configured to not only recognize but be authenticated by the WLAN that they are attempting to access. For example, the connecting device will typically be prompted for the service set identifier (SSID) of the network being connected to. Once the SSID is configured for the connecting device, that device will automatically be able to connect to that network in the future, assuming the SSID is unchanged. For devices that require adapter cards or USB radio capability, usually software drivers must be first installed and configured in order for these added components to function.

For networks utilizing a base station or access point of some type, this device, too, requires configuration. Things that the network administrator may need to configure, modify, activate, or change for a base station/access point include security protocols such as Wi-Fi protected access; the default password that usually comes with the manufacturer supplied unit; whether to turn off the broadcasting of your network's SSID, which in effect closes the network to unwanted devices; and the default network name that may come with the unit. Based on the capability of your base station/access point, that device may be able to be configured with MAC control tables. As you are now aware, a MAC address is unique to a specific device. If your base station/access point supports MAC control tables, you can then enter into the table only those MAC addresses for devices that you have verified.

Testing

When all devices have been acquired and then configured, the next step is to test their functionality, responsiveness, and networking capability. It is always possible that a device has not had a software driver properly installed or that some other element in set-up, perhaps a missing SSID, has not been configured. Testing often takes places when end-users of the network are off-site or during off-hours, perhaps during a weekend or very late evening or very early morning.

Securing

Wireless LANs have security issues that in certain key ways make them more vulnerable to unauthorized access and to potential loss or corruption of business critical data and applications. Most WLANs will broadcast their presence so that wireless devices within range of the network's signal are aware of the network. This is certainly flexible, but such network identification broadcasting is also inherently insecure. That is why WLAN network administrators usually pay close attention to securing the network from unwanted and unintended access.

We have mentioned that base station/access points usually have a manufacturer default SSID and/or password. These manufacturer default settings are public knowledge and as such can be used by unauthorized users who are trying to "hack into" a network. Such an intruder could configure a rogue base station/access point with such default settings in an attempt to trick networked devices into communicating through the rogue device. The rogue device could then obtain access to such sensitive data as MAC addresses, SSIDs, passwords, and other materials. It is usually a good practice to change any manufacturer default settings involving passwords and network IDs to ones that are more secure and privately held.

A term has been coined to describe individuals who drive through neighborhoods and business districts specifically seeking out wireless networks that broadcast their SSID. The term is called **war driving**. War drivers search out vulnerable wireless networks and then use the data gathered to configure their own unauthorized devices to appear as legitimate network users. The vulnerable network in effect is tricked into allowing access to a device that appears legitimate, but which is actually unauthorized.

As noted earlier, with certain base stations/access points MAC control tables can be utilized that specifically identify authenticated network devices. One mechanism that unauthorized users may deploy to break into a network is through a process called *MAC spoofing*. It involves an unauthorized device having its MAC address purposefully changed such that the device appears to be a legitimate user of the network. Hacking programs are available that generate strings of random MAC number addresses with the hope that one of these random strings is recognized as an authenticated address by the network and so allowed access to that network.

Users of a network, whether wired or wireless, can be creative in what they do to that network without the intent of doing harm. However, harm is sometimes the result of a user's unexpected, and usually unreported, creativity. In a WLAN it is possible for a user, in order to enhance his or her accessibility to the network, to deploy an unauthorized base station/access point. These unauthorized devices may not have the same degree of security measures applied to them. In effect these unauthorized devices become security holes in the network, leaving the network vulnerable to attack and exploitation.

The Ethical Perspective

I Know Where You Are

Later in this chapter we introduce the Bluetooth technology. As a wireless technology, Bluetooth devices have what is referred to as a *discoverability* mode. What this means is that one Bluetooth device can recognize or "discover" another Bluetooth device operating in close proximity, approximately 30 feet, or 10 meters. Indeed, one of the marketed advantages of Bluetooth as a technology is this automatic recognition of other Bluetooth devices. This works well when you have several Bluetooth devices that you want in communication with each other. But what if you are out and about in the public at large with your Bluetooth phone and its discoverability mode is turned on?

Would you anticipate that other Bluetooth users can become aware of your presence, or at least of the presence of your Bluetooth device that you are likely carrying in your pocket, purse, backpack, or bag? And if other Bluetooth users can discover your presence, how might this otherwise be used in ways you may not have anticipated?

It is possible, for example, for someone or some business to set up an array of hidden Bluetooth receivers along a street, within a store, inside a restaurant, or pretty much any place where people are likely to gather. Assume these receivers are spaced approximately 20 feet apart. As you stroll along your street, store, shopping mall, or restaurant, your Bluetooth-enabled device with you and its discoverability mode "on," these other hidden Bluetooth receivers are able to track your route.

Perhaps you are being tracked for security reasons? Perhaps for marketing purposes so that vendors can determine where customers are most likely to spend time? Perhaps for no reason at all except that it is possible? Regardless of the reason, do you think such tracking represents an ethical issue, especially if the tracking capability is not posted or is hidden? What if the tracking were posted, alerting people that they could, if they wanted, disable their Bluetooth discoverable mode? Would this make a difference in your opinion?

For each of the preceding steps, documentation will be essential. As with other aspects of network management, all documentation needs to be accurate, understandable, securely housed, and very importantly, current.

OTHER WIRELESS TECHNOLOGIES

Worldwide Interoperability for Microwave Access: Wi-Max

Although Wi-Fi has proven to be a very popular and widely deployed technology, one of its major constraints is the limited physical range that its radio signals can span. This limited range is one reason that Wi-Fi implementations have produced so many "hotspots." A **hotspot** is a Wi-Fi network that offers Internet access. These hotspots can easily be found in such places as airports, coffee shops, banks, restaurants, retail outlets, residential neighborhoods, and a host of other places. Wi-Fi demonstrated that wireless access has huge consumer appeal. Given this success, it is not surprising that other wireless technologies have developed. One such technology is referred to as **Wi-Max**, or Worldwide Interoperability for Microwave Access.

In a number of ways Wi-Max is similar to Wi-Fi. As with Wi-Fi, the IEEE has an umbrella of standards under the **802.16** designation for Wi-Max services. Table 13.5 lists basic 802.16 IEEE specifications. Also like Wi-Fi, Wi-Max allows data to be sent from one device to another using radio signals. The advantages of Wi-Max include higher data speeds covering greater physical distances potentially providing wireless services to a far larger number of users.

Businesses that offer the 802.16a version of Wi-Max will compete directly with DSL and cable Internet providers, particularly for the home user and small business market. Version 802.16a operates in the 2–11 GHz spectrum, providing data transfer rates of up to 70 Mbps and spanning a distance of up to 30 miles. This form of Wi-Max supports both line-of-sight and non-line-of-sight connections. *Line-of-sight* services utilize a fixed dish antenna that points directly, hence the term line-of-sight, at a Wi-Max signaling tower. These types of line-of-sight transmission use higher radio frequencies, usually resulting in less interference, fewer errors, and more bandwidth. The disadvantage is that many users and businesses lack a line-of-sight connection to a Wi-Max tower. *Non-line-of-sight* Wi-Max services operate at a lower frequency range. A device utilizing non-line-of-sight Wi-Max requires a small antenna that connects that device to the Wi-Max tower. Figure 13.4 depicts a possible Wi-Max configuration.

A Wi-Max signaling tower is similar in concept to a cell phone or microwave tower. Coverage for a typical metropolitan area network provides a signal radius of about 30 miles, or 50 kilometers. A Wi-Max tower can connect directly to the Internet

Table 13.5 802.16 Standard Specifications	
Feature	**Value**
Range	30 Miles (50 Kilometers) from Base Station
Data Rate	70 Mpbs
Supports	Line-of-Sight Transmissions
Supports	Non-Line-of-Site-Transmissions
Frequency Bands—Licensed	2 to 11 GHz
Frequency Bands—Unlicensed	10 to 66 GHz

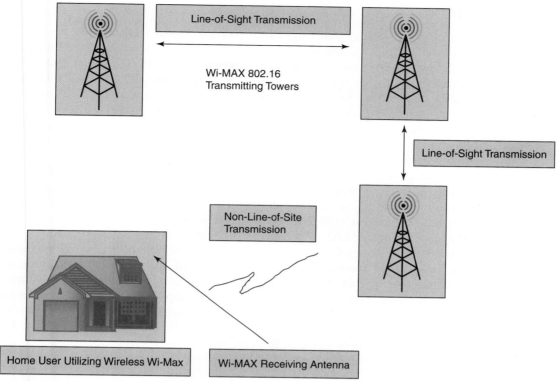

FIGURE 13.4   Conceptual View of a Wi-Max Installation

using a wired connection such as a T3 line, and also can connect directly, via line-of-sight, to another Wi-Max tower and thereby expand the geographic range covered. Wi-Max services could be used to provide wireless connectivity to some remote rural areas. Here are several areas in which Wi-Max can be utilized:

Remote Asset Management and Surveillance

Mobile Workforce Connectivity

Smart Device Metering—Utilities, Parking, Traffic

Voice-Over IP

Emergency Communications

Rural Wireless Communications

Metropolitan Backbone Connectivity

As with Wi-Fi and its Wi-Fi Alliance, Wi-Max also has a formal group associated with it: the **Wi-Max Forum** (*www.wimaxforum.org*). An important function of this group is to certify products and services that are Wi-Max based. As with the Wi-Fi Alliance certification, Wi-Max Forum certification confers a degree of confidence in products and services that customers may want to buy, lease, or rent. Finally, note that the Wi-Max 802.16 standard was developed with fixed devices in mind, meaning that 802.16 services do not perform well for highly mobile devices. Recognizing this, the IEEE has designated the 802.20 standard, released in 2008, for high-speed mobile devices. In addition, the IEEE is developing the 802.16n standard that will provide for 10 Gbps fixed communications and 1 Gbps for mobile communications.

Bluetooth

Another wireless technology that has proven very successful is **Bluetooth**. Named for a tenth-century Viking king, Harald "Bluetooth" Gormsson, the technology Bluetooth operates via low-power radio waves. Communicating at the 2.45 GHz range, Bluetooth-enabled devices do not require line-of-sight communications. In addition, Bluetooth devices can communicate through nonmetallic materials, such as brief cases, bags, pockets, walls, and windows. Because Bluetooth devices transmit using very weak signals, approximately 1 milliwatt, they will not interfere with other wireless implementations. However, the low power range of Bluetooth also restricts the distance at which Bluetooth devices can communicate to about 30 feet, or 10 meters.

An advantage of Bluetooth is that it allows multiple devices to communicate simultaneously. So your Bluetooth-enabled printer can "talk" to your Bluetooth-enabled computer while your Bluetooth-enabled cell phone is communicating with your Bluetooth-enabled car radio. In effect, Bluetooth creates what is referred to as a **personal area network (PAN)**, also called a **piconet**.

Bluetooth makes use of a technique called *spread-spectrum frequency hopping*. Using this technique, a Bluetooth device will use up to 79 individual and randomly selected frequencies, within its frequency band, changing frequencies 1,600 times every second. Because a Bluetooth device changes, or hops, frequencies so frequently, it is unlikely that two Bluetooth devices in proximity to each other will be on the same frequency at the same time. As such, Bluetooth device A does not interfere with the communications of Bluetooth devices, B, C, D, and E.

The earlier version of Bluetooth, 1.0, allowed for data transfer rates of approximately 1 Mbps. Version 2.0 allows for transmission rates of between 2 and 3 Mbps. Bluetooth version 2.0 is backward compatible with Bluetooth 1.0. However, a Bluetooth 2.0 device, when communicating with a Bluetooth 1.0 device, has to operate at the lower data transfer rate of the 1.0 device. So a given piconet, or PAN, might be composed of 1.0 as well as 2.0 Bluetooth-enabled devices. The devices in the piconet will automatically communicate with each other without the user having to initiate or start the process—for example, by issuing a start command or pressing a button. Once in communication, Bluetooth devices in the piconet can determine whether they have data to exchange or if one device needs to control another.

Automatic communication can be a real advantage, but there are also potential problems, especially as they relate to security. Since wireless systems have their own security issues, as a wireless technology Bluetooth is no different. As it is possible for unwanted others to send or retrieve data from your Bluetooth-enabled devices, they typically provide for several possible security modes that the user of the device can configure. Table 13.6 lists four security modes that can be established between two Bluetooth devices.

Bluetooth users also have the option of creating "trusted devices" such that the trusted devices exchange data with each other without having to seek permission. Or a Bluetooth user might select to change his or her Bluetooth mode to "nondiscoverable."

Table 13.6   Bluetooth Security Modes

Security Mode	Security Type
Mode 1	Nonsecure
Mode 2	Service Level Enforced Security
Mode 3	Link Level Enforced Security
Mode 4	Link Level Enforced Security with Encrypted Key Exchange

A Bluetooth device running in a nondiscoverable mode will not be visible to other Bluetooth devices within transmission range. Two types of security problems that a Bluetooth user might encounter are "Bluejacking" and "Bluesnarfing."

With *Bluejacking,* someone you do not know may send your Bluetooth phone contact information or text messages that you may inadvertently add to your phone's electronic address book. If these data are unintentionally added to your list of contacts, messages from that unknown user could be automatically opened because to your Bluetooth phone, the message is from a known source. *Bluesnarfing* is perhaps more dangerous in that it allows an unauthorized user, or hacker, to remotely access your Bluetooth phone to make calls, send messages, or change data on your phone, all of which you may not be aware. There is a formal user group associated with Bluetooth. Information about this group and Bluetooth, in general, can be found at *www.bluetooth.com.*

MOBILE WIRELESS IMPLEMENTATIONS: 4G

As with the other technologies presented in this chapter, 4G is a wireless implementation that depends on radio frequency bandwidths. 4G, for Fourth Generation, is a wireless mobile broadband technology targeted particularly at mobile phone use. As its name implies, prior to 4G there was 3G, 2G, and long, long ago when purely analog land phones ruled the world, 1G.

HOW THINGS HAVE CHANGED

We live in a mixed world of technologies. Although 4G networks and services are rapidly gaining ground, there are still infrastructures, devices, and services being utilized by 2G and 3G technologies. Each generational change has brought with it expanded capabilities and improved services. As an example, a typical 3G network has data download speeds that top out at about 1 Mbps. In an ideal environment, still in our future, 4G networks hold the promise of up to 100 Mbps.

Mobile phone users today increasingly require their devices to deliver data of all types seamlessly, with little to no latency, and with error-free content. The expectation is that as these mobile devices move rapidly from one physical geographic spot to another—perhaps traveling with you by car, bus, train, other means—no data, particularly voice, are dropped. What this means is that 4G devices can offer global roaming across multiple heterogeneous networks. Also, 4G will retain interoperability with existing wireless standards.

As a delivery technology, 4G is a purely IP-based packet switched service. The intent behind 4G is to provide mobile data services that have end-to-end quality of service, high security, low latency, and availability. Types of services supported include wireless broadband access, multimedia messaging, video chat, video streaming, mobile TV, gaming, texting, and, of course, voice communications.

Chapter Summary

In 1990, the IEEE formed another committee to develop protocols for wireless LANS under an 802.11 working group. This working group proposed protocols for both the physical and the data link layers. For the physical layer, the defined subdivisions are the physical medium dependent (PMD) and the physical layer convergence procedure (PLCP) sublayers.

In its creation of the 802.11 standard, the IEEE allowed for three types of physical wireless media: (1) infrared, (2) frequency hopping spread spectrum (FHSS), and

(3) direct sequence spread spectrum (DSSS). Of the three, infrared has proven unpopular due to two major constraints. Both FHSS and DSSS are a type of "spread spectrum" radio frequency transmission, as opposed to a "narrowband" transmission.

For FHSS, the frequency spectrum is divided into channels. In the United States, the number of channels available is 70. On these channels a data packet is split up, spread, and transmitted using a pseudo-random pattern that is known only to the transmitter and the receiver. For DSSS, the transmitter using a mathematical key spreads the data across a wide range of radio frequencies. The receiver has access to the same mathematical key so that the receiver can then decode the message once received.

Under the 802.11 umbrella, a number of workgroup variants has been developed. Each of these standards is associated with a technology referred to as Wi-Fi, or wireless fidelity. The 802.11a IEEE specification utilizes the five GHz spectrum band. Standard 802.11b extended the original DSSS scheme by extending data rates from 1 and 2 Mbps to 5.5 and 11 Mbps. With the intent of developing a standard that incorporates the best aspects of 802.11a and 802.11b, the IEEE created a workgroup referenced as standard 802.11g.

The 802.11n standard was brought forward to address further improvements to the physical layer and MAC sublayer with the intent to enhance throughput. The IEEE has created a wireless security workgroup under the 802.11i standard. This standard defines security and authentication mechanisms at the MAC sublayer.

As with a wired LAN, planning and management are essential elements in configuring and deploying a WLAN. Wireless LANs, by their nature, face issues and concerns that have to be addressed differently from a wired LAN. But WLANs also offer significant benefits, including mobility, flexibility, scalability, a wide array of products and services that support wireless technologies, and interoperability.

There are five general steps that a networking administrator, or business owner, might take in configuring a small WLAN: (1) planning, (2) acquiring, (3) configuring, (4) testing, and (5) securing.

In a number of ways Wi-Max is similar to Wi-Fi. As with Wi-Fi, the IEEE has an umbrella of standards under the 802.16 designation for Wi-Max services. The advantages of Wi-Max include higher data speeds covering greater physical distances, potentially providing wireless services to a far larger number of users.

Bluetooth is a technology that operates via low-power radio waves. Communicating at the 2.45 GHz range, Bluetooth-enabled devices do not require line-of-sight communications. In addition, Bluetooth devices can communicate through nonmetallic materials, such as brief cases, bags, pockets, walls, and windows. Because Bluetooth devices transmit using very weak signals, approximately 1 milliwatt, they will not interfere with other wireless implementations. However, the low power range of Bluetooth also restricts the distance at which Bluetooth devices can communicate to about 30 feet or 10 meters.

Another wireless implementation, 4G also depends on radio frequency bandwidths. 4G, (for Fourth Generation) is a wireless mobile broadband technology targeted particularly at mobile phone use.

Keywords

4G *275*	802.11g *267*	Barker spreading
802.11 *262*	802.11i *267*	code *265*
802.11a *266*	802.11n *267*	Bluetooth *274*
802.11b *266*	802.16 *272*	Channels *264*

Direct sequence spread spectrum (DSSS) *264*

Dwell time *264*

Frequency hopping spread spectrum (FHSS) *264*

Hopping code *264*

Hotspot *272*

Logical link control (LLC) *263*

Media access control (MAC) *263*

Narrowband *263*

Optical frequency division multiplexing (OFDM) *266*

Personal area network *274*

Physical layer convergence procedure (PLCP) *262*

Physical medium dependent (PMD) *262*

Piconet *274*

Pseudo-random *264*

Spread spectrum *263*

Unlicensed National Information Infrastructure (UNII) *266*

War driving *271*

Wi-Fi Alliance *268*

Wi-Fi protected access (WPA) *268*

Wi-Fi *265*

Wi-Max *272*

Wi-Max Forum *273*

Wired equivalent privacy (WEP) *267*

Chapter Questions

Short-Answer Questions

1. What umbrella IEEE standard addresses WLANs?
2. What advantage, if any, does 802.11a have over 802.11b?
3. What is meant by a narrowband transmission?
4. Identify one way in which FHSS and DSSS differ.
5. Describe the purpose of function for the PLCP 802.11a sublayer.
6. List the five elements that a WLAN administrator might consider when configuring a WLAN.
7. Both Wi-Fi and Wi-Max have distance limitations. What are they?
8. What is meant by the "discoverability" mode as it relates to Bluetooth?

Hands-On Projects

1. Sketch a simple WLAN that utilizes a gateway or access point.
2. Visit the Wi-Fi Alliance website (*www.wi-fi.org*) and identify at least three certified products. What is their purpose?
3. What is the current status of the 802.11n workgroup?
4. Investigate changing a Bluetooth device's discoverability mode setting.

Research in Brief

1. Research and report on one of the following IEEE 802.11 standards: 802.11e, 802.11f, 802.11h, or 802.11k.
2. The Wireless LAN Association (*www.wlana.org*) provides case studies and implementation discussions. Visit that website and report on a current topic under review.
3. The 802.11i provides for what is referred to as the advanced encryption standard. What is this standard? For what use is it intended? What advantages does it offer? What might hinder its implementation by some businesses?
4. A technology this chapter did not review that is associated with 4G networks is long-term evolution (LTE). It is an alternative to 4G Wi-Max delivery. Research 4G LTE and report on your findings.

Topic in Focus

TROUBLESHOOTING A WIRELESS NETWORK

Whether wired or wireless, large or small, networks experience problems, errors, or issues that may require hands-on intervention. The intervention may be running a software diagnostic program, replacing a faulty connector or cable, verifying and resetting a configuration parameter, or any number of other corrective measures. Here we list just a few common-sense steps that one might take to troubleshoot a problem in a wireless network. Some of these steps may seem obvious, but perhaps for that very reason they can also be easily overlooked.

Even though we are discussing a "wireless" network, there will still be physical connections required of the devices in the network. Certainly it is possible for physical connections to become loose or dislodged. Verify that all cables required of the network are properly engaged and that they are in fact the right type of cable. Are key devices, such as routers, modems, access points, gateways, and so on, properly connected to a power source.

Wireless LAN clients depend on appropriate signal strength from their access point or wireless router in order to connect to the network and communicate effectively with other devices. Many WLAN clients that utilized wireless adapter cards have configuration utility programs you can run that provide information as to signal strength. The signal strength may be represented in terms of horizontal or vertical color bars, or by simply stating excellent, good, fair, or poor.

If your WLAN clients are using adapter cards, verify that the installation of the wireless adapter has been properly installed and configured. This may require to you to reinstall the adapter and verify the settings.

Further WLAN clients, routers, and access points may be dependent on how their wireless antennas are positioned. It may be that one or more of these antennas need to be repositioned in order to create an effective wireless connection. Also, the position of the router or access point in relation to where the client is located may be a problem. There is the potential for sources of electromagnetic interference that might be corrected if the access point or router were relocated in relation to the clients being supported.

A simple test to determine if two devices—the client and the access point, for example—can recognize and communicate with each other is to ping the access point from the client device. *Ping* is a programmatic method, or tool, for sending messages from one computer to another. It is often used in networking to determine if a particular device is capable of receiving messages. If the ping test does not work, it is very likely that there is a configuration problem. If there is a configuration problem, you will need to verify whether the issue is with the client or the access point. If ping is successful between another client and the access point, it is likely not the access point that has the issue.

Verify that your security settings for your client are in agreement with any security settings that have been established for the router or access point. Also verify that your client's TCP/IP settings are properly configured.

Besides problems associated with software configurations, TCP/IP settings, antenna issues, and weak signal generation, there are other factors that can cause interference and thereby prevent communications from occurring. For example, physical objects such as masonry, buildings, and concrete and/or metal walls can make it difficult for a wireless signal to pass through successfully.

Keep in mind that wireless networks use radio frequencies, as do many other types of devices such as cell phones and microwaves. Devices that share the same frequency channel may cause noise, resulting in weakening of signal strengths.

14

Business and Social Networking

The Business Benefit

The past decade has seen networking technologies evolve in ways that have made communications faster, easier, highly mobile, and globally available, not just for businesses but for consumers as well. For businesses in particular, however, this communications technology revolution has brought not only opportunities but also distinct challenges. How can a business make the most effective use of rapidly evolving communication technologies that permit that business to remain relevant, visible, current, and, perhaps most importantly, competitive?

It is not unusual for a technology to be conceived and developed for one purpose, only to find that once that technology is unleashed, it begins to be utilized in ways not anticipated. Social media networking technologies fall into this category. When social media networking technologies arrived on the scene in the fairly recent past, they were viewed primarily as a means of enabling individuals, regardless of their location, to have highly interactive and collaborative shared experiences. These shared experiences, often in real-time without having to be in the same physical space, create social networks that can span the globe.

How can businesses benefit from such social media technologies? There are, in fact, several ways a business might use such social networking tools for a competitive advantage. For example, social media applications allow for person-to-person interactions. This type of individual interaction and attention permits a business to provide responsive customer service in a manner that is personal and timely. Businesses can also use various social media networking sites to gain name recognition. Thousands, if not millions, of social media users might gain awareness of your business and transform from onlookers into customers.

Many social media networking sites are designed for a dynamic exchange of ideas, opinions, recommendations, and criticisms. By monitoring such sites a business can get a sense of what is being expressed, whether good, bad, or indifferent, regarding that business. Knowing what potential customers may be encountering regarding your business, especially if what they are finding is inaccurate or critical, allows a business to take appropriate corrective measures. Businesses can also discover what comments and conversations are occurring regarding their competitors. Finally, by reviewing various social media networking sites a business may get a better feel for trends or directions for that industry.

Learning Objectives

After studying this chapter, you should be able to:

- Identify the elements of convergence in data communications
- Understand how convergence affects security, privacy, and ethics
- Define unified messaging (UM)
- Name four social media applications or tools
- Describe possible social networking business applications
- Understand potential social networking vulnerabilities
- Be familiar with a variety of social business networking demographics

It is essential for businesses to secure their data communications infrastructures. Businesses not only depend on their data communications resources for their own purposes, but customers, vendors, and business partners depend on these resources as well. Businesses also need to keep abreast of where new technologies are heading so that they do not lose their competitive advantage. Although many businesses do not want to run their operations on the leading edge of technology (and for good reason, as the technology may be unproven), it is important for a business to know what tools its competition could be planning to use or are using. Are such technologies secure? Is there a cost associated with the technology? What business advantages, and disadvantages, might they offer? How might they be utilized by a business as a competitive advantage? This chapter explores some of these leading-edge technologies, and in particular social networking and social media tools and applications.

THE CONVERGENCE OF PERVASIVE NETWORKING

This text began with the idea that instant communications, in our present, and moving into our future, regardless of a person's location, can be available at the push of a button to retrieve news articles, stock quotes, customer contact data, movie reviews, gaming, video chat, and other information and applications. When networking technologists discuss the world of pervasive networking that we have entered, they are talking about the integration of data, voice, and video, all carried seamlessly over one infrastructure. And more to the point, all of these elements will be accessible from many types of devices, not just from a desktop or laptop computer. Such technology is intended to build networking intelligence into any device, small or large, inexpensive or expensive, high or low power.

The issue of power is critical to the development of these networked capable devices. Many users of laptop computers or other battery-operated mobile devices appreciate these devices' portability, but fault them for their inability to power themselves for long periods of time. To succeed, such devices must be smart in how they consume power and extend it. In a very real sense, the goal of always being "plugged in" means not having to plug a communications device into a power supply every few hours or even every few days. With the ideal device, users will not have to think about the availability of that device's power, wondering how many minutes of usage are left. Convenience will be a major characteristic of such devices. Manufactures of technology are still grappling with the issue of battery power consumption and how it can be extended.

Communication technology is well on the road toward invisible mobility, offering devices that are always there but never seen. Users will carry communication technologies with them in unobtrusive places, such as a bracelet on their wrist or a button on their shirt. Of course, such pervasive technologies will raise new social and work-related issues. Many believe that the blurring between home and office has gone too far.

Employees today are already available to or in contact with the corporate office by mobile smart phone, virtual fax, texting, e-mail, and other technologies. Such connectivity will only increase in the future. Mobile technologies are not only transforming how business is done but also how employees work, causing them to take more work into their homes and other private spaces. Some think that this may be too much of a good thing. If employees can be contacted anywhere, what will prevent the office from contacting its employees from literally anywhere at any time, even when they are on vacation, as is already becoming commonplace?

Mobile technologies are thus creating what is often considered pervasive, and some say invasive, computing. **Pervasive computing** refers to technology so prevalent and easy to use, that the technology becomes a second thought, or nearly invisible to the user. Three issues of particular concern involving pervasive computing are security, privacy, and ethics. Consider *security*. The more available the enterprise's information infrastructures, the more open they are to attack. For customers and employees who need to access the enterprise from any location, a major challenge then becomes how to adequately authenticate and validate these users. Undoubtedly, more types of personalized identification information will be required from users, along with new ways of validating this information.

Requiring users to provide more information that may be easily accessible from an open access-from-anywhere network raises questions of *privacy*. Identify theft is a major issue today, and for good reason. Will users of a data communications infrastructure that is accessible from anywhere be willing to provide sensitive data about themselves, such as passwords, account numbers, financial data, addresses, or other privileged information, in order to verify who they are to the network? Can users have confidence that key data about them is secure? The distinction between personal privacy and the communication infrastructure's need to verify users will require a difficult and controversial balancing act. This discussion of privacy, and how it can be used, or abused, ties directly to *ethics*.

The convergence of voice, video, and data into a seamless infrastructure will require technologies that can support such convergence. Users will require persistent connections to high-speed wired and wireless networks; therefore, better and highly reliable delivery technologies will be needed. These delivery technologies will have to be invisible and reliable to the degree that users of the technology take it for granted. Also, protocols that can support these different types of applications must be created.

SESSION INITIATION PROTOCOL

One such protocol is session initiation protocol (SIP). The IETF has a workgroup devoted to SIP (*http://datatracker.ietf.org/wg/sipcore*). In addition, such heavyweight players as Microsoft, IBM, Siemens, and Cisco Systems view SIP as a protocol that can deliver real-time communications for IP-based voice, video, data, and instant messaging. The role of **instant messaging (IM)** as a communications tool has become a major consideration. Instant messaging has become a primary contender in the enterprise-application realm. Three protocols have evolved for the corporate use of IM: session initiation protocol (SIP), security assertion markup language (SAML), and extensible messaging and presence protocol (XMPP).

Session initiation protocol is used for establishing, modifying, and terminating IM communications on an IP-based network. Security assertion markup language is used to enable the exchange of security credentials between communications; it comes from XML. Extensible messaging and presence protocol allows for interoperability between enterprises. Like SAML, XMPP is also an XML-based specification. OASIS offers links to recent articles and research related to XML on its website (xml. coverpages.org).

UNIFIED MESSAGING

Besides IM, another application that has caught the corporate world's attention is unified messaging. **Unified messaging (UM)** is an umbrella term used to describe a unified application system. Such a system is designed to work through a single common interface, most likely through an existing e-mail client application. Being able to receive a message as a voice mail, a fax, or an e-mail sounds like a fairly simple request. But for many users, multiple messaging systems are likely involved.

One voice-mail system is used for a desk or land phone. A second voice-mail system is needed for a cell or mobile phone. A third system is needed to receive virtual faxes. And yet a fourth system is required for e-mail. Then, of course, consider that a single user might have multiple land phones, mobile phones, faxes, and e-mail accounts. As you can see, getting a message to a user can be more complicated than it initially appears. With UM, all of the various messaging systems are rolled into one system, with one access point—the user's e-mail inbox. Of course, although one access point may provide user convenience, it might also provide hacker convenience as well. With UM, the topics presented in Chapter 12—digital signatures, digital certificates, and security in general—become even more important.

So how does unified messaging work? First, a message sent to the user—whether fax, voice, or e-mail—is placed in the appropriate e-mail server's message space. For organizations using traditional PBX voice systems, voice messages from the PBX are copied to a UM storage location. Finally, all messages are ultimately routed to the user's e-mail inbox. Unified messaging vendors include Avaya Inc., Nortel Networks, and Cisco Systems, among others. (Their websites are, respectively, *www.avaya.com*, *www.nortel.com*, and *www.cisco.com*.) The products supplied by these vendors are designed to route messages to a user's e-mail server, perhaps a Lotus Notes, or Microsoft Exchange server. From the server, messages can then be routed to the user's e-mail client application, such as Microsoft Outlook, Gmail, or Yahoo.

In this scenario, all messages, regardless of their source, are ultimately digitized. Users can listen to voice messages, print faxes, or simply view text messages through their e-mail client; the messages are simply e-mail attachments. Web-based e-mail clients enable users to access their messages from virtually anywhere in the world where a Web connection can be made. The goal of UM is to integrate all of the different communication technologies so that they work as an integrated whole.

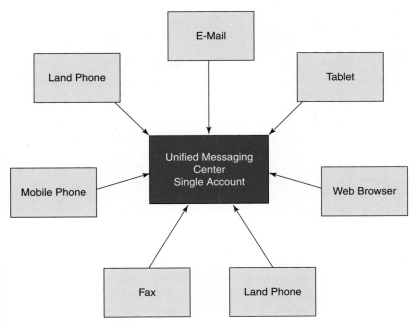

FIGURE 14.1 A Unified Messaging Center

The promise of UM is that users of communication technologies who are using different media and different devices will be able to communicate with anyone, anywhere, at any time. This works both ways, of course, because the user will both send and receive messages. Unified messaging reduces the number of places users must check for all their messages—fax, voice, or e-mail—to one portal. And, with UM, users can send and receive messages from a single interface. Figure 14.1 illustrates this concept.

In practice, a UM application allows a telephone call to switch from voice to data mode while the connection is in progress. In such a scenario, tying a UM technology to a database can be a real payoff. As a client calls in, the UM application, through its database connection, identifies the client by his or her telephone number. If the customer is using a display device of some type to place a call, the UM application can automatically respond with appropriate information based on the client's previous communications with the business. Information can be tracked and stored for improved marketing response to client needs.

Unified messaging utilizes text-to-speech capabilities so that messages can be read back to the user, or, the reverse, verbal messages translated into their text equivalents. A user may want a printed copy of a voice message, so a speech-to-text capability might be convenient. This technique of translating from one form to another can be used, for example, for converting text to fax or speech to fax. Flexibility of message manipulation is the end result.

Providers of UM will have to create solutions that are also flexible enough to accommodate traditional services, such as PBX, until they are replaced by completely digital solutions. Because such services will be digital, scaling the services to expand or contract becomes much simpler. Very likely, as with many technologies used today, vendors of UM tools will rely on open-architecture models and protocols. So, whether you are a corporate employee, a home-based worker, or a student, UM services are likely to be in your future if not already in your present.

The Ethical Perspective

A Chip for Every Body?

Today's users of technology expect to have access to that technology from wherever they are. In fact, some forms of technology are so mobile, and small, that the user can literally have that technology embedded into his or her body.

An organization in Florida, Applied Digital Solutions, in 2004 introduced a controversial technology called the *VeriChip*. The Food and Drug Administration (FDA) gave formal approval to this technology. This intelligent chip is about the size of a grain of rice. The intent is for the VeriChip to be implanted directly into a body, perhaps a pet's, a child's, or maybe even your own. The VeriChip can be used to store security, health, financial, or other types of information about the host into which it is implanted. It can also be used for tracking. However, is it possible for this type of implantable chip and the information it contains to be used for purposes other than for which it was intended?

The potential problem with such technologies that allow you to be tracked and identified wherever you are is the very fact that these technologies can track and identify you wherever you are. This is something of a paradox and for many a frightening reality. Users of these technologies that are now on our doorstep will want assurances that these technologies will not, or cannot, be used in a manner for which they were not intended. The problem with technology, however, is that, like Pandora's Box, once opened it can sometimes be difficult to close or control.

Would you describe this type of embedded technology as "pervasive" or "invasive"? Do you think there are ethical implications? And can any technology truly be guaranteed against abuse?

Probably not.

What do you think about technologies such as those described here? Could such embedded body chips be used unethically? Should those who are incarcerated for serious crimes have a chip implanted? Should parents have the right to "chip" their children? Would such implantation be a violation of basic human rights?

THE ARRIVAL OF SOCIAL NETWORKING TECHNOLOGIES

The past decade has seen the blossoming of a variety of social media networking technologies such as Facebook, Myspace, Flickr, YouTube, LinkedIn, Yelp, and a host of others. These social media sites and tools tend to have several characteristics in common. First, they are usually free. Second, they tend to be interactive, allowing the user to create, modify, exchange, and develop various types of media either individually or as a social group. Third, the applications can be run from any number of types of devices, including desktop computers, laptops, smart phones, tablets, netbooks, and so on. Fourth, they are truly global in reach with users from virtually every country in the world accessing them and sharing experiences and communications through them. Next we take a brief look at several of these social media applications.

Facebook (*www.facebook.com*) in many ways has become the best known site for social media interaction. The intent of Facebook, which arrived in 2004, is to permit its users to create personal profiles, exchange information, create interest groups, add "friends," generate automatic notifications, and allow those who access a profile to "like" the site or profile. Users must register with Facebook in order to create their personal profile and to then share it with others. Social Media Today (*http://socialmediatoday.com*) reported in 2010 that 41% of the U.S. population had a Facebook profile.

Initially viewed as an application for individual/small group social networking, Facebook has now become a resource site for many business organizations as well. From a business perspective, Facebook can be viewed as a mechanism that permits a business to provide a more personal and intimate face to their customer market. Businesses that utilize Facebook review and follow what their customers are experiencing, what sites they are visiting, what comments they are making, how long they linger at the profile, and so on.

Facebook allows registered users to post several types of media, but **YouTube** (*www.youtube.com*) is specifically focused on video and video sharing. Introduced in 2005, YouTube allows its users to upload, share, and view videos of all types: musical, humorous, educational, tutorial, television clips, and others. One does not need to be a professional videographer in order to post a YouTube video. Users must register with YouTube to upload a video, but do not have to be registered in order to view videos.

Created by three former employees of a service called PayPal (*www.paypal.com*), YouTube was purchased by Google (*www.google.com*) for $1.65 billion in 2006. YouTube makes use of such applications and protocols as Adobe Flash Video and HTML5. Typically, videos uploaded are of no more than 15 minutes duration, but longer video lengths are supported. Businesses might utilize YouTube to highlight various services or products. They could post useful "how to" videos that illustrate the different ways their products and services can be used. Many businesses offer types of staff development. YouTube video posts could be generated for staff development purposes. Businesses have been known to post brief employee videos whereby the employees discuss how much they like working at the business. This might be done by an organization to market itself to future employees.

Unlike Facebook or YouTube, **LinkedIn** (*www.linkedin.com*) is designed specifically with the working professional in mind, whether as an independent contractor or as a public or private employee. LinkedIn connects working professionals together so that they can easily exchange ideas, opportunities, training, advice, and knowledge. Using a hosted search application, users of LinkedIn can explore the contents of the site by name, title, company, and location. In addition, using "trusted" contacts LinkedIn subscribers can use tools such as "Answers" and "Groups" to interact with content knowledge specialists in chosen fields of business and industry. On its website, LinkedIn provides the following relevant data:

- It has 161 million members in more than 200 countries and territories as of March 31, 2012.
- Sixty-one percent of LinkedIn members are located outside the United States.
- In 2011, close to 4.2 billion professionally oriented searches were performed.
- Besides the United States, LinkedIn has offices in Amsterdam, Bangalore, Delhi, Dublin, Hong Kong, London, Madrid, Melbourne, Milan, Mumbai, Munich, Paris, Perth, São Paulo, Singapore, Stockholm, Sydney, Tokyo, and Toronto.
- LinkedIn is currently available in 17 languages: Czech, Dutch, English, French, German, Indonesian, Italian, Japanese, Korean, Malay, Polish, Portuguese, Romanian, Russian, Spanish, Swedish, and Turkish.

Additional statistics for 2011 concerning various social networking sites were gathered by *Search Engine Journal* (*www.searchenginejournal.com*):

- Facebook had 310 million daily unique visitors.
- Facebook had 640 million registered subscribers in 2011.
- One in four Americans watched an online video each day.
- Fifty-three percent of employers researched various social networking sites regarding potential job candidates.

- Six billion images were hosted on Flickr.
- Thirty-nine percent of companies in the United States used blogs for marketing purposes.
- There were 95 million tweets on Twitter.

SOCIAL NETWORKING BUSINESS APPLICATIONS

There are several reasons that businesses utilize social networking applications. Users of social media sites are also potential customers who may gain an increased awareness of a particular business or industry simply by visiting these sites. In turn, this can result in directing consumer traffic to a business's website. Also, businesses that monitor social networking groups can often get a sense of what customers, and potential customers, may be saying or commenting on regarding that business.

Based on the conversations being held or posted regarding a business or industry, a business can then take a proactive approach in responding to consumer concerns, perceptions, and market trends. Further, such monitoring by a business could lead to not only improving existing products but also to developing new services or products. Being at the forefront of market trends for an industry can provide a business with a competitive edge, allowing that business to better target its market.

According to a 2011 report produced by AIIM Market Intelligence (*www.aiim. org/research*), finding and sharing expertise was the greatest motivator for businesses of all sizes to pursue social media technologies as a business tool. AIIM surveyed 403 business organizations of varying size from large (5,000 or more employees) to small (10 to 500 employees). From this survey, AIIM discovered that IT and high-tech companies in particular were more likely to view social business applications as useful and to have deployed these applications within their business. Interestingly, AIIM found that mid-sized businesses (500 to 5,000 employees) were most likely to be cautious with social business implementations and that 10% of these mid-sized businesses actively discouraged use of social media sites. Even so, of the organizations surveyed, 51% believed that social business tools were either "imperative" or "significant" to the success of that business.

Compared to a similar survey conducted in 2010 by AIIM, 27% more businesses in 2011 reported that social business applications would be key to the overall infrastructure of that business. Social business applications are being viewed along much the same lines as e-mail and video conferencing, and as another means of communicating not only internally within the organization but externally as well with customers and vendor/supply partners. AIIM found that three business areas in particular were likely to be early adapters of social networking technology: (1) IT, as previously mentioned; (2) marketing; and (3) product development. Because of social media's relationship with branding and product awareness, marketing departments in particular were viewed as the best location for managing and monitoring social media sites.

Because social networks connect individuals and groups at a relatively low cost, they can be particularly attractive to small business owners and entrepreneurs. In particular, for businesses, large or small, social networks can serve as a means providing customer connectivity to that business. For businesses that monitor social networking sites and services for customer and potential customer comments and critiques, it is likely that the business has some type of response mechanism in place.

One response approach is for the business to manually evaluate and review social networking sites and then, depending on the evaluation, have someone from within the business directly contact the customer or potential customer. TweetDeck (*www.tweetdeck.com*) by Twitter, for example, allows the user to monitor for tweet messages or "mentions," search by keywords, or set up a list of "favorites." Based on what is presented, a response can be prepared and delivered.

Software tools are also available that automate the monitoring process. One such product is Radian6 (*www.radian6.com*). As a social media monitoring tool, Radian6 automates the process of "listening" to social network websites. As it gathers data based on parameter settings, what is captured can then be measured and analyzed. Radian6 positions itself as an automated tool that can be used to drive customer service, sales and lead generation, and marketing. Utilizing real-time data analysis, Radian6 can direct alerts to a given individual or department. For alerts that are critical or sensitive in nature, the business can quickly take steps to address the issue or concern.

Tools of the type provided by businesses like Radian6 are referred to as **analytics**. Analytic applications are used by businesses to measure, analyze, and interpret the interactions and commentary that consumers post about a business. In order to effectively utilize social media communications, businesses must be able to interpret these communications. The complexity of social media communications can make it challenging for an analytic tool to accurately measure what is being captured. Such tools have to take into consideration, and be able to discern, differing social contexts, cultural factors, slang, and other linguistic variations. It may be difficult for an analytic tool to correctly interpret the meaning of post or commentary. It should be noted that analytic tools can be used to analyze not just customer data from social media sites but also data related to employees, vendor partners, and competitors in the industry.

Another tool that businesses are increasingly making use of is blogs and microblogs. A **blog** is a posting site on the Internet used for commentary, discussions, information, critiques, and other forms of communication. A **microblog** is similar, but the commentary is limited in size by individual post. **Twitter** is an example of a microblog that limits an individual posting (a tweet) to 140 characters. Commentary posted to a blog is usually displayed in reverse chronological order, meaning the newest entries are at the top. Businesses use blogs as a means of online brand advertising. Such blogs also provide a business a means of interacting with customers and potential customers. Blogs are usually interactive in that those visiting the blog are also able to post commentary. So not only can a business utilize a blog to post product and service information, but it can also to monitor customer input. Although primarily textual in nature, blogs can also incorporate graphics, audio, and video.

SOCIAL NETWORKING VULNERABILITIES

Many businesses that utilize social networking technologies also have in place formal usage policies and procedures that employees are expected to adhere to when interacting with social media sites. Such policies can clearly define what is and what is not permissible within the organization if an employee should be engaged in a social media experience. A security policy regarding passwords is an example. The business may have rules that determine how a password is configured, how long the password can remain active, and whether the same password can be used for more than one area or service.

If a business does permit use of social networking applications, there can be a defined policy as to what types of information an employee is allowed to post and the types of information that are prohibited. Particularly because social networking sites are usually constructed for "group" interaction, should sensitive business data be posted, the business may be put at risk. Another policy might address the tone or nature of any communications posted to a social site. For example, political commentary or personal opinion might not be considered acceptable. Especially when keeping current and potential customers in mind, business policy dictates that no derogative, negative, or inflammatory language be used.

It would not be unusual for a business that makes use of social networks to designate employees or departments to monitor and respond to questions, corrections, or other matters that might come up. By limiting, as policy, which employees or departments are allowed to post or respond to social sites a business can more tightly control the message it wants to communicate and provide a set of consistent responses it wants to present to the world.

From the AIIM survey previously referenced, 21% of responding businesses indicated that security issues with social media technologies were a major concern. Two particular vulnerabilities associated with social networking are the introduction of malware into an organization and the unwanted release of sensitive business data or information. In another 2010 report produced by Sophos, a vendor of security tools (*www.sophos.com*), creators of malware specifically targeted Facebook, Twitter, and LinkedIn as a means for spreading their viruses and attack applications.

There are a number of ways that social media sites can be used by hackers to infiltrate the business networks. Previously we mentioned that businesses may enforce a policy regarding passwords. A strong password policy can strengthen a business's security. Passwords are used to authenticate a trusted user to a given system. If the password used is too simple, that is a weakness. Also, if a given password is used for multiple applications or services, once the password is broken several areas of the business are at risk. Hackers might use brute force algorithms to discover passwords.

Another approach a hacker might use to breach network security is a mechanism referred to as **cross-site scripting (XSS)**. Attacks by XSS take advantage of web-application and web-browser weaknesses to embed malicious scripts into webpages. In this event, the user's web application or browser is tricked into executing malicious code. Once executed, the malicious code can make it possible for the hacker to steal personal information, thus allowing the hacker to impersonate the victim. Or the malicious code may cause the user's computer to launch attacks of its own without the user's knowledge.

Another method used by hackers is to trick an unsuspecting user into clicking onto a link or URL (uniform resource locator) that takes the user to a website that is infected with malicious code. Typically, this type of attack comes through an e-mail message where the user is urged to click a link in order to browse an interesting story, image, or video. Again, this is where a good security policy may state that links sent by others that have not been verified should not be clicked or accessed. It is possible that an email received from someone you know may have been generated and sent by a hacked device with the user of the sending device unaware of the message sent.

Social media and social networks are very much a one-to-many–based application, meaning that a single user is typically sharing or posting to multiple people and/or groups. The nature of social networking applications is to generate a sense of community, even intimacy. Employees who post to various social networking sites may be lulled into a false sense of trust. The problem here is that the information posted, over time, might be gathered, compiled, and used in ways that employees did not intend or desire, especially by competitors who are also monitoring these sites.

A number of the ways in which social media enhanced networks are vulnerable has been a problem for many years prior to the introduction of such networks technologies. However, the nature of social networking, with its rapid sharing of data, communications, and information, with hundreds, if not thousands, of other people make the problem larger and harder to correct once unleashed.

SOCIAL BUSINESS NETWORKING DEMOGRAPHICS

In 2010, the *Harvard Business Review* published a study based on surveys from 2,100 business organizations, large, medium, and small. They found that many businesses are still trying to find their way in how best to utilize social media networking. For example, 75% of respondents did not know which social media sites their customers access and post to. This has important implications because a business will not know how best to respond to customer concerns, questions, or complaints if the business does not know where these comments are being made. Almost a third of businesses surveyed did not believe they were effectively measuring the effect of social media for their industry. Less than a quarter, 23%, was using some type of social media analytic tools, such as Radian6, mentioned previously in this chapter.

Most businesses (69%) believed that the use of social media by businesses would grow significantly over the next few years. Almost as many (61%) believed businesses faced a difficult learning curve in discovering how best to utilize social media. Only 11% of the 2,100 businesses surveyed felt that social media was a passing fad. In terms of using social media, the two biggest challenges businesses reported were understanding the potential of how best to use social media to make a difference in the business and then how to effectively measure the effects of social media on that business. The most-reported benefit was increased consumer awareness of the organization's products and services. The second-highest ranked benefit was the increased flow of consumer traffic to the business's website.

In terms of what types of social media avenues were being utilized, 87% of businesses used social networks such as Facebook, 58% used blogs, 58% used multimedia sharing sites such as YouTube, 53% used microblogs such as Twitter, and 22% made use of review or discussion forums. On average, most businesses utilized at least three types of social media, with the most common combinations being: (1) blogs, social networks, and multimedia sharing, and (2) blogs, social networks, and microblogs. Smaller businesses tended to view social media as a means of increasing consumer awareness, website traffic flow, and generating new customers. Larger businesses viewed social media as a means of monitoring and measuring consumer perceptions and comments, both positive and negative.

Industries that were most likely to be using social media were education (72%), communications (71%), services (66%), and retail/wholesale (61%). The least likely industries to use social media were utility companies (41%), manufacturing (32%), and government organizations (27%). Within the organization, the three areas most likely to be responsible for management of social media development and monitoring were marketing, communications, and public relations.

The use of analytic tools was mentioned earlier in this chapter. The *Harvard Business Review* survey found that 41% of reporting businesses have plans to incorporate analytic tools within the next two to three years. Of particular interest to businesses is the ability of these tools to report accurately on customer opinion, find marketing solutions and opportunities, measure the effect of online conversations, and provide predictive analysis.

Harvard's survey revealed several interesting characteristics regarding "effective" business users of social media. Effective users were more likely to have a dedicated budget specifically for social media activities. In addition, effective business users reported using social media to monitor industry trends, provide an online location for customer user groups, collect and analyze customer commentary, and generate ideas for new products and services. Also, businesses successfully using social media were likely to know where their customers were posting commentary.

Chapter Summary

When networking technologists discuss convergence and pervasive computing, they are most likely discussing the integration of data, voice, and video all carried seamlessly over one infrastructure. Communication technology is also on the road to invisible mobility. Three issues of particular concern involving pervasive computing are security, privacy, and ethics. The convergence of voice, video, and data into a seamless infrastructure will require protocols and technologies that can support such a convergence. One protocol in particular that is attracting notice in the convergence industry is SIP, or session initiation protocol.

With unified messaging, all of the various messaging systems used by an enterprise are rolled into one system with one access point—the user's e-mail inbox. All messages, regardless of their source, will ultimately be digitized. The promise of UM is that it will allow users of different communication technologies who are operating different media and different devices to communicate with anyone, anywhere, at any time.

The past decade has seen the blossoming of a variety of social media networking technologies such as Facebook, Myspace, Flickr, YouTube, LinkedIn, Yelp, and a host of others. These social media sites and tools tend to have several characteristics in common. Facebook (*www.facebook.com*) in many ways has become one of the best-known sites, if not *the* best known, for social media interaction.

YouTube (*www.youtube.com*) is specifically focused on video and video sharing. Introduced in 2005, YouTube allows its users to upload, share, and view videos of all types: musical, humorous, educational, tutorial, television clip, and more. Unlike Facebook or YouTube, LinkedIn (*www.linkedin.com*) is designed specifically with the working professional in mind, whether as an independent contractor or as a public or private employee. LinkedIn connects working professionals so that they can easily exchange ideas, opportunities, training, advice, and knowledge. Another tool that businesses are increasingly making use of is blogs and microblogs. A blog is a posting site on the Internet used for commentary, discussions, information, critiques, and other forms of communication.

Users of social media sites are also potential customers who may gain an increased awareness of a particular business or industry simply by visiting these sites. In turn, this form of customer access can result in directing consumer traffic to a business's website. Also, businesses that monitor social networking groups can often get a sense of what customers and potential customers may be saying or commenting on regarding a business. Analytic applications are used by business to measure, analyze, and interpret the interactions and commentary that consumers post about a business.

Many businesses that utilize social networking technologies also have in place formal usage policies and procedures that employees are expected to adhere to when interacting with social media sites. Such policies can clearly define what is and what is not permissible within the organization if an employee should be engaged in a social media experience; for example, a security policy regarding passwords.

In 2010, the *Harvard Business Review* published a study based on surveys from 2,100 business organizations, large, medium, and small. They found that many businesses are still trying to find their way in how best to utilize social media networking. Most businesses (69%) believed that the use of social media by businesses would grow significantly over the next few years. Industries that were most likely to be using social media were education (72%), communications (71%), services (66%), and retail/wholesale (61%).

Keywords

Analytics *287*
Blog *287*
Cross-site
   scripting
   (XSS) *288*
Facebook *284*

Instant messaging
   (IM) *282*
LinkedIn *285*
Microblog *287*
Pervasive
   computing *281*

Session initiation
   protocol *281*
Social media *284*
Twitter *287*
Unified messaging *282*
YouTube *285*

Chapter Questions

Short-Answer Questions

1. What components might be present in a UM solution?
2. What is meant by "pervasive computing"?
3. How is SIP used?
4. What is one example of a social networking site?
5. In what key way does Youtube differ from Facebook?
6. Who is the target audience for LinkedIn?
7. What might be included in a password policy?
8. Why might a business monitor a social networking site for commentary?

Hands-On Projects

1. Interview someone who has either a Facebook, Twitter, or LinkedIn account. What does the person most like and dislike about her or his account or the application?
2. Draft a two-paragraph security policy on password configuration and maintenance.
3. Determine if your college or university, or place of employment has any policy restrictions regarding the use of social networking sites. If so, what are they?
4. Hootsuite (*www.hootsuite.com*) is another application similar to Tweetdeck that can be used in conjunction with Twitter. Hootsuite offers a free 30-day trial period. Create a free trial period account and determine what features Hootsuite provides.

Research in Brief

For one or more of the following questions, provide a one- or two-page report based on your findings.

1. Many vendors offer UM solutions. Evaluate UM solutions from two vendors. Compare and contrast them with regard to cost, functionality, and their advantages and disadvantages. Of the two, which would you recommend and why?
2. Research and report on ways in which marketing departments might effectively utilize some form of social media networking.
3. Compare and contrast two different social media sites. What are their characteristics? Who is their primary audience? How do users interact with the sites?
4. In what ways might pervasive networking be used in a given industry—for example, health care, education, or automotive?

Topic in Focus

CAREER CERTIFICATIONS

Research shows that having a formal degree—whether an associate's degree from a community college, a bachelor's degree from a college or university, or a graduate-level master's degree can significantly increase your future earning power. These formal degrees pay for themselves in the long run. However, for many in the technical fields—including programming, database and applications development, and especially data communications—career certifications may also be a factor in one's career advancement. Career certifications may affect base salaries, bonuses, promotions, or other job-related areas. Certifications require that an individual take and pass one or more technical examinations, depending on the certification being sought.

In general, each exam costs approximately $100 to $175, and you are charged each time you retake an exam. However, if your college or university has an academic partnership with a vendor that offers a certification, such as Cisco, Microsoft, or Novell, it may be possible to obtain a student discount. To register and sit for an exam, you must go to a recognized testing center, such as Prometric (*www.prometric.com*), which has testing centers nation-wide . Although you can locate an exam site and register for an exam online, you must go to the testing center, with appropriate identification, to take an exam. The following career certifications (below) are appropriate for those in the data communications field. Keep in mind, however, that certifications have to be kept up-to-date. Very likely, you will have to retake an upgrade certification exam to maintain your credentials about every two years.

CompTIA's A + Certification

Some consider CompTIA's A + (pronounced "A plus") certification to be the first level of certification for a computer technologist. The certification is meant to be vendor neutral and concentrates on two technical areas: (1) the hardware that make up a standard desktop computer and (2) the software (operating system and drivers) that a standard desktop computer would use. To become A + certified, one must pass two exams, covering each of the technical areas described above. The exams can be taken on the same day or on different days. The exams are updated periodically, and you have until the next update to take the second exam. Visit CompTIA's website (*www.comptia.com*) for the latest update on their exams.

The Core Hardware exam tests an examinee's basic knowledge to install, configure, upgrade, troubleshoot, and repair a standard desktop computer. This exam typically has approximately 100 questions that must be completed in 90 minutes. Basic hardware networking is also tested in this exam. The operating system (OS) exam requires the examinee to demonstrate basic proficiency with a command line prompt and with installing, configuring, upgrading, troubleshooting, and repairing client computers. This exam also has 100 questions that must be answered in a 30-minute timeframe. If you need to retake an exam, you must pay for each sitting.

CompTIA's Network + Certification

CompTIA also offers a foundation certification in basic networking called Network + (again, pronounced "Network plus"). This certification is for technology professionals with at least nine months of experience in network support or administration. The intent of the certification is to demonstrate technical abilities in networking administration and support and knowledge of media, topologies, protocols and standards, network implementations, and network support. This certification is also meant to be vendor neutral. Network+ is a single exam.

CompTIA's Security+ Certification

Security has become an area of critical importance. As with the A+ and Network+ certifications, CompTIA's Security+ certification is vendor neutral. The test covers security concepts, tools, and procedures. In preparing for the test, topics covered include:

- Network security
- Compliance and operational security
- Threats and vulnerabilities
- Application data and host security
- Access control and identity management
- Cryptography

ICS^2's Certified Information Systems Security Professional (CISSP)

ICS^2, the International Information Systems Security Certification Consortium (*www.isc2.org*), is a global, not-for-profit provider in educating and certifying information security professionals. For its Certified Information Systems Security Professional (CISSP) certification ICS^2 recommends at least five years of professional experience in the field of information security. The CISSP was among the first testing credentials to be approved by the ISO/IEC Standard 17024. Those taking the exam are expected to have experience and knowledge of networking architecture, design, and management in a security context. Topics covered by the exam include:

- Access control
- Telecommunications and network security
- Information security governance and risk management
- Software development security
- Cryptography
- Security architecture and design
- Operations security
- Business continuity and disaster recovery planning
- Legal regulations and compliance
- Physical security

Cisco Certifications

Cisco (*www.cisco.com*), a major provider of technologies that power the Internet and networking infrastructures, offers several stages of certification. First-level Cisco certification is for the Cisco Certified Network Associate, or CCNA. For this certification, students usually take a series of four classes that prepare them for the CCNA exam. The CCNA exam requires students to demonstrate first-level knowledge of Cisco routers and switches and their installation and configuration.

Second-level Cisco certification is referred to as Cisco Certified Network Professional, or CCNP. Prior to taking the CCNP exam, one must already be a CCNA. The CCNP certification indicates advanced knowledge of Cisco-based networks. It also demonstrates that a network professional can install, configure, and troubleshoot LANs and WANs for enterprise organizations with networks having 100 to more than 500 devices. The exam focuses on topics related to security, converged networks, QoS, VPNs, and broadband technologies. To prepare for CCNP certification, four classes are usually required. The third level of Cisco certification is for the Cisco Certified Internetwork Expert, or CCIE. To sit for this exam, you must already be a CCNP. Also, the CCIE has a required hands-on lab component whereby the test taker must, at a Cisco facility, manually configure and troubleshoot Cisco equipment.

Microsoft Certifications

Microsoft (*www.microsoft.com*) also offers varying levels of certification. First-level certification leads to Microsoft Certified Professional, or MCP, certification. The most likely beginning MCP certification for a networking technologist is certification in a Microsoft Workstation or Server operating systems. An MCP certification can be applied toward Microsoft's next higher networking-oriented certification, the Microsoft Certified Systems Associate, or MCSA. To become an MCSA, an MCP must pass additional exams that can be selected from multiple areas. Following the MCSA, the next higher certification is the Microsoft Certified Solutions Expert, or MCSE. A candidate cannot sit for the MCSE exams until he or she has successfully been awarded the MCSA. As with other vendor certifications, Microsoft's certification requirements change over time. Visit Microsoft's website (*www.microsoft.com*) to find out the most current requirements for the MCP, MCSA, and MCSE certification. As with other types of certification, a fee is required for each exam taken.

Novell Certifications

Like Cisco and Microsoft, Novell (*www.novell.com*) offers several levels of certification. First-level certification is to become a Certified Novell Administrator, or CNA. A CNA is certified to provide support in Novell's NetWare Server Operating System for users in various work environments, including professional offices and small businesses, work groups or departments, and corporate information services. The next level of Novell certification leads to the Certified Novell Engineer, or CNE. For CNE certification, a candidate must pass additional exams. Check Novell's website for the latest certification testing requirements.

VMware's VCP (VMware Certified Professional)

Virtualization of desktop and server technologies as well as the advent of cloud computing have created a significant demand for networking professionals familiar with this technology. VMware (*www.vmware.com*) is a major provider of virtualization technologies. Its certification is intended to demonstrate that the credentialed candidate can successfully install, deploy, and manage a VMware network. Those sitting for the exam are assumed to have had hands-on lab experience and ideally at least six months of professional experience with VMware infrastructures.

Average Salaries by Job, Organization Size, and Educational Level

In Fall 2011, Dice (*www.dice.com*), a professional technology recruiting firm, administered a survey to more than 18,000 technology professionals. The following data reflect some of the results of that survey.

Average Salary by Job Title

Job Title	Average Salary 2011	Job Title	Average Salary 2011
Systems Architect	$111,985	Technical Writer	$76,114
Data Architect	$108,961	Quality Assurance Tester	$75,498
Project Manager	$104,398	Network Engineer	$74,687
Security Engineer	$97,809	Web Developer/Programmer	$71,962
Network Design	$94,898	IT Technical Training	$69,123
MIS Manager	$94,255	Systems Administrator	$68,900
Software Engineer	$93,142	Web Administrator	$65,192
Developer: Database	$92,662	Network Manager	$61,444
Database Administrator	$91,769	Web Designer	$61,307
Developer: Applications	$86,627	Technical Support	$50,913
Business Analyst	$85,979	Desktop Support Specialist	$46,752
Developer: Client/Server	$85,850	Help Desk	$40,245
Security Analyst	$78,396	PC Technician	$37,236
Programmer/Analyst	$76,965		

Average Salary by Company Size for 2011

Size	Average Salary
Fewer than 50 employees	$69,424
50–99 employees	$73,249
100–499 employees	$76,739
500–999 employees	$77,602
1,000–4,999 employees	$82,860
5,000 or more employees	$90,533

Average Salary by Education Level for 2011

Education Level	Average Salary
Vocational/Tech School	$59,729
Some College	$72,197
College Graduate (4-Year)	$81,536
Master's Degree $93,465	$98,911
Doctoral Degree $100,120	$112,775

GLOSSARY

4G A wireless mobile technology.

802 An IEEE implementation specific to the data link layers of the OSI and TCP/IP models.

802.1 The 802 implementation for inter-networking.

802.2 The 802 implementation for logical link control.

802.3 The 802 implementation for Ethernet.

802.4 The 802 implementation for token bus.

802.5 The 802 implementation for token ring.

802.11 The IEEE umbrella protocol for wireless local area networks.

802.11a The 802.11a IEEE specification utilizing the 5 GHz spectrum band.

802.11b Extends the original DSSS (direct sequence spread spectrum) scheme by extending data rates from 1 and 2 Mbps to 5.5 and 11 Mbps.

802.11g Extends wireless data rate transmissions from 12 to 54 Mbps per channel and is backward compatible with 802.11b networks.

802.11i Addresses authentication, key management, and data transfer privacy for wireless local area network communications.

802.11n A standard brought forward to address further improvements to the physical layer and MAC sublayer with the intent to enhance wireless throughput.

802.16 A standard designated for WI-Max services.

Acknowledgment When a receiver responds back to a sender regarding a communication.

Adapter card A hardware component used to associate a networked device to a physical address.

Address classes In IPv4, the 5 address classes defined for network and host logical addressing.

Address resolution protocol (ARP) Used to relate a logical network address to a physical MAC address.

Address spoofing Occurs when a filter is tricked into believing a packet is coming from an addressed device different from its true originating source.

Alphabet The set of symbols used in either an input or an output message by a cryptographic method.

Amplitude modulation Modifying the amplitude of signal in order to assign a given logical meaning.

Analog A continuous form or means of expressing data.

Analytics Applications used by businesses to measure, analyze, and interpret the interactions and commentary that consumers post about a business.

ANDing A process used to determine which subnetwork a device is associated with.

Application filtering The screening or filtering of traffic from specific applications, such as FTP and e-mail.

Application layer The first or top layer in both the OSI and TCP/IP models; provides an interface for the user to other lower-layer services.

Application server A specialized server that provides software application services to other networked devices.

Asymmetric cipher Two separate keys are used: a public key and a private key; one is used for encryption, the other for decryption.

Asynchronous protocol A transmission protocol that requires that every data byte include a start and stop bit before and after the byte.

Asynchronous transfer mode (ATM) A cell-based form of packet delivery within a network.

Attenuation The decrease of a signal's strength as it travels over a communication circuit.

Authentication One of the four elements of the CAIN principle.

Autosensing Enables fast Ethernet NICs to automatically sense and adjust to speed capabilities of 10 to 100 Mbps.

Backbone network (BN) A network topology used to connect other networks, typically local area networks (LANs).

Backward compatible A technology that is capable of working and interacting with earlier versions of that and/ or other technologies.

Bandwidth The capacity of a given circuit to carry data.

Back end A logical process that runs on an application server.

Backbone Used to connect the networks of an organization or enterprise.

Backward-explicit congestion notification (BECN) A bit signal sent to alert a sender of network congestion.

Barker Spreading Code Specifically associated with the DSSS (direct sequence spread spectrum) implementation.

Binary A numbering system based on two values or statuses represented by the digits 0 and 1.

Biphase A means of encoding that provides for at least one transition per bit interval and provides for self-clocking.

Bipolar A data-encoding scheme that uses positive, negative, and zero voltages.

Bit In digital notation a bit is either a binary 0 or a binary 1.

Bit interval The time required to send a single bit.

Bit rate The number of bit intervals per second.

Block check character (BCC) An additional byte appended to a message transmitted using longitudinal redundancy checking.

Blog A posting site on the Internet used for commentary, discussion, information, critiques, and other forms of communications.

Bluetooth A wireless standard for communicating at the 2.45 GHz range; Bluetooth-enabled devices do not require line-of-sight communications.

Bridge A hardware component used in a local area network to divide the network, based on the address of the networked device, for efficient communications among the networked devices.

Broadcast A data packet sent to all devices on an 802.3 Ethernet network.

Browser A software application used for web browsing or access.

Bursty Data that are sent in a burst or group of packets as opposed to a continuous stream.

Bus mastering A technique that incorporates a CPU (central processing unit) on a NIC (network interface card).

Bus topology A topology associated with the IEEE 802.3 implementation.

Bus width Determines the number of data bits that can transmit at one time on a network interface card's circuitry.

Byte Composed of 7 to 8 binary bits, based on the encoding scheme used.

C# A programming language often used to develop web service components.

Cache A temporary memory location used to hold data that are to be immediately processed.

Caesar cipher One of the earliest forms of encryption.

CAIN principle A principle associated with securing a network by means of confidentiality, access, integrity, and nonrepudiation (CAIN).

Capacity sharing The ability of a storage device to pool storage space or tape drives with other processors.

Cell A data packet associated with asynchronous transfer mode (ATM).

Channel service unit (CSU) The end point of a digital link in a switched network.

Chassis The physical case that houses a server.

Checksum checking A means of computing a running total based on the byte values transmitted in a message block and then applying a calculation to compute the checksum value.

Cipher An encryption methodology or technique.

Ciphertext An encrypted version of the original data.

Circuit configuration Determines the way in which two or more communicating devices share their connection or link with each other.

Circuit filtering A circuit-filtering firewall; also called a circuit-level gateway. Evaluates not only a packet's source and destination addresses, but also the circuits that have been established for the packet's communication.

Circuit switching One form of connecting interlinked devices called switches within a network.

Classless inter-domain routing (CIDR) physical address A function of supernetting with the intent to reduce the size of routing tables used by routers on the Internet backbone.

Cleartext An unencrypted, or clear, version of the original data.

Client An end-users' networked device.

Client/server model A networking model in which certain networked devices function as clients and others as servers.

Clocking Allows the sender and receiver in a communication to synchronize their transmission.

Cloud Describes a means of providing technological products and services to an end-user with the end-user not needing to be aware of how the products or services are provided or supported.

Coaxial Cable A form of conducted cabling media.

Codec A device that takes an analog signal on the sending end, converts the signal into digital for transmission, and then translates the signals back to analog of the receiving end.

Collapsed backbone Connects all network segments to a central, single router or switch.

Committed burst rate (CBR) Specifies a maximum bandwidth that will be available during temporary increases in data traffic.

Committed information rate (CIR) Within a frame relay network, a negotiated date rate from a carrier that guarantees a specific level of bandwidth.

Common carrier An organization that provides a commonly needed infrastructure such as telephony.

Common Internet file system (CIFS) A file-sharing protocol used by a NAS (network attached storage) device.

Compression A means of encoding data such that it requires less physical space for storage and/or transmission; data that are compressed must be later decompressed in order to be used.

Conducted media A form of cabling media that allows the transmittal of data based on electrical frequencies.

Confidentiality One of the four components of the CAIN principle.

Congestion avoidance A technique used to route around areas of network congestion.

Congestion control A mechanism used to manage and control network congestion.

Congestion recovery A technique used to recover from network congestion.

Connection oriented A transmission service that provides acknowledgment between sender and receiver.

Connectionless A transmission service that does not provide acknowledgment between sender and receiver.

Connectors Hardware components used to connect various types of cabling media.

Contention A competition for transmission circuit usage among multiple networked devices.

Contention-based topology Associated with the IEEE 802.3 Ethernet protocol.

Cross-site scripting (XSS) An attack that takes advantages of web browsers' and web applications' vulnerabilities.

Crosstalk When two or more signals intrude into each other's transmissions such that the original value of one or more of the signals is lost.

Cryptography A technology used to encrypt data in order to make it usable or readable only to those with the required encryption keys.

CSMA/CD A form of contention control used in an 802.3 Ethernet network.

Cycle The completion of one full pattern of a transmission wave.

Cyclical redundancy checking A form of error checking.

Data center A centralized and secure location for essential servers, switches, and routers often connected to a backbone.

Data communications A subset of telecommunications that focuses on the communications between computing devices.

Data flow The direction that data can travel on a given circuit, simplex, half-duplex, or full-duplex.

Data link connection identifier (DLCI) Used in frame relay networks to identify virtual circuits.

Data link layer The layer of the OSI and TCP/IP models associated with media access.

de facto standard—An informal standard that is generally associated with a technology that is pervasive and not yet formalized by a standard-setting body.

Data mining A technology used to find hidden patterns in data that may be useful for predicting future behavior.

Data service unit (DSU) Converts signals from a connecting device, usually a bridge, router, or PBX, into the type of digital signal, usually bipolar, required by a leased line.

Data sharing The capability of a storage device to share data and files concurrently with other storage devices.

Data warehousing A means of viewing a wide variety of data that can offer a comprehensive view of business conditions at a given point in time.

Database server A specialized server that provides access to database resources.

Datagram Independent data units used by an IP network.

Delineate To define or mark out in a bit stream where characters in a transmission begin and end.

Delivery service Defines the type of frame delivery service provided by 802.2 logical link control.

Deregulation The removal of regulations from a formerly governed or regulated service, product, or process.

Device driver A software component that directs the operation of a hardware device.

Digital A means of encoding data in a discrete form usually based on a binary 0 or 1.

Digital certificate A means of user access verification for security purposes.

Digital signature A means of encrypting data using a specific user's private key.

Digitization The process of converting one type of data, usually analog, into a digital notation, usually binary.

Direct attached storage (DAS) A technology usually used by organizations for backing up data and for the off-line storage of data that are not frequently referenced.

Direct memory access (DMA) The capability of a NIC (network interface card) to directly use the host device's memory.

Direct sequence spread spectrum A type of "spread spectrum" radio frequency transmission, as opposed to a "narrowband" transmission.

Disaster recovery plan A set of policies and procedures to follow in the event of a disaster, whether human-made or natural.

Discrete Having a specific and noncontinuous value range, such as a binary 0 or 1.

Distortion Occurs when a signal changes from its originating form and shape as it travels from source to destination.

Distributed backbone A backbone is considered to be distributed if each network segment has its own cabled connection to the backbone.

Distributed management task force (DMTF) A standards-setting organization for web-based services.

Domain name The logical name associated with a given IP address.

Domain name system (DNS) Used to associate a URL (uniform resource location) to a valid IP address.

Dual stack One of the approaches recommended supporting both IPv4 and IPv6.

Dwell time The time spent at given frequency.

Dynamic host configuration protocol (DHCP) A service provided by a DHCP server that enables a client or host to determine and retrieve an IP address.

Dynamic IP address An IP address that can be changed or modified.

Edge switch A hardware device implemented at the edge of a network.

Efficient From a business perspective, a task performed in such a manner that it is cost-effective.

Effective A task that is performed correctly and accurately.

E-mail server A specialized server used to provide e-mail hosting and services.

Encoding scheme A means of translating one given notation into another differing notation—for example, English into ASCII.

Encryption A means of encoding data such that they become unintelligible to those with the necessary encryption key. Data that are encrypted must be decrypted in order to become usable.

Enterprise Describes all the networks, and associated infrastructure, that make up an organization or business.

Error control Composed of error detection and error correction at the data link layer.

Error detection The ability of communicating devices to recognize that an error has occurred or has been transmitter.

Ethernet The 802.3 IEEE implementation at the data link layer.

Even parity Usually used with synchronous transmissions whereby the number of 1 bits in an 8-bit unit must always add to an even number.

Extensible markup language (XML) A key web service protocol for developing web service components.

Extranet The portion of an organization's network made available to customers and industry partners.

Facebook A social networking site associated with personal, and increasingly business, communications.

Failover A recovery mechanism used in server clusters.

Fair access A networking model that allows each network-connected device equal, or fair, access to a shared circuit.

Fault tolerance The ability of a technology to recover from an error or other unexpected problem.

Fiber optic cable A form of conducted media that uses light as a means of representing data.

Fibre channel An implementation of a switched fabric that is usually associated with a SAN (storage area network).

File-level I/O protocol A protocol used for file sharing.

File server A specialized server that provides access to data files.

File transfer protocol (FTP) An application service that provides for uploading and downloading of files and data to a remote device.

Firewall A protective mechanism used to filter out unauthorized users or services.

Flow control Defines the manner in which data frames are transmitted between sender and receiver.

Forward error correction Requires that redundant data be included in a transmittal in order to correct for potential errors during transmission.

Forward-explicit congestion notification (FECN) Used to alert a receiver of network congestion.

Frame A given structure assigned to a grouping of data bits.

Frame relay (FR) A form of packet switching network.

Frame relay access device (FRAD) A device used within a frame relay network.

Frequency division multiplexing A form of multiplexing that uses frequency ranges separated by guardbands for signal transmission.

Frequency hopping spread spectrum (FHSS) A type of "spread spectrum" radio frequency transmission, as opposed to a "narrowband" transmission.

Frequency modulation Manipulation of a signal's frequency in order to assign logical meaning.

Front end A logical process that runs on a client device.

Full backup A backup of a complete data set.

Full-duplex Data flow that can travel in two directions simultaneously.

Gigahertz A unit frequency of one billion.

Half-duplex Data flow that can travel in two directions, but in only one direction at a time.

Hardware The physical components that make up a networked environment.

Header translation One recommended means of transitioning between IPv4 and IPv6.

Hertz A unit of frequency.

Hexadecimal The base-16 numbering system.

Hexadecimal colon notation In contrast to the IPv4 dotted decimal format, IPv6 addresses utilize a hexadecimal colon notation.

High-level data link control A synchronous bit-oriented protocol.

Hopping code The process of changing frequencies, from one short burst to another.

Horizontal network A networking model whereby one or more networks of a given organization are on a single floor of a building.

Host A networked device on an organizational network.

Hot spot A wireless access point.

Hub A passive device used to connect other devices in a local area network.

Hybrid VPN A virtual private network (VPN) that has both trusted and secure VPN characteristics.

Hypertext markup language (HTML) An application layer protocol used by web servers.

Hypertext transfer protocol (HTTP) An application layer protocol used by web services.

Incremental backup A partial backup of data that only backs up the latest changes made.

Infrastructure as a service (IaaS) A type of service provided by cloud computing.

Input/output (I/O) request A request to read and or write data from or to a storage device.

Instant messaging (IM) A web-based protocol used for real-time textual communications.

Integrated drive electronics (IDE) One type of hard drive interface.

Integrity One of the four elements of the CAIN principle.

Internet A technology service based on the TCP/IP protocol suite.

Internet control message protocol (ICMP) Supports IP by providing for error report and query management.

Internet Corporation for Assigned Names and Number (ICANN) The organizational body responsible for assignment of IP addresses.

Internet group message protocol (IGMP) Primarily used by IP when multicasting is required.

Internet message access protocol (IMAP) An application layer protocol used by web services.

Internet protocol security (IPSec) A protocol standardized by the IEFT usually associated with a secure virtual private network (VPN).

Intranet That portion of an organization's network meant for staff access and use.

IP address A logical TCP/IP address.

IPng Describes IPv6, or the latest TCP/IP version.

IPv4 Internet protocol version 4, the first version TCP/IP protocol suite underlying the Internet.

IPv6 Internet protocol version 6, the latest version TCP/IP protocol suite underlying the Internet.

Java 2 Enterprise Edition (J2EE) A programming language often used to develop web service components.

Kilohertz A unit frequency of one thousand.

Label Edge router A devices used within a Multiple Protocol Layer Switching network.

Layer stack Includes or identifies the components or modules that may make up a single layer.

Layer-2 tunneling protocol (L2TP) A Cisco-sponsored protocol that combines the layer-2 forwarding protocol (L2F) with point-to-point tunneling protocol.

Layered architecture Particularly associated with the OSI and TCP/IP models, such that each layer in the model is associated with specific functions and responsibilities.

Legacy A term given to older technology that may still be in use.

Line discipline Controls which device can communicate and when.

Link A connection between two networked points.

Link access procedure-function (LAPF) Used within frame relay to provide a minimum level of data link control functions.

LinkedIn A social networking site primarily utilized by job-oriented individuals and job networking.

Load balancing A technique used by server clusters to distribute network traffic.

Local area network (LAN) A network that is typically bounded in size to a room or building.

Logical address A networked device address that can be changed and be reconfigured.

Logical addressing A logical address associated with a data packet or frame assigned at the network layer of the OSI and TCP/IP models.

Logical link control A component of the data link layer as defined by the IEEE; logical link control sits above media access control at the data link layer.

Login An authentication often required to validate users of a network.

Longitudinal redundancy checking A method used for error detection.

Loopback address An address in IPv6 composed entirely of zeros except for the very last bit which is set to a binary 1, and used to test if a device has been properly configured for communications without going out of the network.

Media The circuit used for transmittal of data, which may be either conducted or radiated.

Media access control (MAC) A component of the data link layer as defined by the IEEE; media access control sits beneath logical link control.

Medium A specific type of media.

Megahertz A unit frequency of one million.

Metered license A type of license that limits the number of active users that may use a product, service, or application at any one time.

Metropolitan area network (MAN) A network typically bounded in geographic size by a city.

Microblog A social networking tool or application for relatively brief communications.

Modem A device used to modulate a digital signal into an analog signal on the sending end and from analog back to digital on the receiving end.

Motherboard The basic or fundamental circuitry for a computer.

Multicasting The capability of sending a given message to multiple devices across an enterprise.

Multimode A form of fiber optic cabling that allows for multiple paths that light can follow.

Multiplexer A device that can take communications from several slow-speed devices and combine them such that these communications can pass over a single high-speed circuit.

Multipoint Multiple devices sharing a single circuit.

Narrowband A specific, narrow frequency radio band used to transmit data for one specific radio station signal.

Network-attached storage (NAS) A technology used to manage disk storage and optimization.

Network interface card (NIC) A hardware component used by networked devices to provide for physical addressing of these devices.

Network layer The layer of the OSI and TCP/IP models associated with logical addressing.

Network operating system (NOS) A software operating system associated with server devices in a networked environment.

Networking model A logical model used in designing a network of a given size.

Nonproprietary An open standard, technology, product, or service available to for use to the public at large.

Nonrepudiation One of the four elements of the CAIN principle.

Octet An eight-bit configuration of binary data bits.

Odd parity Associated with asynchronous protocols whereby the number of 1 bits transmitted in an 8-bit unit must always add to an odd number.

Off-line A networked device that is not available for access by a given network.

Online A networked device that is available for access by a given network.

Open architecture technology A network technology model that is open for general public use.

Open system interconnection (OSI) model An open architecture model used to describe the services and functions of a given network.

Optical frequency division multiplexing (OFDM) An optical implementation that makes use of multiple carrier signals at different frequencies.

Organization for the Advancement of Structured Information Standards (OASIS) A standard setting body for web-based services and components.

Packet A unit or grouping of data bits.

Packet filtering A type of firewall protection that drops or passes packets based on their destination and source addresses or ports.

Packet switching A form of connecting networked devices in a wide area network (WAN).

Parallel transmission mode The ability of multiple bits to simultaneously travel a given circuit.

Parity checking A means of error detection based on either even or odd parity.

Patch panel A centralized wiring point or location for organizing and connecting networked devices, in particular switches and routers.

Path The route that data units may take from sender to receiver.

Peer-to-peer model A networking model in which a given network device may function as a client, a server, or both when making or granting requests for services or applications.

Period The amount of time in seconds that a signal needs to complete one cycle.

Permanent virtual circuit (PVC) A form of virtual circuit.

Personal area network A personal network limited in scope to approximately 30 feet for communicating devices.

Pervasive technology A technology so commonly used that it becomes part of the culture or society and is taken for granted.

Phase modulation Manipulation of a data signal's direction, or phase, in order to assign a given logical binary meaning.

Physical address The MAC (media access control) layer address associated with a device's NIC (network interface card).

Physical layer The bottom layer of the OSI and TCP/IP models associated with transmittal of encoded data from one point to another without concern as to the meaning of the data being transmitted.

Physical layer convergence procedure (PLCP) One of the sublayers of the IEEE 802.11 physical layer.

Physical medium dependent (PMD) One of the sublayers of the IEEE 802.11 physical layer.

Physical security Securing resources by keeping them in locked facilities available only to limited staff.

Piconet Another term for a personal area network.

Platform as a service (PaaS) A type of service provided by cloud computing.

Point of presence (POP) An access point to a WAN infrastructure that is provided by a common carrier.

Point-to-point Two devices exclusively sharing a communication link or circuit.

Point-to-point protocol (PPP) Provides for a direct connection between two networked devices.

Point-to-point tunneling protocol (PPTP) Enables a point-to-point connection to be tunneled through an IP network.

Polling Utilized in a token-ring network to determine if a networked device needs to use the transmission circuit for communication.

Port scanning A type of attack whereby an application searches out Internet-connected devices looking for open well-known port service accesses.

Ports Logical designators for application layer services.

Post office protocol version 3 (POP3) An application layer protocol associated with e-mail.

Presentation layer The layer of the OSI model associated with such tasks as encryption and compression.

Private Key The key used for the decryption of a delivered message on the receiver's end.

Proprietary A standard, technology, product, or service that is trademarked or copyrighted for exclusive ownership; use will typically require a fee.

Protocol An agreed on set of procedures or processes followed to achieve a given result.

Protocol data unit Contains up to four elements and is used by the 802.2 logical link control.

Proxy server A server used as an intermediary between two communicating devices.

Pseudo-random A sequence of values that appears random but that are not.

Public key The key used for the encryption of a sent message on the sender's end.

Public key infrastructure A technology used to create key pairs that establish confidential communications.

Public switched telephone network (PSTN) A common carrier for telephony services and infrastructures.

Radiated media A form of media that uses radio frequencies for transmission of data.

Random access memory (RAM) A temporary memory used to store data and information actively being processed or utilized.

Redundancy Having multiple copies or sets of a given resource.

Regenerated Issuing or recreating a signal at its original strength.

Request for purchase (RFP) An open bid process for products, services, or other desired elements.

Retransmission An error-correction mechanism that requires data be retransmitted if an error is detected.

Reverse address resolution protocol (RARP) The resolution of a physical network address to a logical network address, or the opposite of ARP.

Ring topology The topology associated with the IEEE 802.5 implementation.

Router A hardware device used to connect separate logical networks.

Scalable The ability of a technology to be flexible in either expanding or contracting as needed.

Secure VPN The use of tunneled encryption creates what is called a secure virtual private network (VPN).

Self-clocking An encoding scheme that has a clocking mechanism built into the encoding scheme such as biphase Manchester.

Serial advanced technology attachment (SATA) One form of hard drive interface used by a computer.

Serial transmission mode A circuit that permits only a single bit to be transmitted at one given time such that bits that make up a transmission are delivered in single-file fashion.

Server A networked device used to provide resources to other networked devices.

Server cluster A collection or group of servers that function as a unit.

Server operating system (SOS) A software operating system associated with server networked devices.

Session initiation protocol A protocol designed to deliver real-time communications for IP-based voice, video, data, and instant messaging.

Session key A way to combine the benefits of both symmetric and asymmetric ciphers that create what is referred to as a "session" key, which is a key pair that is renewed or changed periodically.

Session layer The layer of the OSI model associated with the establishing of a connection between a given sender and receiver.

Signaling method A physical layer component used for conveying, representing, and translating data between communicating devices.

Simple mail transfer protocol (SMTP) An application layer protocol associated with e-mail services.

Simple object access protocol (SOAP) An application used to transport data to and from a web service.

Simplex A data flow that permits transmission in one direction only.

Single mode A fiber optic cable that allows for only a single light path on the cable.

Site license A generalized license that covers organizational access to a product, service, or application.

Sliding windows A form of data flow control that allows for multiple frames to be sent without each frame requiring individual acknowledgments.

Sliding windows buffer A memory resource used to buffer frames utilizing the sliding windows flow control mechanism.

Small computer system interface (SCSI) One form of hardware drive interface used by a commuter.

Social media Initially viewed as applications for individual and small group internetworking, but increasingly viewed as an avenue for business outreach to consumers and vendor partners.

Socket The combination of an IP address and a port number.

Software A logical set of programmed instructions that direct the functioning of hardware devices.

Software as a service (SaaS) A type of service provided by cloud computing.

Spread spectrum A technique for spreading wireless data over numerous radio frequencies.

Standards A set of procedures or processes that have been formalized by a standard-setting body as a means of achieving an end result.

Star topology A networked topology in which networked devices are directly connected to a central controlling device.

Stateful packet inspection A stateful packet inspection firewall evaluates both a packet's header as well as the packet's contents.

Static IP address An IP address that is constant and not modified or changed.

Statistical time-division multiplexing A form of multiplexing that allows multiple devices to utilize transmitting time slots based on need without the necessity of assigning specific time slots to specific devices.

Stop-and-wait A form of flow control that requires each frame sent to have an acknowledgment received back as to the status of that frame.

Subnet mask The use of binary 1s to represent the network portion of an IP address and 0s to represent the host portion of the IP address.

Subnetting Artificially dividing a given IP class address into multiple subnetworks recognized internally by a given organization or enterprise.

Supernetting The combining or aggregation if IP addressing.

Switch A hardware device used in local area networks that significantly increase the physical scale and transmission capability of the network.

Switched network A form of connecting devices within a wide area network (WAN).

Switched virtual circuit (SVC) A form of virtual circuit.

Switches Hardware devices used to segment a network, typically a local area network.

Symbol rate The number of bits that can be encoded in a single signal.

Symmetric cipher A security technique whereby the sender and receiver of the communication must be using the same key for encryption and decryption.

Symmetric multiprocessing (SMP) The capability of an operating system to utilize multiple CPUs (central processing units).

Synchronous protocols Evaluates groups of characters in a transmission rather than one byte or character at a time.

System area network (SAN) A specialized network used for storage of data and applications.

Telecommunications An umbrella term that includes such technologies as telephone, telegraphy, television, and data communications.

Telemetry The use of radio frequency identification tags to identify and track products.

Telnet An application layer program that enables a user to remotely login and use the resources of a remote computer.

Terahertz A unit of frequency measured in the trillions.

Terminal Hardware devices connected to a mini- or mainframe computer allowing user access to that computer.

Throughput Throughput for a NIC is a measure of how many bits it can process within 1 second.

Time-division multiplexing A form of multiplexing that assigned specific time slots on a high-speed circuit to specific devices such that the time slots can be used only by the devices assigned to them.

Token In a token ring network, a token is a specially designated frame used by networked devices in order to gain access to the data circuit.

Token ring The IEEE 802.5 implementation of the data link layer.

Topology Determines not only how devices are connected to each other but also how devices get access to the media they use for communication.

Transition coding A transition coding scheme such that a given value is encoded by means of a voltage transition during the bit interval, not before or after it.

Transmission control protocol/Internet (TCP/IP) model An open architecture networking model usually associated with a four- or five-layer configuration.

Transmission impairment Describes some type of error that can occur when transmitting data over a given media.

Transmission media A means of sending data signals from source to destination using either conducted or radiated media.

Transport layer The layer of the OSI and TCP/IP models typically associated with the segmentation of data into packets for delivery between a given sender and receiver.

Troubleshoot To evaluate, analyze, and repair problems or errors that may occur in a networked environment.

Trunk services Services provided by a Public Switched Telephone Network carrier.

Trusted network A network that is known to be secure and safe.

Trusted VPN Does not allow anyone other than the carrier to affect the creation or modification of the virtual private network (VPN)'s path.

Tunneling A technique that allows packets from one protocol to be wrapped, or encapsulated, within a second protocol.

Twisted wire pair A type of conducted media based on twisted copper pairs of wire.

Twitter A social networking technology based on brief, 140-character, communications.

Unicasting A communication between one sender and one receiver.

Unified messaging A means of providing a single source login or access to multiple communication and application services.

Uniform resource locator (URL) Usually a World Wide Web address, such as *www.pearson.com*.

Unipolar A form of encoding that has a direct current (DC) component.

Unlicensed National Information Infrastructure (UNII) Developed to encourage manufacturers to develop high-speed wireless network applications and appliances.

Unshielded twisted wire pair (UTP) A form of copper-based conducted media.

Untrusted network A network that is not known with certainty to be secure and safe.

User datagram protocol (UDP) A connectionless, unreliable delivery service utilized by IP networks.

Vertical network A network that occupies multiple floors of a building or facility.

Virtual channel identifier (VCI) Used in conjunction with a VPI (virtual path identifier) by an ATM (asynchronous transfer mode) network to identify the location of a destination device.

Virtual circuit (VC) A form of packet switching service.

Virtual path identifier (VPI) Used in conjunction with a VCI (virtual channel identifier) by an ATM (asynchronous transfer mode) network to identify the location of a destination device.

Virtual private network (VPN) A means of creating a secure connection between two communicating devices.

Virtual server A logical server based upon a cluster of physical servers.

Voice-over Internet Protocol (VoIP) The digitization of voice communications over a networking infrastructure.

War driving A hacker technique that attempts to chart and identify open wireless networks.

Wavelength division multiplexing A form of multiplexing based on fiber optic technology.

Web server A specialized server used to host websites and web services.

Well-known ports Logical designators associated with well-known and specific services.

Wide area network (WAN) A networking model associated with the geographic scale of a state, a country, or a global capacity.

Wi-Fi A wireless technology associated with the IEEE implementations of 802.11a, 802.11b, and 802.11g.

Wi-Fi Alliance A key purpose of the Wi-Fi Alliance is to provide WLAN vendors an authoritative body that can test and then verify as to the interoperability of a vendor's product.

Wi-Fi protected access (WPA) A security mechanism used by WI-Fi networks.

Wi-Max A wireless IEEE implementation associated with the 802.16 protocol standard.

Wi-Max Forum An organizational body associated with the IEEE 802.16 protocol implementation.

Wired equivalent privacy (WEP) The initial privacy protection provided by the IEEE 802.11 implementation.

Wiring closet A centralized and secure location typically used to house backbone devices.

Workstation A hardware device typically associated with end-users in order for them to access a network.

World Wide Web Consortium (W3C) A standard setting body for web service components.

X.25 An early form of packet switching network.

Youtube A social networking application primarily associated with video-based data.

INDEX